No H
myh.
Waddera

Where No Nightingales Sing

A Memoir

by

Madalena Cocozza

To Alyson and Stephen my children

'As sunlight on a stream;
Come back in tears
O memory, hope, love of finished years'

Christina Rossetti

Grateful thanks thanks to my family who have given me a precious gift in producing this book.
Thanks to Stephen, John, Colin, Angela, Ruth and Alyson for their constant support, encouragement and putting up with my tears.

CHAPTER 1

Sometime in the late 1890s my grandfather arrived in Scotland from Italy. His journey had begun many, many months before when he left his remote village high in the mountains above Naples and set out on his personal Odyssey. He travelled light, his few personal possessions tied in a bundle slung on his barrel organ, with the little pet monkey perched on top.

His final destination was Glasgow, where several of his extended family had settled. Rather than make his way through Switzerland to France and across the channel to Britain, he determined to cross the Adriatic to Albania, on through Yugoslavia, Poland, Russia and Sweden, then across to Denmark, and take a ship across the North Sea to Scotland, pushing and playing the barrel organ as he went, and sustaining himself with the money and food the little monkey collected.

Behind him he had left my grandmother and three young sons, the youngest, my father, newly born.

Coming at last to Glasgow he settled near his cousins, renting a little tenement house, (Glaswegians never spoke of flats) in Charlotte Lane in the Calton, the east end of the city. By the early 1900s the family had joined him, they taking a much more conventional means of travel, making the crossing by boat.

Within a few years the family had grown, two sets of twins who died in infancy, and four daughters who survived. Grandad or Da-dee as he came to be called opened a little fruit stall to supplement the money he made from his daily perambulations with the barrel organ.

Granny worked the stall and cared for the children, the boys having their allocated chores.

The boys were enrolled in the local Catholic school Saint Alphonsus in Charlotte Street, the girls followed when they were of an age, though to Da-dee the girl's schooling was of little importance, they were expected to marry and produce grandchildren.

My father Eugene did not share Da-dee's belief in the value of formal education for his sons, while he, Eugene would dutifully leave the house with his brothers, and later take on the task of shepherding his sisters to school. Once he had safely delivered them through the school gate, he would scarper. His favourite haunt was down by the river Clyde, where he would watch the great ships coming and going, talk to the sailors, and dream of travelling the world. When he grew tired of the ships, he would make his way to the slaughter house in Melbourne Street not far from where he lived.

There he would make himself useful to the men, fetching and carrying, brewing tea, for this he would be rewarded with parcels of fresh meat, which he would proudly present to his mother. These escapades were a source of conflict between Granny and Da-dee. She thought bringing home meat was more important than going to school, Da-dee thought otherwise, and would take the taws down from their hook by the fire, tell Eugene to bend over and apply the strap with considerable force. The fashion at the time was for schoolboys to wear stiff white collars, with their white shirts and dark trousers, though Eugene never really complained about the beatings, he would struggle frantically to release his collar stud before he bent over, as the restriction caused him to choke and go red in the face.

The beatings were always carried out before the rest of the family as a warning, but usually they were rather a source of amusement. Eugene was not above slipping some sort of padding into his trousers, a ploy known to generations of boys, but what usually afforded the fun was as Da-dee struck each blow he would say in Italian, 'Will you do it again?' to which Eugene, his face buried in his hands would mumble, 'Si Da' 'Si Da' The others would collapse with laughter. Eugene never got the joke, or realised he should have said, 'No Da.'

Eugene loved to please his mother, and was always thinking up ways of making money to boost the family coffers. He found his way to the yard of a monumental mason, where he would tidy away the tools, sweep out the yard, and watch the men as they worked.

Marble and stone fascinated him, and soon he was happily chipping away engraving letters on discarded pieces, regarded as an unofficial apprentice.

On Fridays and Saturday nights when the working men spent their wages in the sawdust strewn pubs that graced almost every corner, Eugene would hover outside with a wheelbarrow, ready to hurl the drunk and incapable to the local police station, where he earned sixpence for each one he delivered. Every penny he made went straight to Granny; he never kept anything for himself. He would bask in her approval. She in turn would try to shield him from the truant officer who constantly sought him out. After a visit from the officer Eugene would solemnly promise to mend his ways and would indeed attend school for a few days, but he was soon back to his old tricks, giving the tawse plenty of work.

The contrast between Eugene and his brothers was very marked.

Antonio, older by several years, was tall and muscular. Where Eugene was, as Granny would say with a smile, 'A stranger to soap and water', Antonio was fastidious in his habits, constantly washing himself and badgering his sisters to mend his clothes and polish his boots. He applied himself to his books but was not a great scholar. He too, made a little money, from carpentry, this he hoarded until he could afford to buy himself a smart coat, leather gloves and a trilby hat. At weekends he was the talk of the Calton, as he haughtily strolled up and down the Gallowgate. At home his sisters danced attendance on him, setting his place at the table with a napkin and his own special cutlery.

The usual noisy Italian meal would begin with Da-dee saying grace, then all eyes would watch silently as Antonio shook out his snowy napkin, inspected his knife, fork and spoon for any traces of 'monkey bran' the paste cleaner used by his sister Mary whose job it was every Friday to spread newspaper on the rough deal table and clean every piece of cutlery in the house.

Mary suffered from a severe heart condition and poor eyesight, and now and

3

then a slight trace of the green cleaning paste would escape her notice. Woe betide her if this showed up on Antonio's place setting He would bang his fist on the table, hurl the offending article to the floor, and shout 'I bring good money into this house, I demand respect.' The others would witness this behaviour in silence, except for Eugene, who would shrug and say 'Who brings in the meat eh? Anyway, a wee bit o' monkey bran will no kill ye.'

Encouraged a sister would pipe up, 'Who is it that buys three cream horns every Friday then hides in the close to eat them, so we don't get a share?'

Antonio would glare at her, while the others kept their eyes on their plate. Da-dee would rap sharply on the table with his fork, and say, 'Basta! Basta! Mangere.'

Dominic the middle brother was short like Eugene, often he was absent from the meal table. His passion was gambling, he would disappear for hours on end, refusing to divulge where he had been or who his cronies were. His was a bluff and generous nature.

Granny, although she would never admit to it loved Dominic above all the others, would bemoan his absence, become distraught and dispatch Eugene to find him, with the strict instruction not to come back without him. Dominic was usually to be found in the dark recesses of a tenement close playing cards or taking bets, from furtive punters.

Being a 'bookie's runner' was an illegal activity, but Dominic never let a little thing like the law stop him. Totally engrossed in what he was doing, he would wave Eugene away with a dismissive hand. Eugene would return, minus the miscreant, spread his hands in exasperation and say. 'He willnae come mammy, ah telt him ye wanted him, honest, but he willnae come, he says he's busy.'

'Is-a he a'right?' Granny would ask anxiously 'Aye, but he's dae'in his bookie's runner,' Eugene would say. 'Oh is-a good, he no play the cards,' Granny had no idea what a 'bookie's runner' was.

She would make thick sandwiches of salami and pickle, pour a jug of milk and send Eugene off to deliver these to Dominic. 'Here, take-a this, he got to keep his strength up.'

Eugene would go, stopping only to consume the milk himself, once he was out of sight.

He knew, though he would never tell Granny, that Dominic preferred something stronger.

Da-dee, Beniomeno Cocozza, had met Granny, Benedetta Pacitti, from the neighbouring village of Cherosole, at a fete; it had been love at first sight, though he was several years older than she. Beniomemo's mother was a Pacitti, from the same village as Benedetta, so the union met with approval. Within a year of their marriage their first son Antonio was born. They were peasant stock, scratching a living growing vegetables and tending sheep and goats. Benedetta would regularly ride over the mountain to visit her family in Cherosole. It was while on one of these visits, Benedetta, riding the donkey side saddle being heavily pregnant with Eugene, went into labour and gave birth by the side of the road. After resting for a while she continued her journey to her mother's house. There she rested only a day, before making the journey back to Filignano. When many years later we children on hearing the story asked how far it was from Filignano to Cherosole, Eugene shrugged and said, 'Two hours by donkey.'

Gasps of astonishment from us.

Another shrug of the shoulders, 'Och nae bother at a'.'

It was a family joke that Eugene born in the dust spent his life covered in the stuff.

For many years young men had left the village to seek a better life, settling in America, Canada, and Britain. With a growing family Beniomeno felt it was time for him to go too. Benedetta did not want to leave her family, yet she knew she had no choice, wherever Beniomeno went she must follow.

Years later she was to tell her girls, she was so grateful he chose to settle in Scotland and not Russia.

If he had, how different this story would have been.

On the 28th of June 1914 Arch Duke Franz Ferdinand heir to the Austrian-Hungarian throne was assassinated in Sarajevo, and war clouds began to gather over the Balkans.

On hearing the fateful news, the ailing Pope Pious X, fainted. By July Austria had issued an ultimatum to Serbia, and by August, at the end of a gloriously warm bank holiday, Britain declared war on Germany, an act which sent crowds surging through the streets to gather outside Buckingham Palace, singing the national anthem.

Herbert Asquith the British Prime Minister was loudly cheered in the commons, as he detailed the governments ultimatum to Germany, reminding her of the treaty of 1839 in which Britain, Germany and France agreed to respect the neutrality of Belgium.

'The Kaiser,' said Asquith 'had dismissed the treaty as a mere scrap of paper.'

The stage was set for a bloody conflict.

Granny's reaction was one of panic; she wanted home, back to the sleepy security of Filignano. Antonio and Dominic faced up to the fact that if Italy got involved they would be called to serve. Eugene who never got ruffled or upset about anything turned the news to his advantage and found work in the shipyards. He was sixteen, earning a small wage as a terrazzo worker. The shipyards offered more. Da-dee opposed the return to Italy; he saw the future of his family in Scotland.

He was deaf to Granny's repeatedly expressed fears for her children's safety. In the end a compromise was reached, she would return to Italy with the girls and Antonio, while Eugene, Dominic and Da-dee would stay behind.

By May 1915, Italy was at war with Austria, after successive attempts to wrest parts of the Tyrol, Trieste and Isteria, as the price for her neutrality. By 1916 the conscription law had widened to take in men from 18yrs to 45yrs. Both Eugene and Dominic were called to serve, both rejected, Dominic for poor eyesight, Eugene for flat feet. Granny, back in Italy with Da-dee's words still ringing in her ears, 'You are taking my girls from heaven to hell,' began to fear he may be right as a massive earthquake struck near Filignano.

By 1919, the family were reunited. It took Granny some time to settle back into the tenement way of life. She became unwell, but would not go to a doctor, besides, doctors cost money, and there was very little of that about. Dominic was by now living the secretive life once more, he was never short of money, and was willing to pay for any treatment his mother needed. Da-dee would not hear of it, the true nature of Dominic's activities had become known, and Da-dee did not approve. Neither did he approve of the flashy, expensively dressed men who occasionally visited the house. Dominic spent most of his time on the 'sou'side', over the river where the Jewish community was very prominent and among whom Dominic had expanded his business. Da-dee had never been south of the river, but finding himself in need of a haircut on a Sunday, to attend a funeral on the Monday, he allowed Dominic to take him over on the ferry to a Jewish barber.

Despite Dominic's willingness to pay for the haircut, Da-dee insisted on paying his own way. Da-dee tried in vain to get Dominic to take up a trade, he deplored the gambling and all that went with it. Granny beamed with pride at Dominic's fur collared coat, trilby hat and doeskin gloves. 'Our boy, he such a swell,' she would say her hands clasped in wonder.

The family moved round the corner to 206 Gallowgate, the house was on the third floor of a grimy tenement, it had two rooms and a large kitchen. The landing at the top of the stairs opened out to a large square lobby, Granny's house on the left, the two others on the landing sharing the lavatory.

The girls, Elizabeth Sophia, Christina, Maria Theresa, and the youngest Philomena, had long abandoned their 'Sunday' names, opting for Lizzie, Tina, Mary and Famie. They had all found work with the exception of Mary, whose health had worsened since her return from Italy. For her the only option was to stay at home and do light housework. Mary was plain and gruff of voice, and it was unlikely she would ever marry, but she was possessed of a sweet nature and everyone loved her.

Antonio had settled in Edinburgh, where he lodged with an Italian family, the Ricardo's. They had several marriageable daughters, and Antonio chose Teeny, but the choice was not a happy one.

Life for Granny was a little easier now the girls were bringing in a wage. Life for them revolved around work and chapel. All the sisters were like Da-dee and Granny devout Catholics, a good part of their earnings went to the church. Every visit from the parish priest to number 206 was prepared for as if for royalty. The little altar on the wall which housed a statue of the virgin and child would be given a clean altar cloth of delicately crocheted lace painstakingly done by Mary despite her poor eyesight.

A fresh night-light would flicker, highlighting a little vase of seasonal flowers, hung with Granny's best rosary beads.

The visiting 'father' would be given the best chair, bar Da-dee's which was always drawn up to the fire. Da-dee was devout, but not that devout.

Sipping delicately at his tea the priest would ask each in turn if they had performed their duties to the church, keeping all the feast days, going to mass, having confession, and taking communion.

The answer was always in the affirmative, at least as far as Granny, Da-dee and the girls were concerned, the boys were another matter.

Antonio safely removed to Edinburgh was not that particular priest's problem, though he did ask after his spiritual health, smiling benignly at Granny's assurance that Antonio did all that was required of him.

As for Dominic, he felt as the Good Book says he could not serve two masters, God and Mammon, so he chose Mammon and happily lived with the threat of eternal damnation. Eugene declared himself a 'Widden Catholic' and said he fully expected the roof to fall on his head should he ever step over the threshold of Saint Alphonsus, where his sisters spent so much of their time. Granny and Da-dee would look pained when asked about their errant sons, but they would never lie.

'Eh leave them be,' Da-dee would say with a shrug, 'they will answer to God, someday.'

'Indeed! Yes indeed! They surely will,' the priest would declare, the veins standing out above the dog collar.

Granny would smile and shake her head, 'Eh they are good boys to their Mama.'

The smile would melt the ecclesiastical heart, and Father would pat her hand and say, 'Well that is good, Mrs Cocozza, that is good.'

So life went on, changing times had meant the demise of the barrel organ, the little monkey long departed, and its tin mug now redundant on the shelf above the coal bunker. Da-dee took to peddling ice-cream from a gaily painted cart. From his little depot in Ross Street he would push the cart to Glasgow Green, not far from the Gallowgate. The Green had been for generations one of the 'lungs' of the city. Though Glasgow boasted many fine parks, the Green held a special place in the hearts of the people. Women used it to dry their washing, children played in the huge sandpit, bands played in the bandstand, boys and girls flirted and paired off on happy summer days.

Though there were many drinking fountains with their metal cups secured on a long chain, the children loved to have a penny to spend on a 'pokey hat', from the Tally.

Glaswegians are tolerant and kindly for the most part, and they had readily accepted the 'Tallies', patronising their ice-cream parlours, and chip shops. For their part the Italians tolerated the nickname 'Tally', taking it in the spirit it was intended.

Granny still longed for Italy; she was confined to the house, rarely venturing out, except to go to mass.

Tina and Famie were avid picture goers, always faithfully relating the whole story, complete with dramatic actions to Granny and Mary. Lizzie was quiet and reserved; she rarely went to the cinema, preferring to spend her time reading or making spaghetti on her little machine. Now and then Tina would invite the cousins and the neighbours in for a sing-song, everybody had to take their turn, performing their own special party piece.

Eugene had left the shipyards, to return to terrazzo, working with stone and marble was in his blood; happiness for him was spending hours on his knees polishing a floor by hand. He seemed oblivious of the skin shredding carborundum stone, or the dust clogging his nostrils.

He was a jack of all trades, yet master of one, his terrazzo work. Because of his versatility, and his ability to completely immerse himself in the job in hand, the firm sent him all over the country. He worked in shops, cinemas, banks, libraries, laying floors, cladding walls constructing stairways.

Sometime in the 1920s he found himself in Edinburgh, and met my mother. The manner of their meeting is not known, they were always very coy on the subject, for reasons which only became clear many years later.

CHAPTER 2

Ada Amelia McPherson Coutts, my mother, had lived in Edinburgh all her life. Her father Henry Coutts came from a good family, and he was a man of refined tastes, well read and artistic and owned a smart hairdressing business in the new town. He had met and married Elizabeth Goodfellow something of a beauty, but socially beneath him.

Elizabeth bore him four children, two sons, Harry and Glen, and two daughters Mary and Ada my mother.

The marriage was not a happy one. Eventually Elizabeth left Henry taking only three years old Ada with her. Henry was furious, but he was not a man to be thwarted, he tracked down his wife and child and took Ada back to the elegant town house, hiring a nanny to look after her. The nursery where Ada slept was in the basement of the house, under cover of darkness, Elizabeth aided and abetted by her brother, entered by a window, snatched the sleeping Ada, passing her through the window to her brother who made off with her.

Henry, enraged, sued for divorce, a shaming and expensive process at that time. Despite his efforts Elizabeth was awarded custody of Ada. Harry, Glen and Mary, who was nine years older than Ada, remained with Henry. This decision sealed the fate of Ada, changing her life for ever.

Born into financial security, brought up in a beautiful house she now lived in the old town, in Waverley Buildings, a warren of tenement rooms with communal privies.

Waverley Buildings was seven storeys high. Elizabeth took rooms on the seventh floor, which were reached by enclosed rickety stairs. On every landing a sagging door revealed a lavatory, the bowl set in a wooden bench, the black cistern high above from which hung a chain ending in a white enamel pull. Squares of newspaper hung on a string from a nail on the wall. Each storey had a balcony which ran the whole length of the building, here the women would gather to gossip as they hung the washing to dry on extended pulleys, which hung precariously over the railings. Noisy, dirty, evil smelling and cramped, the place was totally alien to Ada and she was terrified, but worse was to come.

It was not long before Elizabeth found herself another husband, one James Miller, a ruddy cheeked drayman, whose job it was to deliver beer to the many hostelry's around. James was fond of a 'drappie' and soon the horse knew all the stopping places, where James not only delivered but stayed to sample the wares, the horse quite unbidden would return to the stable complete with the comatose James.

Ada was soon joined by a half-brother, James Robert Goodfellow Miller, (Jimmy) and a year later by a half-sister Agnes Paterson Miller (Aggie). Elizabeth, used to the finer things in life, found coping with three children, a drunken husband, and tiny cramped rooms too much to bear. She began to take a little sip of gin now and then. It was common practice among the women of the Buildings, 'mother's ruin' they would say with a wink to each other.

When little James was six years old he contracted poliomyelitis which left him with a useless left arm and leg, he was fitted with heavy callipers.

Months later little Agnes was stricken with erysipelas the red raised eruptions of the highly contagious skin infection, covering her whole body. The disease affected her eyes, leaving them weak and watery, the sight badly impaired.

Unable to bear all these misfortunes Elizabeth completely succumbed to 'mother's ruin', leaving Ada now aged ten to assume the responsibility for her two half siblings. This she was to continue to do for the rest of her life.

Ada put all her efforts into getting herself as well as Jimmy and Aggie to school. She was determined to get an education, and escape the misery of the Buildings. Little Jimmy would cry as he struggled down flight after flight of stairs to reach street level, while Aggie peering pitifully through blurred eyes was fearful of being alone, and clung to Ada wherever she went.

Harry and Glen along with their sister Mary had meanwhile reaped the benefits of living with Henry Coutts. They had all gone to good schools. Glen going on to university to study law, Harry apprenticed into the family business, Mary married off to a prosperous farmer in Hawick.

Ada longed for better things, though she could scarcely remember the first years with her father. She always felt different to those around her. Elizabeth too, seemed conscious of this, for when the gin got the better of her she would scream that Ada was 'stuck up' like her father. In her misery Ada would escape to her secret hiding place on the roof. She would sneak away, squirming through an opening barely big enough to let a cat through. Sitting with her knees touching her chin she would gaze over the rooftops, dreaming of all the wonderful things she would do when she was grown and free from her drunken parents. Always in these dreams, Jimmy and Aggie would be with her, she could no more think of leaving them behind, than she could jump off the roof.

Ada was a good scholar; she was keen to learn, never missing school, even though her nights were disturbed by the screams and arguments of James and Elizabeth. In the long summer evenings she would play in the High street on the steps of John Knox's house, or swing on a rope tied to a lamppost. Ada would hoist Aggie and Jimmy one after the other to swing, Jimmy always crying with frustration when the heavy calliper dragged him down. He would struggle to keep up with the other boys as they ran with the hoop and cleet.

They, like all the other children, went bare foot, and thought nothing of it; shoes were for winter time if they were lucky enough to have them.

Ada was always hopeful of weaning Elizabeth off the gin, and whenever a visiting lantern show was announced at the Band of Hope Mission in the Grassmarket, Ada would persuade her mother and James to attend. Sitting shamefaced as the preacher denounced 'demon drink,' they would shuffle forward, heads bowed, to sign the pledge, bearing away the card that vowed abstinence and temperance ever more.

Ada would hug Jimmy and Aggie and promise that things would get better, but they never did.

Before long she would find an empty bottle thrust into her hand, and a halfpenny in a twist of paper, with the instruction to buy 1 gill of gin. One day James gave her threepence, telling her to buy porter and ale. She bought two loaves instead. On the way home an army recruiting band came marching up the High street.

Fascinated by the colourful uniforms and the beat of the music, she sat down on the kerb to watch, absently she picked at one of the loaves. When the band had passed she discovered to her horror that she had picked a large hole through the centre of the loaf.

Returning home, she found James in a towering rage, he struck her, tearing the loaves from her hands he demanded the return of his money. Ada fled, scrambling onto the roof space where she stayed until dusk, and she could see 'Leerie' the lamplighter going from post to post igniting the gas mantles. Creeping downstairs she could hear James snoring, Aggie and Jimmy sat huddled in a corner crying, Elizabeth was nowhere to be seen. Quickly she bundled the two children out of the house snatching the bread as they went. Down the stairs they crept, she had no idea where to take them; she just wanted to get away from James Miller. They spent the night huddled together in the wash-house, which was set apart from the main buildings.

Morning found them cold and hungry, the bread having been eaten before they had settled to sleep. Ada judged the hour was still early, she was anxious to get away from the Buildings before some neighbour saw them, or James stirred himself to go to the stable for his horse and cart.

She set out for the Bridges, which would take them into the New Town. Ada held Aggie by the hand, while Jimmy struggled to keep up with the brisk pace she set, his chest rose and fell with exertion as the calliper bit into his flesh.

'Where are we going?' he wailed.

'You'll see,' said Ada sounding more confident than she felt.

'Ma leg hurts,' said Jimmy close to tears.

Ada looked around; they needed to put a good distance between themselves and Waverley Buildings before she could begin to feel safe.

'Try to keep going,' she urged tightening her grip on Aggie's hand as she too showed signs of flagging.

On they went, an idea had began to form in Ada's mind, if she could only remember the way to her father's shop, maybe she could see her brother Harry.

She tried to conjure a picture up in her mind's eye. She had been there once, at least in the street where the shop was, though it was some years ago. Elizabeth had wanted to see her son, but fearful of approaching the shop and risking a confrontation with Henry, she and Ada had stood a good way down the street on the other side looking up at the shop with Henry Coutts and Son emblazoned in gold letters on a dark green background.

Ada was sure she would recognise the street when she saw it, though the new town boasted many fine wide streets with gracious buildings. After a while she allowed the two weary children to sit on the kerb-side to rest. She eyed them critically as they sat listless and afraid, looking to her for guidance. Jimmy's clothes were little more than rags, his woollen jumper was matted and shrunk from too many washes, his elbows protruded through holes, the clumsy parish issue boots were gaping at the toes.

Aggie, her wispy hair clinging to her forehead with perspiration wore the same clumsy boots as Jimmy, two sizes too big the toes stuffed with paper; her thin cotton dress reached her ankles. She squinted at Ada through rheumy eyes that constantly danced in her head.

Ada looked down at the worn and torn smock she herself wore, she had no boots, though it was late autumn, and the wind from the Forth was growing sharper making them shiver.

She was conscious of the stares of passers by. Crossing George IV Bridge into the new town was like entering another world. The people regarded them with haughty disapproval.

She coaxed Jimmy and Aggie to their feet, urging them on, eager to find the shop. She had given little thought to what Harry's reaction would be when he saw them. She hoped he would be kind; Elizabeth had always spoken of Harry's good nature.

As they walked, Jimmy still lagging, still complaining, Ada kept her eyes open for a familiar landmark. At last she saw a shop she recognised, she felt sure she had found the street.

'Come on,' she urged, 'this is the place, I'm sure it is.'

As she walked towards the shop, a knot of fear gripped her stomach, she wondered if Henry would be there, and if he was what he would say.

Looking through the shop window she could see her brother Harry expertly wielding an open razor as he shaved the foam covered chin of a customer. As she gazed, Harry looked up, caught sight of her and for a second lost his concentration, a vivid spot of red appeared on the white foam, heated words were exchanged. The silent pantomime made Ada laugh, Harry made a shooing motion, glaring fiercely.

Ada drew Jimmy and Aggie aside and waited till the irate customer came out of the shop, sporting a white dot of paper on his chin.

'What are you doing here?' demanded Harry, following the customer through the door.

'We've run away,' said Ada.

'Run away, you can't just run away, where do you intend to go?' He nodded towards Jimmy and Aggie, 'Why did you bring them?' he asked. 'I couldn't leave them; they get frightened when James gets drunk.' Harry ran his fingers through his thick mop of dark hair, and frowned. 'What do you want me to do?'

'Feed us, we're hungry, I took some bread from the house but there is none left, and we have no money,' pleaded Ada. Harry's face softened, he fished in his pockets, finding some coins. 'Here, take this, buy some bread and milk, then come back here, but don't come in the shop, children are not allowed, especially not girls.' 'But where can we go?' Ada was anxious.

'I don't know,' said Harry, 'but if father finds you here there will be trouble, you know that.' 'He is my father too,' Ada was defiant.

'Yes I know, but it is difficult, don't argue with me, just believe me when I say he would not be pleased to see you, and even less pleased to see them.'

'Ah want tae go hame,' sniffed Aggie.

'So dae ah,' said Jimmy, 'ah didna want tae come here onyroad,' he glared at Harry, then dragging his leg painfully he began to walk away.

Harry looked at the three pathetic figures before him shivering with cold. He scooped up Aggie in his arms, motioned the others to follow. 'Come on, you can warm yourselves at the stove in the back, I'll get you some soup,' he said kindly.

'But what about father?' asked Ada following him through the shop as the bewildered staff looked on. 'We'll cross that bridge when we come to it,' said Harry.

Ada awoke with a start, to find Harry tugging at her elbow. She sat up. Next to her Aggie and Jimmy lay fast asleep, their arms entwined. 'Come on,' Harry urged, 'I have to get you out of here, the shop is closed and father will soon be here for the takings.' 'Where are we going?' Ada asked, gently shaking the children awake. 'Back to Waverley Buildings, where else? I'm sorry, but there is nowhere else I can think of,' Harry shook his head.

They set off along Princes Street, Harry carrying Aggie on his shoulders. Ada had Jimmy by the arm, trying to give him relief from the pain. Halfway across the bridge, Harry swung Aggie down, and scooped up Jimmy ignoring his protests that he 'Didna need ony help.'

It was Harry's first visit to the Buildings; he slowly climbed the stair becoming more and more depressed at what he saw. On the seventh landing, Ada pointed to a door.

'You don't need to knock, it's never locked,' she said.

Swinging Jimmy down from his shoulders, Harry followed her through the door; it opened straight into the kitchen come bedroom.

James lay sprawled on the floor; Elizabeth lay across the bed snoring gently. Ada shook her awake; she sat up, gazing with glazed eyes at her son.

'Hello mother,' said Harry.

Harry became a frequent visitor to the Buildings. He would bring food and clothing for all of them. Elizabeth would comb her hair, put on her good black dress, and try to reduce her drinking on the days Harry was due. When temptation overcame her, he would find her incoherent and aggressive.

James was civil to Harry, yet in a surly fashion, he pawned the suit Harry had bought him, claiming he needed the money for food.

For Ada, having Harry in her life was the most precious thing she had, often they would sit and talk of the life that might have been, she would cling to his arm and beg him to promise never to leave her. He would laugh, drawing his finger across his chest he would say, 'Cross my heart and hope to die.'

They would stroll in Holyrood Park on Sunday afternoons, sometimes Glen would join them dressed in his smart Lawyer's suit.

Ada secured an apprenticeship at McNiven and Cameron, the long established printer's in the High Street, although only earning a modest wage, she took over from Harry as the provider for Jimmy and Aggie, who although older were still very dependant on her. Jimmy grew tired of being seen as an object of charity, he applied to the Cripple Aid Society, who found

Roused from his sorrow, Da-dee said gently, 'We live, we die, it is all part of life, there is nothing we can do about it, they have to know life is like that.'

Ada was still apprehensive, snatching the children back and carrying them from the room as soon as the flowers were laid. Soon the house was filled with people, they spilled from the room along the long narrow lobby, fingering their rosary beads, and murmuring responses as the priest intoned the prayers.

Benny, pressed on all sides by bodies, became fretful, she tugged at Ada's skirt, saying over and over.

'Ah want a piece an' jam mammy.'

Ada's whispered 'Hush' was to no avail.

The priest raised his head and said, 'Give the child her bread and jam, life goes on.'

Sadly for Benny life did not go on, eighteen months later those same people, that same priest were gathered round a small white coffin, set out as Granny's had been in the big room.

Benny was dead at three years old from a mastoid infection. Ada's anguish consumed her, wracked by pain and sorrow; she mourned Benny with a mixture of sadness, bitterness and blazing fury. She railed at Eugene and Da-dee, reminding them of her premonition that death would snatch her child if she went near Granny's coffin.

'I tried to keep her hidden, I didn't want death to know she was here,' she cried over and over rocking back and forth her arms tight around her body. Eugene, though normally scornful of her habit of seeing omens and signs, was dumb before her grief. Da-dee, in what he thought was a way of helping her deal with her sorrow, took both her hands in his and said, 'Yes it is sad you lost your little one, but take heart, it could have been much worse, you could have lost your breadwinner.' Shocked at what she saw as his callous attitude, Ada never forgave him. As her children, we grew up hearing the story, the anger and bitterness still fresh and raw.

The loss of Granny and little Benny drew the family together. Antonio and his Teeny came to live at number 221 Gallowgate across the street from Da-dee. Dominic recently married and preferring to be known as Tommy also came to live at number 221, in the flat below.

Within a year Tommy's wife Mary had fallen victim to consumption, her once handsome features now pallid with sunken eyes. Tommy became tired of caring for her, he was man who always had to out wheeling and dealing. Mary's dependency irked him, he grudged the time he had to spend at her side. He wanted to be in the casinos, or attending the fine functions where he made his contacts.

In the next close at 211 lived two of his gambling partners, their unmarried sister Agnes had a reputation as a man eater, she was out to snare a man, and Tommy with his fine clothes, expensive cigars and fat wallet, was the man she wanted.

Soon the liaison was causing a scandal. Agnes dyed her hair blonde; she changed her name to Carol, adopting an affected accent, which caused much hilarity among the good folk of the Gallowgate.

Tina and Ada found nothing to amuse them in the situation. They took over the care of Mary, shielding her from the rumours and making excuses for Tommy's long absences.

He, in an effort to salve his conscience, lavished gifts on Mary, baskets of fresh fruit would be delivered to the door, Mary would wake to find elegantly wrapped presents on her pillow, too weak to open them herself, she would smile wanly as Tina or Ada held up the contents for her to see Silk underwear, diamond studded earrings, fine chocolates, with hastily scrawled messages professing love.

Tina berated him for his neglect. Ada refused to speak to him or Carol, and warned if he attempted to let Carol set foot over the threshold she would inform Da-dee, who was quite unaware of the affair. When as expected Consumption claimed Mary's life, Tommy eloped with Carol to Gretna Green with what the family felt was indecent haste. Carol was reluctant to live in the house where Mary had died; Tommy eager to please his new bride rented a huge flat in Allison Street in the south side of the city. He spent most of his time there in any case and it was considered the up and coming part of town. The flat on the first floor of a sandstone tenement graced by a tiled entrance, the much coveted 'wally close' which was every Glasgow housewife's dream, had not only an inside lavatory, but a bathroom, beyond the wildest dreams of the Gallowgate tenants.

Though the sisters visited and gazed open mouthed at the furnishings Da-dee stubbornly refused to acknowledge Carol or set foot in the flat to see its splendours.

Tina, Famie and Mary still lived at home. Lizzie rented a little room from her employers the Rossi family who owned the cafe she worked in. She worked till midnight every night, with a half day on Wednesday which she spent at home reading or making spaghetti on her little machine. The cafe was in fashionable Charing Cross, it was stylish and elegant, each glass topped table with an elegant lamp, reflected in the mirrored walls, and a crescent shaped balcony of fine mahogany housed the resident pianist. The Rossis were from the prosperous north of Italy and were conscious of Lizzie's southern roots and treated her with a degree of haughtiness. Mamma Rossi was especially proud of her handsome sons, both tall, with Italian good looks and easy charm.

Since all the family worked in the cafe, mamma kept an eagle eye on any interplay between her darlings and Lizzie, ready to step on any budding romance.

Lizzie was unaware of her own charms and totally unaware of Mamma Rossi's scrutiny, but the sharp eyed Famie had picked up on it right away.

Tina worked in the local fish and chip shop, a little further down the Gallowgate near the Molendinar Burn, its once broad clear gurgling stream reduced to a dirty turgid trickle.

She too worked long hours, her employers like Lizzie's Italians, but from the south like herself. She was popular with the customers, always having a smile and a joke. She was content to live at home and help to look after Da-dee and go to devotions with her sisters on Wednesday nights.

Famie was the fashionable one, working shorter hours meant she had time to browse in Lewis's and Arnott Simpsons spending her wages on the latest gloves and shoes.

Tina and Famie were incurable romantics and dreamed of meeting their prince charming.

The reality was very different. Pat McCann was a frequent customer to Tina's fish and chip shop, he was surly, unkempt and moody, yet Tina with her silly simple heart was attracted to him - as Famie in turn was to be attracted to his brother.

Mary was too weak to work, her heart condition sapping what little strength she had. She was referred to a specialist, who seemed more interested in her mental capacity than her heart. He interpreted her gruff mumbling voice and downcast eyes as a sign of mental retardation, and suggested she should be put into an institution. Mary, perfectly able to understand what this meant was mortally afraid.

Da-dee turned to Ada for help; she had become the family advisor, in matters of health, marital troubles, family squabbles.

Ada took Mary in hand, coaching her in the answers she needed to give to the board of the institute to prove she was not mentally retarded. Mary had always been shy, she had no skill in displaying her personality Ada spent the intervening weeks before the interview instilling confidence into Mary, impressing upon her that being able to cope with questions they would put was her only chance of avoiding being admitted. The day of the interview arrived, Ada supervised Mary's appearance, borrowing from her sisters, a scarf, a pair of gloves, decent shoes, she brushed the steely rebellious hair into some semblance of order, and put a little perfume behind each ear.

Mary clung tightly to Ada's arm as they were ushered into the austere room, where to their mutual relief only one man was seated behind a huge desk. Motioning them to be seated, he leafed through some notes, now and then darting a look at Mary from under the spectacles perched halfway down his nose. Mary began to fidget with her gloves; Ada reached over and removed them, giving Mary a warning look.

Pushing the papers to one side and reaching for a notepad and pen, the man sat back in his chair and regarded Mary for what seemed an age.

'Tell me Mary. How would you go about dusting my desk?' he asked. Mary looked wildly at Ada, who smiled and nodded encouragement.

'Eh, eh, ah would take a' the things off it, then dust it, then dust a' the things before ah put them back,' Mary answered remembering to hold her head up.

'Can you count, Mary?' 'Aye'

'How much would you have to pay if you bought a half stone of potatoes at 4d, two chops at 1/-, and a piece of cheese at 10d?' Mary's head dropped, screwing up her face she began to count on her fingers, caught Ada's eye, and dropped her hands.

'Well?'

'2/2,' she said hesitantly.

'Very good, now how much change would you get if you gave the man 2/6?'

Mary sighed, looked at Ada, who smiled but said nothing. '4d, ah would get 4d,' said Mary, nodding her head, 'ah would get 4d.'

'Can you tell me who the Prime Minister is?'

The sudden change of topic caught Mary off guard, she stared at him. She knows that, it is one of the things I taught her, Ada thought, willing Mary to remember. Mary was deep in thought.

'Take your time, Mary,' Ada said

'Please do not interfere,' the doctor countered.

'Mr McDonald, Ramsay McDonald,' Mary blurted out.

'Yes, that is right, very good Mary, now just one more question.'

'Can you tell me if we have a King or a Queen on the throne?'

'A King,' Mary said confidently. 'Can you tell me his name?'

'That's two questions, you said just one more,' said Mary accusingly. The doctor looked startled; Ada tried to hide her amusement. 'Very well, as you say it is two questions, but can you tell me the name of the King?' he said impatiently.

'King George V.' Mary was clearly bored with the whole thing. 'Thank you,' he said sitting back in his chair regarding her closely. Mary shifted under his gaze.

She turned to Ada, 'Can we go hame noo?'

Ada took her hand. 'In a bit, we need to wait to see what the doctor has to say and what he thinks should happen.'

Mary slumped in her chair, Ada knew she was in one of her moods; they needed to get away as soon as possible.

The doctor was scribbling quickly on his pad, he drew the sheaf of notes towards him, scanning here and there, drawing his pen through some lines inserting words in their stead.

Ada tried to read his expression, as he pushed the papers away and sat back in his chair.

'Well Mary, I think you have been schooled very well, and you remembered all the right answers, it would seem you have a reasoning capacity.' Mary sat up, alarmed. 'What's that?'

Ada reached out a soothing hand, 'It just means you can understand things Mary.'

The doctor held up a hand, 'Thank you Mrs Cocozza, perhaps you could leave this to me?'

Ada glared at him, 'I'm sorry, but you can see how nervous she is, this has been an ordeal for her.'

'Yes, yes, I understand,' he said testily.

'Well Mary, perhaps I have been mistaken in my assessment of your capabilities, it is best you remain at home with your family after all.'

Mary jumped to her feet, tugging at Ada, 'Come on, come on.'

Ada gathered up the borrowed hat and gloves, and stood waiting.

The doctor was scribbling on a form, he handed it to Ada, and she took it, read it and slipped it in her bag.

'Thank you. It will give me great pleasure to give this report to Mary's Doctor, and to reassure the family,' she said.

Mary never ceased to be grateful to Ada, and became devoted to her, always seeking to do any little service.

Ada in turn felt a continuing responsibility for Mary, just as she did for Aggie and Jimmy.

The weeks spent working with Mary, had helped Ada in her sorrow over the loss of Benny, now it overwhelmed her again and she could not bear to go on living next door to the family, Da-dee's house held too many painful memories.

She began looking for things to blame for their terrible misfortune. Always deeply superstitious, she saw omens and portents in everything. A few weeks before Benny's death, Eugene had bought Ada pearls, she was horrified. Everyone knew that pearls brought sorrow and tears. Elizabeth had always warned her never to wear pearls.

'I can't wear these,' she said opening the box he had handed to her. 'Eh that's all silly nonsense, auld wives tales,' answered Eugene with his usual lack of tact, laughingly he reminded her that the pearls were paste, so they could not bring 'real' bad luck.

Ada was not convinced, the pearls stayed in the box. On Granny's death the family had insisted Ada should have an opal ring as a memento. Granny would have wanted her to have it, said Eugene, to refuse would offend Da-dee. Ada was deeply unhappy; opals were the most unlucky stone of all. She had hidden both ring and pearls under the linoleum in the bedroom hoping the symbolic burial would negate their power to bring misfortune. Now after Benny's death she was convinced their evil had reached out to her. She drew them from their hiding place, laid them on a sheet of newspaper, then taking a hammer she began to smash them into tiny little pieces, tears streaming down her face with every blow.

'In the name of God woman, what are ye doing?' shouted Eugene coming to investigate the noise.

'Leave me alone!' she screamed, shrugging off his attempt to release the hammer from her iron grip.

Soon the pearls and the ring lay broken and twisted, so ferocious her attack the pearls were reduced to powder. She gathered up the paper and fled from the house, running down the three flights of stairs, Eugene at her heels.

'Where are you going?' he yelled, as she flew up the street. She stopped at a drain in the gutter, opening the paper she shook the debris between the slats, sobbing wildly as she turned to face Eugene.

He gripped her arms, fearful she would run.

'Maybe you will feel better now, come on, I'll make you a strong cup of tea.' he said.

Eugene found work in England, taking Ada and the children with him. Lena at two years old was spared the constant change of school Domenica experienced as they moved from town to town. Children would taunt her about her name, making her miserable. On Sundays when Eugene went walking with the family, girls would call out, 'Domenica, Domenica, what a funny name, Dommy, Dummy,' they would taunt.

Eugene would smile and shout, 'Si oggi Domenica, domani Lunedi,' (yes today is Sunday, tomorrow is Monday).

This always silenced the girls, but it made Domenica feel worse, she did not like being called Sunday.

Everywhere they went, letters would come from Da-dee urging Ada to come back to Glasgow and settle for the sake of the children. She was deaf to his pleas, determined to keep her distance from Gallowgate and all the memories it held.

For two years they continued to travel. Wrexham, Thirsk, Barrow-in-Furness, Middlesbrough, each lodging more dismal than the last.

Da-dee was becoming more anxious, taking matters into his own hands he sent word that he had taken a two months lease on an attic flat in Moir Street, only a few blocks away from 206. He urged Ada to come home and try to settle there.

It was late 1934; there were compelling reasons why Ada should return. Lena would need to start school, and Ada was pregnant.

The family did settle in Moir Street, extending the lease for a year, with some relief Domenica enrolled in St.Alphonsus school, where Lena soon joined her aged four and three quarters. On her first day at school she was persuaded to sing a little song on the promise of a biscuit.

The song caused the teacher to raise her eyebrows –

Oh Jenny Cockalea
Come to bed and cuddle me.
Ah'll gie ye a cup o' tea
Tae keep yer belly warm.

Coming home at dinnertime one cold January day, Domenica and Lena found Ada in bed, tired and exhausted, lying in a drawer by the fire, swathed in a white shawl lay a sleeping baby. Tina was ladling soup into bowls. She turned to them with a smile.

'Say hello to your wee sister.'

'Is she ours to keep?' asked Lena.

'Of course. She is your sister, she was only born an hour ago,' Tina said.

'Why is mammy in her bed?' asked Domenica

'She has just had a baby,' Tina was surprised.

'But I thought the stork brought babies,' persisted Domenica.

'They do - but they don't just deliver them straight to the door,' Tina managed.

'Our teacher says they leave them under gooseberry bushes,' piped Lena.

'Don't be daft, there isnae any gooseberry bushes in the Gallowgate,' Domenica scoffed.

'Eh well that's why yer mammy is so tired, she was looking for the bush,'

Tina said quickly.

'Was it very far away?' Lena wanted to know.

'Oh aye, very far,' said Tina.

'How far?' quizzed Domenica.

'Ah don't know, now sit doon an' eat yer soup,' Tina rattled the chairs.

'Has she got a name?' asked Domenica.

'Well Da-dee said if yer mammy found a wee girl she was to be called after his favourite auntie, she is very rich and so she might leave yer wee sister a lot of money some day, her name is Madalena, that's nice isn't it?'

'I suppose so,' said Domenica, 'but she will get name called the same as me, we should have names like Mary or Margaret, then we would be the same as everybody else.'

'Ye don't want to be the same as everybody else, ye should be proud of your Italian names, anyway yer just as good as the next one,' Tina said.

'Who's the next one?' asked Lena.

'Never mind, eat yer soup.'

'I wish a rich auntie would leave me money, then ah could get new shoes,' sighed Domenica.

'Aye well ye never know yer luck!' said Tina.

Moir Street was a tram terminus, all through the day and late into the night, they would rumble in with their own very distinctive sound that clanged and shunted as they changed the points, and the driver pulled the huge levers from neutral into gear, they had a driving mechanism at each end, to avoid having to turn them round. That sound became my lullaby the echo still clear in my mind now, so many decades later.

Years later Lena would tell me that the house in Moir Street was always full of visitors, but none left an imprint on my conscience, only the clanging, banging trams.

I was barely a year old before the family were on the move again, this time to Ardersier near Inverness; Eugene had found work at the army barracks in Fort George. Lena and Domenica enrolled in the tiny school, boosting the roll to nine. Preparations were in hand for the imminent coronation of Albert duke of York, who as George the VI, was a shy and reluctant incumbent of the throne, on the abdication of his brother Edward VIII. Opinion in the country was still divided on whether a king should relinquish the throne for a woman, and a divorced woman at that. There were those who could accept the King's wish to be as he said, 'with the woman I love', and just as many who felt that duty to his country should come first. Ada was in the later camp, she saw dedication to duty as paramount, and indeed had shown such dedication to her siblings, at great cost to herself. She felt no less should be expected of a king. Eugene was commissioned to make a gate to commemorate the event. It was of wrought iron, incorporating the Union Jack and the lion rampant, a triumph resplendent with gilt and crimson paint. The celebrations for the coronation brought mugs of caramels and a day off for the school, happy children each issued with a little flag, lined up for a parade. For me at two years old it brought terror in the shape of a military band which came marching up the High Street, for there following the baton twirling major, was a giant of a man, wearing a leopard skin, with the creatures head almost covering his own, the sight of this monster, coupled with the thunder from a huge bass drum which he beat as he moved, was too much. Terrified I wrenched my hand from Ada's and took off into the crowd. I did not get far, and was soon being consoled by one of Lena's caramels. Though there are happier photographs of my time there, showing me rather reluctantly bottle feeding a lamb, there is no pictorial record of my flight from the strange leopard man.

Domenica who loved to tease would constantly remind me of my fear by draping herself in Ada's fur coat, wind the glassy eyed fox skin boa round her face, and make horrible growling noises. This would send me screaming from the room, and earn Domenica a slap on the ear from Ada. The stay in Ardersier was a happy time for Lena, she and Eugene would go tramping over the hills, picking dandelions for salads and herbal tea. Lena was very close to Eugene, and he loved her company. In her own way she was as spirited as Domenica, stubborn and daring she liked to test her nerve, and would get herself into some perilous situations. She, though, would never try to scare me, or tease me, and would often act as a shield from Domenica's torments.

We lodged with the blacksmith and his wife, who also had a small croft. They had taken on two 'parish children', orphans from Glasgow, and they worked them from dawn till dusk. Though they were allowed to sleep in the house, they were not allowed to eat with the family, instead they were summoned by a bell to the back door, where they were given bread and dripping with mugs of tea. The little girl had a 'harelip', thin and undernourished as she was, she was still expected to do heavy work. She often wet her bed, and was punished not only by beating but by being forced to wash her sheets in cold water. The boy was slightly older, considered to be feeble minded, yet his burden of work was even more demanding. He was given to running away, but always caught and punished by a severe beating with the blacksmith's heavy leather belt. Having witnessed this on several occasions, Ada warned Eugene she was going to 'do something about it'. He advised her to 'leave well alone', saying it was not her business. Ignoring his advice, Ada wrote to the authorities in Glasgow. To her shock and dismay, they responded by sending a junior official to investigate, who after a brief conversation with the blacksmith and his wife, concluded that the punishments handed out were beneficial to the children, and good for the development of their characters. Furious at what she saw as Ada's interference, the blacksmith's wife prevailed upon her husband to tell us to go.

Eugene shrugged and said, 'What did you expect?'

Ada just as furious was anxious to go, her only regret was that things were not going to be any better for the unfortunate children.

Within weeks we were off to England, to Liverpool. We arrived on a foggy November night, Ada tried to cheer us up by saying we were going to cross the river Mersey, on the famous ferry. We were not impressed, huddled together we peered into the fog, unable to see anything at all, the mournful sound of the foghorn booming out continually, as the ferry nosed her way gingerly across the water.

Domenica and Lena were in a sulk, they had not wanted to leave Ardersier and the loss of the friendly little school was hard to bear. For Domenica, it was as if she was back in the bad old days of constantly moving schools. She gloomily predicted that both she and Lena would be no sooner settled than they would have to move on.

Eugene however was in a confident mood, the living in Ardersier had not been too heavy on the purse, Ada had managed to save a few pounds, and there did not seem to be a shortage of work. Ada however wanted to settle but not in England, she kept at him to try to get work back in Scotland. We had been in Liverpool only a few months when Eugene was asked to go back to Glasgow. Ada had hoped for Edinburgh, but Glasgow would have to do.

Faced with finding a house, and feeling confident that the work would not dry up, Eugene set his sights on a new housing development at Garrowhill just outside Glasgow. The city was growing, swallowing up the surrounding villages. Detached villas were going for three hundred pounds, still, in Ada's opinion beyond Eugene's salary. Eugene was impulsive, and had little idea of how to manage money as he left all that to Ada.

She reminded him of how often she had to fight to keep the 'wolf from the door', indeed so often did she speak of this terrible animal that I always expected it to be prowling around every time we went out.

Eugene scoffed at Ada's fears, 'The wolf will never find us because we'll no tell it where we're going,' he laughed.

So against Ada's better judgement he went ahead and bought the house. The flitting to No.5 Douglas Drive took place in a steady drizzle of soft September rain. Eugene borrowed a small van which was loaded with beds, a chest of drawers, our one wardrobe, and the china. The sideboard, lovingly polished every day, was Ada's pride and joy, and she insisted it did not go in the van, but rather on the open cart which Eugene had also borrowed.

'Are ye daft woman? Surely it would be better in the van. It will be dry there,' Eugene protested.

'I want it where I can see it. We'll cover it up with a blanket.' Ada was not to be persuaded.

So the sideboard was loaded onto the cart with all the other bits and pieces. The caravan set off, Ada and Eugene pushing the cart, Domenica and Lena bringing up the rear, pushing me in the pram, half buried under pots and pans. It was a long walk from Moir Street to Garrowhill, and we arrived wet and bedraggled to find the van waiting at the gate.

As soon as Eugene had turned the key, Domenica and Lena rushed in, setting off loud protestations from me at being left behind. Lena released me from the pram and I gamely followed them up the bare wooden stairs, the sound of our clattering feet, and excited voices echoing through the empty rooms. We rushed from room to room, exclaiming in sheer wonder at all the space, come and see this, and this, we called to each other. Rushing into the bathroom we pulled up short, a bath, a real bath, and sink, and lavvy, that was ours and no one else's. We turned on the taps, screaming with delight as the water gushed out. Ada's voice cut through our excitement, calling us to come and lend a hand with the fetching and carrying. Ada was clearly enjoying the experience too, she hovered anxiously over the sideboard as it was carried in, saying, 'Careful, don't scratch the wood!'

Later as the darkness closed in, and the rain now heavier beat against windows, we sat amidst the tea chests and bundles, eating fish and chips out of newspaper. From our little radio, a dance band played 'September in the Rain', Eugene laughed.

'Aye, it certainly is.'

On our first morning we were all called outside, Eugene produced a bottle of whisky, tied with pink ribbon, which he attached to the handle of the front door. Setting us in a circle, he seized hold of the bottle, stood back and said 'I name this house 'The Haven', may God bless her and all who live in her.' With that he let the bottle go, and it smashed against the door, rattling the stained glass panel. We stood in frozen silence waiting for Ada to yell at him for making a mess, but she only laughed and said, 'I might have known you would have some daft idea.'

We all laughed, Eugene clapped his hands and said loudly, 'Three cheers for 'The Haven', hip, hip, hooray!'

As we all clapped our hands in glee, Ada disappeared inside the house, and came back with a brush and shovel, shooing us round to the back door to avoid the glass.

'This place is reeking of whisky,' she said. 'What are the neighbours going to think?'

She looked up to find curious eyes peering through lace curtains.

'Look at that, they probably think we are all mad Italians.'

If the neighbours did think that, events to come would certainly endorse that opinion.

CHAPTER 4

Life at Garrowhill was better than anything we had ever known before. For the first time, Ada and Eugene had a room to themselves. Domenica was also given a room, she became fiercely territorial, and we had to wait to be invited in. Having to share a room with her little sister did not seem to bother Lena, she had a loving and generous nature, and always shared everything.

Ada was at pains to prove to the neighbours that we were just like them, she chatted over the fence as she hung out the washing, and when Eugene made us a swing, she encouraged the two young boys next door to come and play on it. Eugene discovered a flair for gardening. He planted a standard rose tree in the front garden, only to have it stolen the very next night under cover of darkness. Ada was appalled. She could not believe that people would steal from their neighbours, especially in a 'posh' place like Garrowhill. In all the time we had lived in the Calton, no one had ever stolen from us, nor had we ever heard of anyone else suffering such a thing.

Eugene was philosophical. 'There was nothing tae steal in the Calton, cos naebody had anything.'

The best thing about the house for Ada was her kitchen, and she happily baked and cooked, taking pride in washing up and clearing everything away to leave the place spick and span, 'in case the neighbours dropped in.' For us it was the bathroom, even having to go in the night was no longer dread, no fear of meeting the neighbours either.

We had always hated having to share communal lavatories, being forced to hurry as a would-be user rattled the door handle demanding, 'Ur you gonnae be in there a' day?'

On Sunday mornings the smell of frying bacon wafting up the stairs would be enough to have Domenica and Lena tumbling out of bed, and rushing down the stairs. The smell of bacon frying held no such fascination for me. I was like Ada, a vegetarian, something of a rarity in the 1930s. However I was always eager to get downstairs, to see what was going on. One morning I missed my footing and tumbled head over heels landing up with my head stuck through the hall stand, which had toppled on impact. My anguished screams brought everyone running, all thought of breakfast forgotten. Eugene tried to free me, with shouted instructions from Ada, which included smearing my neck and ears with lard, which caused great amusement to Domenica and Lena, but failed to set me free. In the end Eugene, much to Ada's annoyance, had to saw through the wood to get me free. Though he did his best to restore it, the hall stand was never quite the same again.

Ada would complain I had ruined a good piece of furniture, and remind me how many times she had warned me to take my time coming down the stairs.

The first winter brought snow as we had never seen it before. It lay thick and pristine, clothing roofs, window ledges, trees and hedges. It was truly a revelation. In Glasgow the snow was brown, churned to slush within minutes of landing. We children were enchanted with this wonderland, and could not wait to get out in it. Domenica announced we would build a huge snowman, so we trudged up the hill, feeling our feet sink deep, picking them carefully trying to preserve the footprints. Once at the top we began to gather the snow into a ball, which grew and grew as we rolled it down the hill towards our garden, where we struggled to get it through the gate. This done, we rolled a smaller ball for the head.

Closing my eyes now as I write, I can see the golden light spilling out from the bay window, the magical silence of the snow as it drifted down, from the brooding sky, the strange echoing sound of our voices, the holes the snow had eaten away in my gloves, the sudden chill in my neck as Domenica in one quick movement whipped away my scarf, and draped it round the snowman, Domenica sneaked pieces of coal for his eyes and mouth, and a carrot for his nose, leaving tell tale puddles on the kitchen floor. Surveying our handiwork we agreed it was the best snowman we had ever seen. Each night we peered at him from our bedroom windows, tapping on the glass to bib him goodnight, in the morning we would rush to make sure he was still there. With a thaw in the weather, he began to shrink, till there was only a misshapen lump, and our friend was gone.

'Ach there will be plenty o' other years tae build snowmen,' Eugene said confidently, and we believed him.

Auntie Mary still eager to show her gratitude to Ada had moved with us to Garrowhill. Her unfailing patience and good nature made her a wonderful companion to us. She would sit uncomplaining, as Domenica put twists of paper curlers in her wiry hair, laughing at her reflection in the mirror, when the curls were brushed out.

Eugene would tease her and say, 'If we turned ye upside down, we could use ye as a brush.' She would play schools with Lena, sitting among the dolls and teddies, raising her hand to answer that two and two made four. Eugene had given over a sliver of the garden to us as our patch, and I would drag Mary out to help me dig it over and plant apple cores. If she ever grew tired of our demands, she never complained. In the house, she would dust and polish, bank up the fire, bring Ada cups of tea. On Sundays she would walk us to chapel. She was as devout as her sisters, and would never miss mass whatever the weather. Religion had never been an issue between Eugene and Ada, he a 'Widden Catholic', she a non practising Protestant. Neither had worried unduly over the dictates of the Catholic Church that in a mixed marriage the non-Catholic spouse had to agree any children would be brought up in the Catholic faith.

However, to Da-dee it was a matter of great importance, he had insisted Domenica and Lena attend Catholic schools, and perform all the duties the church demanded of them. Every Sunday, he and Tina would walk from the Gallowgate to Garrowhill, to sample Ada's home baking, have a bath, and check up on the spiritual welfare of his granddaughters. Out of respect for Da-dee, Ada had gone along with the Catholic education, and for the most part it had worked very well, but now there was trouble on the horizon. Domenica was very unhappy. School had always been difficult for her, the unsettled years when the family had constantly been on the move and the bullying and taunts about her name had made her insecure. She was suffering even more at Garrowhill, not only verbal abuse but physical too. Being older, coming towards the end of childhood, made everything more difficult somehow. Lena, still at primary school, was popular and happy, but Ada now began to worry about what lay in store for her too. Most mornings found Domenica tearful, and complaining of a sore stomach, begging to stay off school, if on Ada's insistence she did go, she would be sent home sick. Ada decided enough was enough. Domenica must be taken out of the school and sent to another. The nearest was a Protestant one, but Ada was adamant that Domenica should go there. Eugene shrugged, 'If it will make her happy, that's fine.'

The headmaster was not so pleased, thundering as Ada sat before him, holding the trembling hand of a tearful Domenica.

'You must realise your action is endangering your child's immortal soul, the Church requires all children to receive a Catholic education, and enjoy the communion of like minded people, and you are denying all of this to your child.'

Ada looked him squarely in the eye, 'I am not of your faith, so cannot accept what you are saying, my only concern is that my child is happy going to school each day.'

'Is it your intention that she embraces the Protestant faith?' he asked.

'Yes, since she will be attending a Protestant school, it is the religion I was brought up in, the religion of her mother,' snapped Ada.

'Your religious persuasion is of no concern, you married a Catholic, so you are aware that you must agree to bringing up your children in the Catholic faith, you cannot go back on that agreement, if you do the Church has the power to take your children from you. Where is the father of this child? He is the one who must decide.'

'We have discussed this, he has no objection to Domenica leaving this school, he too is only concerned she is happy to go to school,' said Ada.

'As for an agreement, I made no such agreement, Domenica is leaving, and that is the end of the matter as far as I am concerned.'

Within a week, Domenica had not only changed schools, she had changed her religion and her name. Ada reasoned that if she used her second name Elizabeth, it would be a new beginning; Domenica opted for Betty, so Betty it was. Eugene was accepting but surprised,' Ah've never known you to give in to bullies; you always said they should be proud of their names.' 'So they should, but drastic problems call for drastic measures, as all that business was making her ill. Still I suppose we will need to get used to calling her Betty too.'

'Aye, ah suppose so, it will take a bit of explaining to the rest of the family though, still at least it is all over now. She can settle down and get on with her school work, anyhow she will be leaving school soon, and that will be that,' said Eugene.

It was not all over, before Betty had spent her first week in the new Protestant school, the priest came to call.

Eugene saw him coming up the path, Ada was reading, we children in bed. As the priest entered Ada rose, laying the book she was reading face down on the table, the title clearly visible, 'Maria Monk'.

The priest's eye fell on the book and his face darkened and he turned to Eugene 'Who is reading this book?' he demanded.

Eugene smiled, 'Ah don't read books, Ada is the one with the education,'

'Are you saying you are unaware of the nature of this book?' The voice was cold.

Eugene shrugged, 'Ah couldnae tell ye anything aboot it, ah never bother, ah don't read.'

Then you should bother, it is your duty to see no offensive material enters your house, your duty to make sure that what your wife reads is acceptable.'

It was clear the priest was losing patience. Ada was losing patience too. 'What do you mean by acceptable?' she demanded.

'Ah don't see what a' the fuss is aboot, a book is a book as far as ah'm concerned,' said Eugene.

'You are a disgrace to the faith man, this book is propaganda against our Holy Mother Church, not only are you married to a woman who is not of our faith, you allow her to read this filth.'

'Are you going to let this man speak to me like that?' Ada shouted.

Eugene looked pained. He hated confrontation and he was totally unable to cope with anger and argument, he spread his hands in a gesture of sheer helplessness. 'look Father, ah don't want any trouble, my wife is a strong willed woman, she is the one wi' the brains, she takes tae dae wi' most things in the family, ah jist bring in the wages.'

'That is very obvious, you are not in charge of your own household, and I can see now how this wicked act of removing your daughter from a good Catholic school to go to a Protestant one came about.'

'Ech the lassie wisnae happy,' said Eugene.

'She was ill, with all the bullying, being called names, and worse, it was a decision made in her best interests,' Ada told him.

'A decision made by you, no doubt, overruling your husband's wishes,' the priest snapped.

'Well we did talk aboot it, the lassie wisnae happy, as ah said,' Eugene put in.

'Surely being called names is better that putting her immortal soul in danger of being condemned to hell for all eternity?' the priest argued.

'I am interested in what happens to her in this life, nobody knows what lies on the other side, in any case I find it hard to believe a loving God would condemn a child to hell, just because her mother took her out of one school and put her in another,' Ada was scathing.

'Then I am here to tell you, you are wrong, very wrong, every Catholic has a duty to bring children up in the Catholic faith, not to do so is a sin, a mortal sin, and merits damnation,' the priest said pointing an accusing finger at Ada, who stood shaking her head.

'I think you have said enough, Mr. Cassidy,' she said.

'Father Cassidy', corrected the priest.

'No, not to me, you are not my father in any sense of the word,' she said.

Incensed the priest turned on Eugene, 'Have you nothing to say about this total disrespect I am suffering?'

'Ech well, sorry aboot that, but maybe ye should just leave it be, the lassie is at the new school noo, so that's that,' Eugene told him.

'You are a snake in the grass, Mr Cocozza, you are not fit to be a man, a husband, a—a Catholic, in fact you are not a snake in the grass, you are lower than that, I hold you in contempt!'

Red in the face, he turned on Ada, 'As for you woman, I will pray to God to take your children from you'.

Ada flew across the room, grabbing the startled cleric by the throat.

'Get out! get out! call yourself a man of God; you are devil's spawn, to say such a thing.' She shook him like a rag doll, her grip so fierce, he could scarcely breathe.

'Ada for God's sake let go!' Eugene tried to pull her off.

'Not until he is out that door,' she fumed, dragging the red faced priest into the hallway, and pushing him through the front door.

The priest tugged at his collar, trying to regain his breath.

'This is not the last of this,' he fumed.

'It is as far as I am concerned; I want nothing to do with your God, if he would answer a prayer to take children from their parents. He has already taken one of my children, and I can't forgive Him for that'.

'Then that was a judgement on your mixed marriage, you should ask His forgiveness, for what you have done,' snarled the priest.

He jumped back in alarm as Ada lunged for his throat again.

'Go! go! and never come back here again,' she screamed at him.

He walked briskly up the path, turning at the gate, he shouted,

'I shall report this to the Bishop, you will be hearing from him.'

'He'll get what you got, if he puts his foot in this door, Bishop, or no Bishop, you can tell him he has no sheep here, we have minds of our own in this house,' Ada shouted after him.

'Come in, come in, let it be,' Eugene urged.

Ada watched the priest make a hasty retreat down the road, looking up she caught the movement of twitching curtains, she smiled grimly to herself,

'So much for trying to impress the neighbours,' she thought as she closed the door.

So Domenica, now transformed to Betty, settled happily into the routine of the new school. Da-dee was horrified when he heard of the confrontation with the priest, as were the aunts. Mary though did not swerve in her allegiance to Ada, though she said an extra rosary every day, to intercede for Ada, lest the priest's threatened prayer should be answered.

Da-dee insisted Lena stay on at the Catholic school, Ada was happy enough to comply, knowing Lena was quite happy there.

So began the religious dilemma that haunted us for the rest of our schooldays.

For me as the youngest this was kept from me, but I would pick up a word or two, of conversation, before the grownups would catch sight of me and change the subject. Auntie Mary's extra rosary was not lost on me, mainly because it meant we spent so much longer in the chapel, and in our bedtime prayers. I would lie in bed pondering over Mary's murmured pleas to God, not to break Eadie's heart, and fret over what it all meant. Mary would try to cheer me, pushing me on the swing in the back garden, from which I constantly fell, and suffered nose bleeds, the boys next door would come round to play on the swing, but one in particular loved to scare me, by dropping spiders and beetles on me, I was terrified, only four years old and very timid. I was forever running screaming to Ada, as an assortment of creepy crawlies dropped on my head or were pressed into my tiny hand. Ada was endlessly patient with all her children, we seldom got the rough edge of her tongue, but even she was beginning to weary of the tears and hysteria, induced by the mischief maker next door. She finally sat me down and told me my hysterical reaction was giving my tormentor great satisfaction, causing him to repeat the mischief. 'I know you are only four, and it is easy to be scared of these things, but the only way to stop all this, is for you to stop being afraid of these little creatures.' She went into the garden, returning with a worm and a beetle, taking a sheet of newspaper, she spread it out on the table then set the worm and beetle down. I shrunk away in terror, but she drew gently forward and stood me on a chair, so that the worm and the beetle were below me.

'Now,' she said 'see how much bigger you are than the little beetle, and the long thin worm. Don't you think they should be afraid of you?'

I could see why they would be but I was still terrified of them.

'What is it you don't like about them?' she asked.

'They are ugly, and I don't like the way they move,' I said.

She laughed, 'they can only move the way God created them, you may think it is ugly but they know nothing of that, and just get on with being what they are.' She picked up the beetle letting it explore the palm of her hand. I drew back, but she reached for my hand and slowly the beetle walked on to my palm.

'It will be all right, just let him wander, he will do you no harm, she whispered.

As she lowered my hand to the table the beetle wandered off, only to be replaced by the worm which lay like a question mark in my hand, it did not move and I soon realized I was not afraid.

The dreaded 'monsters' which stalked the garden no longer held any terror for me.

Ada smiled, 'Next time that horrible boy from next door tries to frighten you, just tell him you are not scared. Believe it and you really won't be, and my word won't he be surprised?'

Losing my fear of the tiny denizens of the garden meant I could sleep out in the tent Betty and Lena had made from old sheets, and dine on jam sandwiches and drink lemonade.

So the happy Summer rolled on, it seemed things would never change, but change they did. As we lay in bed at night the sound of raised voices would filter upstairs. Eugene and Ada arguing over money, we soon realized though Ada did her best to keep it from us, that the wolf had found our hiding place, and was once again prowling outside our door.

Each night Betty would creep halfway down the stairs and listen, till one dreadful night she burst into our room, saying she had heard Ada say we were going to lose the house.

By September the red van was outside the gate, and Ada's precious sideboard was being carried out by Eugene and uncle Pat. Ada stood her hand covering her mouth, too dejected to bother to warn them not to scratch the wood, as she had done that September only two years before.

Eugene was as philosophical as ever, 'Eh,' he shrugged 'that's life, one day up, the next day down,' he went on ferrying things out to the van and handcart, whistling under his breath, 'September in the Rain', seeming not to notice that Ada wept. The soft rain fell on the bowed branches of the trees, as if an extension of her tears.

Betty ran after Eugene, 'Daddy, stop whistling that song,' she said.

'What? What's the matter?' he asked, balancing boxes on top of each other.

'It's that song, it's upsetting mammy, it was playing on the wireless the day we moved in here,' Betty reminded him.

'Get away,' he said. 'Fancy that.'

Ada was incensed he had not remembered, from that day the song joined the list of songs and music that must never be played or sung in our house. With each family crisis, she added to her list. Woe betide any of us who broke the ban.

Lena had vanished, as the house emptied and the time came for us to climb on the cart, she was nowhere to be found.

Ada panicked; Eugene and uncle Pat were dispatched to search the streets, while Ada asked around the neighbours.

It was Betty who found her, crouched in the garden shed, her favourite doll cradled in her arms.

'Come on,' Betty urged, 'it's time to go.'

'I don't want to go,' sobbed Lena.

'I know, but we have to go,' Betty tugged at her sleeve.

'We don't even know where we are going,' I said, eager to have my say.

'I know,' said Betty, 'We are going to stay with uncle Tony and auntie Teeny, and what's even worse, we are all going to live in one room.

CHAPTER 5

In Auntie Teeny's room, we three sit astride rolled up mattresses, singing at the top of our voices.

Oh Johnny, oh Johnny, how you can love
Oh Johnny, oh Johnny, heavens above
You make my sad heart jump with joy
And when you're near me
I can't keep still a minute
Oh Johnny, oh Johnny, oh Johnny, oh!
What makes me love you so?
You're not handsome it's true
But when I look at you
Oh Johnny, oh Johnny, oh!

'QUIET!' the door bursts open, Auntie Teeny, potato peeler in hand, her face flushed with anger, stands framed in the doorway.
'If this is what ah'm gonna hiv tae put up wi', ah'll be havin' a word wi' your mother. We might as well get one thing straight, ah don't want ye here, it was Antonio's idea, ma Tony is too soft hearted. As far as ah'm concerned you should a' be across the road at 206.'
We stared at her, we had never seen her like this before, and she had always been really nice to us. We slid down from the mattresses and huddled dejectedly on the bare floor. 'I wish mammy was back,' Lena said. Ada and Eugene were at Da-dee's depot in Ross Street, where most of the furniture was to be stored, the precious sideboard swathed in blankets.
Ada erupted in fury, when she heard of Teeny's outburst. 'Who does she think she is talking to our children like that?' she fumed. 'Ach, her bark is worse than her bite, she has a quick temper that's a', don't let her bother ye,' Eugene said easily.
'Don't let her bother me! Everything bothers me, no house, no job, no money, stuck in one room, with barely enough room to swing a cat, being beholden to THAT woman, how can I not be bothered?'
'It'll no be for long, ah'll get work somewhere, it's just life's ups and downs, and we just have to be patient.' Eugene was pulling out pots and pans, spreading them over the floor.
'Patient!' Ada screamed, 'You have the cheek to tell me to be patient, it's just life's ups and downs,' Ada mocked.
'Eh what else can we do? Gettin' upset is no gonna solve anything things will get better, just wait an' see.' Eugene laid out plates and cups.
'For God's sake!' Ada yelled grabbing the plates and firing them at him, 'When are you ever going to understand the mess we are in?' We three sat transfixed, we had only ever heard arguments from upstairs or through a wall, and Lena and I began to cry.
The door burst open again, Teeny stood, her hand on the door knob, her

great bosom heaving with rage.

'What's goin' on here? First it's they damn kids, noo it's you two, you are no five minutes in the hoose, an' the place is in an uproar.' She looked askance at the broken plates, then at Eugene who was dabbing at a cut on his forehead where one of the plates had found its mark.

'At least she can aim straight,' he grinned.

It was war from then on and we kept strictly to our room, only Ada ventured into the kitchen to cook, Teeny watching her every move. Fearful of Ada's wrath she saw a soft target in me; she would corner me on my return from using the communal lavatory, making petty complaints about us for me to relay to Ada. Using the lavatory which was down half a flight of stairs was a real ordeal for me, invariably I had no sooner snibbed the lock when the door handle would be rattled, and a stream of oaths would demand I come out. I was convinced the evil smelling old man next door listened for me going down the stairs and would shuffle after me, his threadbare slippers clacking on the stair, his knarled knuckles clutching his trousers for want of a belt. Quickly as I could I would put myself to rights, unsnib the lock and duck under his arm, my eyes riveted to the ground, panting I would sneak through Teeny's door, slink past the kitchen only to have a hand pull me back and a hoarse whisper in my ear. For the most part Ada ignored the petty complaints, till Teeny dropped her bombshell about the cooker.

'Ye can tell yer mammy fae noo on ah'll be usin' the cooker first, she needs tae wait till big Tony an wee Tony hiv had their tea, an' she will need tae put two shillins in the gas meter, ah'm no lettin' her use ma gas.'

Ada, furious at this was all for marching in to confront Teeny, but Eugene urged patience. Teeny, feeling she had scored a victory, grew bolder and two weeks later she caught me coming up the stairs.

'Here you, tell yer mammy that she canny use the cooker ony mair. Tony is sick an' tired o' the smell o' cookin' especially after he has had his tea.' I stared at her in consternation, what would Ada say if I relayed this to her, but she wasn't finished with me yet.

'Oh an another thing, ah still think youse are no puttin' enough in the gas meter, ye can tell yer mammy, that if it's oor gas money, then youse will hiv tae sit in the dork, ah canny afford tae share ma gas'.

'Right auntie Teeny, I'll tell her,' I said, darting away from her grasp. In the room Ada was gathering the food she was going to cook for our tea she looked up and caught the look on my face.

She smiled. 'What's wrong? You look as if you have seen a ghost.' I stood head down not daring to look her in the eye.

'Is it that old devil next door, rattling away at that handle and scaring you when you were in the lavatory?'(Ada never said 'lavvy').

'No mammy, it was auntie Teeny, she—she said you couldn't use the cooker any more, uncle Tony is sick and tired.' My voice faltered as the storm clouds gathered on Ada's face.

'Sick and tired is he? Right well, we'll see about that,' she marched into the kitchen, me trailing miserably at her heels. Teeny and Tony sat at the table with wee Tony, having their meal, and they all jumped as Ada thumped the table.

'I hear you are sick and tired, just what is it that is bothering you?' Tony stared down at the table, unable to meet her eyes. 'Well?' she persisted, your wife uses a wee lass to tell me I can no longer use the cooker, because you are 'sick and tired', so I want to know what is making you 'sick and tired'?

Tony said nothing; he shot a glance at Teeny, who sat both fists clenched on the table. 'Tell her!' Teeny demanded. 'None o' this has anything to do wi' me,' he muttered sheepishly, 'Ah leave a' that tae Teeny'.

'You seem to be the one that is complaining, too much of a coward to talk up for yourself though,' Ada rasped.

'If ye must know he is sick an' tired of cookin' smells jist efter his tea when he is no' hungry, ah telt the wean tae tell ye.'

'So you begrudge your brother's children getting fed?' Ada demanded.

'Ach well ye know how it is, when ye've eatin',' he said, attempting a smile.

'Oh I know just how it is, you are not man enough to speak up for yourself, you make the balls and she fires them.'

'It is oor hoose an' we can say whit we like,' Teeny shouted.

'Oh we are never allowed to forget that, but we pay rent for that room, the only cooker is the one in your kitchen, if I can't use that what am I supposed to do?' Ada demanded.

'Ye will jist hiv tae use the fire,' said Teeny.

Coming home that night Eugene found Ada juggling with pots on the fire trying to keep everything warm. He listened to the story and dismissed the whole thing as nonsense.

'I'll speak to my brother, make him see sense,' he said.

'No use speaking to him, the man is a coward, anyway I have said my piece and I don't need you to speak for me, I will manage just fine without her cooker,' Ada told him.

Nevertheless Eugene tackled Tony who reluctantly agreed to overrule his wife and allow Ada to use the cooker. Eugene, with his usual lack of tact, used those very words to Ada.

'Allow me! Who does he think he is?' Ada exploded.

'Ach, he disnae mean any harm, he is just tryin' to make things right,' soothed Eugene. 'Anyway that is it all settled now, so you don't need to struggle with the fire.'

'Are you saying I can't manage cooking on a fire? Do you think I am useless? I want nothing to do with their cooker, I won't meekly beg to be 'allowed', you should have more respect for me than that,' she fumed. 'Eh, I was tryin' to make things better,' Eugene pleaded.

'Just leave well alone, we will manage, we won't starve,' snapped Ada. She never used the cooker again, every day Lena and Betty were sent out to buy bundles of sticks, to supplement the coal. Ada would listen out for the briquette man, sending me down to tell him she wanted two dozen. She became quite adept at cooking on the fire; she made pancakes on a griddle, cooked vegetables, and made soup. Even though our diet was constrained by lack of a cooker and lack of money we lived well enough. As Ada had promised, we did not starve.

Of the four Ricardo girls only Teeny and her sister Lucia were married. Lucia had a son the same age as wee Tony, her marriage failed and she found herself having to work to keep herself and the boy. Teeny offered to take little Ronnie in until his mother could get herself settled. Ronnie had the same curly hair and large dark eyes as wee Tony. It was easy to see both boys came of Italian stock, both attended St Alphonsus school, keeping all the statutes of the faith. Glasgow was a city divided by religion, Protestants and Catholics lived mostly in an uneasy truce, but in July as the twelfth approached and the Orange Order marched with fife and drum, tempers grew heated. Groups of boys would accost children in the street and demand, 'Are you a Billy or a Dan?' The wrong answer could earn a beating.

Two days before the twelfth, Ronnie and Tony had been followed home from school. The gang pushed them up against a wall and demanded, 'Whit fit dae ye kick wi'?'

The terrified boys did not know what was meant by the question, they stood mute with fear.

'Whit fit?' demanded the ring leader.

'I-I don't know what you mean,' stammered Ronnie, who suffered from a stammer which grew worse under pressure.

'Ur ye a Billy or a Dan, ye eedjit?'

'Ah-ah-ah'm a Ca-Catholic,' Ronnie managed.

'Wrang answer son,' sneered the boy kneeing him in the groin, as Ronnie collapsed, they attacked Tony, leaving him doubled in agony, and they ran of laughing.

The boys struggled up the stairs. Teeny was out, so they came to Ada, who was horrified.

'Who did this to you?'

'A gang of boys, they must have thought we were somebody else, they asked us if our names were Billy or Dan,' said Tony mystified.

Ada poured them cups of milk, and spread slices of bread with jam. 'They didn't think you were somebody else; they meant are you Catholic or a Protestant.'

'We said we were Catholic and they said it was the wrong answer. Is it wrong to be a Catholic, auntie Eadie?

'No, and it isn't wrong to be Protestant either, everybody has the right to be what they want and believe what they want, different people believe different things, we should all try to accept that and live together in peace. I know they scared you but you must never let yourself be bullied, or show people you are afraid, even if you are underneath.'

'Are you scared of my mammy, even though you don't show it?' Tony asked.

'I'm not scared of your mammy son,' Ada said quietly.

'She says you are. She says that's why you don't use the cooker, even though ma daddy said you could,' wee Tony persisted.

Ada smiled grimly.

'That's not fear son, that's pride', she said.

That night Ada wrote a poem for the boys entitled, 'A Billy or a Dan?'

It was a plea for tolerance and understanding.

Still too young to go to school, I spent all my time with Ada. We would do the family shopping, first to the Maypole Dairy with its blue and white tiled walls, and polite white-aproned assistants. I would watch with fascination the man slice a chunk of butter from the huge glistening yellow block of butter, patting it between two wooden paddles into a square, he would lay a piece of greaseproof paper on the scale, carefully lifting the butter and placing it to be weighed, shaving of slivers to get the right weight. Cheese was cut by pulling a wire through, then weighed and wrapped just as the butter. Below the glass top of the counter was a display of cold meats thinly sliced and labelled, here and there among the trays little pots of jellied meat labelled 'Potted Haugh' were offered for sale. These pots held dread for me, being too young to read I shivered when I heard the women in the queue ask for 'potted heid'. I would stare in horror and wonder whose head they had cut off to make this stuff, and keep a close eye on Ada to make sure she did not buy it.

The butcher on the corner of Kent Street was our next call, the shop window with its trays of rolled sides of beef, fatty chops, glutinous slimy liver, and glistening red stuff called mince, which bore the label, 'home fed'. I could never understand how they fed this thing, it did not look alive, yet it must be, since they fed it. I would follow Ada into the shop with great reluctance, for if the window display was horrific, it was nothing to the horror inside the shop. All along the wall, hung huge carcasses of cows and sheep, split from top to bottom, but with the head still attached, beneath them the sawdust strewn floor dark with blood and dripping fluids. Oblivious of this horror, the women would queue, gossiping as they waited to be served, their headscarves brushing against the marbled flesh. I would bury my head in Ada's coat, squirming with revulsion, scuffing my shoes in the sawdust. Pushing me upright she would scold, 'Mind your shoes, money doesn't grow on trees you know.' When a customer asked for, 'a sheep's heid', the butcher would bring it from the back shop, hold it aloft and say, 'How's that?' then with a grin, 'Will ah leave the eyes in tae see ye through the week?' Laughter all round, even Ada permitting herself to smile. Much to my relief Ada never asked for a sheep's head, but she did ask for a ham bone to make soup, which to me was almost as bad. Most mornings we climbed the three flights of stairs to Da-dee's, to deliver his morning rolls and gammon. Tina would open the door dressed in a flowery cross over apron, her long black hair tied up in a turban, invariably she would have a soup ladle in her hand, and the smell of ham and lentil soup would fill the house. Da-dee would be sitting in his chair by the fire, scraping away at his pipe with a pipe cleaner. Tina would smile and say, 'Ah'll put the kettle on for a wee cuppa, eh hen?' lifting the heavy iron kettle from the range to fill it from the swan necked tap with its thin rim of verdigris round the base. The sound of hammering was the only clue to the presence of uncle Pat, through in the 'wee' room at the end of the lobby. Pat was always holed up in the 'wee' room. What he did there was a mystery; no one ever crossed the threshold. Tina who had caught fleeting glimpses, would roll her eyes and say 'The place is like a midden, an absolute midden.'

'What has he got in there?' Ada would ask.

'Junk, just junk, he tells me he mends shoes fur folk, but ah never see ony shoes, or the money he gets fur mendin' them.'

Ada did not approve of Pat. She would complain to Eugene that Pat was dirty, a lazy work-shy good for nothing.

Eugene in his usual live and let live philosophy would say, 'Well it's her life, if she is happy wi' him that's a' that matters.'

'So you are happy to stand by and let that man ruin your sister's life?'

'It's none of our business' he would mumble sucking at his pipe, then scraping at it, just like Da-dee.

Tina herself, though she would complain about Pat, would defend him in the same breath, when Ada railed against his failure to provide for her and Da-dee.

'Och ah know Eadie,' she would say using the name the family mostly used for Ada, 'Ah know he is no' the best man in the world, it's just his way, ye know whit they say, 'a man's a man fur a' that.'

'I don't think that was what Robert Burns meant when he wrote that,' Ada would say.

But this was lost on Tina; the short quote was the extent of her knowledge of Burns and his works.

As she waited for the kettle to boil, Tina would stir the soup, then using two forks she would carefully lift the steaming ham bone out of the pot and lay it on a dinner plate.

The fatty smell would turn my stomach, catching sight of my face Tina would laugh saying, 'Would ye look at her face!'

Ada would mash the tea, spreading the rolls with butter, and filling Tina and Da-dee's with two generous slices of gammon, she and I opting for butter only. I always ate mine as quickly as possible so that I would have more time to play at shops. Tina would spread newspaper on top of the coal bunker, and empty the potato peelings, carrot tops and any other scraps to stock my shop. From the shelves above the bunker, where she displayed her best willow pattern plates, she would bring down a pair of brass scales, with all their weights, that Granny had used in the fruit stall. These were her pride and joy, and it was a real treat for me to be allowed to play with them. Da-dee would fish in his pockets for farthings and ha'pennies, and the shop would be open for business. I was too small to reach the top of the bunker, so Tina would stand me on an orange box, drawing the usual warning from Ada, 'Mind you don't fall now.'

When I tired of the shop, I would climb on Da-dee's knee, and he would sing songs in Italian, making me repeat every line. He had immense patience and he valued everything and wasted nothing. He would show me how to smooth out the paper bags, the blue ones from sugar, and the brown ones from the eggs. We would sit unravelling knots from string, winding it up and storing it away with the bags in the kitchen drawer. It is something I still do to this day. The kitchen window of 206 looked down on the corrugated roof of Barrowland, the popular dance hall, where on Fridays and Saturdays, young men and women flocked hoping to 'click' and get a 'lumber' to walk them home. Many liaisons ended in marriage. Too young to know or care of such things I would clamber up on the draining board of the sink, sit back on my heels and wait for the rats to appear. They would come scurrying along the grooves of the roof, whiskers twitching, beady eyes shining, big rats, little rats, thin rats, fat rats, safe behind the sash cord window, I gazed in fascinated horror. Mice in the house were a common enough occurrence, and though scared of them I could not imagine what I would do if a rat was to come into the house. Occasionally there would be stories of some woman who found a rat a big as a terrier under her sink. The idea that something to swift and secretive could be lurking under the sink, beds or drawers was a constant dread for me. Seeing them scurrying along the roof of Barrowland was reassuring, as I liked to think they preferred that to the dark recesses of Teeny's house.

For Ada the real rat was Pat. I could never understand her animosity towards him, at least not then, innocent as I was of adult activities, yet sometimes in the close confines of our room sleeping cheek by jowl with Ada and Eugene I would hear Ada rail against Pat, accusing him of being deceitful and hinting at some awful pestilence that he had visited on Tina. I had no idea what the pestilence could be, but the thought that our lovely auntie Tina with her sunny disposition could have some dread disease preyed on my mind.

Pat had a brother Joe, and where Pat was slim, of medium height and swarthy, Joe was tall, thick set, with a florid complexion. Joe considered himself a bit of a dandy, and was always well dressed and clean shaven, while Pat according to Ada was 'as black as the earl of hell's waistcoat'.

Joe had been secretly courting Famie, secretly because he and Pat though brothers were sworn enemies.

Famie the youngest of the sisters was generally considered to be the prettiest, she was a little spoiled, indulged by Lizzie, Tina and Mary, and was the 'apple' of Da-dee's eye. Famie was popular outside the family with neighbours and workmates, but at home she could be petulant and vindictive if she did not get her own way.

Ada would say tartly, 'That one is an angel outside but a devil inside.'

Eugene would shrug and agree with his sisters saying, 'She's young, she will learn.' Famie shared Tina's love of 'the pictures', the two of them taking the tram into Argyle Street to the Argyle cinema, to see Fred Astaire and Ginger Rogers, or Nelson Eddy and Jeanette McDonald.

Tina would get carried away and for days after would waltz round the kitchen with the sweeping brush humming the tunes from the films, or burst into song, her efforts to reach the high notes causing even the patient Da-dee to plead 'SILENZIO!'

Though the news that Famie was to marry Joe McCann was greeted with joy by the sisters, Eugene shared some of Da-dee's misgivings, Ada's only comment being, 'The only good thing you can say about him is he is no stranger to soap and water.'

The origin of the brothers was something of a mystery. Ada who 'had a nose' for this sort of thing was able to discover that McCann senior had disappeared from the scene when the boys were very young, leaving their mother to raise her sons by taking in washing and mending clothes.

Joe had joined the army, before taking up with Famie, she was dazzled by the photograph he presented to her, showing him in smart belted uniform, peaked cap and baton tucked under his arm, Famie was convinced he was the handsomest of men. To my three year old eyes, Joe was fleshy and unattractive, while Pat who was always covered in grime, was handsome under all that dirt, and held a great fascination for me. I was the only one he paid any attention, and I was not afraid of him, as Lena (who loathed him) and Betty were. I had not only seen inside the 'wee' room, his inner sanctum, I had been allowed to explore its contents. It was full of the most extraordinary things, shoe lasts, boxes and boxes of buttons, nails, wire, bits of leather, carpet tacks, old shoes, old clothes, some so old the lapels of the jackets had turned green. There was no room to move, every surface and every inch of floor space was piled high, in one box lay dozens of buckles, brass, tin, bone, mother-of-pearl, and a magnificent silver one which I thought truly beautiful. I would pick it out of the box, turning it over and over to admire it, while Pat would be hammering tacks into the sole of a shoe, stretched over a cobbler's last. He would hold the tacks in his mouth transfer them to the leather, tap them in with a small hammer in one fluid movement. I thought he was very clever, and much more interesting than Joe who would sit and tell tall tales of his exploits in the army, while Famie took off his boots and massaged his 'poor tired feet'. Ada was unaware of my forays info uncle Pat's secret 'wee' room, my visits took place when occasionally she would leave me with Tina 'to mind'. I instinctively knew she would not approve, so when one glorious day Uncle Pat, watching me stroke the silver buckle, told me I could keep it, I knew the gift must remain a secret, not even to be shared with my sisters.

The marriage of Famie and Joe was to be celebrated with high mass at St Alphonsus chapel. As her god-daughter I was her flower girl, Lizzie her best maid, and the best man was Calisto Rossi, whose father owned the cafe where Lizzie worked. Calisto was tall and extremely handsome, in Ada's opinion a man of substance and bearing, and a much better 'catch' for Famie had she not been so besotted with Joe. Of course the chapel was very familiar to us all, yet even though I had been taken to mass by Lizzie several times, I had been so intent in following all her movements I had scarcely raised my eyes to look around.

Now standing behind Famie throughout the long nuptial mass, I let my eyes wander taking in the scene. The white alter gleamed with gold goblets and tall candlesticks topped by even taller candles, and baskets of flowers caught the slanting light through the stained glass window in the roof. Moving my gaze to the sacristy from which the priest and alter boys had emerged, I froze in terror, above the door was a figure with outstretched wings, the face was in shadow, but to me it was demonic, it gazed down menacing and gloomy, its eyes fixed on me.

I stood rooted to the spot, totally forgetting to kneel or move as the mass dictated. Lizzie put a guiding hand on my back, guiding me with a sweet smile.

Following the bridal pair into the sacristy to sign the register, I gripped Lizzie's hand tightly as we walked beneath the demon. That figure was to haunt me for the whole of my childhood.

CHAPTER 6

The new year of 1939 was barely two weeks old when Tommy's mother-in-law died, leaving her little room and kitchen in the next close at 211 vacant. Eugene lost no time in securing the rental, and soon we were happily packing our things and leaving Teeny's thrall. Ada was reunited with her beloved sideboard, which when it was installed along with the dining table and four chairs left precious little room. It was decided we girls would share the long narrow bedroom, and Ada and Eugene would sleep in the recess bed in the kitchen.

Betty left school, found work in an office and felt very grand, lording it over Lena and I, saying she was 'very tired after a hard day.' She was generous though with her pocket money and would buy us sweets on Fridays. I was about to join Lena at St. Alphonsus school, and filled with dread at the thought. I lived in constant fear of losing Ada, and was never happy when separated from her.

On the day she took me to school to register, we stood outside the gate listening to the children recite by rote the three times table. I had no real fear of tables, or indeed of reading, Ada had spent many hours reading to me, and already I had a love of books, matched only by her own. It was the fear that somehow she would vanish from my life if I walked through those gates. All during our stay at Teeny's she had been very unhappy, railing at Eugene over our situation, and threatening 'One day I will walk out of here, you will never find me.'

So I had made it my business to stay with her at all times, now I had to go to school, it was small comfort that Lena was there in another class. It was Ada I needed for my very existence.

My stay at St.Alphonsus was short lived, and within six months I followed Lena across to the school opposite, Our Lady and St.Francis, senior secondary, an impressive red sandstone building. It was a convent school run by Franciscan nuns, who lived at Merylee Convent on the south side of the city. The school took children from primary right through to sixth form. There was a muted rivalry between the two schools, the convent girls being viewed as snobs. Lena was a bit of a tomboy, a mischief maker, making waves as she went through the school, her reputation went before her and as 1 progressed the nuns braced themselves for more of the same. They were surprised (I suspect pleasantly so) to find that I was very different and as Eugene said 'frightened of the day I never saw.' We had barely settled into our new home when news came that Uncle Jimmy had finally married his lady friend and installed her alongside Aggie in the tiny cramped house in Waverley Buildings. Mary his bride was barely four feet tall, she was stick thin but surprisingly very strong. She had been reared in an orphanage and sent to the highlands to earn her keep, where she had been shunted from farm to farm, badly treated and expected to work in all weathers. At her last placement she had been tossed and gored by a bull, and sent back to Edinburgh being of no further use to any farmer.

Her harsh treatment and the need to fend for herself made her totally incapable of making allowances for the dependant timid Aggie who still relied on Ada to supply her every need.

It was not long before the friction in the house came to a head, and I found myself being dressed in my Sunday best, and taking the train to Edinburgh with Ada who was bent on 'sorting Jimmy out'.

I loved visiting the tiny house in Waverley Buildings, to me it was like an over sized doll's house. The floor covered by cheap linoleum, worn and faded, especially at the two fireside chairs where slippered feet had shuffled back and forth, the tiny black range, on which sat a huge cast iron kettle, whose lid jumped up and down with excitement when it boiled. A pair of 'wally dugs' stood sentry at either end of the mantelpiece, their chipped noses sniffing the hop filled air that filtered through the ever open window from the nearby brewery.

The centre of the room was taken up by a scuffed deal table, under which was pushed two black bent wood chairs. The house was a but and ben, the ben being a narrow sliver of a room which held only a mattress resting on orange boxes, the mattress was too big for the room, so dipped in the middle its sides riding up the walls, the little latticed window was deeply recessed its broad sill crammed with Aggie's collection of blue and white jugs of various sizes, all of them chipped of cracked.

I loved the jugs and would make a bee-line for them every time I visited balancing precariously on the lumpy mattress.

As the train chugged its way to Edinburgh, I gave little thought to what we would find, Ada always ensured I had no part in adult things, so I was content to contemplate a happy time bouncing on the squashed mattress.

As for my new Auntie Mary, Jimmy's new wife, I was still unsure whether I liked her or not. Even when she was being pleasant her voice was a rasp which came from somewhere deep in her throat, her face pinched and weather beaten, the skin rough like parchment.

Years of heavy outdoor work had honed the sinews of her arms, drawing the skin tight. Since Jimmy too was weather beaten from long years of working outdoors in the snell winds that blew from the Forth, the two seemed well matched, Eugene's wry observation being, 'no so much wally dugs, as a pair o' Toby jugs.'

As we left Waverley station and made our way up Jeffrey Street, our heads bent against the wind, Ada noticed a bent figure shuffling ahead, going in the same direction as ourselves.

'Would you look at that poor soul, if I didn't know better I'd swear that was our Aggie,' said Ada.

Coming closer, we gasped in disbelief, it was Aggie, looking twenty years older than her thirty two years.

'Aggie?'

On hearing her name Aggie turned and seeing Ada burst into tears, she stood ragged and dejected making no attempt to wipe away the hot tears coursing down her cheeks.

'In the name of God, how did you get into this state?' demanded Ada. There was no answer, just shuddering sobs, Ada pulled a handkerchief from her pocket, thrusting it into Aggie's hand, then impatiently taking it back and wiping Aggie's face as she herself seemed incapable of doing.

'You are coming with me,' Ada said, gripping Aggie's arm. We moved on, but, realising we were heading towards the Buildings, Aggie held back.

'Dinnae make me go back there, they dinnae want me,' she sobbed. 'We'll see about that. Jimmy has some explaining to do,' Ada was grim, and she hurried us on. Jimmy was unrepentant. 'Ah'm no keepin' her, she will dae nothin' fur hersel', an' ah canny afford tae feed anither mooth.'

Mary stood defiant her arms folded across her chest.

'Dinnae look at me, it's no ma place tae look efter a grown wuman.' Ada was having none of it; she thrust the tearful Aggie before them.

'I want an explanation for the state she is in. Look at her, this coat is little better than a rag, it is stained and filthy, the soles of her shoes are gaping, and as for her hair, she looks like Madge Wildfire.'

'Ah dinnae care if she looks like half hingit Maggie Dickson, it is naething tae dae wi' me,' snapped Mary.

'Ye ken she willnae dae onything fur hersel', Jimmy protested. Madge Wildfire and half hingit Maggie Dickson were familiar names to me, and I knew that being compared to them was not a good thing. Many a time Ada would attack my unruly mop with a hairbrush punctuating each furious stroke with the comment, 'This hair is just like Madge Wildfire, that poor mad creature whose hair stood out from her head a tangled mess.'

My curiosity about Madge was settled by Ada's explanation that she was a character (based on fact, Ada assured me) in Walter Scott's 'Heart of Midlothian'. As for 'half hingit Maggie Dickson', it was many years before Ada deemed me of an age to hear her story.

Hung in the Grassmarket in 1782 for concealing the death of her poor illegitimate baby, she was cut down and her coffin borne away on a cart to her native Musselburgh. To the consternation of the bearers a knocking was heard coming from the coffin, from which, when it was opened, Maggie sat up, and was revived by stiff drink. She lived to bear many children and died in her own bed at a ripe old age.

I felt sorry for Aggie as she stood there, head down, tears still rolling down her cheeks. Ada looked at her and said, 'Get your things you are coming back with me.'

Jimmy gripping his withered arm in his good hand, always a sign that he was agitated, shot a glance at Mary then asked,

'Are ye taking her for a wee holiday?'

'No, for good, it is obvious she is not wanted here.' Ada made a shooing motion to Aggie was still had not moved,

'Go on get your things,' she urged. Aggie went pulled out a cardboard suitcase from under the little bed that stood against the kitchen wall. The case contained all she possessed. Ada glared at Jimmy,

'I will never forgive you for treating your sister like this.'

'Weel whit wis ah tae dae, a man has tae put his wife first, ye ken.'

'It is no excuse, you should be ashamed.'

Impatiently she turned to Aggie, 'You can't go on the train looking like that. Give your face a wash while I try to tidy this coat, although there isn't much we can do about the shoes till I get you home. Is there such a thing as a needle and thread? I need to sow these buttons on they are hanging by thread, and I need a comb for that hair.'

Mary sullenly thrust a gap toothed comb into Ada's hand, then rifled in a drawer to produce the sewing materials.

The buttons on, Ada tried to sponge away some of the stains, but it made little difference. Aggie was dabbing at her face with a towel, and Ada sighed and said,

'Here, give it to me, I suppose I better tackle the hair while am at it.'

'Ah telt ye she will dae naethin' fur hersel,' said Mary with great satisfaction. I could not understand why a grown up like Aggie could not do all these things for herself, she had always puzzled me, she was my auntie but so different from all my other aunties, I could not imagine Lizzie or Famie standing as Aggie was standing now, letting Ada tease the tugs out of her hair. It was only as we made our way to the station that I realised what Aggie coming to stay with us would mean. She was going to be with us always, it meant she would have to share our room, it meant one of us would have to sleep beside her, and my heart sank as I knew it would be me.

Eugene raised no objection to the new addition to our household, in his easy manner he accepted Aggie as if she had always been there. We girls were not so charitable, we grumbled among ourselves, while treating Aggie with due respect as an aunt, but it was not long before we realised that Jimmy may have had a point in his complaints against her. As Mary had pointed out Aggie would not do a thing for herself if she could get someone else to do it for her. She would stand, her blouse unbuttoned and wait to catch Ada's eye, who eventually would say with the slightest trace of exasperation,

'Come here, I'll button it for you.' If Ada was out Aggie would try her wiles on us, she would fiddle with a button or a hairbrush, trying to catch our attention. We became experts at avoiding eye contact, but after a while she would sigh and say plaintively, 'Ah canny manage thae buttons, it's ma eyes, ah canny see very well ye ken.'

This would make us feel guilty and one of us would give in, do up the buttons, or brush the thin wispy hair.

We soon found that she carried tales, and was not averse to making up stories, which was a great surprise to us, as we were taught to tell the truth and own up to any misdemeanour. Aggie would break a cup and blame one of us, when we protested our innocence Ada would give us a look and say, 'Tell me the truth, you know I will not have lying, you can stop a thief's hand but you can't stop a liar's tongue, I detest lies.' Aggie would fix us with a stare from behind her thick glasses and defy us to accuse her. She would complain to Ada that our chattering kept her off her sleep, yet there were nights when she was the one doing the talking and we would hide our heads under the covers to try to drown her out. Bedtime was a nightmare. As I had suspected I was the one who had to share a bed with her, Lena now sharing with Betty. Aggie would wriggle into the centre of the bed, forcing me to the edge, hugging all the covers to herself, and tossed and turned all night long. My pleas to Ada went unheeded. She reminded me of the 'misery' Aggie had endured with Jimmy and Mary, and said it was my duty to make her feel at home. I promised not to complain again, but I did, though only to Lena and Betty, who, though sympathetic, did not offer to change places. How we missed auntie Mary, who had been our boon companion in Garrowhill and who had now gone back to Da-dee's. We still saw a lot of her as she was only across the road, but it was not the same. We told ourselves gloomily that we were stuck with Aggie and would just have to put up with it, Ada would never see through her, and Eugene would not understand what the fuss was about. As the year rolled on rumours of war grew stronger. Eugene dismissed Ada's fears, but the news on the wireless was of plans to conscript all young males. Lord Privy Seal Sir John Anderson in charge of air-raid precautions issued the corrugated iron shelters which were to bear his name. Betty came home from the pictures saying Pathe news had shown Londoners erecting these shelters in their back gardens.

'They have to bury them underground and store food and candles and matches in them as well,' she said impressively.

'We don't have a garden,' Lena was worried.

'Nobody needs a shelter it will all blow over,' Eugene assured her puffing contentedly on his pipe.

Ada shook her head, 'It looks bad, they wouldn't give out shelters unless they knew something.'

'Not at all, it will come to nothing, the last war put a stop to all that,' Eugene said.

'Huh!' It was Ada's turn to scoff, 'the war to end all wars, but it looks as if it has all been for nothing, it is going to happen again.'

'Not at all,' said Eugene, 'Not at all'.

At 5am on Friday September 1st Hitler invaded Poland. To prolonged cheers, Neville Chamberlain told MPs that Britain would not stand by and see Poland fall. On September 3rd, a weary and mournful Chamberlain told a hushed nation that the deadline for Germany to withdraw from Poland had passed and Britain had declared war.

Ada listened to the report ashen faced, as we three sat huddled together not quite sure what it all meant, Ada caught sight of our anxious faces and smiled 'It will be all right, we will win this war, we must, right is on our side, and right is might.'

Eugene's mind was on a different track, 'It could mean work, they will need men in the shipyards,' he said.

'Who knows what it will mean, God help us,' said Ada.

Within weeks baffle walls of sandbags were built at every close mouth, 'to absorb the bomb blasts', was Ada's less than reassuring explanation, Two buckets filled with sand stood ready to snuff out flames from any fire hazard.

Soon we were gathering in the gym hall sitting cross-legged watching with a mixture of fear and amusement as a fireman demonstrated how to put on a gas mask, then filing out clutching a square cardboard box, on which we were told to write our names. This was to be our constant companion, slung round our necks or over our shoulder every time we went out, leaving it behind was a punishable offence. What the punishment was, we never really knew.

Mother Philippa imposed her own punishment, for forgetting your gasmask, two stinging slaps from the rope she wore round her waist. It became a common sight to see children, adults, and babies in pram carrying gasmasks. Many mothers complained it 'ruined the look of the pram'. Ada was a staunch supporter of the hated masks, telling us of the pitiful lines of men shuffling along one hand on the shoulder of the man in front, every one with his eyes swathed in bandages.

'These poor souls were blinded by mustard gas, brave men whose lives were blighted forever, just be thankful you have a mask to protect you.' 'Och they will never be needed,' Eugene assured us, 'but at least it is handy for keepin' your play piece in.' Ada sunk him with a look.

Eugene's hope that the war would bring him work proved to be a vain one. Meeting a neighbour from Teeny's close, Ada opened her purse and said 'This is all I have, tuppence ha'penny, yet there is one thing I am grateful for, we have our own place, as God is my witness, never again will we live in somebody's room. Sadly it was one vow she would be unable to keep. To make ends meet Ada did evening shifts in the local chip shop, working alongside Tina. Eugene was not happy, 'Ah'm supposed to be the breadwinner.'

'We have to get money from somewhere, it's only a few hours at night,' Ada answered.

Despite the baffle walls, and gas masks, life seemed little changed by war in those first few weeks. Air-raid sirens had sounded over London but they had been false alarms, however hundreds of children had been evacuated to the country, and every news report on the wireless told of more and more. Eugene and Ada discussed the news as we sat eating our dinner.

'It will never happen here, our kids don't need to be evacuated, ah would be surprised if Hitler knew where Scotland is, never mind Glasgow,' Eugene was easy.

'Of course he will know. The Germans are not stupid, and they will have made it their business to know everything. Glasgow is a famous port, he will try to stop supply ships coming here,' Ada said in exasperation.

'Not at all, anyway even if he does know, the navy will sort him out.' The news about the evacuation preyed on my mind, 'Do you think mammy will send us away?' I whispered to Lena that night.

'I don't know, but I don't want to leave mammy,' she said.

'Neither do I.' I was close to tears.

'Whit are you two whispering aboot?' asked Aggie.

'Being sent to the country,' Lena said.

'What country will they send us to?' I wanted to know.

'They don't send you to another country,' scoffed Betty, they send you to the countryside, where there are fields and cows, sheep an' things.'

'I'm scared of cows and sheep,' I said, petrified at this news. Though we lived in the very heart of the city, sheep and cows were a regular sight in the Gallowgate. Often if we stayed late at Da-dee's we came downstairs to find we could not cross the street to our close, because cows and sheep were being herded up the Gallowgate to 'market' as Ada told me.

We would stand patiently on the pavement as the cows went lumbering by, lowing softly, followed by the skittish sheep that were bent on going anywhere but straight ahead.

The beasts terrified me, but my fear was soon matched to pity when Eugene who had little time for euphemisms let slip the market was really the slaughterhouse, where he had spent so much time as a boy when he should have been at school. In my imagination I translated the sight of these poor live creatures into the ghastly open carcases hanging from those cruel hooks in the butcher shop.

Eugene scoffed at my tears, 'Eh that's the way it is meant to be, people have to eat, we need leather to make shoes, bones to make glue, it's the way of the world.'

'It's not fair, it's horrible, they must be really scared,' I protested through my tears. 'I'm glad I don't eat meat, and I am never going to eat it, anyway mammy doesn't eat it either.'

'Eh, your mammy always had strange ideas,' laughed Eugene. The slaughter of the animals, and the threat of leaving Ada to go to live in the country, coloured my thoughts, filling my dreams at night with nightmare visions, causing me to scream out in terror. Finding the root of the problem, Ada turned furiously on Eugene.

'She is far too young to know about such things,' she fumed.

'She has to learn how the world works, she has to learn to accept things as they are,' Eugene was unrepentant.

Though this diverted my attention from the threat of evacuation for a time, the continual reports of children being sent away preyed on our minds. Our fears were groundless, listening to yet another account on the wireless, Ada declared the last thing she wanted was to be separated from her children 'at a time like this'.

We breathed easy.

CHAPTER 7

When Mrs Keyes died she left behind not only her little flat but her ancient tabby Billy. He had been treated like royalty by the old woman and it was clear he expected us to carry on in the same way. I loved him, but he did not like to be hugged, so when one day Betty brought home a tiny bundle of fur snuggled in her jacket we were all smitten, though Ada said pretending to be annoyed, another mouth to feed.

Betty christened him Tiddles, though after a few days she jokingly changed it to Piddles, at least until he was house trained.

Billy hissed and lashed out, not only put out by this intruder onto hallowed ground, but clearly finding the kitten's energy and constant attention annoying.

Being three flights up meant the cats never went out, and they seemed content to jump onto the draining board of the sink and gaze for hours out of the window.

Ada would buy buff (offal) from the butcher. It was the most revolting thing to look at, and the smell of it cooking made me quite ill.

Well if you want the cats you will have to put up with it, was Ada's response.

Eugene would make things worse by bringing in fish heads from the fishmonger, which gazed glassy eyed from the cat's plates.

Lena and I shared the job of emptying the litter tray, carrying it at arms length down the stairs. Making ends meet continued to be a struggle, so when a piano was delivered one morning Ada told the men there must be a mistake, assured that they had the right address, she waited, ready to pounce the minute Eugene appeared.

As soon as he saw the piano he beamed with pride, 'well what do you think of your surprise?'

'Surprise! Shock you mean. Where did you get the money for this?'

'Well that is the best bit. Ah really didnae spend money on it, it was barter.'

'Barter?'

'Aye, ye see ah met a man ah used tae know. He wanted a wall plastered, and ah happened tae see the piano. Ah mentioned we used tae have one but we had tae sell it, so.....'

'So you plastered the wall in exchange for the piano?' Ada finished.

'Aye, just the job eh?'

'Did you not think we needed the money more than a piano?'

'Eh well ah just thought ye deserved a wee present, ah know you loved that piano, and hard times forced us tae sell it.'

'We are still having hard times, we can't afford presents, how long have you been looking for work, and when you get a wee job instead of money you take a piano.'

'But Eadie you always liked tae play.'

'Maybe, but there are more important things, you think it is all right for the kids to go to bed hungry because their mammy can play them a tune instead?'

'Ach ah just thought you would be pleased.'

'Well you thought wrong, tomorrow you can sell it for whatever you can get for it.'

Eugene looked crestfallen.

'Oh mammy can we not keep it,' we three chorused.

Betty opened the lid.

'We could learn to play it, please mammy.' She sat down and tried to pick out a tune.

'Leave it alone, it goes tomorrow first thing.' Ada reached for the lid.

'Ach let them have some fun; it's only here for one night.' Eugene prised open the lid again.

Betty hammered away, we held our ears, and Ada winced.

'You don't have to strike it so hard. It is supposed to make music, not a racket like that,' Ada shouted over the din.

'You play something mammy,' Lena pleaded.

'No, I want nothing to do with it, and it is going first thing, even if I have to carry it down the stairs myself,' Ada said.

'Oh please mammy, please,' Lena begged.

Eugene tapped Betty on the shoulder, shooing her off the stool.

'Yer mammy is very good; she can play Russian Rose, and the Blue Danube.'

'I can play more than that.' Ada trailed her fingers lightly over the keys.

'Ah but they don't know that, you would have tae show them,' Eugene said.

Ada sat down, trilling the keys with the back of her hand, and then she began to play. It was magic. She went from one tune to another effortlessly, clearly enjoying herself.

Eugene beamed, 'Play Red Sails in the Sunset,' he urged, and then whispered to me, 'That was the song that was popular the year you were born.' As the tinkling notes flowed Betty suddenly burst out laughing, turning we saw Tiddles waltzing across the floor on his hind legs. Ada smiled and softened the tone to see how long the little kitten would keep going. The piano did not go the next morning, or any other morning, even though it took up so much space in our already cramped room. Ada would spend many happy hours playing, and each time Tiddles would waltz across the floor.

Lena and I would play chop sticks. Lena was particularly good and taught herself some tunes. Ada decided that she should have lessons and promised me too, but if would have to wait until she could afford it.

'Will we have to wait for the duration mammy,' I asked.

It was a word I heard frequently, since the war began and supplies dried up in the shops, the assistants would shake their heads and say – 'Sorry we sha'nt have that for the duration of the war.

As I mentioned the word 'duration', Ada smiled.

'That was Benny's favourite word,' she said. 'I remember meeting somebody in the street and talking to them for a while, I had Benny by the hand but she was getting restless and looked up at me saying, 'Are we going to be here for the duration?'

I was afraid, anything that reminded her of Benny usually made her very sad.

We all tried to avoid upsetting her, and I had done just that, but this time she didn't seem upset, she was still smiling.

'I didn't even know she knew the word, she wasn't even three years old, and yet she came away with that.'

I realised Ada was talking to herself, had a strange look on her face and just didn't seem to know we were there. Benny had died four years before I was born, Lena had been only two, and Betty six, so she was the only one who had any memory of Benny. To Lena and I she was only someone we knew through Ada's grief. That grief had never really left her, it could come bubbling up to the surface at unexpected moments, leaving us feeling afraid and strangely cut off from Ada who was everything to us. Sometimes we felt as though Benny would take her away from us, that we were lesser persons because we were not Benny. Not that any of this was ever said between us. I was still only five years old and could not have articulated the feelings Benny engendered in me, but I knew they were there.

I would stare at the photograph of Granny and Benny that hung above our beds. It showed Granny seated with Benny on her knee. Granny's hair was parted in the middle and caught in a bun at the nape of her neck; she wore a rough open necked striped blouse tucked into a voluminous black skirt. Her gaze is slightly troubled, the eyes holding sorrow, she clasps the plump baby form of the six month old Benny, dressed in a white dress, white socks and patent shoes, her eyes, like Granny's hold a hint of fear.

These two, so close in life and in death, were like strangers to me though I was taught to revere them. Not only Ada but the aunts too spoke of Benny and Granny as angels, and left Betty, Lena and me feeling we were lacking somehow.

Eugene never spoke of either Benny or Granny. If he grieved, and I am sure he did, he never showed any sign. It is only as I write this now that I realise I for one never acknowledged that he must have suffered too at the loss of a child so young. Ada was still smiling quietly to herself, her eyes misty.

'Yes, I can see Benny as clear as day, tugging away at my hand wanting me to move on. Are we here for the duration, she said. Fancy her knowing a word like that at her age, but then she was so clever.'

She had forgotten my question about the piano lessons, but I did not remind her. Whether we would have to wait for the duration of the war hardly seemed to matter, I knew we would most certainly have to wait a long time.

Carol came to visit. She was not a favourite of Ada's, but Eugene seemed taken by her long blonde hair, expensive clothes and heavy perfume. He would gush over her treating her with all the deference due a lady, much to Ada's disgust.

'What are you making a fuss of that one for? That hair colour comes out of a bottle, you can smell the peroxide even over all that perfume, and she gives herself such airs and graces, but they don't wash with me. I remember that she is not this fancy Carol, just plain Agnes Keyes, born and bred in the Gallowgate.'

Eugene would shrug, 'Eh she is my brother's wife, ah'm just showin' respect.'

'How much respect did she or your brother show for his first wife, Marygodresther?'

Whenever any of the family spoke of someone who had died, God was always asked to grant them rest by stringing the whole thing together, so I was used to hearing Ada, Eugene and the aunts talk of Grannygodresther, or Bennygodresther. I had long been puzzled by this expression, but finally convinced myself that when people died they got a new name.

Ada was put out by Carol's surprise visit; she always liked to have 'snicesters' in to offer with a cup of tea, especially to Carol, to show we were not poor.

Aggie was fascinated by Carol, especially by how she delicately sipped her tea with the little finger extended upwards. She watched Carol closely, her eyes dancing behind the thick glasses, and then reached for her cup holding it in the same fashion, it wobbled and sent hot tea cascading down the front of her blouse. Screeching and flustered she jumped up from the table. Ada quickly led her through to the room to change her.

Carol followed, clearly surprised to find Aggie standing arms at her sides as Ada removed the blouse, placed a clean one round Aggie's shoulders, lifting her arms in turn into the sleeves, then buttoning the buttons. Carol's eyes swept the room, taking in the beds, wardrobe, chest of drawers and piano, she grimaced.

'It must be a bit of a crush for you all, the house is so small,' she said.

'No smaller than when you lived here,' said Ada pointedly, 'we manage.'

Carol smiled, 'Maybe I could help.'

'I don't see how,' Ada turned back into the kitchen, and Aggie and Carol followed.

'I could take one of the girls to stay with me. I could take Lena.'

'Lena was full of excitement, 'Oh can ah go mammy?'

Ada shook her head, 'No, there is no need, we manage fine, Lena is better off with her sisters.'

'It wouldn't be Forever.' laughed Carol, 'You know how Tommy dotes on her.'

'Yes I know,' said Ada, 'it is good of you to suggest it, but she should be with her family.'

Carol looked amused, 'She would still be with her family, we are her family too.'

'No,' said Ada, 'it is out of the question.'

'Ah think it is a good thing, ah don't see any harm in it,' said Eugene.

'There is no harm; I only want to ease the pressure you are all under as far as space is concerned. Tommy and I have more space than we know what to do with.' Carol smiled.

'Oh mammy please, please,' pleaded Lena.

'It would be such a help to me too,' Carol pressed, 'you know my young brother Jim has been staying with us, but now he has been called up, I have a terrible feeling he may not come back. Lena would help take my mind off things.'

Eugene nodded, 'Let Lena go Eadie, you know how you felt when your brothers went to war.'

'Aye ah mind the day when the telegram came tae tell ye Harry had been killed,' said Aggie mournfully.

'Don't talk about Harry, that was different,' Ada snapped.

'Ah don't see how, men get killed in every war,' said Eugene.

'Oh please, don't talk about it.' Carol was near to tears.

Ada sighed, and she topped up Carol's tea and passed her the sugar.

'Men come home safe and sound too. Jim is a nice lad, and we all hope he will be fine.'

'I hope to God you are right', Carol sipped delicately at her tea.

She leaned over the table, her heavily made up eyes fixed pleadingly on Ada.

'Say you will let me have her, just for a little while. It would mean so much to me.'

Ada stirred her tea, the spoon going first one way then another. Carol sat the cup poised halfway to her lips.

'She can go for two weeks, no more.' Ada withdrew the spoon and carefully placed it in the saucer.

Lena jumped up and down with joy. I began to cry. I didn't want my sister to go away, especially not with 'that Carol Keyes'.

'I will get her things ready, and of course she will need to take her ration book with her.' Ada stood up pushing her chair away.

'We won't need her ration book.' Carol smiled.

'How else do you propose to feed her?' Ada looked surprised.

Eugene laughed, 'Ah'm sure Tommy makes sure they don't go short.'

Carol smiled again, 'You could say he has 'ways and means'.

Ada frowned, 'You mean the 'black market'?' No child of mine will take anything that has been come by illegally. The ration book will go with her. We are all in this war together, and the rations are meagre but they are fair. The 'black market' steals out of people's mouths.'

Eugene looked pained, 'Och Eadie ye know Tommy has always had his contacts.'

'I mean what I say. The book goes with her, or she does not go at all,' Ada answered.

'I'll take the book,' Carol said.

That night Lena went off, clutching her little cardboard suitcase, and her favourite doll. As she clattered down the stairs, Carol assured Ada that she would see Lena got to school on time every morning. Ada closed the door with a shake of her head, 'I don't see her getting up every morning to put a child to school. It will be no surprise to me if the school board are knocking on the door, mark my words.'

'Ach Tommy will see to it,' Eugene shrugged.

Tommy did see to it. Knowing Carol's habit of rising late, he hired a car complete with driver to deliver Lena to Charlotte Street, and take her back again.

At the end of the two weeks Tommy appeared begging Ada to allow Lena to stay longer.

'The wee lassie is happy wi' us, she wants tae stay.'

'You think she is not happy with us?' demanded Ada.

'No, no, ye know ah don't mean that. It's jist that we take her tae places she has never been before, and she gets on well wi' Jim, tho' he will be away soon. Carol needs the lassie, honest tae God Eadie, she needs her.'

'She needs a child of her own, and I don't see why she should have mine. Lena is my flesh and blood, her place is here.' Ada was adamant.

Tommy spread his hands in helplessness, 'Eugenio, can ye no speak tae yer wife?'

'Eh, she has a strong will, you know that.'

'Look,' said Tommy, 'if I promise tae bring her tae see you every week, how will that do?'

'Every week. Just how long do you intend to keep her?'

'Well the thing is she is quite settled noo, she likes Carol fussin' over her, she likes goin' tae tea shops, and getting new dresses made. Carol has a wee wifie that makes curtains an' things and she is making some lovely dresses for the wee Lena,' he smiled sheepishly as he caught the look on Ada's face. 'Och don't worry it's a' above board, coupons and that.'

'I'm sure,' Ada said grimly.

'Och Eadie I don't want to fa' oot wi' you aboot this. I'm just thinking aboot Carol. I want tae make her happy and the wee lassie as well'.

'Let Lena stay, where is the harm. He says he will bring her every week, what's wrong wi' that?' Eugene asked.

'You will see she still gets to school?'

'Aye nae bother, though it is costing me a fortune,' Tommy laughed.

'We will leave it for a month,' said Ada.

Every week we trooped over to Da-dee's to see Lena. Carol was afraid she would get homesick if they came to our house.

'My, are you no the posh one,' Tina would say as Lena turned up in a new outfit every time, her long hair tonged into ringlets. At the end of the four weeks, Tommy pleaded for more time. Jim had been posted overseas and Carol was distraught, even Ada could see she needed Lena for solace.

Christmas came, and my stocking held a little doll made from a wooden spoon.

It had a painted face, and bits of wool for hair, with arms and legs made from pipe cleaners, and a dress made from a scrap of material. I really loved it, and the big storybook of my favourite Hunky Dory. When Lena arrived, she carried the loveliest doll I had ever seen. The beautiful doll was almost a mirror image of Lena, it wore the same dress and had long ringlets. The only difference was the doll was blonde, while Lena was dark. When she saw my doll Lena laughed saying how funny looking it was, and I put the doll away ashamed. The doll was the final straw for Ada; she sat quietly fuming not wanting to cause a scene in Da-dee's house, but when Carol and Lena had gone, and we were safely back in our own house, she exploded in anger.

Pointing a finger at Eugene she hissed, 'You will get over to Allison Street first thing in the morning and bring Lena home. No ifs or buts, she is coming back here where she belongs.'

'What's the rush? She is happy. You saw her wi' a' thae fancy things. She is like a different wee lassie.'

'Exactly, that is why she has to come home. I am not going to lose my daughter to that woman. Lena is getting spoiled, and she is beginning to feel she is different from her sisters. It is not right, and I am not going to let it go on. Our Lena is the sweetest, kindest, wee girl you could imagine, but she was spiteful to her wee sister tonight when she laughed at that wee wooden dolly.

It is not her nature to be like that, I want her back before she changes for good.'

'Get away woman, she is still the same wee lassie. She was just carried away wi' that fancy doll.'

'Yes, and being driven to school and back every day in a fancy car is enough to turn any child's head, and it has to stop. I mean it; you will bring her back tomorrow.' Ada would not be moved.

Eugene sighed, 'Aye ah'll go, tho' Carol will be upset.'

'Then that is just too bad,' Ada said witheringly. So Lena came home. She spent the first few nights crying for Auntie Carol, and her lovely bedroom, which was like something out of the pictures, she said, with wonderful draped curtains and a carpet that covered the whole floor. She would wince at the cold linoleum under her feet and remind us that Auntie Carol's house had carpets in every room, even the bathroom.

I was happy to have her back home, though it meant I had to share with Aggie again, but now we were more used to her we seemed to get on better. She surprised us by developing quite an impish sense of humour, and she bought us treacle toffees and sherbet dabs.

Ada had hung all Lena's fine dresses in the wardrobe and there they stayed. To Ada's mind it was unfair for one child to be dressed in finery while the others were in hand-me-downs. Lena never complained about not being allowed to wear them, and she seemed content just to take them out and look at them, when she knew Ada was not around. Gradually Lena adjusted to the Gallowgate way of life once more and soon is was as if she had never been away.

Within weeks of Lena coming home Carol received the dreaded telegram, Jim was missing presumed dead. Lena wept at the news, and she told us how funny and kind Jim had been. He was the youngest Keyes brother and only nineteen. Tearfully she told how she had gone with Carol and Tommy to the Central Station, to say goodbye to Jim as he left for his posting. He had wound down the carriage window, and began to sing, the other boys joining in -

> 'We'll meet again, don't know where don't know when,
> but I know we'll meet again some sunny day.
> Keep smiling through, just like you always do,
> till the blues skies chase the dark clouds far away,

and if you'll just say hello, to the folks that I know,
tell them I won't be long
they'll be happy to know, that as you saw me go,
I was singing this song.
We'll meet again don't know where, don't know when,
but I know we'll meet again some sunny day.

Betty teased Lena saying she had a crush on Jim. This only made her cry all the harder. She was only eleven years old and had never experienced the emotions that engulfed her.

Though several years her junior I too was experiencing the first pangs of unrequited love; the object of my affections was a red haired daredevil named Frank Mailey. He was in my class at school, which in itself was remarkable as Our Lady and St.Francis was an all girls school, but for some reason ten boys had been admitted, though their reign was short lived.

Frank was totally unaware of my existence. His parents ran a newsagents shop at the corner of Ross Street. Every Saturday I would spend my pocket money there in the hope of seeing Frank, and now and then I would glimpse his impish freckled face peering out from the back shop, but he never acknowledged me and gradually my love withered on the vine. The experience left me dejected, and seemed to reinforce the feelings of inferiority that plagued me.

The only real memory I had of Frank's attention was when being paired off with him for school races, he objected to being paired with 'that lassie with the funny name.'

The 'funny name' was to prove an even bigger problem in the months to come.

Ada's patriotism knew no bounds, and she would berate 'Lord Haw-Haw' as he spouted his pro-Nazi propaganda. She bought me a little Union Jack telling me it was the flag of freedom. Britain, she declared was the finest country in the world, a free nation that would always remain free, even if we had to fight to the 'last drop of our blood.' I was apprehensive about all of us having to give our last drop of blood, but to me Ada was the fount of all wisdom, she was never wrong, and if she said I had to give all my blood I would do so, though I did not know who to give it to.

The knowledge of how it would be if the Germans won the war was too horrible to contemplate. Ada said it would be 'the end of civilisation', and she prayed to God, asking him to end the world rather than give victory to the Germans. I was very afraid, sure that God would listen to her, and that everything would be gone in a flash.

We gathered round the wireless to hear the Prime Minister Winston Churchill's speech –

'We shall defend our island, whatever the cost may be. We shall fight on the beaches. We shall fight on the landing grounds. We shall fight in the fields and in the streets. We shall fight in the hills. We shall never surrender.'

Ada nodded vigorously in agreement.

I prayed that God was on Mr.Churchill's side.

By September blackout was introduced, women queuing to buy yards of black material. Winter came, the usual dark northern gloom descending, the gas lamps struggling against the black curtained windows.

The gas mantles were in short supply, and Ada would travel far and wide in her search, and would return home clutching the little square cardboard box with its extremely fragile contents as if she had struck gold.

We would sit taut with tension as Eugene climbed on a stool the little globe of gauze cupped in his hands.

'Careful, careful, mind you don't break it,' Ada would warn.

'How often have I done this eh?' Eugene would ask mildly exasperated.

'Just be careful, I had to go round half of Glasgow for that thing.'

The mantle safely installed Eugene would gingerly strike a match from the Swan Vestas box and gently apply it to the mantle.

The soft light would play on the brass kettle and the long toasting fork that hung by the fire. It was only here in the tiny kitchen with my family all around me, with the shutters shut masking the ugly blackout cloth, the soft gaslight vying with the light from the coal fire, that I felt really safe, sure that we were beyond Hitler's reach, that he would never win and end 'civilisation' whatever that was.

But in the cold light of day my fears would return, I was fearful of going to school in case the world ended when we were not all together.

I told no one of my fears, not even Lena.

One Thursday after Ada had left for her evening shift at the chip shop, Eugene said he was going out to see a man about some work. Lena and Betty were at devotions with Lizzie, meaning I would be left with Aggie.

'Can I come with you daddy?' I pleaded.

'Aye, if you like, get your coat,' Eugene said much to my delight. 'Ah don't think Eadie would want her oot on a night like this,' Aggie warned.

Eugene shrugged and looked at me, 'It's up to you.'

'I want to come,' I scrambled hastily into my coat.

'Right then, it's only along to the Saltmarket, we'll no be long.'

The wind drove the rain into our faces. Though still early evening it was very dark, with blackout everywhere, and here and there a pinpoint of light from hooded torches as people hurried by.

I held Eugene's hand as tightly as I could, but when we reached the Saltmarket, he released my hand, and told me to wait as he went into a cafe.

I huddled miserably in the doorway praying he would not be long. When he came out, I grabbed his hand, 'Did you get a job, daddy?'

'Ah'm too late the work has gone, but he says there is a man in Jamaica Street that might have something for me.'

We walked on and all I could think of was that Jamaica Street was where the zoo was, and there was a lion in that zoo. People pushed by heads bent against the rain. I entwined my fingers into Eugene's hand terrified we would be separated. At Jamaica Street we stopped at the mouth of a close, and Eugene struck a match to light up the brass nameplates on the wall.

'He is on the third floor, wait here,' he said and vanished into the close before I could stop him.

I waited, everything around me filled me with terror, - what if the lion escaped? The darkness made it almost impossible to see the people as they shuffled past. The mournful clanging of the trams as they lumbered out of the darkness and the pinhole of blue light they were allowed to show made them look like ghost ships.

Eugene seemed to have been gone an age, the noise of the street grew fainter as shops rattled down their shutters, the workers calling goodnight to each other, and the darkness seemed to press in all around me. I felt as if I was the only person in the world.

What if I was the only person left, what if God had answered Ada's prayer and ended the world? I thought of the news on the wireless in the past few days, it seemed the Germans might be winning. I began to cry, God could end the world anyway he liked, silently like this, and leave me. I had no idea how to get home, but there wouldn't be any home. I cried and cried. I wanted Ada, I wanted my mammy. Suddenly a hand clasped my shoulder. I screamed and ran for my life. I could hear feet pounding behind me, then a hand gripping my arm and spinning me round.

'What are ye running away for; it's me, yer daddy.'

I clung to him the sobs racking my body.

'I- I thought the world had ended.'

'What! What made ye think such a daft thing?' said Eugene laughing.

'Well - the Germans are winning-an' mammy says-'

'Aye ah know what she says, and it is all daft nonsense. Ye shouldnae always believe what yer mammy says.'

He lifted me on to his shoulders, 'Come on ye daft wee thing, you should be in yer bed.'

How could he tell me not to believe Ada? Everybody said she was the wisest person, even Eugene. I decided I did not understand grown ups, not understand them at all.

Aggie wasted no time in relating the whole thing to Ada. Ada was furious.

'What were you thinking of leaving that wee soul by herself, in Jamaica street of all places?'

'I thought she would get tired climbing up all the stairs, anyway ah wisnae away that long,' Eugene protested.

'Long enough for a kiddie of that age,' Ada answered.

'How was ah tae know she would think the world had ended. That's your fault for puttin' daft ideas intae her head,' he laughed.

'That is no excuse. She is only a child, left on her own like that. How do you expect her to feel?'

'Och she canny go through life bein' scared a' the time. Ah've said before she needs to know her way aboot the world,' Eugene argued.

'She will learn soon enough. Let her have her childhood,' Ada answered.

CHAPTER 8

Ada sat at the table head in hands. Before her, spread out in a semi-circle, lay the ration books for the family.

She drew columns on a scrap of paper, headed butter, sugar, raw bacon, cooked bacon, and then pencilled in the figures under each heading - 4oz of butter, 4oz raw ham, 3oz cooked ham, 12oz sugar.

'I've registered with the Maypole dairy, they know me in there,' she said.

'At least we can still have mince and tatties,' Eugene laughed.

'I don't know about that. All slaughtering has been stopped till they work out a scheme,' Ada told him.

I picked up my ears at this news; maybe the government would be too busy to get around to setting up a scheme, and so spare the poor animals that long walk up the Gallowgate to their doom.

It was not to be. By March everyone was required to register with a butcher, and meat coupons were issued.

Rabbit, offal, poultry, game and fish were not rationed. Soon the offal that had only been bought for the cats had to feed the family. Ada invented ways of disguising it, and while she and I never touched it, the others ate it without complaint.

Tina decided she would try rabbit stew when Pat presented her with a fairly large rabbit. He declined to say how he had come by it, and she in turn did not tell him she had no idea how to cook the thing.

Arriving for an early morning cup of tea, Ada was horrified to find the rabbit cooking in a large pot, still intact, fur and all. Rabbit never figured on Tina's menu again.

By June 1940 Italy finally showed her hand and declared war on the Allies. The New York Times thundered- 'With the courage of a jackal at the heels of a bolder beast of prey, Mussolini has now left his ambush. He wants to share in the spoils, at the least cost to himself.'

President Roosevelt declared 'Italy has scorned the security of other nations.'

Hot on the heels of Italy's declaration of war, mobs the length and breadth of Britain attacked Italian owned businesses. In Glasgow the destruction and looting of cafes and chip shops, often accompanied by physical attacks went on for days, and in the smaller surrounding towns of Hamilton and Motherwell, Italians who had been living there for fifty years were attacked, many of these families had sons fighting in the British army.

At school Lena and I found our 'funny name' a target for derision, and I was terrified and totally bemused to find that my father, the placid generous Eugene, was viewed as an enemy, even a spy. Eugene in typical laid back fashion dismissed the hysteria with a shrug.

'What have I got to fear? People know who I am. I want no truck with Mussolini, the man is a dangerous buffoon.'

'It makes no difference. Look at what has been happening to people who have been here even longer than you,' Ada was worried.

Tina and the others reported people had cut them dead in the street, and Ada had sensed a coolness in the neighbours.

Call-up papers for the Italian Army arrived. Eugene took one look and threw them on the fire.

'If I have to fight, I will fight for Britain,' he said.

His failure to return the papers brought a second lot, this time Ada stayed his hand as he made to burn them.

'I don't think you should burn official papers. There may be some kind of comeback about it.'

'What comeback? I don't want anything to do with Mussolini.'

Ada took the papers and hid them in a drawer.

Each day the papers carried reports of aliens being rounded up and sent for internment, and most could expect to be kept for the duration of the war.

Ada worried that Eugene would be taken too.

He scoffed at her concern, but when news came that the Arandora Star taking hundreds of internees to Canada had been torpedoed, even Eugene was disturbed. He sat reading the list of names of the four hundred and seventy Italians who had lost their lives, along with over hundred Germans and others.

Now and again he would call to Ada as he recognized another name on the list. Some of them were the same age as Da-dee.

'My God! I never thought that Da-dee could be in danger, or my brothers.'

He was really shaken.

'Nobody could doubt the sincerity of your father,' Ada reassured him, but she did not sound totally convinced.

'I'll go across and see how he is,' Eugene said folding the paper and putting it in his pocket.

He found Da-dee in tears, a copy of the paper opened on his knee.

I had never found it easy to make friends at school, and after the riots against Italians I felt unworthy, so I kept myself amused at break time by playing doublers, bouncing two balls at the same time under leg and over leg.

I was still only in primary, but had already seen the start of bullying when my name was suddenly 'funny peculiar'. The girl who had started the name calling was Molly McKay a freckled faced girl with tight red curls.

Soon she was following me around the playground taunting me that I was different and should not be in the school.

'Ma mammy says folk like you and your mammy and daddy should be put away. Ma mammy says your daddy is a spy,' she shouted at me.

I tried to ignore her, but a little group had gathered and she was happy to be in the spotlight.

'Is your daddy a spy?'

'Don't be stupid, my daddy says he wouldn't know how to be a spy,' I retorted.

'But if he did know he would be?'

'No!'

'Ma mammy says he would.'

'It's not true.'

'Ma mammy says your daddy will be put away, ma mammy says he could be sent far away for ever!'

'Stop it, stop it, my daddy is not going away.'

'Ma mammy says he is, an' they might take you and your sisters as well.'

I start to cry, and they all laugh.

Each day the taunts grew worse.

'See your mammy. Does she speak like us?'

'No'.

'See, ah told you,' Molly tells her gang.

'I mean she speaks properly, not slang like you,' I answer back.

'Ah bet she cannae speak English, jist Tally Wally, cos you are Eyeties.'

'Eyeties, Eyeties,' shout the gang, circling round me.

I push my way through them. Molly sticks out her foot, and I go sprawling on the ground. I stumble to my feet and run, their chanting ringing in my ears.

I say nothing to Ada or anyone else about Molly and her gang, though I dread having to go to school each day.

Ada had chosen Our Lady and St.Francis, because it was a senior secondary. She intended both Lena and I to stay on till we were eighteen. Lena's ambitions were not academic; she wanted to be a dancer. I wanted to go to university.

It was a convent school, run by Franciscan nuns, who also employed a few lay teachers, all of whom dressed in black flowing gowns and mortar boards. Our Lady and St.Francis enjoyed a good reputation.

The lower school formed two sides of the 0-shaped complex. The high school occupied the much grander red sandstone building, graced with a sweeping stairway, adorned by elegant statues.

We lesser mortals were permitted only on special occasions.

Our English mistress, Miss McCrindle, was a tall young woman with a sweet nature. Her flowing red hair was too springy for her mortar, which sat upon her head at a rakish angle.

She was an inspirational teacher, and on Fridays as a reward for good behaviour, which she always achieved without recourse to the use of the belt, she would indulge her love of poetry by reading to us. We had become familiar with many poems and already had our favourites - 'Young Lochinvar', 'Upon Westminster Bridge', 'Sea Fever'. But above all we loved 'The Lady of Shallot'.

She would bring her high stool from behind her desk, placing it centre stage, and perch there, her long legs crossed at the ankle, the black robe falling in folds from her shoulders, the mortarboard laid aside on the desk behind. Eagerly we would sit watching as she turned the pages of the slim volume, going to each marker and pausing for a moment or two. We all knew where in the book this poem lay. She would reach it, pause and then turn back, skimming through the pages.

Knowing all eyes were on her she would look up with a smile.

'Which one?' she would ask.

'The Lady of Shallot Miss,' we would chorus.
'Again?' She would feign surprise.
'Yes Miss.'
The slim fingers would find the page, smooth out the book with the flat of her hand, steady herself on the stool and begin –

> 'On either side the river lie,
> Long fields of barley and of rye,
> That clothe the wold and meet the sky;
> And thro' the field the road runs by
> To many-tower'd Camelot;
> And up and down the people go,
> Gazing where the lilies blow
> Round the island there below,
> The Island of Shallot.'

Her soft voice lulled us into a dreamy trance as she told of the doomed lady who could only see the world through a mirror, and was cursed in a way she did not know.
We listened as Sir Lancelot came riding by, seeing him with his coal black curls flowing from beneath his burnished helmet, and waited with bated breath for the terrible climax.
Suddenly Miss McCrindle would jump down from her stool, throw her arms wide, and declare -

> 'She left the web, she left the loom,
> She made three paces through the room,
> She saw the water lily bloom,
> She saw the helmet and the plume,
> She looked down to Camelot.
> Out flew the web and floated wide;
> The mirror cracked from side to side;
> "The curse has come upon me," cried
> The Lady of Shallot.'

And as she finds the boat, and lies robed in white, singing as it gently drifts, we watch as Miss McCrindle leans forward one hand raised palm outward, stilling us to silence once again.
We see the boat drift; hear her song die away, as the blood freezes in her veins. Still we sit, watching the dust motes dancing in the sunrays, slanting through the window. Miss McCrindle sighs, her voice dropping almost to a whisper.

> 'Who is this? And what is here?
> And in the lighted palace near
> Died the sound of royal cheer;

> *And they crossed themselves for fear,*
> *All the knights of Camelot:*
> *But Lancelot mused a little space;*
> *He said, "She has a lovely face;*
> *God in His mercy lend her grace,*
> *The Lady of Shallot".'*

Silence.

Then a shifting of bottoms on seats, a loosening of tense shoulder muscles, a nervous cough.

Miss McCrindle slips the bookmark in place and closes the book, and carries the high stool back behind the desk, looks up and smiles.

'Gather your things children, and stand at your desks, the bell will ring soon.'

Noise and clatter, as each one scrambles to their feet to stand behind their chairs, some laughing and pushing each other, till a sharp rap with a ruler calls them to order.

I gather my stillness round me like a cloak, the dreamy spires of Camelot still dance before my eyes. The bell shrills its summon of release, and the children file through the door. As I pass Miss McCrindle we exchange a smile.

Eugene and Ada rarely went out in the evenings, most nights Ada was behind the counter in the chip shop, but for over a week they had been mysteriously disappearing, leaving Aggie and Betty to squabble over who was in charge. The matter was usually settled by Betty doing the work and Aggie supervising from the armchair.

We were really curious as to where they went each night, but they were tight-lipped, talking to each other in Italian, so that we could not understand.

On the second Saturday they were out all day, and this time, much to Betty's relief, they had taken Aggie with them.

By ten o'clock I was getting tired but I was determined not to go to bed before Ada came home.

Betty had really got into the swing of bossing us about. She put the kettle on the range, telling me that as soon as it boiled, she would fill the sink for me to wash before bed.

Complaining loudly I climbed onto the little three legged stool to reach the sink, and tried to take as much time as I could get away with. As I lathered my leg with the flannel I heard the key turn in the lock. Ada always locked us in.

I rushed to the door, the flannel dripping on the linoleum.

'What's this? No in yer bed yet?' Eugene said in mock anger, and smiling broadly.

Behind him Aggie stood, hands at her side, waiting for Ada to unbutton her coat. She was clearly excited, her eyes dancing in her head.

'Well tell them, tell them,' Eugene urged Ada.

'Tell us what?' Lena wanted to know.

'Let me get my coat off first,' Ada protested though she too was pleased about something.

'Yer mammy has got a shop,' Aggie blurted out.

'A shop! What kind of shop?' we clamoured.

'An ice-cream shop. It is in St.Vincent Street,' Eugene said.

Lena and I danced around, 'We've got an ice-cream shop. We've got an ice-cream shop.'

'Hold your horses,' cautioned Ada, 'it's not our shop, I am going to manage it.'

We stopped our dancing, Lena was deflated, 'Well, who's shop is it?'

Ada hung up Aggie's coat then her own, 'Put the kettle on Betty, I need a cup of tea, after all that talking.'

I scrubbed at my leg now prickly with dried up soap, and pulling on my nightdress, I squatted at Ada's feet. I was not going to bed till I heard all about it.

Ada took a sip of tea, 'Ah that's better. I suppose you all want to hear all about it?' she laughed.

'Well it is called the Favourite Cafe, and as Daddy says it is in St.Vincent Street, just where it meets Argyle Street.

'Aye at the gushet,' chipped in Eugene.

'The Favourite Cafe,' Lena said softly to herself. 'So what is it like, is it nice?' demanded Betty.

'Oh it's lovely,' Aggie said, 'It has a lovely glass counter, and tables wi' long benches on either side.'

'And a back shop,' said Eugene.

'Remember it is not ours. I will just be managing it for the people who own it,' Ada warned.

'Does it mean we will be rich?' I wanted to know.

Ada laughed, 'No, I will have to give most of the money to the owners. I'll just get a wage.'

'Aye, but it will be better than the chip shop, a lot better,' Eugene said.

'What about the people who own it? Are they going away on holiday?' Lena asked.

Eugene's smile was grim, 'Aye, a long holiday.'

'How long?' Betty said

'For the duration?' I piped up. They all laughed.

'Aye, they're Italians,' Aggie said. 'They've been attacked.'

'That's enough!' Ada snapped.

'Who attacked them?' Betty wanted to know.

'A mob,' Eugene told her.

'Basta! Basta!' Ada shouted. She stood up pulling me up with her, 'Time you were in your bed,' she said as she steered me into the room.

'I want to hear about the shop,' I protested.

'Tomorrow is another day. Get to sleep now.' She helped me into bed, pulling the covers round my ears, 'Get to sleep it's late,' she turned away.

'Mammy, what did the mob do?' I asked.

'It is nothing for you to worry about. They are just bullies. Go to sleep now,' she left me. I jumped out of bed and followed her back into the kitchen.

'I want to hear about the bullies. Were they wee girls?'
Ada was so surprised she didn't order me straight back to bed.
'Wee girls, what made you think of that?' she asked.
'There are bullies at school, they don't like .....' My voice trailed away as 1
realized I would have to tell her about Molly.
'What don't they like?' Ada asked.
'Eh just a lot of things, they just bother some of the girls in my class.'
'Do they bother you?' Ada said sharply.
'No,' I said trying not to look her in the face.
'Are you sure?' Ada persisted.
'Yes.'
Betty butted in, anxious to get back to hearing about the shop.
'What happened to the shop people, mammy?
'Wait until this one is in her bed,' Ada said, taking my hand.
'Och let her stay up, it's Saturday night, anyway she's nosey, like the rest of
them,' Eugene laughed.
Betty poured out more tea, and we sat huddled round the table.
'Well the people who own the shop are called DiMarco. They have a young
son, and Mr. DiMarco has brought his old mother over from Italy to stay
with them,' Ada began.
'He's a Blackshirt,' Aggie chipped in.
'What's that?' Lena was puzzled.
'Och he supports that Mussolini,' Eugene said.
'More fool him,' said Ada.
Mr. DiMarco had made no secret of the fact that he would be willing to fight
for Mussolini. He was one of Mussolini's Blackshirts, and held a huge
collection of propaganda in the form of books and pamphlets He also had his
Blackshirt uniform. Eugene and Ada had found him frantically ripping all
this to shreds and burning it in the kitchen range. He was expecting to be
interned at any moment and did not want to make things worse for himself.
They had been living above the cafe, but a few months earlier had taken a
lease on a much bigger flat in the fashionable area of Charing Cross, just
opposite the cafe where Lizzie worked. He had decided to move all of the
family to the new flat, as already there had been trouble with the local gang,
and even some formally friendly customers had been threatening.
When the police did come for him, the word got round and a mob gathered
pelting the family with stones and rotten fruit. The women and the child had
been terrified though unhurt. They were taken to the Charing Cross flat, and
he was kept in custody until transfer to the Isle of Man. Mrs DiMarco had
gone to Lizzie in the Charing Cross cafe to ask her to beg Ada to agree to
take on the shop, because although they had been talking for over a week,
Ada had been reluctant to do it. The Rossi's who owned the Charing Cross
Café, although not supporters of the Fascists, had been on holiday in Italy at
the outbreak of war and were stranded there for the duration. Ada's initial
reluctance was due to the Fascist sympathies of the DiMarco's. Eugene was
still vulnerable, she did not know what would happen to him, and to take

over a business from a known Blackshirt was a risk. Eugene scoffed at her fears. No matter how many times Ada reminded us that shop was not really ours we could not wait to see it.

We were not disappointed; the glass door was set in a mahogany frame, the benches and dado rail were of the same dark wood, the table tops white marble, the floor terrazzo tiles. The tables and benches ran halfway up one wall and all the way up the other with the long glass counter filling the rest of the space. Behind the counter row upon row of glass shelves, lined with Grecian urn shaped bottles of sweets of every colour. The wooden shelves below held all the soft drinks, or 'ginger', as the Glaswegians termed it.

The ice-cream freezer was very basic; a small galvanized steel tub within a larger one, the space between was where the ice was packed to freeze the revolving mixture.

Ada's pride and joy was the oval mahogany framed mirrors which hung above each table. The back shop, though quite small, held most of what was needed to carry on the business. An ordinary domestic gas cooker, on which stood a huge urn, which covered all four burners, a jaw box sink, kitchen range, and against the remaining wall, a drop leaf table and two bent wood chairs. As Betty, Lena and I scurried around looking at everything and served imaginary customers, Eugene was standing on top of a step-ladder at the front door, nailing up an oblong board, which Ada had handed to him.

When he was finished he called us out to see it. We were puzzled, as it read, 'Ada Coutts Proprietor'.

'Well, we daren't put up Cocozza,' Ada said.

So began our dual identity.

CHAPTER 9

The war was making its presence felt more and more. On practically every wall, in the shops, even on trams posters warned, 'Careless talk costs Lives', 'Be like dad keep mum', 'Walls have ears', and as you rattled along on the tram, the accusing, 'Is your journey really necessary?'

At Ada's insistence Eugene criss-crossed the windows with tape against flying glass, should there be an air raid.

'It will never happen,' Eugene said, but crossed the street to do the same to Da-dee's windows. When Pat protested that was his job, Eugene shrugged and said easily, 'Och ah had plenty stuff left over. What does it matter who does it, as long as it gets done?'

Pat let the matter drop, knowing the truth of Tina's observation, 'If ah had waited on Pat tae dae it, the war would have been ower.'

The air raid warden came to tell us our nearest shelter was right next to us, under the Saracen Buildings in Little Dove Lane.

Eugene laughed and said, 'Aye thanks, but we will probably never need it.'

The warden wagged a warning finger, 'Mark my words, Gerry will find us.'

'Not at all, not at all.' Eugene went back to his pipe.

It was the government who found him first. Days later answering a thundering knock on the door, he found two policemen with an order to take him to the station, to answer some questions as he was an alien.

Ada paced the floor till he returned ashen faced and shaken.

'I knew it, those call up papers, you should never have burned them, not official papers. It makes it look as if you have something to hide,' she railed.

'Aye,' Eugene said wearily, you were right.'

'What happens now? Are you to be interned?'

'Will they take daddy away?' Lena was close to tears.

'Nobody is going to take me away,' Eugene said.

'What did they say?' Ada was exasperated.

'They wanted to know if I had agreed to fight for Italy, if I was a Blackshirt, if I knew anything about their movements,' Eugene told her.

'What did you say?' she asked.

'Eh ah told them it was a load of nonsense. I wanted nothing to do with Mussolini, or his army. I said ah had burned the first set of call up papers, and that you had hid the second lot.'

Fingers and thumb pressed together Ada shook them in his face, 'Tu sta matto! Stupido! Stupido!'

Eugene spread his hands, 'Eh it's true.'

'You should think before you speak; it looks bad, as if we have something to hide. If they find out about the shop, the connection to DiMarco, it will make them suspicious. Oh my God, what will happen now?' Ada was shaking.

Aggie was jiggling the shop keys nervously, the noise grated on our nerves.

'Will you stop that?' Ada shouted.

Aggie burst into tears.

Ada rounded on Eugene, 'Tell me exactly what they said.'

'Ah told you, the usual stuff, they want me to back for more questioning.'

'Did they say you were a spy, daddy?' I asked.

'Be quiet!' Ada snapped.

Eugene laughed, 'Not at all, not at all.'

'Did they mention the Isle of Man?' Ada asked.

Eugene hesitated.

'Did they?' Ada demanded.

'Eh well they said ah could be interned, it depended on what the chief constable thought aboot what ah had to tell him, that's the trouble, there is nothing to tell him,' Eugene laughed again.

'This is no laughing matter. You could be imprisoned for the duration of the war,' Ada said.

'I've done nothing wrong. I'm no spy. Eh where would I spy? I wouldnae know where to start, it's daft, a lot of nonsense.'

'You worked in the shipyards, and maybe they think you saw something there you shouldn't have,' Ada said.

'What? Men playin' cards when they should have been workin?'

'Oh I don't know; who knows what is on their minds, it is enough that you are Italian,' Ada said.

'Are you scared daddy?' Betty asked.

'Not at all.' Eugene's laugh was uneasy.

'We will just have to pray that the good Lord will have mercy on us all,' said Ada.

He did.

Eugene was freed, the only restrictions placed on him were that he was not allowed to travel, and must report to the local police station every week.

He came back beaming all over his face.

'Ah have to report to the Bobbies every week for the....'

'Duration!' I shouted.

We all laughed.

From the first the cafe had taken all of Ada's time. She and Aggie would take the tram every morning from the Gallowgate to open the shop by nine o'clock, and it would not close till midnight. She was anxious to keep Eugene away as much as possible, because there had been a lot of trouble with the Bath gang who hung around outside the pub at the corner, the Breadalbane Arms. Several Italian owned shops in the vicinity had been attacked, especially since most were run by women, the men having been interned. Ada was banking on the name of Coutts above the door to avoid being targeted, but she knew that once Eugene was seen around, the gang was likely to strike.

Next to the cafe separated only by a close was Mr.Angelini's chip shop, which the gang saw as a soft target.

The Angelinis were elderly and frail, their daughter, though extremely bright, was confined to a wheelchair, and their son Armando, at sixteen several years younger than his sister, was lazy and of little help to his parents, spending all his time smoking Woodbines and telling tall tales. Coming to help out for a week, Tina watched the boy as he lounged on a bench dunking water biscuits into a cup of Bovril.

'Ah can see why they never sent old Mr.Angelini away, but why did they no' send him away?' she jerked her thumb in Armando's direction. Ada touched her forehead, 'He's, you know....'

'Daft?' asked Tina.

'Well, not quite right,' said Ada.

'Aye, daft the right way,' scoffed Tina.

Eugene wanted to be in the shop. He hated being idle, besides preparing the mixture for the ice-cream was a full time job in itself. It meant filling the huge vat with all the ingredients and standing over it constantly stirring it all the time to make sure it did not 'catch on' and burn.

He persuaded Ada that if he stayed in the back shop it would be all right, and reluctantly she agreed. He would leave the house each morning with Ada and Aggie, leaving Lena to take me to school.

Ada was proud of her ice-cream made to a recipe given to her by the people who had owned the cafe in Elm Row in Edinburgh. Since Italians like to keep their recipe secret she had been privileged indeed.

At weekends we all worked in the shop. Eugene, shirt sleeves rolled up, sweatband round his head, a long white apron round his middle, its strings wound round twice since he was so small, would be perched on his stool for hours on end. My job was to keep him supplied with glasses of water, handing them up through the steam that engulfed his head. Betty and Lena would drain off the mixture into galvanized buckets, lining them up along the wall to cool.

The air would be filled with the sickly sweet aroma, like thick creamy custard. As we worked we would dip spoons into the mixture, supping it till we felt quite sick. Eugene would bellow at us threatening to come down from his stool to 'tan our hides', but we knew he never would. Ada meanwhile would be hammering at the huge block of ice, breaking it into manageable pieces to pack into the freezer. As Betty and Lena ferried through the buckets of cooled mixture Ada would tip the mixture into the inner vat, and gripping the paddle in both hands begin the laborious job of stirring until the ice-cream formed.

Aggie meanwhile would be coping with the customers, serving Bovril and tea, soft drinks and sliders.

She was slow but surprisingly tireless, working long hours and doing most things reasonably well. The skill always deserted her when she returned home, where she would resort to her helpless self, waiting for someone to take off her coat and unbutton her overall.

We three girls would also take on the task of clearing tables, heating pies and washing dishes.

Ada, still fearful of Eugene being attacked by the Bath gang, would insist he left early with us.

She and Aggie would stay on till after midnight, long after the last tram had gone and they would walk home through the blackout.

She carried the day's takings in a bag strapped round her waist, under her coat. Always on the alert for possible attack, she carried a pot of pepper in her hand.

'Who would attack two wimmin?' Eugene would comment.

'You never know who is about, especially under that Central Bridge, the war has brought all sorts,' Ada insisted.

She refused to be parted from her pepper pot, even when a policeman told her it was against the law.

Whoever she was expecting to encounter under the Central Bridge it certainly was not Joe McCann, but one night there he was, in civvies, with a group of men dressed like himself.

They emerged from the railway station deep in conversation, and vanished.

'Ah thought he was abroad wi' his regiment,' Aggie said.

'He can't be on leave. Famie would have said, and you know how she makes such a fuss. I think he has deserted; I wouldn't put it past him. Thinks if he goes around in civvies no one will notice, and hasn't got the sense he was born with.' Ada was scathing.

'Do you think Famie knows?' Aggie asked.

'I doubt it, but even if she did she would stand by him, he can do no wrong in her eyes,' Ada said.

'What are you goin' tae dae?' Aggie's eyes danced with excitement.

'Nothing. It is none of my business, though I would dearly like to give him a piece of my mind. No, the redcaps will find him soon enough and he'll cool his heels in the glasshouse. Men have been shot for deserting you know,' Ada said grimly.

'Are ye sure it was him?' Eugene queried.

'Oh it was him all right. You couldn't mistake him even in the dim light of the station entrance.' Ada was adamant.

'Aye, but you don't know if he has deserted. He could have been....'

'What? On a secret mission? You are as gullible as your sister. Why she ever chose him over Calisto Rossi I will never know. She could have been living in the lap of luxury,' Ada fumed.

'Eh love is a funny thing, you know what they say, love is blind,' Eugene shrugged.

'It is your sister that is blind. He is in big trouble, mark my words. It is only a matter of time before he is picked up. Hardly a day goes by without the redcaps coming into the shop checking up on any uniformed lads'.

Within two weeks it was all over.

Joe was arrested at home. Famie, in the mistaken belief he was home on leave, welcomed him with open arms, only to be terrified and bewildered when the early morning knock on the door heralded the arrival of the redcaps.

Joe was marched away to face court martial and imprisonment, at the end of which he was given a dishonourable discharge.

'He is too sensitive to be a soldier,' Famie said in his defence. 'He is chicken hearted, he canny stand violence.'

'He is chicken all right,' said Ada darkly.

Joe joined his brother Pat on fire duty, spending long hours on the roofs of buildings or in draughty closes fire bucket and stirrup pump at the ready.

'Ah'll bet he wishes he had stayed in the army,' laughed Eugene.

The dreaded disease which had troubled Auntie Tina as far back as when we lived with Auntie Teenie had flared up again.

Ada would lower her voice and speak to Eugene in Italian as a double precaution against my hearing what the terrible thing was, and terrible it seemed to be as even I could catch the anger in Ada's tone and recognize the name of uncle Pat which she spat out.

Aggie was clearly having trouble keeping the information to herself, and one night, in the blacked out darkness of our bedroom, she wondered aloud how Tina was coping and expressed sorrow for her plight.

'What is the matter with her?' asked Lena alarmed that anything should upset her beloved Godmother.

'Your uncle Pat has passed on a terrible disease tae her,' said Aggie.

'What kind of disease, you mean like measles or mumps?' asked Lena.

Aggie laughed in the darkness.

'No. Nothing like that.'

'Well what kind of disease?' Lena demanded.

'Ah'm no supposed tae say.' Aggie was enjoying her power.

'She is my Godmother, I should know,' Lena persisted.

Betty half asleep said wearily, 'I think you don't really know yourself.'

'Aye ah dae,' Aggie said angrily.

'You do not. Mammy speaks in Italian, and you don't know what she is saying any more than we do.' Betty turned on her side.

'Ah do know. It's syphilis,' Aggie blurted out.

'What is that?' Lena said.

'It is something dirty, tae dae wi' sex,' Aggie said.

'What is sex?' I wanted to know.

'Nothing, go to sleep,' Betty and Aggie said together.

There were many taboos in my life as far as Ada was concerned, and sex was definitely one of them.

It was a word seldom if ever heard, certainly not in school, the home, the radio or indeed the press, save for 'the Rags' as Ada called them, but they never entered our house.

I was totally ignorant, and Ada wanted me to stay that way. So Aggie's 'cat out of the bag' revelation was a total mystery to me. Yet that did not stop it being something dark and monstrous in my mind. Lena, though older, shared my ignorance to some extent and all of my horror. She had always loathed Pat and this news justified her hatred. Betty being much older and very 'grown up' professed to know a lot, but stayed tight-lipped, saying she could not explain it to us as we were much too young to know. Lena and I suspected that even she had no idea what syphilis was either.

Tina continued to be her sunny self whenever she was around us, but even we could tell she was far from well. She no longer helped out in the cafe. Aggie enjoying being the bearer of sensational tit-bits, told us in another of her nocturnal chats that Ada had 'put the bar up' on Tina till she was better. Lizzie sacrificed her saving sending Tina to a nursing home for treatment. Tina stayed six weeks and came home looking much better.

Ada's standard of housekeeping was very high, and being so busy in the shop meant most chores were entrusted to us, except the washing. None of the houses had hot water, which meant the women had to use the communal washhouse in the back court or haul the washing through the streets to the steamie. Monday was washday, and the use of the back court washhouse was strictly regulated, each landing taking its turn. Living on the third floor the turn of the washhouse seemed to take forever to come round. When it did Ada would certainly use it. It meant an early rise since the other women on the landing were snapping at her heels. The night before no matter how tired she was after being in the shop all day, she would sort out the clothes into separate bundles. Whites, some to be boiled, some to be steeped, woollens for delicate wash, coloured on their own.

At dawn she would be down in the washhouse getting the boiler going, then up stairs to carry down a huge zinc bath of clothes, with two blocks of Sunlight soap, and the washing board perched on top.

I hated 'backcourt Mondays'. Ada was always in a bad mood, exhausted from carrying load after load of soaking wet clothes up three flights of stairs.

At dinner time as soon as I came through the door Ada would hurriedly ladle soup into a bowl slap down the 'heel' of a loaf and say, 'Quick as you can, I need a hand with the mangling before you go back.'

I would eat, one eye on the clock willing the hour to pass.

Helping Ada with the mangling filled me with terror. I always seemed to end up in the 'black books', by letting the clean sheets touch the floor.

'Stop dreaming and watch what you are doing,' she would shout.

Anxiously I would grab at the sheet as soon as it appeared through the rollers.

'Mind your fingers, they will get caught! Don't bunch up the sheet like that it makes it harder to iron.'

The whole thing would be repeated time and time again, making me more nervous as time went on, till the inevitable happened, three of my fingers got caught and burst in the rollers.

My screams of pain mingled with terror as I saw the newly washed sheets spattered by bright red spots of blood.

Ada seemed not to notice as she rushed me to the sink letting the cold water run over my fingers, the blood changing to a dull pink as it swirled down the drain.

Later tucked up under a blanket in Eugene's arm chair, supping saps of bread soaked in warm milk and sugar, and reading my favourite book 'Hunky Dory'. My fingers throbbing and strangely hot I drifted off to sleep.

I awoke to the hot steam that rose from the clothes on the airer round the fire. It caught at my breath, plastered my hair to my forehead and curled the edges of my book.

To my relief and delight Ada decided to use the steamie for a few weeks. I

74

loved the steamie, but to Ada it meant the same hard work with the additional bother of borrowing a 'bogie' from a neighbour to pull the zinc bath the quarter mile to Laundressy Street where the steamie shared the building with the public baths.

She would go late afternoon so that I could come along after school to help her. I would run as fast as I could to have the longest time possible in that magic place.

It was a huge vaulted hall, the roof of iron girders almost invisible in the steam. Ghostly figures emerged and disappeared in the gloom, the rows and rows of booths each with two sinks, a boiler and mangle, separated from the next by a wooden partition. The women clad in wrap round aprons often with a rubber apron on top, their ill shod feet splashing in the water which covered the floor, their hair caught up in a turban, stood bent over a washing board, slapping each garment over the board, rubbing it over with a block of soap, then scrubbing it over and over the corrugated grooves. Some exchanged gossip as they scrubbed shouting to make themselves heard over the din. Seldom did they stop and talk. Time was precious, each minute had been paid for and there was always a queue of women waiting to come in.

Aside from the small mangle in the booth there was a larger communal one for sheets and blankets. This was considered dangerous for children and we were forced to keep our distance. This suited me, and I would happily run on into the drying room to bag a place for Ada by hanging a piece of our washing over the rail.

When Ada appeared I would help her hang the clothes and stand guard as they dried while she went on with the next batch of washing.

When the clothes were dry I would take the smaller things from the line fold them and lay them in the bath ready to be pulled home. The sheets and blankets had to be left till Ada came. This was the only part I did not like, folding the 'big' things with Ada. I worried again about letting .hem touch the floor.

She would tug at two corners, tell me to grip them then motion me to walk backwards pulling the sheet further from the rail, when she would catch the last two corners.

'Hold it open, right out as far as it will stretch. That's it, don't let it sag, and keep it up from the floor. Now bring your corners together, make sure they are even. Now grip each corner and stretch the sheet.'

Tongue clamped between my teeth I gripped each corner knowing what was coming next.

Ada shook the sheet with such force it made a snapping sound, I tightened my grip I had let go before and rued the day.

Then we went into the dance, coming to meet each other, matching the corners, she taking over mine, me gripping the two at the bottom, moving backwards, while she gave another snap, moving towards her to repeat the process till the sheet was duly folded.

So we went on till all the 'big' things were folded to Ada's satisfaction.

With the clean dry clothes neatly folded in the bath, covered with her rubber apron, the washboard and soap placed on top, and the whole thing secured by ropes, we were ready to go home.

Home to tea free from choking steam, from wet clothes round the fire and hanging from the pulley, dripping on your head, clinging to your cheeks.

Yet Ada could not rest.

'Hurry up with your tea. I need the table to iron. These things need to be done and put away tonight, and then I gain a day to get on with things in the shop.'

We ate in silence, then Betty washed the dishes, while Lena got out the thick rubberised mat from the cupboard, spread it over the table, placed an old blanket on top and set the two flat irons on the range to heat, as Ada untied the clothes and selected 'flat things first' as she could 'get through them quicker.'

As she ironed she would come across holes or tears, and these she would pass to Lena to repair. Lena had twenty-twenty vision and could thread a needle as quick as look at it. She was a natural seamstress, sitting happily stitching away, never complaining as the pile grew faster than she could sew.

My eyesight was much poorer than Lena's so I was of little help with the mending, truth to tell it took me many minutes to get the thread through the eye of a needle, and if I did succeed no sooner had I put the needle through the material than the thread would snag.

Ada would remove the sorry mess with a sigh and tell me to go to bed.

I would go willingly enough since it gave me a few hours revelling in the joy of having the bed to myself before Aggie came home.

CHAPTER 10

The attack had been quick and unexpected, two bottles hurled through the door in rapid succession. Thankfully both Aggie and Eugene were unhurt but badly shaken. The Angelinis next door had been hit too, old Mr. Angelini cut above the eye.

'We need to bring charges,' Ada said.

'We don't know who did it,' Eugene argued.

'That crowd at the corner, who else?' Ada snapped.

'But we didnae see anybody, it happened so quick,' Aggie sobbed.

'Then I'll ask Mr.Angelini, he was hurt, he needs to charge them too.' Ada left the shop.

She was back within a few minutes, shaking her head in disbelief.

'He doesn't want any trouble. What does he think having bottles hurled through his door is if it isn't trouble?' she fumed.

'Did he see who threw them?' Eugene asked.

'The Lang brothers, he is in no doubt, he was just coming from the back shop when they burst through the door, and it was definitely the Lang brothers.

'Ah think we should just leave things for now, it is no' likely to happen again, is it?' Eugene shrugged.

'Of course it will happen again, especially if we don't do something about it,' Ada was furious.

'Ach they will soon be called up, and we'll get rid of them.' Eugene reached for his tobacco pouch, filled his pipe with his beloved Erinmore tobacco and struck a match.

'They are too young for the army, why else would they still be here? In any case I doubt if the army would take hooligans like that, they are not fit to be soldiers,' she said.

'The army needs all the men it can get,' Eugene said through a haze of aromatic smoke.

'The British army is the best in the world, and the Scottish regiments the bravest, this lot are cowards,' Ada told him.

'Aye, well a few weeks square bashing is just what they need,' Eugene said.

'Whether they go to the army or not does not solve our problem,' Ada said decisively.

'Leave it for a while,' Eugene urged.

'All right, but it is against my better judgement,' Ada said wearily.

In the following weeks there were several more attacks on both shops, and threats of physical harm.

Ada had had enough.

'I've said all along we need to involve the police, I'm going to talk to Mr.Angelini, if we complain together we will have a stronger case.'

'We might just stir up more trouble,' a worried Eugene said.

'We need to stand up for ourselves, they are just bullies, and the only way to get rid of bullies is to stand up to them. Why do you think we are in the mess we are in today as far as this war is concerned? Because Chamberlain did not stand up to Hitler, he tried to appease him, and look what happened,' Ada told him emphasizing each word with a stab of her finger on the table.

Eugene laughed nervously, 'Eh ah don't think it is the same thing.'

'What! Of course it is, a bully is a bully, and to them appeasement is only a sign of weakness.

She took her coat from the hook behind the door and slipped it on.

'Where are you going?' Eugene asked.

'To talk to Mr.Angelini, and then to Cranston Street station to report what has been happening.'

She came back jubilant, 'He has agreed to do it, and I've spoken to the police and they are going to look into it.'

'So you think it might end up in court?' Eugene seemed concerned.

'I hope so, that is the whole idea, but they say they will need evidence so they will be keeping watch over the next couple of weeks.'

'If it goes to court and ah have to give evidence, it will mean giving ma name, ma real name, some of the gang will be in the dock and they will hear.'

'Then we will have to make sure you are not called. I am a British citizen with citizen's rights, they won't be able to pin anything on me,' Ada was adamant.

'Aye, no like me, wi' ma Roman nose, roamin' a' over ma face,' Eugene said with a wry smile.

He shrugged, and reached for his pipe, 'Och the whole thing is daft, it is only that crowd that cause trouble, the rest o' the folk are fine they call me 'Tally Joe', and ah....'

'Answer to it, more fool you,' Ada put in.

Eugene sucked at his pipe which refused to light, 'Eh ah take it in good part, and ah don't mind.'

'Ah don't like folk callin' me "Tally Aggie". Ah tell them my name is Agnes Paterson Miller and ah'm from Edinburgh,' complained Aggie.

'Quite right,' agreed Ada. 'I only answer to Mrs. Coutts, nothing else.'

Ada thought over what Eugene had said. She knew he was afraid; he was not a violent man and could not bear confrontation of any kind.

'I think you should stay away from the shop for a while,' she told him the next day.

He looked surprised, 'Not at all, how would you manage, what about boiling the mixture?'

'Betty can come in and do that; she wants to leave her job anyway. She knows what to do with the mixture. I just want you out of the picture till this thing blows over.'

'If you think that's best,' Eugene conceded.

The next attack came when Betty and Aggie were alone in the shop. Four of the gang came in sat at a table smoking and drinking beer. Aggie eyed them nervously as did the other customers seated at other tables.

'What do you want, Bovril, Vimto?' Aggie asked.

'We waant you dirty Tallies oot o' here,' one said.

Aggie ignored him and repeated her question.

'We telt ye', they sneered.

'Ye cannae sit here withoot orderin' something,' Aggie persisted.

'Away ye go,' the ringleader said giving her a mighty shove.

They all laughed and began to sing the national anthem stamping their feet and thumping the table.

The commotion brought Betty from the back shop.

'Stop that noise or get out,' she shouted above the din.

'Try an' make us,' they taunted.

'Get out now! 'Betty demanded.

For answer they got up, going from table to table shouting, 'She waants us oot, we're no rotten tallies we belong here, we can dae whit we like, it's oor country, right?'

The customers looked away refusing to answer and one or two got up to leave.

'Whit ur yus goin' away fur? It's them that should go, they ur makin' money off us.'

Soon all the customers had gone.

Betty stood hands on hips shouting, 'Get out! Get out!'

'Keep yer hair on we're goin', but we'll leave ye a wee message.'

They ran the length of the shop, clearing the contents of the tables to the floor, laughing as they ran out the door. Betty rushed to bolt the door after them.

Aggie was still shaking from her assault. She looked wild eyed at Betty.

'Whit are we go in to do?'

'I need to report this, and get the police here to see the damage,' Betty said.

'Don't leave me here ma sel'. They might come back,' Aggie pleaded.

Betty was listening at the door.

'Shush, they're next door. I can hear Mr.Angelini shouting.'

As Mrs. Angelini's voice rose in a piercing scream, Betty winced.

'I wonder what's happened. It sounds as if she is really hurt.'

Aggie burst into tears, 'Ah wish Eadie was here.'

'Well she isn't so we will just have to think of a way to get to Cranston Street to get the police,' Betty snapped. Then more gently, 'I wish we had a back door to this shop.'

As time wore on, people came to the door testing the handle.

'We're closed,' Betty shouted.

After a while there would be another try of the handle.

Betty shouted again, 'We're closed.'

'It's me, Hammy,' came the answer.

Betty peered through the glass into the darkness. She could just see the tall slightly stooped figure she knew very well. She opened the door.

'Come in quickly,' she urged.

Hammy's tall skinny frame squeezed through the gap.

'What happened?' He eyed the debris scattered across the floor.

'We had a visit from the Bath gang, what else?' Betty sighed.

'The chip shop is shut as well,' said Hammy.

'They went there too, and I think Mrs Angelini has been hurt. I heard her screaming,' Betty told him.

'What are you going to do?' Hammy asked, cracking his knuckles nervously.

'I need to get word to Cranston Street, but I can't leave Aggie, she is too scared. Would you go and report it for me?'

'Me!' Hammy jumped in alarm.

'There is nobody else, we can't stay closed all evening, and we can't open till the police have seen the damage,' Betty explained.

'What if the gang know where I'm going?' Hammy said.

'How will they know where you are going, they never take any heed of you do they? Have they ever even spoken to you?' Betty said impatiently.

'No, I always go round Dover Street way if I see them at the corner.'

'Well then!' Betty steered him back towards the door.

'Go, as quick as you can!'

'Wh-what will I say?' Hammy whispered.

'Just tell them what happened, go!' Betty shoved him through the slightly open door, and quickly bolted it again.

'Do you think he'll go?' Aggie asked, still wiping the tears that rolled down her cheeks.

'Yeh, he will. He's scared, but he is even more scared of not "doing the right thing", as his mother would expect, and you know what she is like,' Betty said.

'She is a nice woman, they are a nice family,' said Aggie.

'I know, Hammy has been brought up to be polite to everyone, but he is scared of his own shadow,' Betty answered.

'He is only a boy, fifteen of sixteen no more. People think he is older because he is tall. Yer mammy likes him,' Aggie finished.

'I like him too, we all do, but we need help and he is the only one who could do this for us. It is just a pity he is such a scaredy cat. We may as well have a cup of tea while we wait,' Betty said moving through to the back shop.

An hour passed, and another, Betty paced up and down.

'What is going on? Why don't they come?' she fumed.

'Maybe he was too scared to go,' Aggie said gloomily.

'We can't wait much longer, if they don't come within the next half-hour, I will need to go myself,' Betty decided.

'No, ye canny,' Aggie pleaded.

'You will be all right if I lock you in,' Betty reassured her.

They watched the hands of the clock crawl slowly round, then a thundering knock at the door, and a sharp 'POLICE!' had Betty rushing to draw the bolt.

The two officers were no strangers to Betty. Ever since Ada had taken over the shop they had came in for the odd cup of Bovril especially on a cold bitter night, when, away from the prying eyes of their sergeant they enjoyed a quick cup and a cigarette.

Aggie stumbled tearfully through her statement. Betty adopted her usual flippant bantering tone, unable to resist flirting a little.

The big highland policeman snapped shut his notebook and fixed Betty with a stern look.

'You realize you will be asked to repeat all this in court lass, are you prepared to do that?'

'Yeh, of course,' Betty assured him.

'And what about you?' he turned to Aggie.

'She will, of course she will,' Betty said quickly.

'I need to hear her say so.'

Aggie sniffed loudly, 'Aye, aye ah will.'

'Right,' said the policeman. 'We will leave it there, what I need to do now is speak to Mr. Angelini.'

Betty opened the door, and as they left Hammy appeared still cracking his knuckles nervously.

'Can I come in?' he asked his nose almost in the door.

'Yeh, come and give us a hand to clear up this mess, we need to open for the last hour or two,' Betty said letting him squeeze through the opening.

'Do you know if Angelini went ahead with the charge?' Ada asked as they told him what had happened.

'I don't know, I think he would, because Mrs Angelini was screaming.'

Though Mr.Angelini had indeed decided to bring charges, in the weeks that followed while waiting for the case to come to court, he was finding it difficult to keep his nerve. Some of the gang members tried to intimidate him, as they did Ada, but she was not to be moved and spent much time with the frightened man, trying to 'stiffen his backbone'.

At last the case came to court, Betty and Aggie called as witnesses.

To Ada's shame Betty received a reprimand from the magistrate for chewing gum in the witness box, and as if this was not enough she earned a second ticking off. When asked if a certain statement was true she answered 'uhuh'. She was sternly reminded there was no such word in the English language, the expression was slang and there was no place for slang in his Magistrate's court.

Betty got her own 'sentence' from Ada when she got her home.

The gang members were given the option of a fine or thirty days in prison. They opted for the fine.

Ada was pleased enough with the outcome but would have preferred they had gone to jail. Still she felt they would feel 'the draught' in their pockets.

She was furious when Armando, let slip his dad had been 'leant on', and had paid the fine from his own pocket.

'Why did you do it?' she asked in exasperation as Mr.Angelini stood head down avoiding her eyes.

He shrugged, 'I got no fight left, I'm too old, and my Maria she say just pay, so they leave us alone.'

'No, no they won't. You have made things worse, don't you understand?' Ada pleaded.

He soon found out the truth of what she had said, as hardly a night went by without some sort of incident in his shop. Ada barred the Lang brothers from the cafe, and when with the rest of the gang they congregated outside the shop chanting and intimidating customers, she would march up to Cranston Street station and report the disturbance. The police would swoop with the 'Black Maria' pile them in and leave them to cool their heels in the cells for the night.

Soon they adopted a new tactic, targeting other Italian owned shops, and forcing Mr.Angelini to pay any resulting fines.

Trying to cope with this and the restrictions on supplies for his business eventually proved too much for the old man. He collapsed behind his counter one day and had to be taken to hospital. Armando was left in charge of the shop. He was even more afraid of the gang than his father, and soon put up the shutters, and they were to stay up for some months.

Though the gang never seemed to notice me, or bother me in any way, they terrified me.

While to Ada and Eugene they were 'lads', to me, a child, they were grown men, men who carried razors. I lived in constant dread of what they might do to Ada and Eugene.

At school there was still Molly and her gang, who had not let up on baiting me. At break-time and home-time they would gather round me, name calling and spitting, jostling me among them and laughing as I tried to run away.

I kept it all a secret from Ada, from everyone in the family. Ada would have told me to stand up to them, I knew I couldn't.

CHAPTER 11

It was May, the month of Mary the virgin, this meant taking flowers to school for the altar, and going to Merylee Convent to process the statue of 'Our Lady' round the grounds. I loved Merylee; the buildings were honey stone, nestling in beautiful grounds of manicured lawns and outstanding trees. At Easter we would process a huge cross to 'Calvary', a large mound, which would be the cross's final resting place. Easter was a mixture of sadness and joy, remembering the suffering of Christ, and then rejoicing in His resurrection. The procession of the Virgin was an occasion for joy, a celebration of her beatification, Mary the mother of God, Mary, ever a virgin. During a religious education period I had innocently raised my hand to ask the nun taking the lesson, 'Please sister what is a virgin?' There was a pause, then she said in her soft Irish brogue, 'You do not need to know that child, it is enough that our Lady was in that blessed state.'

I felt cheated by this explanation, but concluded that it must be some sort of landmark on the way to sainthood, so I resolved to strive to be a virgin too.

I found my Catholicism hard going. Though Ada had gone along with the Catholic schooling, she never really supported the going to mass and all the other duties incumbent upon a follower of that faith, so I was frequently arriving late at school on the mornings. The class was lined up ready to march the short distance to St.Alphonsus for mass, being caught by Mother Philippa, and to compound the sin clutching my hat squeezed into a tight wedge, rather than set on my head at the regulation angle. Mother Philippa would demand I stretch out my hand to receive two strokes of the rope all the while berating me for my tardiness and my slovenly appearance. This would be a great cause of amusement for most of my classmates and ammunition for Molly to throw at break time.

Going to mass on Sunday was another difficulty. All the family were at the shop on Sundays, so there was no one to see that Lena and I got to mass, and Ada would not let us go on our own. For Lena in the senior school it was less of a problem, since the sister who took the religious education class left it to the girl's own conscience that they would attend mass every Sunday. Lena never volunteered the fact that she did not. For me in the junior school it was an entirely different matter. I would arrive at school on the Monday conscious that I had a mortal sin on my soul, and hoping against hope that Mother Philippa would not choose my class to pay a surprise visit, and ask awkward questions. She would sweep in, her gimlet eyes taking everything in, seeing into your very soul, the face beneath the white wimple was stern and cold. Taking her place before the class, she would stand silent and erect regarding us as we shifted uncomfortably in our seats.

The voice when she spoke was cold and unemotional.

'You all know as good Catholic girls you must attend mass and take holy communion every Sunday. If you do not you have committed a mortal sin, and should you die with this sin on your soul, you will go straight to hell from which there is no escape.'

She began to walk slowly up and down each isle, as she passed each child lowered her eyes, terrified that she would stop and pick her out for special attention.

Sweeping down to the front once more, she continued.

'To prove to me that you all attended mass yesterday morning, each child must put out her tongue. If you have a mortal sin on your soul because you have missed mass yesterday you will have a purple mark on your tongue, so you cannot lie to me.'

We would sit tongue extended as she slowly walked up and down each isle. Always she would find some unfortunates with the mark on their tongue, and I was always among them.

The hands would be extended, the rope would descend, each whimpering child promising that she would go straight to confession to expunge the shameful sin from her soul.

At break time we would rush to the toilets putting out our tongues and asking each other if the purple mark was visible. Strangely enough it always seemed to have vanished by the time break time came along. We told each other perhaps we could not see it because we were in a state of sin.

As Mother Philippa swept from the room, the sister in charge of the class would scold us for our wickedness, we had let her down and our classmates and she would be sending a note to our mothers.

As we guilty ones blew on our stinging palms, sister would rap sharply on her desk for our attention.

'You may think that you suffer now, but because you have been justly punished you should show gratitude to Reverend Mother for her care for your souls. Think of the risk you run of dying with a mortal sin staining the pure soul that God has given you, think of the torment of hell, from which Reverend Mother is seeking to save you'.

She would finish by making us repeat the prayer we had to say each night before sleep.

> Matthew, Mark, Luke and John,
> Bless the bed, that I lie on,
> If I should die before I wake,
> I pray the Lord, my soul to take.

The sister seemed so sure that there was a good chance that we would indeed die in our sleep that I tried hard every night to stay awake for fear it would happen.

We sinners would be excused from class to take confession. The priest was none too pleased to see us, and would add his warning of the dangers of not being in a state of grace. He would go further, adding his own terrors for our consideration, reminding us that a bomb could fall from the sky at any time, and should we have the mortal sin on our soul we would have our descent into hell assured.

The priest knew all of us, as he was a regular visitor to the school. The anonymity of the confessional was not always observed and on occasions, recognizing my voice, he would sigh wearily.

'You are an unfortunate child, having as you do a mother who is not of our faith, and a father who has never acknowledged his duty to Holy Mother Church, so it is no surprise to me that you find yourself with a mortal sin on your soul, not once but many times. I fear child, that you will never attain the state of grace required of you to attain union with the blessed saints.'

I would burst into tears truly terrified at this awful prediction. I told him that I was trying, that one of my aunties had bought me three little books on the lives of the saints, which I had read over and over, and could relate to him any story he chose to hear.

'Then you must not only read them but try to emulate them, you must strive with all your might to be like the blessed saints.'

Encouraged by this I told him that I had resolved to try to be like Our Lady, the blessed mother of God and work toward being a virgin. He gave a strange cough and said quickly, 'Say three Hail Marys and one Our Father, in penance for your sins, now go in peace my child.'

Famie had been the donor of the little books; as my Godmother she felt responsible for my spiritual welfare. Having virtually cut herself off from the family after Joe's desertion, she now decided on hearing of my teetering on the brink of hell-fire, that she should take me under her wing, and ensure my attendance at mass.

Though I would not admit to it, I found the lives of the saints harrowing reading, most of them had met with the most horrific deaths, and I despaired of ever finding the courage or faith to follow them in their martyrdom. Yet I was convinced it was what was expected of a good Catholic girl, especially me, as I had already sinned. Eugene would shake his head and complain to Ada, 'The wee one is too serious, she will end up in a nunnery.'

The aunts agreed, but while to them this was a desirable prospect, to Eugene it meant heartache.

So I sat up in bed each night before Aggie came home from the shop, and read of the fate of St. Catherine, tied to a wheel, and broken and in agony left to die. Then of St. Francis who was my favourite as he talked to animals and birds, called the sun his brother and the moon his sister. I read his story over and over, and began to think I could emulate him.

I told Aggie the story of St. Francis.

'He seems a nice man,' she said.

'He wasn't a man, he was a saint,' I was annoyed she could not see the difference, and view him in the same light.

'Aye but that was a long time ago, and it is only a story, it's no really true,' she said.

This shook me, what if she was right? If I tried to follow St. Francis and he never existed, then I would never be good enough to get into heaven.

There was still the goal of becoming a virgin, but I felt that would take some time, as Mary was very special being the mother of God, and if it was easy to be like her, other girls would have done it.

I ran to Famie, as my mentor pouring out my fears.

'Aggie is talking nonsense, you shouldn't listen to her, she is not a Catholic, so how can she know what is true and not true?' Famie consoled me.

Famie was right, what could Aggie know? So I found my faith in St. Francis restored, and felt a little easier.

I thought long and hard about it all, and decided that fond though I was of St. Francis, I should aim for higher things; as a sinner I had a lot to make up, so no matter how hard it was to become a virgin I must try.

Being like Mary meant becoming more devoted to her too, so as it was May it was the perfect time to start, and I looked joyfully forward to the procession at Merylee.

The whole school would attend. We juniors would walk before the statue, singing and strewing rose petals from our little baskets to sweeten the path as the statue passed. The mothers would line each side of the route, watching with pride as their offspring went by. Ada would not attend so Famie came in her stead. The procession would circle twice round the grounds before entering the beautiful little chapel for mass and communion. While I had been looking forward to the event for weeks, on the day itself I was in a panic. It was a requirement to fast before communion, no breakfast could be eaten, and partaking of breakfast, even a cup of tea would render the soul in mortal sin, with the ensuing threat of instant death at the altar rails as the holy host touched the tongue.

If I was going to early mass with Tina or Famie, Ada would allow me to skip breakfast, on the understanding I ate immediately I came home. While the procession at Merylee started early it was some time till the mass and communion, too long Ada felt for a child to go without breakfast. She insisted I ate two slices of toast and drank a cup of tea.

Nothing was said to Famie when she came to pick me up, but as I sat on the coach with all the other children chattering happily around me, I grew more and more terrified as we drew nearer to the convent.

All through the procession I agonized over what I should do; should I tell Famie I had eaten? I knew she would be very angry with me. Should I tell one of the nuns, who would be absolutely furious with me? The prospect scared me even more than telling Famie, but it would probably save my life, she would probably put me in the punishment corner, and give me the belt, but at least I would be spared taking communion, and she would tell Mother Philippa, and she would...., it just went round and round in my head. We entered the chapel, filing into pews we began to sing as the statue made its way down towards the altar.

> *The sun is shining brightly,*
> *And all the world is green:*
> *The beautiful trees and flowers*
> *On every side is seen,*
> *And we will go rejoicing,*
> *With joy we sing today,*

For it is the month of Mary,
The lovely month of May.

Oh Mary dear mother,
With joy we sing to thee,
Thou art the queen of heaven,
Thou too our queen shall be,
Oh rule us and guide us,
Unto eternity.

The mass began, and as we knelt to pray, I felt the panic rising, as the communion bell drew nearer and nearer. I tried to catch the eye of Sister Mary Joseph who sat at the end of the pew waiting to usher us out to the altar rail, but she ignored me. I sank back in despair.

I would have to walk down that isle to my certain death. All we children knew that if you took Holy Communion on a full stomach not only did you die instantly at the altar rail, but your face turned black as the sin made itself manifest for all to see.

I tried to imagine what Ada would feel when she heard of my terrible end, would she feel guilty because she had made me eat? What would Da-dee say? He would blame Ada and Eugene, and maybe even me for not resisting the tea and toast. If I had disobeyed Ada and not eaten it would have been a sin too, but only a little sin, not this terrible thing that I had done which was now going to kill me.

The silver notes of the communion bell rang out, Sister Mary Joseph stood up, the girls began to file out joining all the others as they made their way to the alter.

My knees felt weak, as I moved nearer. The choir of nuns kept singing, and I thought of all my plans to be a virgin, to attain union with the saints. Suddenly a thought struck me. St. Catherine, though she died a martyr, had in her past life committed sin, yet by sacrificing her life she had gained sainthood, and a place in heaven. Maybe God would accept my life as a sacrifice, and allow me in, as I had not really wanted the tea and toast in the first place. I felt a little calmer as I reached the altar and knelt alongside my classmates, our tongues extended to receive the host. As the priest made his way along the line, placing the wafer on each tongue, I panicked. I didn't want to die; I wanted to go home to Ada, and Eugene, Lena and Betty and Aggie too. The priest was before me, he lifted the small wafer, and I looked up, watching it as it descended.

Suddenly I jumped to my feet, and ran screaming up the aisle, vaguely aware that someone was running after me.

I ran and ran, stumbling over my own feet, found the heavy door and pulled it open, running on and on till finally I collapsed sobbing on the grass.

Moments later Sister Mary Joseph was pulling me to my feet, and dusting me down, she held me at arms length. 'What in heaven possessed you to do that terrible thing child?' she asked.

I could not stop sobbing, there was an awful pain in my head and I shook from head to toe.

'Are you going to tell me what this is all about? Do you realize that you have disrupted the holy mass, and you have screamed in the holy chapel?'

'What am I going to say to Reverend Mother when she hears of your astonishing behaviour?'

No words would come, I felt absolutely terrified.

Sensing she was getting nowhere, Sister Mary Joseph led me through a little white gate into the nuns' quarters, and ushered me into a small room, telling me to sit on one of the two chairs that stood against the wall. She knelt before me, brushing the damp hair from my forehead, and then taking my hands in hers, she began to pray.

'Oh blessed mother, take pity on this child for she has surely committed some dreadful sin, and now this day she has compounded this sin, by unseemly behaviour in your holy chapel, on your holy feast day.'

She stood up, saying calmly, 'I am going to leave you now for a moment or two, you must compose yourself, and then get on your knees to ask our Blessed Virgin for forgiveness.'

With that she went out, closing the door softly behind her. I slid to my knees, but no words would come, I felt so tired, my eyes heavy, I let my head fall on my hands as I leaned on the chair.

I was still there, half asleep when Sister Mary Joseph returned.

'Sit up child and take this, it will make you feel better.'

She placed a little tray on the other chair; it held a cup of warm milk and two digestive biscuits.

I sipped at the milk it tasted wonderful, and as I nibbled at the biscuits I realized they were probably her whole ration for the week, and I felt a rush of affection for Sister Mary Joseph.

She smiled at me and said 'now, are you going to tell me what it was all about?'

Haltingly I told her about the tea and toast, about Ada not being a Catholic, and Eugene being a 'Widden Catholic', even though I didn't really know what that was.

She sighed, 'perhaps Reverend Mother needs to have a word with your mother.'

'Oh no, please Sister.'

'Well something needs to be done child, who is with you today?'

'My Godmother, Sister.'

'Very well, I will speak to her. Finish up your milk, and we shall go and wait for her by the chapel till the mass is over.'

Famie stood listening to Sister Mary Joseph, two bright spots of colour on her cheeks. I knew she was very angry, and that she was ashamed of me. I did not know how I was ever going to make up for the disgrace I had brought on her.

We sat in uneasy silence all the way home, she dropped me off at our house but did not come in, only kissing me briefly on the cheek and leaving without a word.

If she ever spoke to Ada about it, I never knew.

I was summoned to Mother Philippa's office, and given a note for Ada. Ada did go to see Mother Philippa, but I never knew what passed between them. Ada's mood was dictated by the events of the war; she avidly read the newspapers and listened to every news report on the radio. The secret and sudden arrival of Rudolph Hess, Hitler's deputy in a field in Lanarkshire, brought a glimmer of hope. He demanded to see the Duke of Hamilton, insisting he would speak only to him. Everyone speculated that Hitler wanted a deal; the rumour was he had never wanted to go to war with Britain.

Ada assured us that Churchill would never make a deal with the devil, who Hitler surely was. Had not Churchill at the end of 1940 made his truly memorable speech about fighting on the beaches, in the fields, from street to street, but we would never surrender? Whatever Hess's mission had been, it came to nothing. By July, 'Winnie', had invented the V sign, the BBC broadcasting it to Europe at midnight, urging all Europeans to adopt the sign, to go out in the night and paint it on walls and pavements.

Soon everyone was greeting each other with the sign, saying V for Victory. Ada lost no time in having Betty paint it on the shop window.

No matter how much of a morale booster the victory sign was, there was no denying the fact that things were bad, the rationing was really biting and the black market was flourishing as never before.

Ada detested cheats, and labouring under severe restrictions on supplies for the shop, she was furious when she read of a woman caught with black market sugar.

'Enough sugar to supply 104 weekly rations, and to add insult to injury she was carrying it home in a Rolls Royce, so she had illegal petrol too,' she shook the newspaper in Eugene's face.

'Och she must have had a sugar daddy,' he said.

'Can you take nothing seriously?' demanded Ada.

'Eh, she was caught, wasn't she?'

'She was fined £75, it should have been more,' Ada snapped.

'Whew! That's a lot of money,' Eugene said.

'It would be a drop in the ocean to a woman like that, it makes me sick when I think of what the rest of us have to suffer,' Ada fumed.

'Ah know things are bad, but there is a war on,' Eugene tried to lighten the mood.

'Do you know how bad things really are for us?' Ada was not amused.

'We are not making enough to keep us and the DiMarcos. Every week when I go to give that woman her money she pulls a face as if I am cheating her. She has no idea how difficult things are, with rations cut to the bone.'

'Things could be worse I suppose,' Eugene ventured.

'I don't see how,' said Ada.

The morning post brought an official envelope with the dreaded stamp O.H.M.S.

We sat round the table staring at the letter it contained, a letter from the Food Ministry, informing us it was now an offence to sell ice-cream.

'We'll just have to shut up shop,' Eugene said gloomily, his usual optimism deserting him.

'I'm damned if I will, there must be a way round this,' said Ada.

'What, do you mean you would break the law?' Eugene was amazed.

'No, find a way round it, a lawful way.'

Ada had joined the Ice-cream alliance when she took over the shop, she had been a regular attendee at meetings, always taking me along with her for company.

Since the outbreak of war the meetings had been suspended, but now in the face of this new directive a meeting had been called. There was a serious threat to all the cafe owners. It was now not possible to use milk, there was a further cut in sugar allocation, and there did not seem to be a way round it at all.

Without the shop we had nothing. Ada was irritable and snappy in the days leading up to the meeting. It could not come quick enough for me.

'Is it worth going, what can they do, what can anybody do?' asked Eugene.

'I don't know, make representation, start a petition, anything,' Ada snapped back.

The meetings were held in a room above the Argyle Arcade, in Argyle Street. This was a favourite place of mine, there were so many wonderful shops, but the meetings were always held after hours, the creaking iron gate opened for us by an ancient man who's great bunch of keys rattled eerily through the empty mall.

With the shops in darkness, you could not see the doll's hospital, or Dido's umbrella shop, or the little toy shop, with the Hornby train set that chugged around the window, during the day.

At the Buchanan Street end there was the specialist tobacconist, with its rows and rows of little drawers, each holding a special blend, its name written in spidery handwriting, but the jewellers and the fur stores were my least favourite stores, especially the furs in the window. The glassy eyes of the fox stoles seemed to follow me as I passed.

The stair to the meeting room was dank and gloomy, the steps worn away in the middle. As we climbed to the top for that first meeting after the directive we could hear the chatter of excited voices, through the open door.

Everyone seemed to be talking at once, in Italian, and Ada was soon in the thick of it while I sat in my usual place at the back of the hall and watched the scene.

Not understanding the language, I found the facial expressions and hand gestures amusing. The meeting when it was called to order seemed to go on for ever, till at last there was a show of hands, murmurs of assent, then a lot of shaking of heads and shrugging of shoulders. I could see Ada was angry, she got up and pulling me to my feet headed for the door.

'What are they going to do mammy?'

'Shut up shop, by the looks of things.'

'For the duration?'

She smiled grimly, 'maybe, but we can't afford to do that, come on.'

We clattered down the stairs, the murmur of voices receding, and as we headed for home on the tram, Ada was quiet. It was clear she had something on her mind.

'Did you cancel the ice?' Ada asked Eugene at breakfast next morning.

'Aye we don't need it,' Eugene said.

'Go round and re-order, I have an idea,' Ada told him.

As soon as the ice arrived next day she set to work experimenting. For days she tried mixture after mixture, boiling, churning, freezing, and then scooping the mixture up with a spoon to test its consistency.

At last she came up with a formula, the exact ingredients she would not divulge, 'The less people who know, the better, that way nobody can steal it.'

Dipping spoon after spoon in the mixture she passed it round, watching our faces.

'It's good!' we said in surprise.

'Right! That's the one we go with, and you must remember never to call it ice-cream,' she warned.

'What are you going to call it then,' Lena asked.

'This!' With a flourish she produced a large white card on which she had printed-

TRY OUR NEW BLANCMANGE
IN THREE FLAVOURS
LIME-COLA-CREAM SODA

'Blankmangy,' said Aggie.

'No, no, no, blancmange, it has a much softer sound,' said an anxious Ada. We rolled it around on our tongues, saying it over and over till Ada was satisfied.

'Do you think it will sell?' Lena asked.

'It had better, or we are in deep trouble,' Ada was grim.

She gathered up the spoons, dropping them in the sink.

'Remember it is against the law to sell ice-cream. This is not ice cream, so we cannot sell it as such, and we need to tell people that.

'People might want to know what it's made of,' said Betty.

'You can't tell them what you don't know', laughed Eugene.

'We need to be constantly on our guard that we do not say it is ice-cream,' Ada drummed in to us again and again.

The mixture proved a hit from the start, though children called it that 'mangy stuff', much to Ada's annoyance.

'Och, what does it matter what they call it as long as they buy it?' Eugene soothed her.

One Saturday afternoon Aggie was alone in the shop, the weather was nice and there was a steady stream of customers.

A little girl came in and asked for a penny cone with pink ice-cream. Aggie served her and out she went, only to return immediately with two men in trench coats and trilby hats.

'You have just sold this child ice-cream, which is a contravention of the Food Act,' they told a startled Aggie.

'We don't sell ice-cream, it is blancmange,' Aggie protested.

'This child asked for ice-cream, and you did not correct her, therefore you have committed an offence, and will be charged under the act.'

'She is only a wee lassie, the kiddies don't know any better,' Aggie pleaded.

'Nevertheless the responsibility lies with you, you should have corrected her.'

'Ah'm awful sorry Eadie, she was only a wee lassie, ah didnae think,' a tearful Aggie told Ada.

'It was bound to happen sometime. The cowards, fancy using a child to do their dirty work. We will just have to wait and see what happens next,' Ada fumed.

As proprietor it was Ada who was summoned to appear before the sheriff.

The charge was that she had deliberately misled the public by passing off a concoction as ice-cream.

The second count was that in contravention of the food directive prohibiting the making and sale of ice-cream she had continued to do so.

Ada gave a spirited defence.

She had concocted the mixture as an alternative to ice-cream; she had instructed her staff to inform the public that it was an ice-cream substitute. There was no intention to defraud, no intention to break the law. She was only trying to make a living in difficult times, and regretted the court had little more to do with its time than persecute a law-abiding citizen, when others were blatantly breaking the law every day on the black market.

Stung by the last comment the sheriff imposed a fine of £30.

'You could have got away with ten if you had kept your mouth shut,' said an unsympathetic Eugene.

Two months later, Aggie again fell foul of the men in trench coats, this time they took away a sample for analysis.

Ada appeared before the same sheriff.

She was told artificial sweeteners had been detected, and these were now to be banned.

She was fined £30 again for Aggie's failure to point out they did not sell ice-cream.

Ada, not to be outdone, requested permission to make a statement, and wearily the sheriff agreed.

'Though I have protested my innocence, it seems that I have been deemed to have broken the law. I have always upheld the law, and held it in high esteem. However, these are difficult times, and I have to make a living, as I have dependants. I would also like to point out that by keeping my shop open I am making a contribution to public morale, especially that of the children. I shall continue to offer this service to the public as long as I am able. I believe I have right on my side, and right is might!'

The sheriff gave her time to pay, and told her he did not want to see her again.

Back home she set about altering the mixture to compensate for the lack of artificial sweeteners. She succeeded, and though slightly changed in taste, it was as popular as ever.

Ada was well pleased.

'I would have gone to parliament itself, if I had been banned from making a living,' she told us.

We knew she meant it.

Getting cakes for the shop was proving increasingly difficult. Certain shops were able to offer a service to cafes, hotels and restaurants. We got our supplies such as they were from Bilsland's bakery in Argyle Street. The cakes were sold on a Saturday. It meant a six o'clock rise to get a good place in the queue, and it was a case of first come first served. Each person in the queue was allocated six small cakes or two large ones as long as stocks lasted. It was all hands to the pumps, Ada, Aggie, Lena and Betty with me tagging along out of curiosity. We knew we were in for a long wait, but there was a lot of friendly banter among the women in the queue. Across the street from the baker's on the site where decades later Marks and Spencer would stand, there was a huge canteen used by all three branches of the forces. The women would watch the men coming and going, giving marks out of ten for good looks. Further along the street the Argyle cinema was showing 'Gone with the Wind', starring Clark Gable. Even the sight of his face on the billboard caused women to swoon, and by common consent he was the most handsome of men, the servicemen coming a poor second. Betty, Lena and to my great surprise Ada had all fallen under Mr. Gable's spell. When I complained to Lena that I could not see what all the fuss was about, she laughed and from the great supremacy of her almost thirteen years told me I was too young to understand.

'You would be in trouble with mammy if you could see the attraction at your age,' giggled Betty.

Too young to get an allocation of cakes, my reward for the long wait was to gain the shop itself and see the girls putting the customers money in a little metal tube and send it whizzing along to the cashier in her little booth, who in turn would send the change back the same way. So fascinated was I with this contraption I struggled with myself as to whether I should still aspire to being a virgin or get a job as a cashier and play with the little tubes all day.

Three weeks before Christmas, the Japanese bombed Pearl Harbour. A stunned President Roosevelt knew America's neutrality was over.

He addressed the nation –

'Our enemies have performed a brilliant feat of deception, perfectly timed and executed with great skill.'

Japan had declared war on Britain too; it seemed too much to bear.

CHAPTER 12

We were becoming used to the restrictions the threat of air raids laid upon us. It became second nature to carry the gasmask slung over your shoulder everywhere you went, and to walk through the corridor of sandbags piled high on either side of the close, and to draw the blackout curtains over the window to deny 'Gerry' the advantage of light to identify targets.

There was one light that could not be hidden by blackout curtains, the moon, and if it was full Lena and I would climb Dove Hill to the railway line checking for the red light that warned of a possible air raid. Ada never tried to hide the news from us and we knew things were not going well for the Allies. The hated voice of Lord Haw-Haw would burst from the air waves and have Ada screaming at the radio, 'Lies! Lies! It's all lies.'

'Jairmany calling, Jairmany calling,' he would intone, 'the British Army is losing on all fronts, the British people are starving and ready to surrender.'

The constant drip of his poison was having an effect on the British public, Londoners were sleeping on underground platforms, and the life expectancy of young British pilots was put at six weeks. News that the Channel Islands had fallen to the Germans was almost the straw that broke the camel's back.

The Government responded by forming a Citizen's Army of men aged 45-65. The Local Defence Volunteers (LDV) had no uniforms, and no weapons. They practised with broom handles and ancient cutlasses borrowed from museums. Though they were dubbed 'Dad's Army' and looked a motley crew in their 'civvies' they were deadly serious in their intention to protect their native shores.

Women 20-45 were conscripted into a Land Army, freeing more men for the front. To help the war effort metal was collected; railings disappeared from public buildings, schools and hospitals. Housewives were asked to give up pots and pans, anything that could be used. Ada depleted her stock, leaving herself with only two.

'It is a small sacrifice, if it helps us win,' she told us.

Reports of air raids came almost daily, London, Coventry, and Southampton.

'It will be our turn next, you'll see,' warned Ada.

She insisted we went to bed with most of our clothes on, our coats on a chair nearby, together with flasks, flashlights and gasmasks. When a dog was heard howling in the night, she was convinced it was an omen, the dog knew that death was near.

'RUBBISH!' Eugene scoffed.

'It is not rubbish!' Ada countered.

'How can a dog know what is going to happen?'

'Animals know these things they are sensitive to vibrations in the atmosphere.'

'Where is this dog anyway?' Eugene asked.

'Across the road in Kent Street he has been howling for days, you must have heard him,' Ada said.

'No, never heard a thing. You honestly believe that this dog knows Adolf is pouring over a map of Glasgow and picking out Kent Street to drop a bomb on,' Eugene laughed.

'Mark my words, that animal howling is an omen', Ada insisted.

To cheer her up Eugene decided to distemper the walls and cover the chimney breast with brown Rexine which was the latest thing. He was just finishing it off when the siren sounded. Ada and Aggie were in the shop, Lena and I in bed. Since he was in charge of us he was under strict instructions from Ada, to drop everything and take us to the shelter. We scrambled out of bed, grabbing the coats, and all the other things Ada had left out ready, rushing through to the kitchen to the door we found Eugene calmly smoothing the sticky rexine over the chimney breast.

'Daddy, come on, there's an air raid,' Lena shouted.

'Get yersels doon there, ah want tae finish this,' he answered.

'But mammy says we have all to go to the shelter,' Lena was frantic.

'Away ye go, ah'll be fine, if ma name is on the bomb then it will no go by me, shelter or no shelter,' he pushed us out of the door, and closed it behind us.

We ran down the stairs, tears blinding us, convinced we would never see him again.

The shelter was already packed, and we knew most of the faces, neighbours and those who lived nearby. We had been in there many times as the sirens went off, and mostly the atmosphere was almost party like, especially the children who would play silly games of 'I Spy' or 'Knock Knock'. Somebody would start a sing-song, 'Roll out the Barrel', Run Rabbit, Run Rabbit, Run, Run, Run'. As the time wore on the children would nod off, the mood would turn melancholy, an elderly voice would say, 'Haw Jeanie gies "ma ain folk"', and Jeanie would oblige in a thin reedy voice, in a key that was too high to let her reach the high notes, but the crowd would join in at the crucial moment to spare her blushes, and Jeanie would receive a round of applause worthy of the finest soprano.

That night the atmosphere seemed different, people were tense, mostly silent except for the children. We could actually hear the drone of the planes, but had no idea if they were friendly or not. I clung to Lena, remembering Ada's warning. Suddenly there was the most horrendous blast; it seemed to go on and on. The children woke up screaming. The warden appeared mouthing something no one could hear above the din.

'Fur God's sake can somebody no shut thae weans up? The warden is trying to tell us something,' a woman shouted.

'The weans ur feart, whit dae ye expect?' somebody answered.

'Wheesh! The man is trying tae tell us something's been hit,' another voice said.

A cry went up. 'It's Barraland, thae've bombed Barraland.'

'Da-dee!' We screamed at each other, 'maybe they've got Da-dee and Auntie Tina.' We knew there was no chance of getting out of the shelter till the all clear sounded, even then we would have to wait till the warden counted us out as he had counted us in.

The blast of the bomb had sent Eugene flying across the room, the bucket of distemper he had been using to paint the walls, went spinning in the air, splattering the newly applied brown rexine, but Eugene was past caring about that. The blast had shattered the windows, though the tape had kept them from falling out, and it had lit up the room so he knew it was very close. Staggering down the stairs, he could see flames leaping from the roof of Barrowland, there was debris and shrapnel everywhere, and over to the left Kent Street was a mass of flames. He raced across the street to 206, anxious to find Da-dee and Tina; he could hear voices, on the top landing and rushed up the stairs towards them. Two wardens were trying to persuade Da-dee to come downstairs. Da-dee was rattling off in Italian telling them in no uncertain terms, that he was staying where he was. Tina was urging him too, but he was stuck firmly in the doorway and was not going to be moved.

'Come on da,' Eugene urged as he arrived breathless from the stairs, the men are right it is too dangerous to stay here.

Da-dee shook his head, 'lasciare, partire da.'

'Da. Pericolo! Pericolo! Incendio! Eugene urged.

Da-dee shook his head, he was growing more agitated, barefoot and clutching his trousers which had no belt, he had been wrenched from sleep, and was confused.

He pulled back into the house, the wardens pulled him forward, as he moved he let go of his trousers and they fell at his feet. Reaching down to pull them up he stumbled, and before he could right himself the wardens grabbed him, and carried him trouserless and protesting loudly down the three flights of stairs.

To our joy we saw Eugene and Tina squeezing through the narrow door of the shelter, followed by Da-dee still struggling and protesting, being shoe-horned in by the red faced wardens. A voice from the back shouted, 'There's an auld sowl wi' naething on but his combinations, God bliss him.'

Da-dee was urging Eugene to go back for his trousers, and he still had not grasped what had happened. Tina was shaking with a mixture of relief and fear, she put her face close to Da-dee, 'Aspet tare Da, you need to wait, it's an air raid, never mind aboot yer trousers.'

She turned to Eugene, 'we might no have a hoose tae go back tae, never mind his trousers.'

'You know,' said Eugene shaking his head, 'Eadie kept on aboot that dog howlin' in Kent Street. She said it meant it knew somethin'. Said it was an omen, an' she was right. From what ah could see there is no' much left o' Kent Street.'

As the grey dawn broke, the mournful but welcome sound of the all-clear sent us trooping fearfully out of the shelter, Eugene urging us up to the house to assess the damage.

Later that day we stood among a stunned silent crowd and watched as firemen sifted through the rubble that had once been Kent Street. The dog, a large Alsatian, still howled pitifully, as it would continue to do for the next two or three days. The sound a fitting dirge for the scores of people who had lost their lives.

When the dog no longer howled, I asked what had happened to it.

'Och they will have taken it to Cardonald, the cat and dog home,' Eugene said. I knew that too was a death sentence. The fact that the bomb was so close shook Ada to the core. She kept saying over and over, 'I could have lost my girls.'

'Ah suppose we were a' lucky,' said Eugene.

Lena, who had lost one of her school friends to the bomb, kept a daily vigil till the last body had been removed.

'The whole family is gone,' she sobbed as Ada put a comforting arm around her shoulders.

'Eh we all have to die sometime,' Eugene said.

Ada silenced him with a look.

'What's on your mind?' Eugene asked Ada a few days later.

'We need to be together. I can't rest knowing half the family are down here while I am in the shop,' Ada said.

'Och you know what they say. lightning never strikes in the same place twice, and that probably goes for bombs as well. Anyway ah think it was a mistake, that raid the other night, where is the sense in bombin' a place like Barraland, or Kent Street, for that matter,' Eugene said placidly.

'Mistake, or no mistake, those poor people are still dead. No we can't go on like this. I would be happier if we were all together,' Ada told him.

'You want to move? To where? The lasses are handy for the school here,' Eugene protested.

'Well it won't be long before Lena leaves, and one of us could take Madalena on the tram in the morning and pick her up at home time,' Ada persisted.

'But where do ye want tae go?' asked Eugene.

'Well the house above the shop is empty. Two rooms and kitchen, and an inside lavatory. It's heaven sent,' Ada said.

'Another one o' yer omens?' queried Eugene.

'Don't mock, you know I was right about that poor animal,' Ada snapped.

We all trooped up to inspect the house above the shop; the space was amazing compared to our cramped little house in the Gallowgate. Though it was dirty and full of odd bits of junk, including an old rusty bedstead, minus a mattress, we agreed it was good. Ada secured the tenancy in her name.

'She raised a warning finger, 'remember, now that we are going to be living over the shop, we need to be on our guard that our name is Coutts. It won't be as easy as it has been up to now, because you don't really mix with the people round here, but you will make friends, and they will come about the house, so you need to be on your guard.'

The plan was we would stay in the Gallowgate until Eugene had cleaned and painted the new house. Then he would hand in the keys to our tiny abode, at number 211, and leave the Calton for good. It soon became clear that 'Gerry' was not quite finished with Glasgow and the surrounding area.

Two weeks before we moved to St.Vincent Street, a massive series of bombs hit Clydebank and the Finnieston docks, which were just over the hill from the shop. Unsure where the nearest shelter was, Ada and Aggie had taken refuge upstairs. Betty had just started as a 'clippie' on the trams and had come home after her first late night shift. She joined Ada and Aggie upstairs and spreading her coat on the rusty bedstead fell fast asleep. When the blast came she was thrown off the bed, and landed under it, still fast asleep. She slept on undisturbed as the savage bombardment went on.

As soon as the all clear sounded, Ada and Aggie ventured downstairs. They found they had no need to unlock the shop door it was no longer there, and everywhere they stepped glass crunched beneath their feet. It was difficult to see by the feeble beam of a torch, but Ada guessed there was substantial damage. Upstairs Betty was still asleep, Ada shook her, 'wake up, there is work to be done.'

Betty gazed around her half awake, 'how did I get here?'

'Courtesy of Adolf,' said Ada. 'I always said it would take more than a bomb to wake you up, and I was right.'

As well as the door being blown away, the window was too, and all that remained was splintered wood and shattered glass. It was no better inside - shelves, bottles, display jars and mirrors, all smashed, even the heavy plate glass of the counter was split in two.

When news filtered through of the total devastation of Clydebank, the terrible loss of life, and the wrecking of Finnieston docks, Ada counted herself lucky.

'Glass and wood can be replaced, people can't,' she said.

I was terrified; it was as if Hitler knew where we were. It didn't look as if our side was winning, which meant the end of Civilization was getting nearer.

Through for a visit some weeks later, Mary and Jimmy wanted to see Clydebank.

Eugene agreed to take them on the tram, and after much pleading with Ada I was allowed to go too.

The sight was horrific; the ruins of Kent street multiplied a thousand times. The famous Singer's factory was no more; survivors had lost both home and work. Those who had survived were living in the hills which surrounded the town, yet showing great bravery coming down each day to help with the clearing up, or continue with their jobs if it was possible.

I cried at the sight of stray cats and dogs sniffing disconsolately among the ruins.

'Och dinnae waste yer time worryin' aboot beasts,' said Jimmy. 'It's mair like the puir folk ye need tae worry aboot.'

When we got home we found Ada trying to make a meal for all out of a little bacon, fried bread and an omelette of dried egg.

Eugene switched on the wireless, and the whining voice of 'Lord Haw- Haw' filled the room.

'Germany calling, Germany calling, our brave invincible Luftwaffe have wreaked havoc on British ports and supplies, stopping all food convoys, and the British people are starving.'

Ada grabbed the frying pan and shook it at the wireless.

'That is a damn lie,' she shouted. 'We can still have ham and eggs for our tea.'

'Aye even tho' you could sole yer shoes wi' the eggs,' Eugene quipped.

We all laughed, even Ada who in the heat of the moment had broken one of her golden rules, 'never swear in front of the children'.

Jimmy and Mary had wanted to see the shop, now it was too late as all its splendour had vanished.

'Och ye have seen enough bomb damage for one day, ye can see it when it is repaired,' Eugene told them.

That was to prove more difficult than he thought. Everywhere he went to find replacement glass he heard the same story. There had been so much damage that suppliers could not meet the demand, 'there is a war on you know,' he was told time and time again.

He set to work doing the best he could with wood. The window was completely boarded up, and also the door, making the shop very dark. Fortunately the shop had electricity, but it meant the lights had to be on all day.

Eugene taped the counter with the same tape he had used for the windows in the house. He wiped his hands on his trousers saying, 'that's the lot, what do you think?'

Ada looked around in dismay, saying nothing.

'It's the best ah can do,' Eugene said.

'I know, I can see you have done your best, but it's not the shop it was, it will affect business,' she sighed.

'Not at all, anyway, there is a war on,' Eugene grinned.

Since the huge raid on Clydebank had been followed by several others, people were not venturing out at night. For several nights there had been few customers, despite the huge notice Betty had nailed to the boarded up window, proclaiming, 'Business as Usual'.

Any customers there had been had been mostly sailors from the ships docked at Finnieston.

Even Hammy Little who could always be found in the shop in the evenings had not been seen since that fateful night of the blitz. Ada had decided to keep herself busy by starting on the cleaning of the house upstairs, with the help of Betty.

Eugene for his part was more optimistic and prepared the urn for a new batch of mixture, ready for the weekend as none had been made for some time. He lit the gas under the urn, and climbed up on the stool, leaving Aggie to deal with any customers who might appear.

Since the door had to be kept closed because of the blackout, it wasn't possible to see anyone approaching, so Eugene had rigged up a bell which rang whenever the door was opened. The street outside was quiet, till around half past ten, when Aggie heard shouting and swearing outside.

She hurried through to Eugene, her eyes dancing nervously behind the thick glasses.

'The gang is oot there, and by the sound o' things they have been drinkin'.'

'How many?' asked Eugene.

'Ah don't know, do you think ah should look an' see?'

'Aye, if they don't see you,' he grinned.

She drew him a look and made her way cautiously to the door, easing it open and forgetting about the bell, which clanged loudly. Snatching a quick look round she shut the door, setting the bell off again. Her nerves at breaking point she appeared once more at Eugene's elbow.

He looked down at her, shaking his head.

'Well if thae didnae see ye thae must have heard ye. Did ye see how many there was?'

'Aboot five ah think. The Lang brothers and one or two others,' Aggie said nervously.

'We might be in for trouble then,' Eugene said.

'Will ah shut the shop?' Aggie asked.

'What at half past ten? No, it will be a'right, jist keep yersel' busy, and the time will pass,' Eugene said.

Reluctantly Aggie had gone back behind the counter, making a half hearted effort to tidy the shelves.

Suddenly the door was flung open, the bell clanging noisily, as the gang rushed into the shop. Aggie let out a scream, at which one of the gang struck her a blow, knocking her glasses to the ground. As she bent to try to retrieve them, he came round the counter, and ground them under his foot.

Aggie had recognized most of the gang, but just before she had lost her glasses she caught sight of a huge thickset man in a long overcoat.

She had never seen him before, but he acted as if he was in charge, and she heard him shout to them to 'get the wee B******.'

They had rushed through to the back shop and dragged Eugene from the stool. Without her glasses she could see very little, but she heard Eugene cry out, heard the thump, thump, thump of blows.

Aggie began to scream. The younger Lang brother punched her in the stomach, and told her to shut up. He dragged her through to the back and threw her on the floor.

'Leave her, get the f****** fags an' money,' the big man growled. Aggie could hear them rifle the till.

'Come on Butcher.'

'Ah'm comin'. Youse beat it,' he shouted back.

Standing astride Eugene, he opened the valve of the urn, and the burning hot mixture flowed on to the floor, forming a pool around Eugene, burning into his flesh. Eugene tried to scramble to his feet, but the big man knocked him down.

'Ah'll call the police,' Aggie shouted.

The big man swung round, and, lifting the kettle from the range, he poured it down on her, as she drew up her legs, trying to get away.

'That will stoap ye callin' the polis,' he laughed and drew the door firmly shut behind him.

Eugene was trying to get to his feet, the sticky mixture making it hard to get a foothold.

'Are ye hurt bad?' he asked Aggie trying to steady her and guide her to the door; she stumbled through collapsing onto the nearest bench.

'Ah'll get Eadie,' Eugene said.

Neither the shop or the house had a phone, but since Ada and Betty had been spending time upstairs cleaning the house, they had devised a way of communicating with the shop, by the simple means of banging on the floor or roof with a sweeping brush.

Eugene was working his way carefully towards the brush which stood in a corner of the shop. He raised it a high as he could and banged a staccato of notes on the ceiling, pausing for a second or two, before repeating.

After what seemed an age, the answering knock came. Eugene resumed a frantic assault trying to convey the urgency of the situation.

He was answered by a series of thumps, which seemed to echo his own, and in a few minutes Betty appeared, demanding to know what was wrong.

Always cool in a crisis, she quickly assessed the situation, applying ice from the freezer to help the burns.

'Get Eadie,' Eugene said, beads of sweat standing out on his forehead as the pain became acute.

Betty banged on the ceiling, and then filled the kettle to make a restoring cup of tea.

There was no reply from upstairs, as Ada was already on her way down.

'Who did this? Was it the Lang brothers?' she demanded.

'Aye, but there was another man, a big dirty brute, I've never seen him before,' Aggie stammered through her tears.

'Ah heard the name Butcher,' said Eugene.

'We need to get the police, right away,' Ada said.

'I'll go,' Betty volunteered. 'It's dark and it's a long way to Cranston Street, they might still be hangin' aboot,' Eugene warned.

'We need to do something, they can't get away with this,' Ada fumed.

'I'll go, mammy, it's not that far, just over the hill, I'll go up and get my coat and torch,' Betty said.

While Betty was gone Ada quizzed Aggie and Eugene for the whole story. Aggie could remember everything, and she repeated the tale over and over.

'You would definitely know this brute again?' Ada asked.

'Aye, nae bother,' said Eugene, 'no jist his face, he stank tae high heaven.'

Betty was gone a long time. At last she returned flanked by two burly sergeants.

Once more Aggie told her tale, but both she and Eugene were none too well; bruises had started to come up on Eugene's face, his burns needed attention. Aggie, by instinctively recoiling as the water was poured on her, had escaped with minor burns, which nevertheless hurt, and she was very badly shaken and the loss of her glasses was a severe blow.

For several days after the attack there was no sign of the gang. Hammy had appeared a day or two after, and on hearing the tale, apologized for not being there to get the police.

'We know you would have helped if you could,' Ada told him. He listened with interest to the description of the unknown gangster.

'Ah've seen him talking to the Lang brothers. He comes and goes, maybe I can find out something.'

'You be careful, I don't want anything to happen to you, your mother would never forgive me,' Ada warned. Hammy's detective work paid off, and within days he was able to tell Ada more than she had hoped.

'He's from the Gorbals, his name is Tarn Butchard, but they call him butcher because - he paused eager to see the effect of the explanation - 'because he cuts people up'.

'How did you find out?' Betty was impressed.

Hammy tapped his nose with a long bony finger, 'Ah just did, and I found out something else.'

'What,' Betty asked giving him his moment.

'His gang was in a big fight with another gang and he was run out of the Gorbals. He can't go back, or they will get him.'

'How did you find that out?' Betty asked again, really intrigued.

Hammy shrugged, 'I know somebody that knows somebody.'

Ada was vigilant, and she put us all on alert to spot any member of the gang, once again enlisting the eyes and ears of Hammy.

It was Ada herself who spotted them first; she lost no time in reporting the sighting to the police. Within days they were arrested, and then released on bail.

Eugene still not fully recovered still had to make the weekly visit to Cranston Street to register as an alien. Coming out of the police station he had made his way down towards home when he was pulled into a close and beaten up. He knew immediately who his attacker was by the smell. The beating was more severe then the last, and as he lay groaning on the ground a voice growled in his ear.

'Listen ye wee Italian bastard, ah told ye no tae go tae the polis. If ah'm gonnae hiv tae go doon fur ye ah want ma money's worth.'

Eugene staggered home, his eye burst, his jaw dislocated. Ada was furious. She watched as Eugene was patched up by the doctor, then settling him as comfortably as she could, she left the house without a word.

At the police station she left them in no doubt how she felt.

'I have always believed in British justice, and that every law abiding person has the protection of the police regardless of nationality, even if we are at war. I demand that the person who is responsible for this attack on my husband be arrested and held in custody. If he had not been bailed for the first attack this would never have happened.

'Butcher' was duly lifted and held in custody till the trial, where he had to answer to both offences. He got ninety days, and the others got thirty.

Ada was not impressed, 'that is hardly a deterrent. They will be out in no time and back to their old tricks, just you wait and see. I am ashamed of British Justice. It was once the finest in the world,' she complained loudly in the corridor of the court, much to Lena's acute embarrassment.

Aggie's recovery was much slower than Eugene's. She sat by the fire, half blind and very nervous, weeping and shaking. Though Ada tried her very best to have the glasses replaced it was proving very difficult. She was reminded as with every other commodity that there was a war on and it would be some weeks before they were likely to be delivered.

Meanwhile Lizzie has received word through a circuitous route from the Rossis that they were well in Italy, but concerned for their property in Glasgow, knowing the anti Italian feeling. They wanted the cafe closed and boarded up for the duration of the war.

Out of work, Lizzie was happy to take Aggie's place until she was better. Lizzie's nature was similar to Eugene's; she rarely got upset, always opting for the line of least resistance, always the peace maker. Barely over five feet tall she was slim and pretty with a mop of dark hair that refused to be tamed. It was not long before she had a string of admirers among the service men who visited our cafe, a situation which caused her much amusement and embarrassment. Betty now seventeen also had her admirers, some of them unwanted, like Eddie Gillan. Eddie lived with his sisters and brothers on the next landing to our newly acquired house above the shop.

The family was close, having lost their parents when they were young, and they had been brought up by their older sister. The three brothers had joined the HLI the famous kilted regiment. They were all handsome boys though Eddie was much shorter than his brothers. He cut a slightly comical figure in a kilt that was too large and too long, yet what he lacked in stature he made up for in valour, and was to distinguish himself in active service.

Though some years older than Betty he set his cap at her making no secret of the fact that he was smitten.

Betty found the whole thing amusing, towering above him she would rib his mercilessly, but it made no difference.

Betty was interested in having a good time, she was not ready to settle down, and she was much more interested in the various service men who passed like ships in the night and demanded no commitment.

While Ada felt Eddie was too old for Betty, she did not approve of Betty's attitude towards him. She felt he merited some respect. Eugene shrugged and said Eddie was a daft wee bugger and should have more sense, than to go after a girl so much younger than himself.

Eddie was posted overseas, putting the problem on hold for the time being.

Ada meanwhile was still worrying about trade, the shop was so gloomy and dull in appearance.

Betty who had a flair for decoration, unearthed some enamel biscuit tins, and crepe paper, from which she cut out frilled edging for the sturdy wooden shelves Eugene had made. To Ada's great joy, three of the mahogany mirrors were found in the cellar wrapped in sacking.

Ada insisted that Eugene hung them on the wall opposite the counter.

'They could get damaged in another raid,' Betty warned.

'They are going up. I'm not going to let 'Gerry' get the better of us,' said Ada defiantly.

CHAPTER 13

Sister Constanza ran a little tuck shop beneath the stairs of the dinner hall. The shop was tiny with space for only two customers at a time, and Sister Constanza was very old, very deaf and very slow. Each day a queue of noisy girls hopping from foot to foot would press impatiently forward anxious to be served before the bell rang for afternoon classes.

I loved the little tuck shop; it made me feel like the girls in the 'School Friend' that I read avidly every week.

Now we had sweet rationing, it was new and nobody knew just what it really meant. That first day we stood clutching our coupons and gasping in disbelief as each girl emerged with her meagre ration.

Molly McKay thrust herself in front of me and held out her hand.

'Hand them ower.'

'What?'

'Yer money an' yer coupons.'

'No.'

'You better or ah'll belt ye.'

'You have your own.'

'An' ah want yours as well.'

'No.'

'Right!' She grabbed a handful of hair and pulled me over kicking viciously at my shins.

I struggled to get free, and she pulled me out of the queue, twisting my arm behind my back.

I struggled to get free, but she held on to my hair, the pain was excruciating. A monitor came by, Molly let go and smiled.

'Something wrong?' asked the monitor.

'No, we're just playing,' Molly told her.

As the monitor passed on I took to my heels, Molly in hot pursuit. Panting, half bent with pain I stumbled into a narrow opening between the Junior school and the main block.

A quick glance showed Molly had run on and I stood with my back against the wall trying to get my breath back.

Suddenly I realised I was not alone; a quick movement had caught my eye. Turning I saw a tall thin girl staring at me in consternation. I smiled, but she just went on staring.

'Hello,' I said.

For answer she turned her back to me.

I studied her, and as I did not recognize her I knew she must be in another form, possibly a year ahead of me.

I was shocked at how thin she was, her shoulder blades stood out under the thin short sleeved blouse under which her arms were blue with cold.

The blouse was loosely tucked into a blue serge skirt which may have fitted at one time but now hung low on her hips. Remembering Molly I took a quick glance out to the playground. She was nowhere to be seen, but as I turned inward once more I caught the girl looking at me.

'Hello,' I said again, 'what's your name?'

She dropped her gaze. I waited.

'Want to know mine?' I told her.

She weighed me up for a moment, then shyly, 'Marian Cuthbertson.'

Suddenly she was seized by a violent fit of coughing; it shook her whole frame, bending her double.

I took a step nearer, but she turned from me, frantically she fished in the waistband of her skirt producing a large white handkerchief, holding it over her mouth as the coughing went on and on.

I could only stand helplessly by, watching as the sharp shoulder blades strained under the thin blouse.

'What can I do?'

She warded me off with a backward motion of her hand.

As I backed away, the bell rang. What could I do? I didn't want to leave her.

She spun round, the handkerchief covering most of her face, and her eyes pleaded with me to go.

Next day at first break I went in search of her. She was standing leaning against the wall, head bent, her long lank hair hiding her face.

She wore the same blouse and skirt as the day before, her bare feet thrust into worn black plimsolls.

'Hello, are you all right?' I asked.

'I'm OK.'

'You don't look OK.'

'I'm - -.' The coughing seized her again, and she snatched at the handkerchief.

I moved closer, she turned her back, but not before I had seen the blood.

'I'll get a monitor.'

She couldn't speak, but gripped my arm, shaking her head.

'There is blood on the hankie!'

'I'm...I'm used to it, it's no...nothing.'

'Does your mammy know?'

'No! Nobody knows.'

'Except me!'

She tightened her grip.

'You need to promise you won't tell.'

'But you're not well, your mammy needs to know, or Mother Philippa.'

'No! You canny tell them, promise!'

'But, if you are really not well, I mean really not well ....'

'Ma mammy is ill, she misses ma daddy, cos he is away in the navy, she thinks he'll get killed, she cries a' the time, and I canny tell her.'

I nodded. 'I have things I canny tell my mammy.'

'How do you mean?' she asked looking a little better.

'Och just about being bullied, that Molly McKay and her gang, because I'm Italian. My mammy hates bullies; she stood up to the Bath gang when they attacked our shop.'

'Your mammy has a shop?'

'Yes an ice cream shop, but I don't want Molly to know, so you need to promise you won't tell her.'

'If you promise not to tell on me.'

So we each hid from our own particular demons, becoming close friends. Marian always wore the same clothes, whatever the weather. She was the only girl in the school who did not wear the regulation uniform.

I wondered that the nuns had not done something about that.

I kept away from the tuck shop, and brought what I could from home, always sharing with Marion.

Though we had become friends there was something very private about Marion, a kind of barrier that kept me at arms length.

We would hunch down, leaning against the wall exchanging scraps, or dressing paper dolls, if Marion felt well enough, often she would just lean on the wall for support, and endure the coughing. At these times I could not help beg her to let me get some help.

Molly had her spies and it was not long before she discovered our hiding place.

At first she completely ignored Marion, who as soon as Molly came close would retreat as far up the alley as possible.

I knew Marion was worried that Molly would find out about the coughing and tell someone.

I caught a cold and Ada insisted I stay off for a day or two, and when I got back to school Marion seemed more distant than ever.

That first day back Molly sought me out and I braced myself for the usual abuse. Instead she invited both Marion an I to join in a game of skipping ropes.

Marion shook her head and retreated as usual, I cautiously agreed to join the game, wanting Marion to be left in peace.

Two girls cawed the rope while the rest of us stood in line ready to jump in and out.

Molly pushed her way up the line and stood right behind me.

Just as I was about to jump in, she gripped my arm.

'That lassie you play wi' says your mammy has an ice cream shop.'

I pretended not to hear, waited for the right moment and jumped into the cawing rope.

Molly raised her voice. 'Has your mammy got a shop?' 'Yes,' I shouted and went on jumping.

'Does it sell sweeties an' cigarettes?'

'Yes.' I came out the rope and ran to the end of the line for my next turn.

Molly stood behind me. 'What kind of sweeties?'

'Same as the tuck shop,' I told her not wanting to talk about the shop at all.

'Right,' she said.

Next day she caught hold of me, the rest of the gang surrounding me.

'Ma mammy says it's no right that your mammy an' daddy are making money out o' British folk, ma mammy says your daddy should be locked up cos youse are Tallies.'

I ignored this and tried to get away, but the gang closed in.

'We want you tae bring us sweeties, an' cigarettes fur ma mammy, and you better bring them in the morra or we'll bash you.'

'I can't. I'm not allowed to take things from the shop. Anyway you need coupons for sweeties now.

'Ma mammy says you willnae need coupons cos your mammy gets everything on the black market.'

I was horrified. I knew all about the black market, Ada was forever railing against it; she hated it and would never take anything she suspected of coming from it.

'That's not fair, and it's not true, my mammy would never do that.'

I could just imagine Ada's fury at the very suggestion.

'Well we don't believe you, sure we don't?' she turned to her gang.

'No!' they chorused obediently.

The bell rang for assembly. Molly brought her face close to mine.

'You better bring thae things, or we will really bash you. Mind you bring them or else.' She pushed me against the wall, and then walked off her gang at her heels.

At break time I hurried to find Marian, hurt and disappointed that she had broken her promise.

'Why did you tell on me? I never told on you,' I demanded.

'I'm sorry, they scared me, but I was tryin' to stick up for you.'

'They said I shouldn't play with you, cos you are a Tally, and Tallies could kill ma daddy, an' nobody should play with you.'

'What do you mean you were sticking up for me?'

'Well, ah said that even tho' you are rich cos your mammy has a shop, you were kind to me. You didn't care that ah'm poor, you are still my friend.'

'My mammy only manages the shop, it isn't ours. We're not rich ma mammy has to give most of the money to..to the people who really own it, because....'

I trailed off reluctant to let her know the whole story.

I could see she was confused. 'We're not rich, we're not,' I repeated.

'Well I think you are, anyway I'm sorry, honest I am.'

'You shouldn't have broken your promise.'

She was really upset. 'Are you going to tell on me?'

'No, we are still friends, but now Molly wants me to get her things for nothing, and I can't. My mammy won't ever let me take anything. She won't let any of us take anything without paying for it.

'Maybe you should tell your big sister.'

'No, she would only tell mammy, then she would come and complain to Mother Philippa, and that would be worse.'

That night I lay next to a snoring Aggie, trying to think of a way out of the mess. Lena was in Senior school, and I rarely saw her. She was very popular, and no one ever tried to bully her, she would have stood up to them in any case. Though she was sweet natured she could be cocky and rebellious too, always in the forefront of any mischief that was going on.

My only hope was to think of a way to outwit Molly and her gang. Next day

Molly just gave me a threatening look when I arrived. She kept this up all day, passing notes to her gang in class, each in turn staring me down. They dogged my heels at dinner time and afternoon break, not saying a word. I kept away from Marian, not wanting her to get into any trouble.

I knew Molly would be waiting for me at home time. I had thought of a plan, but even that was not without danger. The Junior school came and went through a little green door that led straight into the Junior playground. The Senior girls used the main entrance, through which a Junior went at her peril. However if (God forbid) a Junior was late even by a few minutes she would find the green door locked and be forced to use the main entrance, where like a preying mantis Reverend Mother lay in wait. She stood half hidden by the heavy chenille curtain that hung at the entrance to the corridor which led to her office.

From this vantage point she would observe each girl as she came through the door, checking that the full uniform was worn, that it was clean, pressed and free from stains, that the blazer was buttoned, and the much hated hat was at the regulation angle, with the school badge clearly visible.

Over at the green door Sister Mary Joseph performed the same scrutiny of the Juniors but with much less rigour.

As she clambered breathlessly up the marble steps to the entrance hall, the unfortunate Junior would be unaware that Reverend Mother was still on guard after nine o'clock, waiting for late comers.

The tall imposing figure would glide towards her blocking her way, the cold piercing eyes fixed on the quivering face.

'You are late! Why are you late child?'

Mother Philippa never bothered to listen to the excuse uttered in a strangled whisper, the chin firmly on the chest.

Circling round the girl flicking real or imagined flecks of dust or worse still dandruff, she would finally turn the child to face her.

'Hold out your hand!'

Slowly the hand would be extended, and the tears would start to the eyes as the heavy knotted rope the nun wore round her waist descended on the tender skin

'You are dismissed. You may go to your class and inform the sister or mistress in charge that you have received your punishment for being late. Now run along.'

The child would take off at a run, only to hear.

'Walk! Young ladies do not run!'

More than once both Lena and I had experienced the stinging blow from that rope. We were often late due to helping out in the shop and getting to bed late. Once I had earned an extra slap for the heinous sin of having my hat squashed in my pocket, something which particularly incensed our Mother Superior.

Telling the form mistress that you had already been punished invariably cut no ice, especially if your class was with one of the few lay teachers in the school.

She would take the strap from her desk and deliver her own stinging slap.

Most days Mother Philippa would be there at four o'clock too, nodding with grim satisfaction as the Senior school filed past in orderly fashion on their way home.

This was the hazard I faced in my plan to outwit Holly.

There was one other hazard. Both doors opened on to Charlotte Street, and were in truth only a few yards apart, so Molly could spot me. It also meant heading down Charlotte Street towards Glasgow Green, where I had been warned by Ada never to go near alone.

The route home would take me round the Green, up Bain Street, across London Road, down Kent street into the Gallowgate.

The risks seemed worth it, the alternative being 'a real bashing' from the gang. Going home with bruises to my face would alert Ada that something was going on, and the whole thing would come out. The afternoon seemed to drag on forever, my preoccupation with my plan earning me a 'ticking off' from the teacher. I was angry that I had drawn attention to myself. I needed to slip away.

At last the bell rings for the end of the period. There is a rustle of books being stuffed into schoolbags, and all eyes are on the form mistress for the signal to stand. I watch the second hand of the huge clock above her head jerkily make its way towards the hour. I willed the second bell to ring.

'You may stand by your desks.'

Frantic scraping back of chairs, hubbub of chatter.

A rap on the desk with a ruler, 'SILENCE!'

A hush descends, stifled giggles, jostling for space.

The second bell rings, 'You may go.'

Somehow I gain the door ahead of the rest. I speed down the corridor out of the Junior building, sprint across to the Senior school, up the stone-flagged steps from the playground into the entrance hall, straight past the dreaded chenille curtain, down the marble steps, and out the door into the street.

A quick glance towards the green door reveals Molly's red curls snapping this way and that looking for me.

I run.

A cry goes up, they have spotted me.

I run, pain burning in my chest. They are on top of me. Molly has me by the hair, and she pulls me over aiming kick after kick at my shins.

I hear but do not see the pounding feet as they draw nearer, now I am on the ground doubled up from a kick to my stomach.

Suddenly Molly lets out a yell as she is yanked away from me. I look up, she is squirming like a fish on a hook trying to free herself from the grip of a swarthy boy about twelve years old.

He releases her, she runs off screaming, safely out of reach she turns and yells defiantly.

'Jist you wait till ma mammy gets you.'

The boy takes a run at her; she scampers off the rest of the gang at her heels.

'Ar...ar...are y...you al...al...alr...r...right?'

'I think so, but she has ripped my blazer pocket, ma mammy will be furious.

'S...sew it be...be...before sh...she s...s...sees it.'

'I can't sew, I can't knit either.'

'W...well d...don't look at me, th...that's L...L...Lassie s...s...stuff'.

My shins are smarting from the kicks; I pull up my socks to hide the red marks that I know will be purple by the morning.

'W...why d...do they p...p...pick on you?'

'That girl Molly McKay, she wanted me to bring her sweeties and cigarettes from our shop, she and her gang are always picking on me because I'm Italian.'

'S...s...so am I, c...canny hide w...with m...my name, D...d...Dario B...B...Benedetti.'

'Do you get picked on?'

'Oh aye, b...but I g...gave as g...g...good as I g...got, they d...don't b...b...bother me n..now.'

I thought how hard it must be for him, not only because of his name but the terrible stammer too.

'Y...you sh...should try t...to s...s...stand up t...to them.'

'Ma mammy is good at standing up to bullies.'

'Is y...your d...d...daddy interned?'

'No, is yours?'

'Aye in th...the Isle of M...man.'

'My daddy can go no further than ten miles from home, and he has to sign on at the police station every week for the du...'

'D...d...duration!'

We burst out laughing.

'You go to St. Alphonsus?'

He nods, then chuckles, 'Y...you g...g...go to the s...s..snobs s...s...school.'

'We are not snobs.'

He laughs.

'Where do you live?'

'R...R...R...Ross S...S...Street.'

We walk up Charlotte Street, cross to Ross Street, he stops at a close. 'I s...s...stay h...here,' he takes out a key.

'You have your own key? I am amazed; no one gets a key till they reach twenty one.

'M...ma m...mammy is a...always out, sh...she ha...has to w...work.'

I nod.

'S...s...see y...you t...t...tomorrow,' he goes in.

I felt so sorry for him; it could not be easy with that stammer, as well as being Italian. Yet he seemed unfazed by it all, it reminded me of Eugene's laid back attitude.

Dario appointed himself my guardian angel, waiting for me at the green door every day.

Molly left me alone when he was around.

As we became good friends, his stammer bothered him less.

Having Dario waiting at the gate had a sobering effect on Molly, she confined herself to whispering and giggling with her gang as I walked by, this was bearable and I did nothing to provoke her.

Just as things got easier on that front, I soon found myself in trouble again.

We had a change of teacher for English, our pleasant young lay teacher departed and in her place came the stern faced sister Ignatius.

As she walked up and down between the desks she suddenly stopped at mine.

'Hold the pencil in your right hand, you stupid child.'

'Please sister, I am left-handed.'

'Nonsense, you will write with your proper hand in my class.'

'Please sister I can't.'

'I cannot, you say I cannot,' she corrected. I say you will, you will certainly not write with your left hand in my class.'

She took the pencil from my left hand and forced it into my right.

'Write!'

I tried with great difficulty to grip the pencil, and guide it across the page; the result was an unseemly scrawl.

From then on it became a battle of wills, she would haul me out to the front, tell me to hold out my left hand and deliver two hefty strokes of the belt, then send me back to write with my right hand

Fearful of upsetting Ada, I confided in Da-dee, he understood, he was left handed too. Tina laughed and said, 'Jist tell the sister you are corry- fisted, like your Nonno and your Auntie Lizzie.'

Da-dee promised to write a note to sister Ignatius, but it made no difference.

5isler Ignatius seemed to take it as a personal affront that I insisted on writing with my left hand.

Determined to make me conform she called me to the front of the class, ordered me to remove the sash from my gym slip, and as the whole class watched in silence, proceeded to wind the sash twice around my left wrist pull my left arm behind my back, then secure the sash around my waist.

'You will return to your desk, take the pencil in your right hand and continue with the lesson.'

The ritual sash tying took place before every English lesson, and soon every other teacher adopted the same method. Since I could not deliver neat work with my left hand I earned a few strokes of the belt along the way.

Da-dee was puzzled by the nun's behaviour, but declined to interfere any further. He was however determined that I should still be able to write with my left hand, insisting I go to him every Saturday morning and practise with my left hand.

The whole thing was a torture to me, and to make matters worse my eyesight seemed to be failing. I had difficulty seeing the blackboard.

The teachers and nuns lost patience with me and brought me down to the front row of desks, a position usually reserved for slow learners.

This was seized upon by Molly and her followers who would snigger and call me dummy. I began to have nightmares, giant figures in flowing nun habits would screech at me, causing me to sit up in fright sobbing and shaking.

A visit to an optician confirmed my eye problem, and I was issued with hideous wire spectacles, which Molly and her gang found screamingly funny. My misery was complete when Dario announced he and his mother were moving to Edinburgh to stay with relatives.

Bereft of my knight in shining armour, I was once more fair game for Molly.

I found I had difficulty speaking, the words would form in my mouth but I could not utter them. When challenged by the teachers I would struggle to get the sound out, but it would not come, and without exception they viewed my behaviour as insolence, and I would be forced to stretch out my hand for two or three strokes of the belt. At home, though not dumb, I stammered almost as bad as Dario had done. The more Ada and Eugene asked me what was wrong the worse the stammer seemed to be. Ada blamed herself, saying perhaps she was not spending enough time with me, since she worked all hours in the shop.

'Eh what can we do? She has always been too timid, she just needs to toughen up a bit,' Eugene told her.

'I think she is upset about having to wear glasses,' Lena suggested. 'That is silly, if she needs glasses she has to wear them, don't fuss, she will get used to it,' Eugene insisted.

Betty took me aside. 'What's the matter? You can tell me.' I shook my head, I could not tell anyone.

I sought refuge more and more with Marion, who accepted my stuttering without comment, but really she was too ill to have the strength to react to anything.

We would just hide ourselves away, swapping our scraps, and reading the 'School Friend'.

So the year wore on, it seemed there was little to cheer not only me but everyone else, the war was not going well, Ada voiced her fears that even The Almighty seemed to be turning a deaf ear.

'Och don't be daft woman, what will be will be, it will a' turn out for the best,' Eugene told her.

His refusal to get upset infuriated her, they would argue non stop.

Ada was furious on hearing reports that Churchill was to face a vote of censure over his conduct of the war effort.

'What are they thinking of?' He is the best man we have. 'Cometh the man cometh the hour'. Churchill is our only hope.'

'Och it will a' be sorted, they are no gonny get rid o' him,' Eugene said.

The vote was easily defeated; Churchill triumphed by 475 to 25, his grinning face and famous V sign salute on every front page.

'Thank God common sense prevailed,' Ada said.

She was further heartened when it was announced 'Bomber' Harris was warning the Nazis that he intended to scourge them.

'Maybe the tide is beginning to turn,' Ada said with satisfaction.

'Och ah told ye things would take their course,' Eugene reminded her.

The autumn brought a further cut in milk ration to two and a half pints a week.

This was a further blow to the viability of the shop and plunged Ada back in the doldrums. However by November, church bells were ringing in London to celebrate The 'Desert Rats' stunning victory at El Alamein.

Ada had 'felt it in her bones' that 'Monty', Field Marshall Montgomery, would be the man to topple Rommel.

'See, I was right! I knew he was the man for the job,' she told us all at tea time.

'Aye, cometh another man, cometh another hour,' grinned Eugene.

'You can mock but we need to win this war, or the world is finished.' 'Aye, ah know,' said a chastened Eugene.

As usual Churchill had the last word, and we gathered round the wireless to hear that familiar growl:

It is not the end.

It is not even the beginning of the end.

But it is perhaps the end of the beginning. 'Eugene scraped at his pipe reflectively.

'God help us, the war had been going for nearly four years and he says it may be the end of the beginning.'

Ada smiled, 'It will be all right, there is nothing can defeat the British Tommy, when his dander's up, and they have the finest leaders, so we will be all right.'

Eugene struck a match and puffed at the pipe.

'Well lasses, ye have heard yer mammy, and if she says it will be fine it will be fine. Betty put the kettle on and we might jist squeeze enough milk to have another cup o' tea.'

As the winter took its grip, an outbreak of diphtheria claimed victims among the children. In the Gallowgate a little six year old was taken. The mothers all around were fearful of who would be next, but the fear did not hold them back in offering solace to the stricken woman who's child was taken.

Ada helped as best she could, telling Eugene she knew what it was like to lose a child, and despite the lingering threat of the disease she could not turn her back on grief.

I stood with Ada watching the solemn procession follow the little coffin to St. Alphonsus chapel, people wept openly, Ada too dabbing at her eyes. I had no idea that within two or three weeks I would be shedding tears for Marian too. Too weak to withstand the illness she died at home, her mother at her side.

The whole school was talking about her. She, who had always been so private, who had been ignored and left alone, was now the main topic of conversation.

I found it hard to truly believe she had gone, and, running to the alley, I stood staring at the space she had occupied for such a long time. There was a requiem mass celebrated for the repose of her soul. All the junior school filing into St. Alphonsus in their neat school uniforms, remembering one of their number who had never possessed a uniform, or a winder coat to keep out the cold.

No one had ever bothered to find out how ill she was, now they knelt and offered prayers, sang the funereal hymns, none of which would ever help her. Coming before God in the chapel demanded a pure and loving heart towards God and your fellows. I knelt and prayed, joined in the singing with nothing but anger and bewilderment in my heart. I looked up with dread to meet the demon eyes above the sacristy door, and felt a chill as if those eyes could see the hurt and anger within me.

Famie consoled me that Marian was now in heaven, free from all pain and suffering.

'But she was only a little girl like me, she never missed mass, even though she was ill,' I protested.

'That is why God took her then, he wanted to take away all her suffering, you will see her again some day, when you go to heaven,' Famie assured me.

I wanted to tell her that Marian did not want to die, she wanted to be better and run about like the other girls, she wanted to see her daddy come home from the war, and her mammy get better, but I knew it was no use telling Famie all that, she would just say Marian was better off in heaven.

Each night as I lay with my back turned to Aggie, I held a silent dialogue with God. I railed against HIM, angry yet fearful HE would strike me down for my insolence. I felt I needed to know the answers to so many things. Why did HE allow Marian to suffer, why had the little six year old girl have to die, why did he allow the war, and all the people get killed and injured, and why oh why, was there such a thing as death?

When I had grown old enough to realise there was such a thing as death, I was astounded. I went to Ada who knew all things and asked her how long mankind had been on earth.

'Oh for thousands of years,' she said.

'For thousands of years, yet they still have not found a way of stopping death?'

'Well, that is a matter for the Almighty, he has his reasons for all things,' was her enigmatic reply.

Despairing that even Ada could not give me the answers I sought I badgered God to tell me.

Each night my pleas fell on deaf ears, frustrated my silence gave way to mumbling, till Aggie demanded to know who I was talking to, I burst out that I was talking to God, because I was very angry with HIM.

'Ye canny be angry wi' God! Who do you think you are tae be angry wi' HIM?'

'Well I don't understand why he lets all these bad things happen.'

'He can do whit He likes, He is God, He made you, He gave you life, and He can take it away whenever He likes.'

'But who made God?' Lena piped up in the darkness.

'I don't know, He has jist always been there,' Aggie told her.

'But how did He get there?' Lena persisted.

'Nobody knows, so will you all just shut up and go to sleep,' Betty said wearily.

'But I want to know, same as Lena,' I chimed in.

'Then ask yer mammy, she'll know,' Aggie said.

'No she doesn't, I already asked her,' I protested.

'Then nobody knows,' Betty sighed loudly, 'anyway what does it matter?. Maybe God is not there at all.'

There was a stunned silence, then Lena said in a worried tone, 'You will never go to heaven.'

'GOOD NIGHT! Betty snapped.

Marian's death continued to haunt me. At school I could not bring myself to go anywhere near the little alley we had spent so much time in. In an effort to avoid Molly I kept moving round the playground trying to keep out of her line of vision. She never let up though, and really enjoyed pushing me against the wall asking me questions and falling about when I tried to get the words out and they would not come.

At home Betty tried to take my mind off things, she made a silly little jacket and bonnet for Tiddles, dressing the squirming cat and walking it across the room on its hind legs. She would twirl it around in an upturned umbrella till it staggered off unable to steady its legs, then she would scoop him up and carry him to the piano striking the keys with its paws to play 'chopsticks'.

'Oh stop it, he doesn't like it,' I would protest, but she rarely took notice of me.

'He knows I don't want to hurt him, sure you do pussums?' she would laugh, giving the poor squirming creature a hug.

Lena took a softer approach, she whispered to me that she would tell me her very best secret .We huddled on the bed heads together. Her secret which was no secret at all was that she wanted to be a dancer. We both knew it was unlikely to happen, but she was certainly pretty enough to go on stage.

Slim and graceful with long shining hair that hung to her waist. Her hair was her special pride, every Friday night she would wash it with Amami shampoo. 'Friday night is Amami night', the billboards screamed. It was the latest thing and Lena liked to keep up to date.

After the shampoo, she would rough dry it with a towel, then sitting crossed legged on the bed she would run her fingers through it to get rid of the tangles till it was almost dry, and it was time for the hundred strokes of the brush that all the magazines recommended.

Perched on the pillow beside her, I would silently count the strokes of the brush with her, clapping my hands when she reached one hundred.

Shaking her hair loose she would slip from the bed and begin to dance to music only she could hear. As she moved the long shining hair swung like a silken curtain.

Ada did not really bother about the length of our hair, she allowed mine to grow until there was an outbreak of lice in school.

We juniors were all examined regularly by the nit nurse, standing in line, heart thumping in case you received a yellow card trumpeting to all that you had nits.

Ada cut my hair not too short but shorter than I would have wished.

No sweet smelling Amami for me, the nostril stinging Derbac soap was lathered through my hair and Ada or Betty's strong fingers scrubbed at my scalp.

Once washed a sheet of newspaper would be spread on the table and the 'bone comb' would be set to work, bent over as I was my eyes were riveted on the paper looking for any black speck that moved.

Aided and abetted by Tina, Lena found the courage to ask Ada for dancing lessons. She was pleasantly surprised to hear Ada say she would make some enquiries. Within weeks, Lena was enrolled in Diamond's school of dance (all forms of dance taught to the highest grade), the school was on the south side of the river.

Eugene was detailed to take her and bring her back. I went along for the tram ride, and he and I spent the hour of the lesson in a nearby cafe, he sipping Bovril, me a glass of lemonade.

Ada was a firm believer in fairness, Betty was of an age when she chose her own amusements, Ada felt to be fair to me I should have the long promised piano lessons, and engaged Miss Buise (instructor in pianoforte to young ladies). I was a very young lady indeed, but this did not seem to trouble Miss Buise.

She was very old, and smelt of lavender and something else less pleasant, she was very sweet, and took to the whole family, especially Lena, who ended up being taught too.

Tiddles the cat, fully recovered from Betty's less than tender mercies, still reacted to music by waltzing across the floor, causing Miss Buise to abandon the lesson and give long discourses on the wonders of the animal creation. We were avid listeners as we shared her love of animals.

Ada however was less than pleased at our slow progress towards actually being able to play the instrument. She would diplomatically remind Miss Buise that she was being paid to teach us to play. Miss Buise would sniff slightly ,finish the lesson then disappear for a few weeks.

She would return without warning as if she had never been away. When pressed by Ada to account for her absence she would clasp her chest and say the three flights of stairs to our house affected her 'tubes'.

Meanwhile Lena was progressing well with her dance lessons, Diamond's school of dance having an altogether more professional approach to teaching.

On the rare evenings Ada was at home, we would rush to get the supper dishes washed and put away so that Lena could perform her dancing skills. I would try to copy her tying myself in knots in the process.

Lena would scowl at me and shoo me away.

'Go away! You are putting me off my steps.'

Eugene would chuckle and say impishly, 'She canny do it because she hasnae got your 'Willy Woodbine' legs.'

Her eyes would flare with fury, and tossing her head defiantly she would turn her back on him and dance on.

Later we would gather round the fire. One of us would start to sing, the others would join in, and we would sing song after song, Lena and I harmonizing.

Ada who insisted she had been taught to sing by an enthusiastic school mistress would berate us for our sloppy posture, and going off key.

'No, no, no, you were definitely off key there, stand up, you can't get air into your lungs sitting slouched over like that, the lungs need room to breathe.' With that she would stand erect, chest out ,hands clasped lightly together at her midriff, flaring her nostrils she would take a deep breath and sing out.

'Now you try it, do a few scales.' We stood up reluctantly sighing and rolling our eyes as Ada adjusted our posture.

'Now sing out, doh-rae-me-fa-soh-lah-te-doh.' We echoed her.

Depending on her mood Ada would sing the old Scots songs, or the music hall hits of Vesta Tilly and Marie Lloyd.

We would roll our eyes in despair, dismissing all this as 'before our time', never knowing that these songs were entering our consciousness and would evoke Ada again for us when she was long gone.

After a while we would begin to get ready for bed, Ada reminding us to polish our shoes and lay out our clothes for the morning. Lena and I would sing as we worked, Lena always singing the descant.

> *With someone like you*
> *A pal so good and true*
> *I'd like to leave it all behind, and go and find,*
> *A place that's known*
> *To God, and God alone*
> *Just a spot to call our own*
> *We'll find a perfect peace, where love will never cease,*
> *And there beneath a kindly sky*
> *We'll build a sweet little nest*
> *Somewhere in the west*
> *And let the rest of the world go by.*

Our chores complete Ada would be ready with the jar of malt and the bottle of cod liver oil.

'Open up.'

We obediently opened our mouths while she measured the dose of cod liver oil and passed it to us, then as we screwed our faces at the taste, she would twirl two spoons in the malt, and we would suck its sickly sweetness.

As time passed the age difference between my self and my sisters grew more marked. Betty, ten years my senior, lived in a completely different world to me, and Lena, who for a while had very similar tastes to mine, suddenly grew away from me, the six years between us more marked.

Along with her dancing, Lena was a fine seamstress; she had an eye for textiles, and could cut out and follow patterns. The clothing coupons we were allotted bought dreadful utility clothes, and as the war went on things got more difficult, with even the height of women's heels reduced to save wood.

Lena, always happy to spend time with her beloved auntie Tina, would rummage through Tina and Famie's wardrobe, selecting dresses and coats to alter, or practice on.

Tina had a Singer treadle sewing machine, at which Lena spent many happy hours.

None of this interested me, and I was increasingly thrown on my own resources.

For me the radio and books were my escape to happiness. It was the radio that introduced me to the wonderful enduring classics.

'Tess of the D'Urbervilles', 'The Mayor of Casterbridge', 'Silas Marner', 'The Mill on the Floss', 'Lorna Doone', 'Little Women' and 'Black Beauty'.

Besides the classics, there was Children's Hour, with Auntie Kathleen, with her kind but firm voice, a lot like Ada's. There was Toy Town, with Larry the Lamb, with his tremulous bleating voice, there was Down at the Mains, a farming story that opened up a new world to me, a city child.

The whole family would listen to 'ITMA', with Tommy Handley, a show full of wonderful characters, and catch phrases.

Molly Weir's Mrs Mopp, 'Can I do you now sir?' Colonel Chinstrap, 'I don't mind if I do'.

Of course there were jokes I did not quite understand, but I knew 'ITMA', 'Worker's Playtime', 'Music While You Work', and 'Housewife's Choice', were all part and parcel of our lives.

'The British sense of humour never fails, it is what will see us through the dark days,' Ada would tell us.

On Sundays, there was the familiar voices of Cliff Michelmore and Jean Metcalf, and at night, as Betty bone-combed my hair in her never ending scourge on lice, there was The Palm Court Orchestra, who's last notes dying away saw me sent to bed.

Ada made sure we were introduced to all kinds of music, but of the three of us I was the only one to like opera and classical, Betty and Lena coming to appreciate them much later in life.

Ada would sing snatches of arias, one favourite being Pagliacci, she told me the song was the lament of the tragic clown, but when I asked why he was so sad and tragic, she said I would not understand.

Aggie bought me a book of Burns poems, and so began my long fascination and love of the man and his works.

I found Burns's poems 'chiefly in the Scottish dialect', hard to understand, and his poems in English sometimes too flowery and overblown.

In vain I searched for a voice I recognized, characters who spoke in a language similar to mine.

Ada was very strict about our language and would not tolerate 'Glesca slang', of course all Glaswegian children were bi-lingual in as much as they spoke English in the classroom, and 'Glesca' in the playground.

This class divide was forever making itself felt, with the rare exception of the portrayal of characters like Maggie Tulliver in 'The Mill On The Floss', John Ridd in 'Lorna Doone', and the lilting Welsh tones of 'Under Milk Wood', the voices on the radio spoke what Ada called 'The Queen's English', and seemed to live lives a world away from mine or anyone I knew.

Betty would take me to the pictures, where most of the films were American, which was the accent she used all the way home, whether consciously or not I could not tell.

If the film did happen to be British, the class divide was to be found in people who spoke with 'cut glass' accents lording it over 'cheerful cockney sparrows'. In war films it was always the lesser ranks with their uneducated accents that got killed off. It was always the lot of Scots characters, who were invariably few and far between, to be a thug, a whisky swigging sot, or a loyal batsman to some exulted being of high rank and pedigree, for whom he would lay down his life, his passing being marked by the raising of a glass in the officer's mess to the memory of 'Jock, a mad Scottish bastard but a damn good soldier'. The women in British films were just as divided, tweed suited ladies with felt brimmed hats dispensed tea, organised jumble sales, waved brave goodbyes to their cleaning ladies who in overalls and turbans took on the jobs the 'Tommies' left behind.

Even when surveying the bombed ruins of their homes, these refined ladies still in their smart costumes and hats would never flinch. They could be seen, reading letters from the front, a lace handkerchief wiping away an errant tear, as the disembodied voice of the letter writer said, 'Chin up old girl, don't let Gerry get you down. I need you to fight on the home front while we tackle the blighter out here. Remember it is only the thought of England and all that it means that keeps us chaps going. After all darling it is England and freedom we are all fighting for, and if we all do our bit we just can't lose'.

Who can forget Greer Garson as the stoical Mrs Miniver as she beheld the destruction of her suburban home with never a hair out of place? Though Garson was not English, the Americans had caught on.

It was clear to me that these were beings far above my station, and for the most part I was the only one who seemed concerned. Ada would tell us that if we were not better than others we were just as good, adding the caveat that it depended on honour and integrity. Eugene on the odd occasion he overheard the radio would laugh and say, 'Thae a' talk wi' bools in their mooths.'

Even levelling this criticism against the sainted Auntie Kathleen, who was a Scot and broadcast from Glasgow's Queen Margaret Drive, but spoke 'The Queen's English' nevertheless. Ada would lose her patience with him, saying. 'These are educated people; it will do her no harm to speak as they do. You can't even speak proper Italian, only that slovenly Neapolitan dialect, which is as bad as 'Glesca' slang.

'Aye, well, that's because ah'm a peasant,' Eugene would answer good naturedly. As indeed he was.

Despite her defence of the English language Ada decided it was important to acknowledge the Scottish heritage around us.

She taught us the songs of Harry Lauder, and would occasionally take us to the Metropole, to see Tommy Morgan and Harry Gordon, the Short family who became better known as the Logans were the up and coming stars of the variety shows, each member more talented than the next. The youngest son Jimmy was our particular favourite; he could sing and play the clown with equal ease. Christmas brought pantomime and saw Jimmy playing a simple lovable Buttons with a broad 'Glesca' accent, it was the language of the audience and they responded with happy recognition.

We would queue on dark bitter winter nights for a seat in the 'Gods' where for a few pennies you could sit high above the rest of the audience, engrossed in the show which helped you forget the bum numbing rough wood benches.

In comedy sketches Jimmy would play the fool to his father's straight man. He had several catch phrases which Lena and I would copy, 'sausages is the boys', 'oh ah love ma daddy'.

We would go around the house saying them ruffling our fingers through Eugene's fast disappearing hair, till he would lose patience and push us away, 'Basta! Basta! enough, enough.

Often a huge placard would slowly descend printed with the words of a song. Jimmy would invite the men to compete against the women to see who could sing the loudest.

We would join in with gusto.

'Roamin' in the Gloamin', Keep Right On To The End Of The Road', 'Ah Love A Lassie', all Harry Lauder songs which thanks to Ada we knew by heart.

It was great fun, and we would call for more, Jimmy would feign exasperation, 'Och no' again.'

'More! More! More!' we would chorus, the placard would be hauled up and another descend in its place, to thunderous applause.

'Right this better be the last wan,' Jimmy would remonstrate.

The music would begin and we were off, happily following the little red dot as it danced along each line.

It's a fine thing to sing
Singing is the thing
It makes you smile, when you're feeling dreary
It lightens up the road
When you have a heavy load
Singing is the thing to keep you cheery.

Applause, shouts of joy would all but drown out Jimmy's 'thank you and goodnight'.

Out we would go into the dark night still singing to ourselves, as we hurried to catch the tram home.

Live performance had a totally different appeal for me. The films were fine but nothing could give that rush of excitement being in a theatre could bring, yet our outings were confined to variety shows and pantomime, it never occurred to us to go to a play, or any other kind of performance.

Though it was never voiced there was an unspoken acceptance that such

120

things were not for the likes of us.

It was some years later that Jimmy Logan appeared with another fine actor Gordon Jackson in the film 'Floodtide'. I sat through the whole thing scarcely able to believe the people up on the screen were talking like me.

CHAPTER 14

The long awaited move to St. Vincent Street finally arrived. Eugene decided to try to hire a van big enough to take everything.

Though posters everywhere asked 'Is your journey really necessary?' he felt ours was, but still got the stock reply, 'There's a war on'.

One ration of petrol for one small van, managed three journeys from east end to west end. It was not enough and once again the beloved sideboard swathed in blankets made an undignified trek on a handcart. Lena and I were given the job of ferrying the smaller things caught up in bundles on the tram. Glaswegians had a great affection for the trams, they may have been supplied by the Corporation, but the people claimed them for their own. It was not uncommon to have to push your way past rolls of linoleum, baskets of pots and pans, or the odd chest of drawers, or mattress.

The good natured Glaswegians would shove up uncomplaining to make way. Even the fierce 'clippies' would squeeze round the obstacles with only a long suffering sigh.

The 'clippies' had a love hate relationship with their passengers, and a razor sharp sense of humour.

A hesitant passenger would ask, 'Dis this bus go tae the university?'

Quick as a flash would come the reply, 'Naw, it's no clever enough.'

At tram stops if punters spotted the 'clippie' was upstairs they would pile on blocking the gangway, only to have her swoop down the stairs with a roar, 'Come on, get aff!'

Some would sheepishly do as they were told, while others would push and shove, hanging on the straps for dear life, eyes fixed on the floor. Arms akimbo, the 'clippie' would fix them with a steely eye.

'Can youse no count? Nae mair than ten staunin' passengers. If ye canny count use yer fingers, ur somebody else's. Come oan, dae ye think ma heid buttons up the back?'

An irate finger would stab at the bell and the tram would lumber to a halt, as shamefaced passengers decanted.

On Friday and Saturday nights when the pubs closed, wee men in cloth caps and dungarees would cling to the tram stop complaining that it was swirling round them. They would try to board the tram while still clinging to the pole for support, if they let go their legs would buckle under them.

The 'clippie' would shake her head, 'Dae ye waant this tram?'

'Aye hen.'

She would grab his lapels, and haul him on, 'Some ither folk wid like tae get hame the night, if that's a' right wi' you?'

'Sorry hen, ah've had a wee bevvy, a wee refreshment, ye know.'

'A wee bevvy!, yer steamin' so ye ur', she would dump him in the first vacant seat, grim faced, her hand extended for the fare.

To us as children, these men were very old, but in truth they were mostly around their mid fifties. They were always good natured, sometimes sitting quietly weeping for someone or something lost.

Some merry revellers would insist the other passengers join them in a chorus of 'I belong to Glasgow', or 'Keep Right on to the End of the Road'.

The sight of a child would have them fishing in their pockets for pennies, 'fur sweeties'. There was nothing to fear from them, mothers did not pull their children away, and everyone accepted no harm was intended. The wonderful Glasgow trams were a microcosm of the warm heart of the city. It took several trips for Lena and I to move all the bits and pieces. We loved to ride on the top deck and would lug the bundles up the steep narrow stairs, teetering precariously on the way down as the weight of the bundles threw us forward.

The cats were left till last. Ada was sure they would try to escape from the shopping bags, so Betty came along as chaperone.

The ancient irascible Billy would not tolerate Tiddles, so each had a bag of his own.

Billy kept up a low mournful growl, while Tiddles did somersaults clawing at the bag to get out.

An old man on the tram eyed the bag with curiosity, 'Whit hiv ye got in there then, a pair o' ferrets?'

'No,' said Betty keeping a straight face, 'it's two hens; we like to have our own eggs.'

'Is that right? Dae ye have a wee bit gairdin then?'

'No, we live up a close,' answered Betty matter of factly. 'An' ye are goin' tae keep hens in the hoose?'

'Oh yes, we have always had hens in the house,' said Betty, ignoring Lena's scowl.

'Well, ah've heard a'thing noo,' said the man shaking his head. When they were finally released the two cats took a quick look round then shot under a bed, and they did not surface until the next morning when hunger drove them out.

My hope that with the move I would no longer have to share a bed with Aggie was in vain. Ada and Eugene took the recess bed in the kitchen, Betty and Lena would share the settee in the big room. The settee had been specially bought, so the room could also be a place to bring visitors.

Aggie and I were given the wee room; it was the same bed, and the same problem.

The first time I ventured into the big room, Betty and Lena sent me out again telling me I had to knock, as I was only small fry. I dutifully did as I was told until Ada found out, and gave the two of them the rough edge of her tongue.

They laughed and said it had been a joke, but let it go on as I had not complained.

Apart from the luxury of having an inside lavatory again, the house in St. Vincent Street had electricity. The first night we spent in the house, Lena kept switching the light on and off, refusing to give me a turn as I was too small to reach the switch.

The light made everything so much brighter, and when the kitchen range was going full blast the place was welcoming and cosy. Ada complained the range was so much bigger than the one in the Gallowgate, and it ate up all the coal ration. Lena and I were always out scouting for wee shops that sold bundles of sticks, and chasing the briquette seller as he moved from street to street. All the kitchen scraps went on the fire, some newspapers were laid aside to use as wrapping paper at the shops, and the rest were soaked and compacted with coal dust to make slow burning briquettes when the supply of bought ones ran out. I hated these things; they dampened the fire glow and sent out billowing smoke.

Ada told us we just had to put up with it, there was a war on; it was the stock reply to any complaint.

We also acquired a washing machine. Eugene had got it from a man who knew a man who was selling this monstrosity, it had an enormous fat bellied tub with all sorts of tubes attached, and a mangle, with slightly worn rubber rollers. When it was filled with water and switched on it jumped and juddered across the floor, spewing suds everywhere. Despite its shortcomings Ada declared it a great help in coping with the laundry, and it was much admired by the aunts when they came to visit.

Eugene was like the cat that got the cream, the washing machine was one of the few things he had bought Ada that met with her approval.

The move to St. Vincent Street meant a twenty minute journey on the tram to school, and it also meant having to stay for school dinners. Lena had no problem with this, she had lots of friends and was involved with activities such as helping with the school library, and she was also a meat eater. The juniors had dinner at different times from the seniors, and on that first day as I stood in the queue nervously clutching my buff dinner ticket the smell of meat cooking gripped my nostrils. Within minutes the dinner lady had punched my ticket and I was seated in front of a plate, staring down at a brown and white mess, of runny mince and dry mashed potato. Each day a nun would act as duty monitor in the dinner hall, she would glide up and down the isles, her eagle eye missing nothing.

I was suddenly aware that she was standing by my side. She picked up my fork and placed it in my hand.

'Eat!' she said.

'Please sister I don't eat meat, I only eat vegetables,' I stammered.

'We do not say don't, we say do not,' she corrected, 'Also it is a sin to refuse the wholesome food the Lord in His goodness has provided for us. There are little children in Africa who would be only too pleased to have such food, sure do we not collect every week for them to relieve them of their lack?'

'Yes sister.'

I knew all about the black babies, they were constantly being invoked on all children to shame them into eating their greens. I would have happily given them my mince and potatoes.

The nun plunged the fork into the potato covered it with mince and thrust it at me.

'Eat, you ungrateful child.'

I sat lips tightly shut, my stomach churning at the smell of the mince.

'Are you going to eat child?'

'No sister it will make me sick,' I pleaded.

She forced the fork into my mouth, filling it again and ramming it in. I spat it out, and it spread all over her robe.

'You disgusting child!' She hauled me from the bench, frogmarching me from the dinner hall, to a chorus of giggles from the other children. I found myself before Mother Philippa trying to explain, her steely gaze told me she did not understand.

The misdemeanour merited two strokes from her rope.

Over the next two weeks I tried many ploys to get around the problem, though the other nuns on the rota were not so sharp eyed as the first nun, they nevertheless would question why food was not being eaten. I managed to persuade one or two fellow pupils to take my meat, and having noticed that the windows of the hall were always open regardless of the weather I would try to get a seat under the window and throw my meat out, there was always a passing stray dog that would gobble up the evidence.

It was not long before the rota brought my tormentor back; she had not forgotten me and watched me like a hawk. As I moved along the queue to collect my dinner I would say as quietly as possible to the dinner lady that I only wanted one spoonful of mince, this I would spread thinly around my plate, then mop it up with the slice of bread we were always allowed, this I would conceal in my gym pocket until I could get to the toilets where I would dispose of it, and scrub the inside of my pocket with wet toilet roll.

I was very afraid of being found out, and eventually confided in Betty who despite my pleading told Ada.

Ada sent a note to Mother Philippa explaining that my vegetarianism was not a fad, and indeed she was a vegetarian too.

Mother Philippa was not impressed, Our Lady and St. Francis did not countenance vegetarians.

She also used the old argument of the poor black babies whose plight was obviously exacerbated by my refusal to eat meat.

Ada's response on reading the note was mixed, she did acknowledge that we should be grateful for what the Lord provided, but on the other hand personal preferences should be honoured.

It was decided that I would go to Da-dee's for my dinner. While I loved Da-dee, Auntie Tina and Auntie Mary, actually getting up the three flights of stairs to their door was a challenge. Since Barrowland had been bombed the rats had fled to the surrounding backcourts, and they were to be seen running along the walls of the stairs even in the daytime, some had even got into the houses. The stairwell at 206 was gloomy and dark, some neighbours left a candle flickering outside their door, but there was always the dark unlit close to negotiate before that. I would take a deep breath and dash in, knowing the rats ran along the wall I was careful to keep to the centre of the tread. Once I reached the first landing I would shout as loudly as I could, 'OPEN, OPEN.' Tina would open the door ready for me to dash in almost doubled by the pain in my chest; she would laugh and say, 'Come in, feartie gowk.'

Tina loved to feed people, any caller, be they insurance men, priest or the tally man who hawked his wares around the doors would be pressed to sit down and join in the family meal. Always there was pasta or soup simmering away, and she and Da-dee took offence if the offer was declined Many a polite refusal was overruled as the reluctant guest was steered to the table and presented with a steaming bowl of soup and the heel of a loaf, or a plate piled with spaghetti.

They soon found it was easier to comply, eat and make their excuses. Da-dee who loved to have someone to talk to would shake his head sorrowfully and say, 'Eh, mangiare scattare', eat and run. Tina was convinced that as a growing girl I needed to be fed on large quantities of spaghetti, and she and Da-dee would watch indulgently as I gamely tried to get through it. My breakneck dash down the stairs would result in indigestion for the rest of the afternoon; it also earned me many a strap as I kept nodding off during lessons.

I tried to explain to Ada that Auntie Tina gave me too much to eat; she would have none of it.

'Your Auntie Tina is the salt of the earth, she would give you the clothes off her back, and you should be ashamed of yourself. Don't forget there is a war on, she is probably denying herself to give to you.'

On rare occasions Tina would be out, and I was allowed to buy penny buns and a drink of Vimto on those days I felt I was in heaven.

There was a slight difference of opinion as to what the name of the district we now lived in was. Some said it was Finnieston, others favoured Sandyford. This was Ada's preference and she went so far as to get a map to convince us, so Sandyford it was, Finnieston being deemed to start over the hill, where the docks were.

When Lena and I were not at school we were helping out in the shop, which meant we had little opportunity to make friends. We lost one old friend Billy the ancient tom. He had never really settled in the new place, and one day when the door was left open took his chance and vanished. We hunted for him for several days. A week later Tina spotted him at the close mouth of 211, looking tired and bedraggled. We took him home, but he went AWOL twice more, always turning up at the old address. It was clear he was not going to settle in St. Vincent Street Ada persuaded the people in our old house to take him in, so he happily spent the rest of his days in his old haunt.

'Cats get attached to places rather than people, that is why Billy went back,' Ada told me, trying to make me feel better.

'Maybe there is a better class of mice in the Gallowgate,' Betty said mischievously.

The shop had always been a Mecca for the servicemen who came in on the ships at Finnieston, and now we had Americans too. They had a certain glamour, wooing the girls with nylons and chocolate. While they were welcome on the whole, not everyone was pleased to see them. Ada already concerned at Betty's busy social life, dancing at the Locarno in Sauchiehall Street, or Barrowland. Betty would spend far too long on her appearance for

Ada's liking. She would emerge from the room; hair swept up in combs, and piled high on her head, legs stained with tea, a seam drawn with black pencil. This was something she did for her friends too, as she was judged to have the most steady hand.

Often they would miss the last tram home, and would come rolling home linked arm in arm, singing the latest hit song.

'You will get a name for yourself, my girl, different men almost every time, already some of the neighbours have commented.'

'We are doing no harm, it is only a bit of fun,' Betty told her. Ada complained to Eugene, 'I intend to put a stop to this, she is only a young girl, anything could happen.'

'Let it be, she is just enjoying herself, you are only young once.' Eugene said mildly.

Ada could not leave it, 'You will be seen as a loose woman, it will ruin your reputation,' she told Betty.

'Oh for goodness sake they are all nice boys, they are lonely and missing home. We all just want to live a little while we still have a life to live,' Betty protested.

'Maybe so, but I want no daughter of mine taken advantage of, they are here today gone tomorrow, and if anything happened you would be left to cope, there is no more precious thing than a good name,' Ada warned.

'A good name will not be much use to me when I am dead!' Betty screamed, slamming the door behind her.

Betty had no interest in 'going steady', she was having too much fun, but some of 'the boys' were looking for a serious relationship. One such was Harry Kaufmann, a young Canadian from Toronto. He really took a shine to Betty, bombarding her with gifts, trying to monopolize all her time. She would sit with Lena and I, all three huddled on the bed, sharing the chocolate Harry had given her, listening to her devising ways to let him down gently. Harry seemed incapable of taking the hint; he would come into the shop and if Betty was not there would plead to be told where she was.

He left a message with Aggie that he was going to be posted abroad. Ada told Betty to stay away from the shop till he sailed, but Harry was determined to see Betty. He came every day to the house, banging on the door pleading with Betty to let him in. She grew really afraid and would sit hunched up on her bed, willing him to go away.

On the fifth day he arrived early, banging on the door at regular intervals. Betty banged frantically on the floor in a desperate bid for help. Ada came upstairs and tried to reason with him, eventually agreeing to let him see Betty if he would then leave her alone. So they spent a fraught ten minutes together, before a crestfallen Harry kissed her goodbye and left.

Two days went by, Betty was back working in the shop. On the third day, alone in the house she heard the familiar knock, and she refused to answer. The knocking went on and on, Harry calling through the letter box begging her to open the door. After a while the knocking stopped, and hardly daring to believe he had gone, but fearful of opening the door to find out, Betty crept along the lobby, and carefully lifting the stepladders from the lavatory, she gingerly set the ladder up, and tiptoed up it to peer out of the fanlight. To her great shock she found herself at the top of the ladder looking straight into Harry's eyes. Weak with shock she skimmed down the ladder, leaning against the door, her heart pounding.

'Open the door Bet, I gotta see you, I'm sick to my stomach for the sight of you,' he pleaded.

'Go away! Go away, please', she shouted through the door.

Rushing through to the kitchen she banged noisily for help from the shop. Soon she could hear Ada giving Harry a piece of her mind.

Finally, he agreed to go, shouting a last lovelorn message to Betty.

Confident the coast was clear Betty opened the door. Ada stood there holding a ladder.

'God knows where he got this from, he was certainly determined to see you one way or another,' Ada said grimly.

'I feel sorry for him, he is a nice enough lad, just can't take no for an answer,' Ada said.

'Well I don't feel sorry for him, he scared me out of my wits,' Betty shivered.

'It bears out what I say. You can't be too careful, let's hope you have learned your lesson,' Ada warned.

Betty was a bit subdued for a few days, but it was not long before she was out and about again with her friends, dancing and going to the pictures with different boys.

Ada in an effort to curb her flighty ways cut her pocket money, but soon began to suspect what she called 'sticky fingers in the till'.

'Och it is your imagination, it is only the family that work in the shop, so who could be stealing?' Eugene said.

Ada kept watch for a few days, and she was astonished to see Betty slipping money that should have gone into the till, into her shoe.

Saying nothing Ada left the shop, returning with a suitcase containing Betty's clothes. She called Betty through to the back shop, and minutes later Betty emerged crying, the red weal of Ada's fingers clear on her face. She hurried to the door, carrying her case.

'Where will she go?' Aggie asked, when all was explained to her.

'That is her business, I will not have a thief in my house,' Ada stormed. We were all devastated, and there was the most horrible atmosphere.

'How long do you mean her to stay away?' Eugene asked.

'I have no indention of having her back, to think a daughter of mine would steal from her own, it is terrible thing to do,' Ada replied. 'Maybe she is sorry,' Lena said.

'Oh she is sorry, sorry she got caught, no doubt,' Ada said sharply.

We knew Ada was implacable, if she felt someone had betrayed her, she would never forgive.

'You talk to her,' Eugene begged Lizzie.

'It is really none of my business, Eadie knows her own daughter best,' was the diplomatic answer.

'But Eadie would listen to you,' Eugene urged, 'it is no use me talkin' to her, the trouble is the two of them are alike, stubborn and headstrong.

'Well they are mother and daughter. Betty is a law to herself, she has always been different,' Lizzie said quietly.

It was true, though I has never heard any of the aunts say so before. I knew they treated her differently from Lena and me. Even at family gatherings, Betty always seemed to be just outside that close warm family circle, though never overtly slighted.

If Betty was sorry it was clear Ada was too, but her pride would not let her admit it. What Eugene had said about the two being alike was true. Both were proud, quick to take offence, bold and adventurous; what Ada saw in Betty was her young self.

Now Betty had gone and nobody knew where she was.

'You were tryin' to keep her on the straight and narrow, now she is on her own. God knows what she is up to,' Eugene said.

'I told you she is not my concern any longer,' Ada snapped, but a look of fear had crossed her face, and we all knew she was worried.

The beat Bobbies coming in for their usual cup of Bovril missed Betty and asked where she was. Eugene told them there had been a row and she had left, and he tipped them the wink that he would be grateful if they could find out anything.

'We'll see what we can do,' they promised.

Within a few days they found her working in a munitions factory in Bishopton. She was lodging with one of her workmates.

'Oh my God! A munitions factory,' Ada was shocked.

'Well at least you know where she is and that she is safe,' Eugene said.

'You call making bombs safe?'

'The lassie had to earn money to keep hersel'. Send word, tell her to come back,' Lizzie urged.

'No! She has made her bed, she can lie on it,' Ada said firmly.

No amount of pleading from Lena and me would change her mind.

'It's nae use, you know what she's like, nothing we can say will change her mind,' Eugene told us.

The weeks passed. Late one Friday night a young girl came into the shop asking to speak to Ada. She introduced herself as a workmate of Betty's, saying she had some news.

'If you have come here to plead for her, you are washing your time. What happened is a private matter, and I won't discuss it, or listen to any pleas.' Ada told her.

'The thing is Mrs Coutts; Betty has lost her job and her lodgings. She doesn't even know I am here. I only got your address from her work record.

'Lost her job you say? Has she done something wrong?'

'No she's got scabies, and as it's very infectious they just sacked her.

She turned away, then came back and said earnestly,

'I just thought you should know.'

There was an uncomfortable silence, as we watched Ada's face and waited for her to speak.

'You better tell her to come home then.'

So Betty came home. Ironically she had to be separated from the rest of us, using her own soap, towel, bed linen and eating utensils. She even slept on the floor on a makeshift mattress.

To treat the disease she had to coat herself in a foul smelling cream each night, and have a hot bath each morning.

Since we had no bath in the house it meant a long uncomfortable trek to the public baths in Elliot Street across the road from the shop.

She complained she was segregated there too, and found the whole thing very depressing.

I was curious to see the baths, and begged Ada to let me go with Betty.

I wrung a promise from her that once Betty was cured, I could go with her and have a bath myself.

My first visit proved to be a scary experience. I handed over my sixpence entrance fee and was given a small bar of carbolic soap, a thin towel with 'Property of Glasgow Corporation' stitched in red thread along the hem, then followed a stern faced woman dressed in a drab green overall with the Corporation crest on the breast pocket along a narrow passage with cubicles on either side. I could hear splashing and tuneless whistling. As we passed along the woman would bang on a door now and then and bellow, 'Yer times up.' Selecting a key from a huge bunch hanging from her belt she opened a door and stood aside for me to enter.

She leaned over the bath, pointing to each verdigris covered tap.

'Cauld watter, hoat watter. There's a wee stool tae sit oan an' a duckboard tae staun oan when ye get oot the bath. Ye only get six inches o' watter mind, but if it's good enough fur the King an' Queen it's good enough fur you.'

She gave me a stern look.

'I'll be back tae check by the way.'

'Six inches will be enough,' laughed Betty. 'She is so wee, if it was any more she would probably drown.'

The joke fell flat. The woman rattled her keys and opened the next door.

'You kin hiv this wan, so ye can keep an eye on her. Ah hiv enough tae dae.'

I heard her go through the ritual contents of the cubicle, and warn of the regulation six inches of water.

I heard Betty's repeated, 'Yes I know.'

The woman's voice rose, 'Listen hen, whether ye know ur no', it's ma joab tae tell ye, right!'

The door of Betty's cubicle slammed shut. Moments later the lined face topped by brown hair trapped in a hair net peered round my door.

'Ye hiv goat twenty minutes, nae longer, right? So when ah open the door ye better hiv yer claes back on, right?'

I stared at her petrified as the water gushed into the bath, and she leaned over turning off the taps, shaking her head and sighing. It was really impossible to tell through the steam whether the six inches had been reached.

She went out pulling the door behind her with a resounding click. I was panic struck. She had locked me in. I had a horror of being locked in.

I gazed at the bath as the steam began to clear. It was enormous, and I was scared to get in, in case I could not climb out again.

I sat on the little stool gazing at the water. How could I know when twenty minutes had passed?

'Are you all right?' Betty shouted.

'Yes, but I think I am locked in,' I shouted back.

'That's all right, she will let you out when the time comes,' Betty shouted.

I scrambled onto the edge of the bath, letting my feet dangle in the water. Splashing it up on my legs, then jumping down, I lathered the soap in the water, swirling it round and round trying to make bubbles.

Ada always said Glasgow water, coming as it did from Loch Katrine, was soft, and of the highest quality, so gave a good lather, but my carbolic bar was so thin it soon disappeared. Hurriedly I rubbed myself all over with the scummy lather, and dried myself as best I could with the scratchy towel.

Quickly I pulled on my clothes and sat once more on the little stool, eyes firmly fixed on the door. I could hear Betty splashing noisily and singing, 'I left My Heart At The Stage Door Canteen.'

I jumped up and let the water drain away, swishing the remaining soap suds this way and that to get them away.

The door opened with a jangle of keys, and the wrinkled face appeared again, eyes sweeping round taking everything in.

'Well! You must hiv been clean tae start wi',' she said eyeing the empty bath. 'Maist times there is a ring o' muck roon that bath thick enough tae grow tatties. Ye hiv nae idea the dirty buggers we get in here.'

I darted past her into the passage.

'Haud yer horses, ah'm no gonny keep ye prisoner,' a glimmer of a grin creased her face.

Betty emerged, hair clinging to her forehead, face flushed with the heat, and she looked at me in surprise.

The woman catching the look, said knowingly,

'Ah think she gave hersel' a lick an' a promise, an' if ye ask me ah think she wis scared o' the whole thing,' she pulled a face at Betty and shook her head.

'Did you have a bath?' Betty asked.

'Y-es I'm all clean,' I said

'Aye so ye ur hen, but ah think ye didnae need a bath in the first place.

She turned to Betty.

'Ah wis jist tellin' the wee lassie, we get some dirty buggers in here, so we dae.'

Betty frowned at the profanity but said nothing.

'So did you not like it then?' asked Betty as we made our way down the hill.

'It was a bit scary,' I said.

'Well, you lived to tell the tale. You were curious to see the place, and you know what curiosity did?' she laughed.

'Killed the cat!' I grinned.

CHAPTER 15

For weeks the talk of the class was the forthcoming Birthday celebration of Shirley Finlay, and who would be invited to what promised to be an occasion to remember. Shirley was the girl who had everything, everything that is except her parents. They were on the stage, travelling round the circuit of Variety Theatres.

While this lent a certain glamour to Shirley, the reality was she was a lonely little girl who lived with her grandmother in the same close as my Auntie Teeny. From these less than glamorous surroundings Shirley would emerge at weekends dressed in the most beautiful clothes, her auburn hair caught up in extravagant bows. Always she carried a doll dressed in the same flamboyant style as herself. Even her school uniform was of superior material to ours, her blouse and tie of tussor silk. Having parents who were on the stage made her very glamorous in the eyes of her classmates, and girls tried to ingratiate themselves into her circle. Shirley had her own set, among them Molly McKay and her gang. I had no expectation of being invited to the birthday bash, so it was with great astonishment that a pink card written in a spidery hand was waiting for me one day when I returned from school.

'Isn't that nice,' said Ada, a statement rather than a question.

'Y-es,' I said hardly daring to believe my eyes.

'You don't seem very excited,' Ada looked at me closely.

'It-it's just that I was not expecting it. All the girls in the class want to go to this thing, but Shirley has her own friends, and I'm not really one of them.'

'Shirley would not send out the invitations,' said Ada, 'It would be her granny. I always got on very well with Mrs Finlay, so she has remembered you.

Realizing the truth of this made me feel even more uneasy. Shirley might not know her granny had invited me, and she would be furious when I turned up. I had to find a way of getting out of this. In panic I turned to Lena for help, asking what I should do.

'I don't really see what you can do, except go. Mammy will be very angry if you snub Mrs Finlay. Anyway you will probably find that half the class have been invited, and you won't stand out like a sore thumb.'

I turned to Betty, she was always full of ideas, but she too was of little help.

'Listen, I would go and enjoy myself. Tea at Miss Cranston's Tea Rooms, and a pantomime. You may even get to go backstage, because her folks are in the business, so take the chance when you can, that's what I say. Anyway, Shirley will be so excited with her presents and everything, she will probably not really notice who is there at all.'

I realized it was no use talking to them, they knew nothing about the bullying, so they could not understand.

There was no help for it, so I duly turned up at the Tollbooth at the foot of the High Street, where we were to meet.

Dressed in my party best, a new frock, white ankle socks though it was the middle of December, black patent shoes and my 'new' coat, with a mock astrakhan collar. The coat was a hand me down from Lena, that Ada had altered.

Ada assured me there would be many other children in hand me downs.

All the way down in the tram I had tried to imagine how Shirley would react when I turned up. Ada kept up a stream of instructions on how I was to behave during the evening.

'Remember to say please and thank you to the waitress, and don't speak with your mouth full. If you are offered spam, don't make a fuss and just leave it on the side of your plate. The waitress will not ask you why you did not eat it; she will just take it away. Keep close to Mrs Finlay all the time and don't stray. Don't shout or laugh too loud at the pantomime. Remember your manners. Remember to say thank you to Mrs Finlay at the end of the evening, and I will thank her again when I come to collect you at ten o'clock as arranged.'

'You won't be late will you?' I asked anxiously.

'Of course not, I will be there at ten o'clock on the dot,' Ada assured me.

There were a clutch of parents delivering the privileged guests. Ada was so engrossed exchanging pleasantries she failed to notice the look of horror on Shirley's face when she caught sight of me.

I stood shivering with a mixture of cold and embarrassment on the periphery of the excited chattering throng. Molly strode up to me eyes blazing.

'What are you dae'in here? You need an invitation to come to this.'

'I have an invitation, it is in my pocket,' I told her.

'Let me see it then,' she demanded.

'How did you get that?' She stared at the slightly dog eared card in disbelief.

'Through the post,' I said innocently.

Shirley was scowling; she glared at me, and then turned her back. Molly went to Shirley's side, and they stood arm in arm.

Mrs Finlay was all smiles, and taking Shirley by the arm, she steered her round the group, telling her to thank each one in turn for coming.

When they reached me, Shirley gave the briefest of nods and moved on, but her grandmother pulled her back.

'Don't be so rude and say thank you properly to your friend. We must always remember our manners.'

'Yes granny,' Shirley bared her teeth, waggled her head at me, and turned away.

With much wagging of warning fingers, to remember to be on best behaviour and assurances to be on time to pick their offspring up, the parents departed. Mrs Finlay marshalled us all into a crocodile and we headed for the tram to take us to Miss Cranston's celebrated tea rooms.

The girls had paired off, and I was the odd one out. I found a seat at the rear of the tram, and was joined by a slightly out of breath Mrs Finlay.

'Oh dear, we seem to have an uneven number, never mind, you can have me for company can't you?'

'Yes thank you,' I said remembering my manners.

The evening over we arrived back at the Tollbooth to find the group of parents waiting. I searched anxiously for Ada but she was not there. I sent up a silent prayer that she would come on the next tram, but as the parents and children melted away, and tram after tram came and went, my heart sank. Soon I was the only one left apart from Molly, who was going home with Shirley and her granny.

The night was chilly, and Molly stamped her feet and blew on her hands. She glared at me, obviously wishing to see the back of me. Shirley whined that she was cold and wanted to go home.

'We can't leave your little friend here alone. I'm sure her mother will be here soon.'

There was no sign of Ada. I stood in abject misery, trying to avoid Molly's murderous glare. Shirley turned her back on me and huddled into her grandmother's coat for warmth, even Mrs Finlay was beginning to get agitated.

At last I saw Ada stepping off the tram, and she hurried towards us, already apologizing for her lateness.

Mrs Finlay smiled politely and assured her it had been no trouble at all, she and the girls were only too pleased to keep me company till she arrived.

I slipped my arm through Ada's and tried to steer her away, but she turned back and to my horror I heard her say.

'Because the girls have been so good, standing in the cold, why don't they come to our house next Saturday for a visit?' She turned to me, 'You would like that wouldn't you?' I nodded dumbly.

Mrs Finlay said, 'Oh that would be nice and the girls will love it. Molly often talks about your shop. I think they think having a shop must be wonderful.'

'Well I wouldn't say that exactly, but they are very welcome to come and see it. Next Saturday would be fine, if it suits.'

'They will look forward to it, thank you,' Mrs Finlay smiled. We went our separate ways, Molly turning as they went and pulling a face at me.

'You are very quiet, did you not enjoy yourself?' Ada asked as the tram trundled its way along Argyle Street.

'Yes, the pantomime was really good, I enjoyed that,' I said.

Mrs Finlay is such a nice lady, and those two little girls are just the kind of friends you should have. You all play together at school, don't you?'

'Eh no, not really. Shirley has her own set of friends, and I'm not really one of them. I told you, that's why it might be difficult when they come to the house,' I blurted out.

'Difficult? What can be difficult about having two little school friends on a visit?' Ada said.

'But they are not my friends,' — I trailed off seeing the look on Ada's face.

'Nonsense, they were kind enough to stay with you tonight, and we must do something to repay that kindness; all that time standing in the cold,' she said.

I stared at her in amazement, but said nothing. It was as if it had been my fault they were standing in the cold. 'It was because you were late, like you are always late,' I thought rebelliously, but had not the courage to say so.

'Well they are coming next Saturday, and that is that, so we need to think what we can give them to eat,' Ada said.

'Eat!' I said.

'Yes of course, they will be there all day, and they have to eat. I think I'll make my special spaghetti, it is a good filling dish.'

I was horrified. Molly hated all things Italian, so we couldn't have spaghetti.

'I don't think they like spaghetti, could you make something Scottish?'

Ada gave me a funny look. She was quiet for a moment or two. I was biting my tongue, wishing I hadn't said anything.

'I'll make stovies, nothing more SCOTTISH, than that,' she said letting me know she had got the message.

All week at school I watched Molly and Shirley, as they stood heads bent conspiratorially. I was convinced they were talking about the forthcoming visit, and now and then they would look up and stare at me and burst into laughter. I cringed at the thought of the coming Saturday.

Betty was detailed to collect the two from the Gallowgate, and bring them to St. Vincent Street.

I stood at the bedroom window watching for the three figures to come off the tram. I had a sick feeling in my stomach, and hoped something had happened to stop them coming. Betty seemed to have been gone a long time, but at last as the tram pulled away from the stop I saw them, each holding Betty's hand as they waited to cross the street. I rushed down to meet them, anxious to see what their first impression of the shop was. They were all smiles when they saw me, and I realized they had decided to put on an act.

I wondered if they would be able to keep it up all day. Shirley had probably been told to be on her best behaviour, and did not want any tales getting back to her granny about misbehaving.

I took them on a tour of the shop. They went behind the counter, Aggie letting them pretend to serve customers, then through to the back shop where Eugene, perched on his stool, was busy stirring the mixture for the blancmange.

They stared at him, taking in the stool, the huge vat that was almost as big as himself, and tried to stifle a giggle as his whole body bent forward with each turn of the paddle which he clutched with both hands. For the first time I realized how comical he looked. Eugene wiped his brow with his huge handkerchief, took off his glasses which were fogged by steam, and peered down short-sightedly at the grimacing faces.

'Get Aggie tae gie the lasses a slider, or better still there should be some shells left, and they can pick what colour o' blancmange they like.' He grinned down at them showing toothless gums. I wished the floor would open up and swallow me. We went through to the front, Aggie fussed around getting drinks and looking for the shells and Ada was busy churning the blancmange in the freezer. They seemed genuinely interested as she told them how the substitute ice cream was made.

We sat eating our shells and drinking our Vimto as Aggie recounted the air raid, and Betty being thrown under the bed by the blast. She told them of the way the shop once looked, and how the window had to be boarded up and the door too, making the shop so dark and gloomy. I was beginning to feel a little better, and we were just about to go upstairs when Armando Angelini came in. It was his habit to just hang around the shop most days, generally making a nuisance of himself. He peered into the freezer, as Ada turned the handle.

'What flavour is that you are making Mrs Coutts?'

I saw the look that passed between Molly and Shirley. In my concern about all the things that might go wrong, I had completely forgotten about the double name. I could see from their faces that they would want an explanation.

Upstairs Betty has set a nice table, and she, Ada and Lena had sacrificed their egg and sugar ration to make a small sponge cake. The stovies were simmering away on the stove, the smell pervading the kitchen. While we waited for Ada to come upstairs, Betty suggested snakes and ladders. After a while we grew bored and went through to the big room where Shirley played the two tunes she had already learned in her piano lessons. Not to be outdone Molly banged away tunelessly for a while. Betty 'played' a tune on paper and comb, which made them laugh, and beg to try for themselves.

Ada came upstairs, and we sat down to eat. They took such a long time to eat, picking the tiniest amount up on the fork, pushing the food around the plate, fishing out the pieces of onion and leaving them on the side of the plate.

'If it is not to your liking you can leave a little,' Ada said rather sharply. She hated to see food wasted, and even though the children before her were guests she was not for letting them off the hook. They bent their heads and ate some more, nipping the food off the fork with bared teeth and swallowing it with an exaggerated gulp. Giving them a stern look, Ada finally cleared away their plates. Betty cut the sponge and poured more Vimto. Molly and Shirley relaxed. There was little conversation, and alarmed by the silence I caught Betty's eye, pleading with her to do something.

'We could play Ludo,' she suggested, shrugging her shoulders at me. At last it was time for them to be taken home. They said polite goodbyes to Ada and went tripping gaily down the stairs after Betty, giggling and chattering as if released from school.

Ada closed the door and turned to me.

'I think that went very well.'

'Yes, I said, but I knew different.

Standing in line on Monday morning I could see Molly and Shirley up ahead pulling faces and giggling.

There was a strict rule of silence in the line, so I knew they would say nothing till break time.

When playtime came I made straight for my special part of the playground but Molly and her gang followed me, with Shirley at their heels.

'Her daddy stands on a wee stool, an' stirs this big pot; it's like a witch's cauldron. Is it a witch's cauldron?' Molly sneered. I ignored her.

Her gang hung on her every word.

'We had this funny Italian stuff fur oor dinner, an' her mammy made us eat it,' she told them.

'That was not Italian, that was stovies, and stovies are Scottish,' I was stung into replying.

'Stovies? Hiv you ever heard o' stovies?' she asked the gang. They shook their heads.

'That was made especially for you,' I shouted.

'Well we didnae like it, did we Shirley?' Molly said.

'It was like nothing I had ever tasted before,' Shirley made a face. 'Stovies! Stovies!' shouted the gang.

'It was funny, everything about you is funny,' Shirley said.

'Aye an' yon funny name yon boy called your mammy.'

'She's got a funny name?' said one of the gang'.

'Aye, but this wis a different name,' Molly said.

'Aye, what was that name?' Shirley prodded.

'I don't know what you are talking about,' I said.

Molly put her face close to mine.

'Is your mammy an' daddy trying tae kid on youse are no Italian?'

I was staggered that she had worked it out, and I shook my head.

'I don't know what you are talking about. If you didn't like my house you should not have come,' I said.

'We didn't want to come, it was only because my granny said we must,' Molly nodded as Shirley finished.

'Ma mammy wis nosey aboot your shop.'

I walked away. What would Ada say if she could hear all this, I thought.

Shirley shouted after me, 'and another thing. I didn't want you at my party, so there!'

'I didn't want to come,' I shouted back.

Having a double identity was difficult, and I was always on my guard that school and home would not mix, but now it was too late, Molly had worked it out, and she kept up her harassment.

So far the few friends I had made in Sandyford had no reason to doubt our name. The school broke up for the Easter holiday. As I swung down from the tram on the last school day, I noticed a group of boys idly kicking a can along Breadalbane Street, and as I crossed the road they caught sight of me. Bored with nothing to do I was an easy target for sport.

They surrounded me and grabbed my bag, tossing it from one to the other, laughing as I tried to grab it back, pushing me and tripping me up. The bag fell and burst open, spilling out my books.

The boys swooped on them, tossing them from one to another, reading aloud my essay, and shouting out my marks.

Suddenly one of them noticed my name on the front cover.

'I thought your name was Coutts.'

'It is.'

'Then this isnae your book.'

'It is, give it t o me.'

'This name is Co-c-coco-.'

Another boy laughed, 'let me see.' He took the book,' Cocozzzzz,' he laughed.

'Give me my book,' I screamed.

'It's no your name.'

'Just give me the book, give me all of them,' I pleaded.

He gathered up the books, stuffed them into the bag and ran off followed by the others.

I chased after them. I needed to get my books back before it was all round the street about the name.

The boys were too quick for me, and I gave up, a sharp pain in my chest from running. What would Ada say if all this came out? She was forever drilling into us to make sure we used the right name in the right place.

I thought it was daft anyway, everybody guessed that we were Italians, we certainly looked Italian.

I let myself info the house, slipping into the bedroom to change my uniform and hang it in the wardrobe for the holiday.

Lena was in the kitchen peeling potatoes, and she looked up, as I said I was going out.

'Be back in half an hour,' she said.

I slammed the door shut and ran down the stairs. Rounding the corner into Breadalbane Street I could see no sign of the boys, and I hung around waiting. After a while I spotted them coming down the street carrying a shoe box. Seeing me they ran towards me, surrounding me and pinning me to the wall.

'I want my school bag and my books,' I said.

'Only if you tell us something first.'

'What is your real name?'

'Coutts.'

'We don't believe you. Tell us or you will be sorry. We hiv somethin' in this box you willnae like.'

'Are you gonnae tell us?'

'Coutts, my name is Coutts.'

They all laughed. One opened the box. Inside was a dead rat. It lay on top of my books, and the boy lifted out the rat dangling it by the tail in front of my face. I cringed back against the wall, averting my face. One of them grabbed me by the hair, forcing my face round.

'Are ye gonnae tell us?'

I squirmed. I had always been terrified of rats, dead or alive.

'Coutts,' I said.

He pushed the rat right into my face. A quick flash of the worm and the beetle when I was younger, and Ada's words, 'even if you are afraid, you must not show it.'

I put up my hand and grabbed the rat. It felt cold and stiff, and I felt my stomach churning.

I pushed it with all my might into the face of my tormentor, and he jumped back spitting furiously, wiping his mouth with the sleeve of his jersey.

All the other boys were falling about laughing.

'Give me my books!' I shouted.

'Here!' he thrust the box at me I dropped the rat, took the box and fled. I was horrified that the thing had lain on top of my books, but at least I had them back. Of my schoolbag there was no sign, and I would have some explaining to do to Ada.

Dumping the box in the lobby I ran to the kitchen, straight to the sink, scrubbing and scrubbing at my hands, trying to wash the feeling of the stiff cold body from my hands.

'What's up?' asked Lena

'Nothing.'

She gave me a funny look but said no more.

Lying in bed that night I relived the whole thing, still feeling the stiff body of the rat, remembering its face distorted with the rigour of death.

Next day the boys passed me by without a word.

If only I could deal with Molly in the same way, but there was no rat, no beetle or worm to physically come to grips with.

Molly and her gang made me feel worthless, an outsider, an alien. I was something less, not fit to even live in the country, I belonged somewhere else, somewhere I had never even seen, and knew very little about, and it was official, for did not Eugene have to register every week, because he was this thing, this alien.

CHAPTER 16

If I had any talents, sewing and knitting were not among them. For Domestic Science we had one of the few lay teachers Miss Docherty, a short stout matron with wrinkled stockings, two pieces of charcoal for eyes and a mouth that was a thin line of disapproval, especially for me. If I had learned anything from Miss Docherty it was that she had a great hatred for all things German and Italian, the two being interchangeable in her eyes. She had been the only teacher in the school who had made Lena feel uncomfortable about her origins, and now she was bent on doing the same thing to me. At least she had to acknowledge Lena's expertise in sewing and knitting. Whereas I gave her lots of scope for derision as I was no needlewoman, and useless with two knitting needles let alone four, which was the scary prospect before me now, as we were 'learning' to knit a sock.

For several weeks I had laboured to get the thing started, my wool was wrinkled and wavy from the constant ripping out of my efforts. Finally after much slow painful effort I had come up with a respectable four inches of plain and purl, but now horror of horrors we were at the heel, what is more it was given as homework.

Travelling on the tram on the morning of our next lesson with Miss Docherty, I gazed in consternation at the sorry mess that was my heel. As we trooped into class passed the gimlet eyes of Miss as she sat perched like a vulture on her high stool, my heart pounded.

'Good morning Miss Docherty,' we chorused.

'Hands up any girl, who has not done her homework,' she rapped out.

Not a hand was raised, we were all too aware of the consequences of not doing our homework.

We may not have done it to the standard she wished, but all without exception had at least tried.

'Very well, take out your knitting, and we shall have a look at your efforts.

We reached into our bags, pulling out the sewing bags we had laboured so long to make, and unwrapped the socks.

There were furtive glances all around as each girl tried to compare her own efforts with those of her neighbour. The thing that hung from my needles bore no resemblance to a heel. Judging from the really good heels I could see, I suspected that some girls had enlisted the help of their mothers or grannies.

I had solicited the help of Aggie, who despite her poor eyesight could knit and crochet, but Ada had forbidden her to help saying it was my homework and I must do it myself.

'If you don't do it right, the teacher will show you how it should be done, at least you will have made an honest effort to do it,' Ada told me.

So now I sat, waiting for the moment when the sword of Damocles would fall upon my head.

Molly was sitting opposite me. She laid her well turned heel on her desk in full view of anyone who wished to look. She looked across at my desk as I tried to hide my tangled mess behind a book. It was too late, Molly had spotted it, and she began to giggle,

'Molly McCann would you like to share with us what you find so funny?'

'Please Miss, it is Madalena Cocozza's knitting,' she giggled again.

'Indeed, perhaps we should all see this specimen and judge for ourselves.'

She beckoned to me, 'bring it here girl.'

Reluctantly I walked towards her.

'Well hurry up child, it is hardly going top get any better if you walk slower,' she snapped.

The class giggled, and I felt my face go red.

Reaching her desk I placed the tangled mess in her outstretched hand. She turned it this way and that, laid it on the desk, and studied it for a moment or two. The eyes of the class were riveting into my back, and there was a deathly hush.

Miss Docherty held the sorry mess in the finger of one hand, raising it aloft for all to see.

'What is this?'

'Please miss, it is a sock,' I muttered.

'Speak up girl, what is it?'

'Please miss a sock.'

'A SOCK?' her voice rose in feigned surprise.

'Yes miss.'

She gripped the needles, pulling them apart to reveal the misshapen lump that hung from them, 'and this?'

'Please miss a heel.'

'Oh it is a HEEL!' she said as if having a sudden flash of understanding

'Yes miss.'

'Then I must tell you child this is like no heel I have ever seen.'

The class giggled.

She paused, playing to her audience, clearly enjoying my humiliation.

'Perhaps it is a Mussolini heel,' the tone was heavy with sarcasm.

Loud guffaws from the class, Molly holding her sides in exaggerated mirth.

'Go stand with your face to the wall, you imbecile.'

She pointed her stubby finger at the corner by the blackboard. I went feeling all eyes upon me and wishing the ground would open up and swallow me. As I gazed at the wall I consoled my self that at least I had, as Ada wanted, made an honest effort.

When the break came, I was last out of the classroom, and Molly and the gang were waiting for me. They followed me around chanting, 'Mussolini heel, Mussolini heel.'

I had never set eyes on Mussolini, but I hated him.

'Well, did you learn what you needed to know?' asked Ada later.

I looked at her blankly.

'I mean the sock heel; did the teacher tell you where you went wrong with the heel?'

'We didn't do knitting today,' I lied, 'we did sewing instead.'

'Oh well, I'm sure when she gets around to it, she will see that you tried your best, that's all anyone can do,' Ada said.

Betty came in, and glanced at my woebegone face.

'Who stole your scone,' she grinned.

I fled into the 'wee' room, slamming the door.

'What's the matter did something happen at school?' Betty shouted through the door.

'NO!'

'Best leave her alone, she will get over it whatever it is,' I heard Ada say.

I cried myself to sleep.

Travelling on the tram to school the next morning I wished I had the courage to run away, I did not want to go to school, it was all too much. Coping with the constant bullying from Molly and her crowd, and now the hostility of Miss Docherty, whose humiliating put down about the sock had caused other girls to point at me and giggle.

I wished I knew the rules, what to do to be normal, accepted, but I didn't. I was a left handed, vegetarian Italian, who could neither knit or sew, who was somehow responsible for all the things that Mussolini did, even though I was a child, had never seen him, and could not have stopped him if I tried.

Because Ada drilled into us that we must be honest, play fair, put others before ourselves, be prepared to give the last drop of our blood to save our way of life, I carried it all like a black dog on my back.

I was constantly scanning the newsvendors' placards, eager for news of Allied success. I sat in silence listening to the news from the BBC, and spent a long time on my knees praying for the Army, the Navy and the Air Force, for the prisoners of war, and the people who had been bombed. Ada said we should pray for the Germans too, as it was Hitler, and not the ordinary people, who was guilty of all the horror.

None of the other children seemed to worry about the war, occasionally someone would cry about their daddy or big brother, but mostly they grumbled they wished they could get more sweets, and not have to lug around the stupid gas mask all the time.

Betty usually took me to school in the mornings, and she was happy to sit upstairs on the tram and to let me have the window seat. I would stare out of the window at the people going about their business, heads down against the biting drizzle, or stare inquisitively into the tenement houses, with the soft glow of the gas mantle shining through the steamed up windows. Sometimes as the steam cleared I could see the glow of the range, an elderly man reading a paper, or children fighting over a piece of toast. I longed to be at home with Ada, for that part of the morning before she opened the shop, and sat drinking tea by the fire, our feet in slippers, and our thick red dressing gowns keeping us snug. Betty was always half asleep in the mornings, leaving me to my thoughts, which as we drew nearer to school, centred on Molly, and what she would do that day. As I swung down off the tram at the top of Ross Street, Betty would follow me down; say cheerio and cross the road to get the tram back home, leaving me to join the stream of girls heading down Charlotte Street.

My trials with the sock and Miss Docherty were not over, each week she would call me out before the class and ridicule my 'progress'. The sorry article got no better, and I couldn't hold the needles steady, so nervous was I about the whole thing.

My salvation arrived when Miss Docherty was struck down with flu, and one of the nuns took over her class.

She smiled and shook her head at my tangled mess, wisely decided knitting a sock was asking too much of me, and allowed me to try a scarf, with alternate rows of plain and purl, and my painstaking progress went unremarked.

At home I shut myself in the 'wee' room, which I had to myself until Aggie came when the shop closed.

I would draw or read, or stare into space, only emerging when called out for meals. I felt a lethargy in my bones, everything was an effort, getting ready to go to school was almost beyond me, and Ada was constantly shouting at me to hurry up.

The shop did not close till midnight, and often I was still up, sitting on my bed waiting for Ada. She never scolded me for not being asleep, but sometimes let me have a cup of tea.

Every night she brought up the days takings, which had to be counted and sorted for the bank. Ada did this at the kitchen table, almost always on her own.

One night she asked me to help her. We sat down at the table, and she poured the contents of a fat-bellied pot out on to the Rexene, pennies, halfpennies, threepenny pieces, florins, and half crowns. We began by separating them, raising them up in piles before counting them.

'You can count the pennies and halfpennies, here I'll show you what to do,' Ada said.

She toppled the piles and drew some towards the edge of the table, 'you do it like this.' She skimmed the coins into the palm of her left hand with the forefinger of her right, setting them up in little piles of twelve for the pennies, and twenty four for the halfpennies.

I soon caught on and happily worked until all the coins stood in rows of shillings.

'Good, now we roll them in newspaper like little sausages,' Ada told me. She placed the column of coins in a strip of paper and began to roll it tightly, twisting the ends and laying it on its side.

This I found a little difficult and the roll of coins would scatter across the floor, but Ada was patient with me and I soon got the hang of it. The ritual became a feature of each night, and my expertise grew to match Ada's. All the money was stored in a cupboard in the 'big' room, till there was sufficient to merit a trip to the bank.

Though I knew the money was kept there I had never seen inside the cupboard, it was kept locked and Ada had the only key.

One Saturday afternoon the shop was particularly busy, and Ada handed me the key to the cupboard and asked me to bring down some coppers and other change. Upstairs I had no difficulty opening the cupboard, or reaching the rolls of paper wrapped coins which were on a shelf about level with my chest. As I closed over the door to lock it, I noticed a box on the top shelf. Curious, I dragged a chair over and climbed up to reach the box.

It was an old King Edward cigar box, the colours faded, the corners soft and curled, and it seemed to be full of something and was stopped from springing open by a thick elastic band.

Carefully I slipped off the band, and as the lid sprang open I found myself looking at a lock of blonde hair tied with a blue ribbon, and lying alongside was a little white silk tassel, which I recognized as coming from a coffin. A chill ran through me as I realized these things belonged to Benny, my sister who had died five years before I was born.

I felt a pang of guilt, feeling I should not be seeing these things; these were surely among Ada's most precious possessions. Laying them back together I turned my attention to the other article in the box. This was what caused the box to be bound with a band. It was a fairly large black leather purse which was stuffed so full that like the box it too was bound with elastic, several bands each wound round again and again.

I lifted it out, weighing the heavy bulk of it in my hand. What could be in it that stretched it to its limit, the metal clasp unable to meet?

I began to struggle with the tight bands of elastic, careful not to break them, and the contents of the purse spilled to the floor. Stooping to pick them up I realized they were bundles and bundles of postal orders, each in turn bound with elastic.

Carefully I opened a bundle. Each counterfoil was for the sum of one pound, made out to Mrs E Cocozza, and a quick flash through the other bundles proved they were all the same, each for a pound, each to Mrs E Cocozza, and stretching back over many years.

'What's keeping you?' Ada's voice made me jump, and I rushed to the window. She was standing on the pavement looking up.

'I'm just coming,' I shouted back. I hurriedly bound the purse again, taking care not to stretch the bands to breaking point, set it back in place, and closed the lid of the box. The elastic that had held the box together seemed to be reluctant to stretch so much again, and as I struggled, I could hear Ada shouting again. I panicked knowing she would come up to find me if I did not get down soon. At last the band yielded, I scrambled up on the chair and replaced the box exactly, to fit the marks it had made in the dust, locked the door, and put the chair back by the window.

Ada was waiting for me at the foot of the stairs.

'What on earth took you so long?' she asked.

'I dropped a bundle and had to re-roll it,' I said. It was the first thing that popped into my head.

I kept out of her way for the rest of the day, feeling that if I had to look her in the eye she would know I had looked in the box. I realized that the box was the real reason the cupboard was locked, and why she was the only person to have a key.

The postal order stubs haunted me, what could they mean? Who was Mrs E.

Cocozza? They seemed to reinforce the atmosphere of secrecy; the hint that there was something too awful to talk about, something all the adults knew which had to be kept from me and my sisters. I thought of the whispered words between Eugene and Ada, always in Italian for added secrecy, the looks that passed between the aunts or the quick warning frown if I entered the room.

I made me afraid, as if I was walking on shifting sand, nothing and no one seemed to be what they really were, and nothing was permanent.

It seemed I could trust no one in my life, from my family to Shirley and Molly who had acted so sweetly to Eugene and Ada when they came to visit, and yet held everything up to ridicule to the rest of the gang.

I retreated even further into myself, miserable and afraid of what each day would bring.

Christmas was almost upon us, and it was a time I loved, but even that could not lift my gloom.

Ada and Eugene busy with the shop seemed unaware of my misery, but Betty who liked to tease me had noticed my disinterest.

'I know what will cheer you up,' she said, coming into the room and spilling coloured paper and scissors onto the bed.

'You can start your Christmas cards, and then we can make decorations.

I just sat and stared at the paper, taking no notice of the new crayons tumbled into my lap.

'Come on, let's make the chains first, I have nothing else to do,' she drew a chair towards the bed.

We made the chains, cutting strips of paper, shaping them into circles, linking them together with glue. We worked in silence for a while, and then Betty stood up.

'Right, I know there is something wrong, so you may as well tell me,' she said. She put her hand on my brow, 'you feel normal enough.'

'I'm all right!' I said shrugging her hand away.

'There is something bothering you, is it school, that awful Miss Docherty?'

'Leave me alone,' I jumped from the bed and ran into the kitchen.

After a few minute Betty followed, she said nothing.

Ada and Betty took turn about to collect me from school. I would walk to the tram stop, outside The Salvation Army hostel, and next to the rag store. Usually I had to wait, neither Ada nor Betty were good time keepers.

The men that came and went from the hostel were poor creatures, dirty, ragged, and unshaven. Often they were unsteady on their feet, sometimes from drink, sometimes because of the 'baffles' they wore on their feet, old worn things that had long lost any resemblance to shoes.

They didn't smell very nice either, and if they hovered about the door of the hostel I would move away, and stand looking into the rag store.

There were great piles of rags on one side and piles of bones on the other. The women would scramble up as if they were scaling a mountain, and perched on the top, they would begin sorting out the rags, tossing the different materials down to the floor, where other women bundled and tied them, then slung them in a corner.

The women working on the bones had made small hollows in which to sink their feet, to stop them from slipping. They too were engaged in sorting bones from pieces of metal and other objects which had no doubt been brought to the rag and bone man by children eager to get a balloon or some other trinket. I liked to listen for the rag and bone man, trundling along on his little cart pulled by a mournful donkey. Most times Ada had little in the way of rags as she would always find a use for things; when sheets were showing signs of wear, they would be cut in two, the frayed edges becoming the outside edge, the sturdier pieces sewn together up the middle. Shirts had their collars turned, socks were darned, and clothes were handed down. Only when a piece of material had clearly come to the end of its days would it be used as a duster, and finally passed to me to gain a balloon or ribbon from the rag man.

1 loved to watch the women in the rag store, mostly they were small and spare with skin like leather, round their heads they wore bright coloured turbans, round their waists hessian aprons over long tweed skirts. Sometimes they would sing as they worked; songs that were familiar to me, since Ada sang around the house too. 'Roamin' in the Gloamin', 'Keep Right On To The End of the Road', 'Annie Laurie', though singing this was sure to bring on the rain, Ada always said.

Watching them in the gathering gloom of a winter day passed the time for me as I waited for either Ada or Betty to take me home. Not long after Betty had quizzed me about what was bothering me, I came up to the tram stop to find her there, on what was one of Ada's days.

'Where's mammy?'

'She's busy, she asked me to come instead,' Betty smiled.

As we boarded the tram it was already dark. Since it was black-out, only the dim blue light allowed for the tram lit up the rail ahead, and from the shops muted glows pierced the gloom.

I made to go upstairs, knowing Betty took the chance to smoke, away from the prying eyes of Ada, but Betty held me back.

'We'll be getting off quite soon,' she said steering me into the lower saloon.

'Where are we going?' I asked.

'Christmas shopping,' she grinned.

'Woolworth and Lewis's?' I felt a stirring of excitement.

'Yes, if you like, I have some money, and I'll share it with you,' she laughed.

We peered out of the window, trying to see where we were. As we moved along London Road into Glasgow Cross and on into Argyle Street, there was the bustle of people on the streets, some with pinpoint torches already lit, but pointing carefully straight down, lest 'Gerry' was about in the sky.

We got off at Lewis's. Betty took my arm.

'We will go to Woolworth first. There is something I want to buy in Lewis's, but I don't want to carry it around too much,' she said. I loved Woolworth, except for the first row of counters as you entered the shop. There were rows and rows of artificial flowers, corsages for buttonholes and dresses, these were drenched in perfume that caught at your throat and stifled your breathing. I could not stand the onslaught of heavy scent and would scurry on as quickly as I could. Further in the store, was an Aladdin's cave of rubbers, pencils, rulers, jotters, pencil cases, and sharpeners.

Then all the household things, the handkerchiefs and gloves, the bottles of Californian Poppy and Evening in Paris. There were toys too, and the meagre sweets stall, which guarded its wares and demanded your coupons before yielding its treasures.

Betty shared out the money, and I went ahead eager to find a present for Ada and Eugene. Presents were always modest, and usually for Ada and Eugene the same every year at least from me.

For Ada, Evening in Paris, in its little distinctive blue bottle, and for Eugene pipe cleaners or handkerchiefs, which truth to tell he never used, usually using his sleeve, and incurring Ada's wrath.

No matter that the presents were the same each year, they were always accepted with smiles of delight and surprise.

I made my way to the perfume counter, agonising as I always did, whether I should chance a bottle of Californian Poppy, just by way of a change, but lost my nerve and settled for the tried and tested Evening in Paris.

Now to the handkerchiefs, and if I had enough money I would buy Aggie a handkerchief with her initial, although she never complained if the funds didn't run to such extravagance.

As I browsed I noticed the gents initialled handkerchiefs, running my eyes down the alphabet I came to the letter E - E for Eugene – and a slight shudder went through me. E for Eugene, Mrs E Cocozza, and the picture of the postal order stubs flashed into my mind's eye.

Mrs E Cocozza, suddenly I thought of the letters that arrived addressed to Ada, Mrs E Coutts, but really Ada was Mrs E Cocozza, so who was the other Mrs E Cocozza?.

I stood staring at the handkerchiefs.

'Finished?' Betty said at my elbow, making me jump. She looked at the handkerchiefs.

'Maybe it would be better to try something else, he has enough of those to start his own shop, and never uses them anyway,' she laughed.

'I know, too posh, he says,' I said turning away.

'Lets go to Lewis's, you might find something there. We left the store, and crossed the road.

I loved Lewis's most of all; it was a wonderland from floor to roof. Floor after floor was full of interest, it had escalators, and it was always a treat to travel up and down on these wonderful moving stairways. The Christmas displays of Lewis's windows always drew the crowds, and the toy department at Christmas time was the most wonderful experience, full of light and colour even in those dark days of black-out. Santa reigned supreme in his grotto, flanked by his ever faithful elves and fairies, all of them impervious to any threat from Adolph Hitler.

I followed Betty as she went from floor to floor, up each escalator, until they ran out; they only went so far in store as not every floor had them. To my surprise Betty kept going, leading me out to the stairs to reach the fifth floor. I looked around. Furniture and carpets. Was this what she was going to buy and hadn't wanted to carry around?

'What are you going to buy?' I asked.

'Wait and see. Come on,' she marched off to the far corner away from the furniture.

I was trotting to keep up with her. She stopped, turned to look at me and smiled, 'Look!' she said.

We were in pets' corner. I ran from rabbits to canaries, to budgies, to kittens, and finally to puppies.

'You are going to buy something here? Is it a budgie? The cats will get it,' I was bewildered.

'Well I thought you might like one of these. She tapped on the glass to attract the puppies.

'You mean, I can have a dog?' I was speechless.

'If you want one,' she laughed.

'What about mammy? What will she say?'

'It was her idea,' said Betty.

'Really? I can pick any one I like?'

'Yes, take a good look; take your time, because you will be the one who has to look after it.'

I crouched down to look at the little huddle of puppies that were asleep in a corner, piled one on top of the other.

I tapped gently on the glass, and one puppy opened one eye to look at me, but didn't move. I tapped again, and this time he sat up, and advanced toward me on unsteady legs.

'Oh that one. He wants to come home with us. He is lovely,' I said.

'He costs ten shillings,' Betty said.

'Have you got ten shillings? Oh we must have him, he wants to come,' I pleaded.

Betty laughed, 'Yes I've got ten shillings, and enough left over to buy a collar, a lead, and a dish.

I tapped the glass again, and the pup put its nose to the glass.

'Hello Rover,' I said.

Minutes later we were heading down the stairs, the little pup huddled inside Betty's coat, me skipping alongside her, carrying all his things.

'Well, you have picked a little beauty,' said Ada, stroking the little bundle who was shivering with fear.

'His name is Rover,' I said, knowing she would be pleased.

'Oh, Rover, my dog was called Rover, he was my very best friend,' Ada smiled.

'I know, I remember the stories about him,' I said. 'Rover was a golden retriever,' Ada said.

'This is a Collie cross,' said Betty.

'You mean it's a Heinz, fifty seven varieties,' laughed Eugene ruffling the pup's head.

'What do you mean?' I wanted to know.

'Take no notice, it just means the pup is not a thoroughbred, he is a cross between two breeds, but he is a handsome dog none the less, and will be just as faithful,' Ada said drawing Eugene a look.

'Ada put the pup down on the floor, and it stood on shaky legs, uncertain what to do.

'We bought the lead and things,' said Betty.

'You should have bought a mop as well,' laughed Eugene, as a little puddle spread across the floor.

Rover was installed in his cardboard box, specially cut down on one side for easy access. The next day the cats were introduced, Billy having been replaced by Smokey, who was now pregnant with Tiddles' kittens. They hissed their disapproval at the poor bewildered pup, but as the day wore on and he offered no threat to them, they went about their business, choosing to ignore him.

Within a week or two they were all sleeping together, and harmony reigned.

Aggie was delighted with the pup; she was a real sucker for animals of all kinds.

'Yer mammy got ye the dog tae try tae get ye oot o' the hoose,' she let slip one night as we lay in the darkness.

'We've a' been worried aboot ye keepin' tae the room a' the time,' she added.

I was totally surprised, but felt a warm glow at this news.

CHAPTER 17

Rover changed my life, just as Ada had hoped he would.

He was the passport to a much more normal life, and he was the entrance ticket to a group of boys and girls, all of whom fell under his spell. He was growing into a very handsome dog indeed, even Eugene was impressed.

More importantly he was the most placid, gentle creature you could hope to find, and as he grew, his tail grew into a huge plume, which he carried curled over his back and which was never still.

Arriving home from school, I would stand at the foot of the close and shout, 'send down the dog,' and within seconds a hurtling ball of fur would shoot out of the close, jump around with joy at the sight of me, his tongue lolling in a silly grin.

I soon found that Rover could be a liability as well as an asset, mostly when playing hide and seek, as his frantically wagging tail would give away my hiding place, but this was a small price to pay for the joy he brought.

Ada was so pleased with the change in me, she even relaxed the strict rule of profit before handouts, and allowed me to dispense the odd soft drink, or slider to a few select friends.

The girl I was most friendly with was Mary Murray. She had a little sister Jennifer, and Mary's parents were spiritualists, and held séances in their house.

Her mother was a thin pale woman, who lived on tea and cigarettes, while her father who worked as a brickie, lived on beer and boiled potatoes.

He liked the potatoes boiled till they were almost a soup, then he would sit with a huge plate of steaming 'broth', since the potatoes were never strained, supping away and finally mopping up with the heel of a plain loaf.

Most of us ate plain bread, which came uncut and on occasions we would buy pan bread, which though considered more refined was also uncut, and with rationing not always an option.

Mary told me about the trumpet her mother used to summon the spirits; this was kept in a locked cupboard in the room where the séances were held which also doubled as Mr. and Mrs. Murray's bedroom.

Mary promised to take me into the room and to show me he trumpet, since she knew where her mother kept the key. I was reluctant to take her up on this offer, yet curious at the same time.

I asked if Mary and her sister were allowed to attend the séances, but she said no, though they did listen at the door, and once had to flee, since the spirits had told her mother they were there.

Mary said her mother spoke about the spirit messages, often giving people news of their sons, fighting in the war. The spirits had also foretold that Germany would win the war, news that sent me into a panic, as I knew that it meant the end of civilization, or even the end of the world.

I told this to Mary, who didn't know what civilization was either, and anyway was not sure if the spirits always got things right, because once they had said Britain would win.

Nevertheless, I thought it wise to keep all this to myself, sure that if Ada found out, I would be banned from having Mary as my friend.

Instead I decided to take Mary up on her promise in the hope that I could allay my fears.

The first time I went into Mary's house I was a little shocked at how untidy it was, there were clothes both clean and dirty lying in heaps, on chairs and on the floor, the sink was clogged with dishes, and the grate choked with ashes. I said nothing, knowing it was not my place to comment.

I knew Ada would have been horrified, she insisted there was a place for everything and everything in its place, woe betide any of us who left things lying around.

Mary and Jennifer always had spotty skin, and I soon found the reason, watching Mary wash her face then reach for her father's sweaty shirt to dry it, and I told her she should use a proper towel.

'We don't have towels, anyway, I've always dried my face with whatever I can find,' she shrugged.

Mary and Jennifer each had a dream of what they wanted to do when they were grown. Mary longed to be a ballet dancer, Jennifer a singer, and even at their young age it was clear they each had a talent for their chosen career, but it was difficult to see where the money would come from to take them to their goal.

The day came when Mary signalled that her mother would be out all day, and we could have a look at the trumpet. I was torn between excitement and fear.

Though I had been in the house, I had never been in the séance room. Mary opened the door to reveal a room shrouded in darkness by the heavy curtains which covered the window.

There was a chill in the room, which I felt was not totally due to the January day outside.

We crept in, hardly daring to speak.

As my eyes grew accustomed to the dark I could make out a table with several chairs set round it. It was covered by a heavy chenille cloth, and alongside the wall there was a bed settee, which looked like it had been folded up hurriedly, as bits of sheets stuck out all round.

Mary made her way to the window and drew the curtains aside a little, and the daylight immediately eased the tension I was feeling.

'I better not pull the curtains right open, they sometimes fall down if you tug them,' Mary said.

'Where's the trumpet?' I asked.

'In here,' she fished around in the hem of one of the curtains, where the stitching was loose and came up with a key.

The cupboard was on one side of the fireplace, the door creaked as she opened it, and I took a step back.

'Are you scared?' Mary said.

'No.'

'Well I am,' she said.

'LOOK!'

She beckoned me forward, and began tugging at the heavy trumpet, trying to lift it down from the shelf.

'Help me,' she panted.

Gingerly I put out my hand, then more boldly as I saw Mary was really struggling, and between us we managed to get the solid brass monstrosity on to the table.

'I don't think I like it,' I said.

'Shush, it will hear you,' Mary whispered.

'What!'

'The spirits sometimes stay in the trumpet if mammy stops the séance too soon,' Mary said.

'I don't believe you,' I stepped away from the table.

'You don't believe in the spirits?' Mary was incredulous.

'I didn't say that,' I eyed the trumpet warily.

Mary peered into the dusty horn, 'ma mammy can hear the spirits, they come when she calls them,' Mary told me.

'But how does it work, do they speak through the trumpet or do they appear out of it?' I peered in after her, curious in spite of myself.

'Och I don't really know, I'm not allowed into the séance, but I've heard the spirits talkin', they talk through ma mammy.'

'Maybe she just makes it up,' I said.

'Ma mammy is a real, a real thingy-you know, the spirits definitely come. I told you they told her Jenny and me were listening at the door,' Mary said.

'Do you think there might be a spirit in there just now?' I asked.

'Maybe there is, we better get it back in the cupboard,' Mary said.

We both reached out to lift the thing, and then drew back.

'You lift it first,' Mary said.

'It's your trumpet,' I said.

'We need to get it back before ma mammy comes back.'

Maybe we could say the spirits got it out the cupboard,' I suggested.

'What! They could come out the cupboard themselves?' Mary looked alarmed.

'I think spirits can go where they like, through doors and everything, they could be all over your house.'

'Oh mammy, daddy,' Mary said and ran out the room.

I flew after her.

'Shut the door, shut the door!' Mary yelled.

I grabbed the handle and pulled the door shut.

'It won't make any difference, I told you, they can go through doors,' I yelled back.

We stood huddled together in the lobby, looking fearfully around.

There wasn't a sound to be heard, except for our breathing.

'We need to get the trumpet back in the cupboard,' Mary whispered.

'I don't wan to go back in that room,' I whispered back.

'But you said they could be anywhere.'

'I know but I think they probably stay near the trumpet, it's like a place they are used to,' I said.

'We need to go in there,' Mary urged.

'O.K.'

We crept back to the door and slowly turned the handle, but the trumpet hadn't moved. It still sat fat and solid on the edge of the table, its dusty metal glowing dull in the small shaft of light.

'I think they only come out at night, in the dark, I don't think they like light, so we need to open the curtains,' I said.

Mary moved towards the curtains, pulling me behind her.

She began to tug gently at the curtains, but they refused to move.

'They won't move,' she let go of the heavy curtain, shaking her hand as if it had something nasty on it.

'What if it is the spirits stopping me from letting the light in?' she asked.

I pushed her aside.

'Here let me have a go.'

I tugged at the curtains, but they refused to budge.

I dragged a chair from the table, climbed up, and I began to tug at the curtains more forcefully. They jerked along the rail, letting in more light. I kept tugging, pulling them further and further apart, I really wanted the spirits back in their dark trumpet as soon as possible.

Now that the room was flooded by daylight, we felt much safer.

We approached the trumpet warily, each grabbing hold of it at the same time, huffing and puffing it off the table and over to the cupboard.

Just as we got there the cupboard door swung shut.

We looked at each other in consternation.

'It doesn't want to go back in,' Mary gasped.

'It must go back in, we need to get out of here,' I hissed.

She rested her end of the trumpet on her knee and tried to reach the door, but she couldn't.

'We will need to put it down so that I can open the door,' Mary whispered

'We can't put it down, we will never lift it up again,' I whispered back.

We lowered the thing to the floor. It settled with a dull thud, we froze, was that a spirit?

Mary opened the door again, and as she stooped to lift the trumpet, the door swung shut again.

We stood rooted to the spot, staring at the trumpet.

'What are we going to do?' whispered Mary.

'Get the chair, open the door, and prop it open with the chair,' I was still whispering too, it seemed the right thing to do.

Mary dragged over the chair and gingerly opened the door, as if expecting some ghostly hand to pull it shut again.

We struggled painfully to lift the trumpet and manoeuvre it on to the lip of its shelf, and with one mighty heave we pushed it back in its place, and it clanged and donged as it hit the back wall.

I grabbed the chair; Mary slammed the door, and turned the key. PHEW!

We both stood palms flat against the cupboard door, trying to get our breath back. Inside the cupboard the last faint reverberations fell on our ears.

'Let's go!' I said.

'The curtains!' Mary whispered.

I nodded, dragging the chair back to the window, and climbing up.

'Get to the door, and open it, but stay in the room,' I told her.

She stood holding open the door, and the dim light from the fanlight above the outside door shone through.

I tugged at the curtains. They were as reluctant to close as they had been to open, but finally they were together, and I jumped from the chair, making a beeline for the door.

'The key! I need to put back the key,' Mary whispered.

'I'll keep the door open,' I whispered, pushing her towards the window. She flew across the room, and fumbled about at the hem of the curtain to find the loose stitching.

'Hurry up!' I hissed.

'I'm coming, give me a minute.'

At last she was back at the door, and we quickly drew it shut behind us. 'I wouldn't like to live in your house,' I told her.

'I just hope the spirits don't tell ma mammy what we did,' Mary said.

'Will we go out to play?' I said.

'Yes, come on,' she opened the door and we flew down the stairs as fast as we could.

For quite a few days afterwards, I kept looking behind me in case I had angered a spirit and it was haunting me. Mary said she felt spooky too, and we both agreed we would never go near the trumpet again. The spirits must have taken pity on us because Mrs Murray never did find out though she did say the hem of the curtain was more ripped than usual, but put it down to one of her clients catching it with a chair leg.

Occasionally I would ask Mary if her mother had any news of who would win the war, I really felt the spirit world would probably know the future, and I agonised over the outcome.

Ada of course kept up with all the news, and though she rarely went to the cinema, would ask Betty for a detailed report on the Pathe News bulletin. Ada had great admiration for General Montgomery; she was heartened by his appointment, saying he was the man for the job. Betty often took Lena and I to the pictures. It was a continuous show, so you could sit on to see the bit you had missed if you came in late. We saw 'In which we Serve' which made me cry, to see the poor sailors dying of thirst lost in the Atlantic.

We saw 'The Best Years of Our Lives', and 'Mrs Miniver' and Ada went to see these too. She impressed upon us the need to pray for victory, and she bought me a little Union Jack and a Lion Rampant.

She taught me all the war songs and the songs from World War 1. I would march around the house, waving my flags and singing at the top of my voice, Rover trotting faithfully at my heels, up and down the lobby, in and out of the rooms.

The whole family always stood for the National Anthem played by the BBC at the end of broadcasting, and when we went to the cinema we joined the audience who stood to a man till the last notes died away. I took my little flags out to show my friends and soon had them marching and singing up and down the street, Rover barking his contribution. But I was to find that the show of patriotism was not appreciated by everyone. It seemed Ada, though in a class of her own as far as patriotism was concerned, was not the only one who held such views. Finding Mary Murray out one day when I called for her, I crossed the landing to Helen Wilson's door to see if she would come out. The door was opened by Helen's mother, who on seeing me scowled. Feeling a little uneasy I politely asked if Helen could come out to play.

The scowl grew deeper, 'Helen will not be coming out to play, certainly not with the likes of you, whose father is an enemy to our people, and should be locked up instead of being free not only to make money from us but spy on our country for all I know.'

I stared at her, and not knowing what to say or do, I turned and clattered down the stairs. She came on to the landing and shouted after me.

'What gives you the right to go around singing British songs, that is what I'd like to know?'

I stumbled on, blinded by tears.

I ran home to tell Betty, she hugged me.

'Better not to say anything to mammy, better just try to forget about it all.'

'But it's not fair, we are all on the right side, mammy is always telling me to pray for all the soldiers and things.'

'I know, but if you tell mammy she will go round there and give that woman a piece of her mind, and it might make things worse,' Betty said.

So I said nothing.

The next time I saw Helen, she turned away from me; I knew her mother had told her not to play with me.

Soon there was a division in our little crowd, some siding with Helen, some quite happy to play with me.

Later Betty told me she had heard that Helen's uncle had been killed in the war.

'That would be her mother's brother,' said Betty, 'so I suppose we can understand why she reacted like that, but it was a shame she took it out on a little girl like you.'

The war would be over before Helen spoke to me again.

Mary and I were still friends, she still wanted to be a ballet dancer, and I wanted to be a writer.

We would sit on the steps of the Grove Stadium in Breadalbane Street, sometimes joined with a few others, boys and girls, and talk about what we would do when we grew up. The boys wanted to be soldiers, sailors, or pilots, and one boy wanted to go to America to live.

'My mother says Britain is finished, America is the best place to be.'

'That's not true, Britain is the best country in the world,' I would protest, hearing Ada's voice echoing in my head.

We all loved the 'Grovie'. It was a boxing stadium which was closed for the duration. We used its steps as our debating chamber, and its deep basement court for games and concerts, persuading our audience of reluctant younger children to sit on the long flight of steps which led down to the court.

Our little sketches and dances were religiously rehearsed; my sketches always had a patriotic flavour, where my oft rehearsed songs of both wars always featured.

The air raids continued, and we would gather in the dark dusty shelters to wait for the all clear. The women would knit and gossip, once I heard my name mentioned and picked up my ears to hear what they were saying. 'She's a funny wee lassie, far too serious fur her age,' said one voice. 'Aye but whit dae ye expect, they ur no like us, ur they, they're Tallies.'

'Och leave the wean alane, we're a' Jock Tamson's bairns,' a gentler soul put in. I tucked my head into my scarf, hiding my face, the familiar feeling of being different churning up inside me.

So the year wore on. We played Rounders, Kick the can, rambled trough Kelvingrove Park, and played on the swings.

Christmas came again, bringing soap in the shape of Snow-white, and her dwarfs, a book of children's poems and rhymes, a new penny and a shiny new pencil with a perfect point.

Ada made a dumpling, which seemed to owe something to grated carrot, but was hailed a success nevertheless. We sang carols round the cardboard crib, and Lizzie took Lena and me to midnight mass. We would walk home arm in arm, ready for the hot drink Ada would have ready.

Ada was rarely in a good mood at Christmas, she always grumbled it was too much on top of everything else she had to do, but she cheered up once it was over and she could prepare for the New Year.

To me she had more to do getting ready for the 'Bells', but it was a good Scottish tradition she said and it had to be observed in the proper manner. She would mobilize the whole family, each of us given a list of chores which had to done to her rigorous standards.

Every cupboard emptied and scrubbed from top to bottom, every mattress turned, but only after a good brushing and shaking, and if any foolish spider had dared to spin a web, it was immediately demolished. The clothes wore one day had to be washed by the next, each garment smoothed within an inch of its life.

Every debt was paid, every hurt mended.

The search would be on for a dark haired first foot, who must be a man, no one had ever heard of a female first foot.

On Hogmanay itself the activity never stopped. Ada, Eugene and Aggie busy in the shop, as customers stocked up on their Iron Brew, Vimto and Lime.

Ada would come up stairs now and then to see if we girls had everything in hand.

Eugene who did not drink himself would stand patiently in the queue at the licensed grocer's for his bottle of whisky, a pale sherry, and some beers. As a treat he would buy ginger wine and raspberry cordial for Lena and I, this too was his tipple for welcoming the year.

The festive table was sparse, rations had seen to that, but where there had been salmon, there was now paste sandwiches, and there was a little Black bun and Dundee cake that Betty and Ada had queued for hours to get.

We would all be spruced up and in our best clothes by eleven o'clock, Eugene having been sent upstairs early enough to ensure he had a 'proper' wash, which Lena was detailed to oversee.

Though Ada would close little earlier than usual it still left her very little time to get herself ready. She would wind her hair in steel curlers, strip to the waist to wash at the sink (the rest of us banished from the kitchen till she had finished).Between them she and Betty would wash and dress Aggie as if she were a doll. Eugene would sit shaking his head as Ada buttoned her blouse while Betty brushed her thin wispy hair.

'Eh, how is it she can work in the shop without any bother yet when she comes up here she is helpless.

Aggie's eyes would fill with tears at this jibe.

'Silencio!' Ada would shake her head at him.

Eugene would busy himself with the glasses and open the sherry bottle, placing them all on a tray on the sideboard for fear that any drop should be spilt on the snowy damask linen tablecloth.

As the clock hands crept round to twelve, Lena would give a final check to the table, put the kettle on, whip off her apron and slice the precious black bun.

Betty would be trying to get the curlers out of Ada's hair at the back while Ada would be fiddling with the ones at the front.

'You mind take that apron off or you will be wearing it all year round,' Ada would warn Betty.

A quick tug of the brush through her hair, a dash of lipstick and she was ready, just as the clock struck twelve, and the sound of revellers from all across Glasgow cheered each stroke of the Tron clock, and reached us via our little wireless.

Eugene would hand round the glasses missing me out, and seeing my crestfallen face would say he had forgotten to buy ginger wine.

'Och don't tease her, give her a glass,' Ada would smile. So we stood, glasses charged, drinking each others health, clinking glasses as we went.

A look from Ada would bring us all to attention as she raised her glass and said with a catch in her throat.

'Here's to GrannyGodRestHer, to MaryGodRestHer, and -- a pause while she drew a deep sigh, to my wee darling BennyGodRestHer.

It was a ritual carried out every year, and for a moment or two we stood silently raising our glasses towards heaven.

'Eh, a wee toast to the future and here's a wee song,' Eugene would smile.

He would refill the glasses and as he went round he would burst into song, 'Jist a wee doch-an'-doris', and as he went his voice got louder and louder. Rover would sit up, throw back his head and howl. We would cover our ears and fall about laughing.

'Come on, it's New Year!' Ada would say, her clear soprano taking over with,

A guid New Year, tae ain an' a'
An' mony may ye see
Frae noo an' a'
The years tae come
Oh happy may ye be
An may ye hae nae cause tae mourn
Or sigh or shed a tear
Tae ain an a'
Baith great an' sma'
A Happy Guid New Year.

We would sip at our drinks and wait to see who would be our first foot. One year it had been Hammy, complete with coal, salt and a wee slice of his mother's black bun.

Usually it was Mr. McCormack from the top landing, soon to be followed by his four sons and four daughters, and finally Mrs McCormack who was never ready for the 'Bells' on account of having so many children to oversee.

Eugene would open the door to find a beaming Mr. McCormack, who had clearly anticipated the 'Bells' and sampled the Irish whisky, from the now half empty bottle he clutched in his right hand, the left hand clutching a piece of coal.

'God bless all in this house,' he would intone in his soft Irish brogue. Eugene would embrace him heartily to the great danger of the precious bottle crashing to the ground.

'Come in! Come in!' Ada would cry, and in they would troop with much hugging and hand shaking, as if they had just arrived from the other side of the world, rather than two floors up, and had only seen us less than two hours ago in the shop.

No sooner had the McCormacks arrived than there was a knock at the door and the Misses Murray our immediate neighbours would saunter in, the door now propped open, the Gillans, and old Mrs. Davis, a rotund Jewish matron, would slowly advance into the room, shaking hands as they went.

Old Mrs. Davis would sip a cup of tea and tell us as she did every year, that this was not her new year but she was very happy to share it with us, and she would begin to sob quietly for her two sons, lost somewhere in Germany, fearing she would never see them again

'Eh this is no time to weep, it is time for celebration, maybe this will be the year we win the war,' Eugene told her.

'Amen to that,' Mr. McCormack raised his glass.

Eugene would grab a beer bottle and standing in the middle of the floor would bellow out his party piece,

An old Bass bottle
Washed in by the sea
An old Bass bottle
Came rolling in to me

And inside that bottle
Was a message with these words
Whoever finds this bottle
Will find the beer all gone

Loud applause and cries of 'Encore! Encore!' would set him off again inviting all to sing along.

Everyone had to do 'a turn', Mr. Mac would sing 'Kathleen Mavourneen', in his soft lilting voice, and then his jolly little wife would oblige with 'Knees up Mother Brown'.

Ada would sit and smile benignly, waiting her turn. It was generally acknowledged that she was the finest singer of all. She insisted that she had been taught to sing, and when the company called her she would take her place before them, back ramrod straight, hands clasped lightly in front of her midriff, this being the 'proper stance'.

The request was always for 'a good Scots song'.

Come ye by Athol?
Lads wi' yer philobegs
Doon by the Tummel
And banks o' the Garry
Saw ye the lads, wi' their bonnets
And white cockades?
Leaving the mountain
To follow Prince Chairlie
Follow him, follow him
Wha widnae follow him?
Lang have we lo'ed and trusted him fairly
Chairlie, Chairlie
Wha widnae follow him?
King o' the heilin' hearts
Bonnie Prince Chairlie.

She would sing all the verses and with a sweep of her hands invite the rest of us to join in the chorus.

Few of us could reach the high notes and Ada's clear soprano would soar to the ceiling.

There was genuine heartfelt applause for Ada, she really did give a stirring performance.

Betty would invite the company to have tea and partake of the goodies, which they good souls that they were had added to. So an hour or so would pass and then the Misses Murray would retire having had their quota of excitement for another year.

The rest of us would set out to visit more neighbours, Rover and all.

There was always a party at the McSween's, 'good God-fearing Highland folk' Ada called them. With the father at sea it was left to Mrs McSween to ensure her family of four girls and twin boys walked the straight and narrow path their father would want them to.

The boys were a year younger than Lena, they would make up a foursome when Lena and their older sister Morag went dancing or to the Ceilidhs in the Highlanders Institute.

That year, the second year in the shop was the first time we had joined in the fun. We could hear the accordion and fiddle as soon as we entered the close, upstairs on the first landing the McSween's door stood open to all comers.

Eugene called out 'Happy New Year', and immediately we were ushered in, people jumping up to give Ada and Aggie a seat.

Rover, a bit put out by the crowd, slunk away under the table, head on paws, eyes swivelling this way and that.

I was keen to see the famous square dumpling, which Lena had told us Mrs. McSween boiled in the enamel bread bin.

It sat square and ginger coloured, the steam still rising, and the smell filling the room.

The younger McSween girls and various cousins were queuing up each thrusting a plate eager for a slice.

Mrs. McSween a tall well built woman, her salt and pepper hair tied back in bun, a small cameo brooch pinned at the throat of her black blouse, stood bread knife in hand ready to cut the dumpling.

'You must all make a wish as the first slice is cut.' she smiled.

We stood eyes shut tight, for a fleeting second fearful someone would get in before us. Soon we had scrambled on to the blanket covered sideboard backs against the wall legs stretched out in front of us eating the steaming hot dumpling with our fingers.

There was little room for dancing, but the music drew people to their feet. I watched as Lena joined in the dance with her special friend Morag and her older sister Kirsty, Lena's dark hair and sallow colouring contrasting with the McSween girls creamy skin, green eyes and flaming red hair. Round and round the dancers went, in a Paul Jones, Lena dragged a reluctant Eugene to his feet and soon he was being carried along by the spirit of the evening.

The music grew fast and furious, the dancers changing partners rapidly. Suddenly as Kirsty came to face Eugene he caught her to him and kissed her full on the mouth. She struggled and pushed him away, the music had stopped and people were staring not quite knowing what had happened. We children though innocent of the implications knew something was very wrong. Ada leapt from her chair delivering a stinging blow across Eugene's face. He fled through the open door, Ada after him, the sound of their staccato footsteps clear on the stone steps. Lena was dragging me down from my perch, pushing an almost hysterical Aggie before her, Rover was cowering at our heels tail between his legs. It all seemed to happen in a heartbeat. I stole a look back into the room, Kirsty was sobbing her face in her hands, Mrs McSween seemed to be holding back her son from following us, and everybody in the room seemed to be talking at once. We hurried down the stairs trying to catch up with Ada and Eugene, who were standing at the foot of our close, Eugene head bent ,hands outstretched saying, 'sorry', over and over again.

Ada was demanding an explanation, her voice steely with rage, and seeing us she waved us away saying, 'leave us , just leave us.'.

We went upstairs, Lena was shaking, great tears running down her cheeks, I felt numb.

Aggie her eyes dancing in her head said with relish, 'yer mammy will never let him in the hoose again.'

'Don't say that I don't want daddy to go away for ever,' I sobbed.

'I hate him, I hate him, how can I ever go back round there, I've lost my friends and it is all his fault,' Lena gulped.

'You still have me and Rover,' I said giving her a hug.

Ada came in she looked grim, snatching up the kettle she filled it at the tap, turning it on full blast.

'We might as well have a cup of tea, they say that is the answer to everything,' she patted Lena on the shoulder, 'your father is a fool, a stupid, stupid fool. You won't be seeing him for a while, I for one could not bear to see his face.' Aggie nodded with satisfaction.

'What am I going to say to Morag and Kirsty?' Lena wailed, 'it's not as if he has the excuse of being drunk.'

'We need to go round and apologize, no matter how difficult that will be, we have to do it,' Ada said.

'No I couldn't,' Lena shuddered.

'You can and you will but no alone I will be with you,' Ada told her.

'Now we all need to get some sleep, things always look better in the morning. Some start to the New Year this is.'

When I woke next day none of the beds had been slept in.

The house was quiet. I went back down the lobby, and pushed gently on the half open kitchen door. Rover came straight to me, his tail still down but the tip wagging in welcome.

Ada stood at the stove stirring porridge, and though I could not see her face, the set of her shoulders told me she was still furious.

Lena and Betty sat head in hands on either side of the table.

There was no sign of Eugene.

I crept in and took my place at the table, Lena looked up and smiled.

'Where's daddy?' I whispered.

She shrugged and spread her hands.

Ada turned and seeing me, told me to set out the plates, which I did at once.

She spooned the porridge into each plate. No one said a word, as we picked up our spoons and ate, eyes fixed on our plates.

Betty gathered up the plates, placing them on the draining board, and filled the huge kettle and set it on the gas hob, while Lena livened up the fire to toast the bread.

She speared the first slice on the toasting fork, looked up and smiled.

'Toast or 'Cocozza' toast?'

"Cocozza' toast,' I said graceful for the normality.

'Cocozza toast' was bread toasted on one side only, we all liked the contrast of one crisp side and one soggy side.

The kettle boiled, Betty made the tea.

Ada sat gripping her cup, lost in thought, and the rest of us sat in silence, not daring to speak. Aggie pushed open the door, she had pulled on her clothes without washing, her hair a tangled mess.

She looked round the room, 'where is he?'

'What do I care?' Ada snapped.

One by one we left the table and busied ourselves in our rooms. It was three days before we saw Eugene again. Though she could not tell us where he had been, Aggie let slip that Ada had insisted he go round to Mrs. McSween and apologize for his conduct.

'What happened?' Lena asked anxiously.

'She accepted his apology, but she wouldn't let him talk to Morag.' 'I'm not surprised,' Lena said.

'Mrs McSween said if Morag's father had been there he would have knocked your daddy down,' Aggie was warming to her subject. He has ruined everything, I will never be able to face them again,' Lena said.

We took our cue from Ada when Eugene returned. She behaved as if nothing had happened, at least when we were around, the incident was never referred to again.

It was hardest of all for Lena, where Morag and the twins had been a big part of her life, now there was no contact at all. Ada encouraged Lena to try to find new friendships, and gradually she became friendly with Geena who lived nearby. Yet we knew it hurt Lena to have Morag pass her in the street without acknowledgement.

CHAPTER 18

Though on the surface everything was fine between Eugene and Ada it was clear to all of us that she had not quite forgiven him for his behaviour over the New Year. As the months progressed the news from the front was not good and when this happened the Bath gang saw it as an excuse to cause trouble for the 'bloody Tallies'.

Night after night they marched up and down outside the shop singing at the top of their voices.

> 'Hello, hello, we are the Billy boys
> Hello, hello, we are the Billy boys
> Up to our knees in Tally blood
> That's what we enjoy
> We are the Billy, Billy, boys.'

They would jostle customers, turning them away, telling them not to buy off the F*** Tallies.

Ada would burst out the door demanding they go away.

'See that name above the door, that's Scottish, that's me, go away and leave us in peace.

They would laugh and jeer at her.

'Whit aboot wee Tally Joe?' they would shout.

Eugene was really nervous and he kept to the back shop as much as possible.

Ada decided it would be better if he stayed away all together. It was an arrangement that suited them both, if he was not around all day every day, perhaps Ada would get over her anger.

He decided to go into business for himself.

He rented a little workshop in Stobcross Street near Anderston Cross.

Here he would spend hours making terrazzo doorsteps. At weekends I would go down to watch him as he worked. I loved the smell of the place, a strange mixture of wet cement and wood shavings, a smell that would always evoke Eugene to me.

He made doorsteps in three designs, a single diamond shape in the centre, its edges lined in black, a diamond set in the centre flanked by other smaller diamonds on either side, and three diamonds joined by a black line.

The terrazzo came in white, pink and cream.

There was not a lot of demand for terrazzo doorsteps and he was forced to travel far and wide to find his customers. Day after day he would load a canvas bag with samples and take the tram to its furthest terminus, Bearsden, Milngavie, Glasgow's affluent outskirts.

He found few takers, but realizing there was a demand for vestibules and garages he began to offer quotes.

Here he was more successful, and soon found he needed to hire two men to help cope with the orders.

He had no real business sense and underestimated his overheads.

He was running the business at a loss, making nothing for himself.

Ada tried to help him, but he would not listen to her, and it became just another bone of contention.

She, meantime, was having to cope with increasing trouble and threats of attack.

Determined to put a stop to it, she armed herself with a shillelagh winding the black leather strap round her wrist, and concealing the rest up her sleeve.

'I'll sort them out, they are a bunch of cowards, and all of them have a big yellow streak down their backs.'

I was really intrigued by this and kept a sneaky eye on the gang whenever I passed them, but to my great disappointment I never saw it.

Eugene was alarmed when he saw the shillelagh.

'That will only get you into trouble,' he warned.

'What do you want me to do? They are affecting trade, and I need to put a stop to it, show them I'm not afraid of them.'

She was as good as her word, the next night they were there again, singing 'The Sash' and 'We are the Billy boys', swearing at the customers, and coming into the shop and causing mayhem.

Ada launched herself among them, swinging her baton right and left, cracking a few skulls. They fled the shop, congregating at the corner of Breadalbane Street chanting and threatening.

Ada employed that shillelagh time after time, even tackling Butcher and breaking his nose.

He made threats that he would have her charged with assault but knowing there was no love lost between himself and the police he never went through with it.

The broken nose did not enhance his already ugly face, but fate had not finished with him yet.

For days the gang had warned Ada that she didn't know what was going to hit her.

'Big Bill is coming on leave, he'll soon sort you oot, ye'll no' scare him wi' yer bloody stick.'

'Is that right? Well we'll see, the bigger they are the harder they fall,' Ada told them.

'Who is this 'Big Bill' anyway?' Ada asked Hammy the next time he came in.

'He is a bad one, the worst of the lot,' said a fearful Hammy.

'Well he is coming home on leave so they tell me, so we will see what he gets up to,' Ada said.

'He's in the Navy, so is his younger brother, but he's a' right. They call him 'Babyface' because he looks a lot younger than he is,' Hammy was a mine of information.

Eugene was really concerned, 'It's no right for only women tae be here tae face them, ah better stay around.'

'You would be no help, you can't stand up to them, it will only make things worse if you are here,' Ada said.

'Aye ah suppose,' Eugene agreed.

Aggie was the first to hear the commotion; she peered out the door, and then flew into the back shop to find Ada.

'There is a terrible fight goin' on, the whole gang are fighting each other an' Butcher is being attacked by a another big man.'

'Is this 'big Bill' I wonder?' Ada said.

As she made her way t the front door, it suddenly burst open and three gang members carried Butcher in, flinging him none too gently on a bench.

'Gies a towel or somethin', he's in a bad way.'

'Get him out of here, I don't want any trouble,' Ada said. 'Get a F**** towel, his heid is split open,' they shouted.

Ada threw a towel at them. Butcher was bleeding badly.

'I want him out now, you can fight your battles outside,' she shouted again.

The door burst open again and a giant of a man thrust himself forward, struggling to get free from three others who held him back.

'Let me get the F*** B***,' he shouted catching sight of Butcher.

He threw off his restrainers and caught Butcher by the throat, shaking him like a rag doll. Butcher half blinded by the blood streaming down his face tried to land a punch, but slumped back, and the gang members fled as the big man threw them aside and whipped out a razor.

Ada dashed past him, blowing her whistle with all her might to summon the police. Butcher was yelling in agony as the man slashed again with the razor. Ada now behind the big man and brought her shillelagh down on his head.

It stopped him in his tracks for a second, turning he threatened her, but she just blew and blew on the whistle.

'Come oan, big man, the polis are comin,' the gang shouted to him.' He staggered out of the shop, and they gripped his arms and dragged him away.

Butcher lay moaning, and Aggie was in hysterics.

'Pull yourself together, the police will be here soon,' Ada said, trying to get her breath back.

She went outside again, peering through the darkness hoping to see some sign of the police.

At last the 'Black Maria' loomed out of the darkness.

'Am I glad to see you,' Ada told the first policeman out.

'What's been going on?' he asked.

She told him.

'Rogue that he is, he needs a doctor,' Ada said looking at the bloody mess that was Butcher's face.

The policemen took him away, one officer staying behind to get the full story from Ada.

'So big Bill is back, none too happy about Butcher muscling in on his gang.'

'He has the strength of a bull, he threw the rest off him as if they were dolls,' Ada said.

'Aye, and you cracked his head, you tell me, not a good idea, not a good idea at all,' warned the policeman.

'How else could I stop him, he would have murdered Butcher, and I did not want that to happen in my shop,' Ada answered.

'Nevertheless, we will need to keep an eye on things, big Bill will not forget what you have done in a hurry.'

'I'll just have to cross that bridge when I come to it,' Ada smiled grimly.

'You have made things worse woman, what were you thinking about?' Eugene said.

There was no time to think; I couldn't let that kind of thing go on, could I?'

'That copper is right, the big fella will no' let you away wi' that.' 'Well time will tell, he can't be on leave forever, and if the Navy hear about this he will be in big trouble,' Ada told him.

'Don't tell me you would report him to the Navy?'

'Just try and stop me.' Ada said.

Ada was on the alert for any sign of big Bill, and sure enough, several days after the fight he came swaggering into the shop. He was quite drunk and stood leaning on the counter demanding cigarettes. Aggie handed them over and held out her hand for the money.

'Ye can whistle fur it,' he sneered.

'Are you refusing to pay?' Ada said coming from the back shop.

'You owe me, it was you that attacked me, the cigarettes are just a start, believe me.'

'We don't give things for free in this shop, if you want cigarettes you will pay for them, and as for me attacking you it was no more than you deserved. I have no time for Butcher but I was not going to stand for that behaviour in my shop,' Ada said, feeling the reassuring weight of the shillelagh at her side.

He smiled and pocketed the cigarettes.

'Ah'll have some for ma mates as well,' he told Aggie.

'Get out, right now before I call the police,' Ada warned.

He lurched towards her and she pulled out the baton.

'You're no scared o' me, ur ye?' he mumbled.

'NO'

'Well too bad, cos you are due a lesson.' He grabbed a bottle from the counter, and smashed the neck off, holding it to Ada's face.

'You touch me with that and I will report you to the Navy, they will sort you out,' Ada said.

He stood swaying in front of her the bottle still in his hand, then turned and walked out the shop.

'He never paid for the cigarettes,' Aggie said.

Hammy stood cracking his knuckles nervously; he had just listened to Aggie's lurid version of the fight between Butcher and big Bill.

'Has big Bill been in since?' Hammy asked.

'Oh aye, he threatened Eadie, though she stood up to him,' Aggie told him.

'What happened? Did he hurt her?'

'No, he went away, we were surprised,' Aggie said.

'They say he is scared o' his wife, and she is only about five feet tall,' Hammy laughed.

'How dae you know that?'

'Ma cousin knows her, she is really a nice wee woman, and ma cousin says he is OK when he is sober.'

'Ah don't think that can be true,' Aggie said.

Things had been quiet for a few days. Eugene, his work slacking off, was back to his usual task of making the mixture.

Suddenly the door opened, in walked big Bill Mathieson, and Aggie jumped. She stayed behind the counter, ready to fly for help.

He looked around him, then sat down heavily on a bench chin on hands staring into space.

Aggie edged her way through to the back shop. 'It's him!' she told Eugene excitedly.

'Who?'

'That -- that big Bill fella, he is in the shop.'

'See what he wants,' Eugene went on stirring.

Reluctantly she went to the table where big Bill sat.

'Dae ye -- want something?'

'Gie's a cup o' Bovril and two cream crackers.'

She hurried through to Eugene, 'he wants Bovril and cream crackers,' she said as he had just demanded the money in the till.

'Well if that is what he wants, you better get it quick.'

She carried the Bovril through, her hand shaking so much it spilled into the saucer, and nervously she put it in front of him.

He sipped the Bovril and made a face.

'Ah need pepper.'

She burst in on Eugene again.

'He wants pepper!'

'Aye well, folk usually ask for pepper, don't start imagining things.'

'You think it's just for the Bovril?' Aggie asked.

'Is he drunk?' Eugene asked.

'Ah don't think so.'

'Well then, according tae Hammy he is supposed tae be OK when he is sober, so jist keep an eye on him, an' you better get oot there wi' that pepper before he gets angry.'

Aggie took the hint; she placed the pepper on the table and backed away.

Big Bill looked up, 'dae ye no waant payin'?'

He fished in his pocket and threw down some coins.

Aggie reached for them and vanished behind the counter.

He finished the drink and sat back.

Aggie never took her eyes off him.

'Whit are you lookin' at? Ah'm waitin' fur somebody right!' he growled.

She nodded.

He sat on.

Almost half an hour later three men joined him. Aggie had never seen them before and they were scruffy and unkempt. They sat huddled together speaking in low tones. She hurried through to Eugene.

'Ah don't like the look o' that three, an' they look as if they are plannin' something,' she said.

'Jist keep an eye oot. If there is trouble, the whistle is hanging up, and we can get help. Eadie will be in later on.

'Ah wish she was here right now,' Aggie told him.

She took up her place behind the counter again; the men were playing cards for money.

It wasn't allowed, but she was too afraid to say so.

'Do you want to order anything?' she called from behind the counter. They ignored her.

They played on, buying nothing. Customers came and went, some raising their eyebrows at the card game, but saying nothing.

Aggie was hopping from foot to foot. The men were getting loud, and one or two had produced bottles of beer, passing them round the table

She went to complain to Eugene, 'Eadie wouldn't let that go on.'

'Eh, let them be, there is too many of them to tackle,' Eugene went on stirring.

'It's no right, it's jist no right!' Aggie's eyes danced excitedly. 'Eadie will be here soon, she'll sort it out,' Eugene said complacently. 'She will no' be very happy wi' you either,' Aggie warned.

Eugene shrugged.

The game went on, the money piling on the table. Aggie grew more and more agitated, and she watched the door hoping Ada would walk in and put a stop to it.

When the door did open it was not Ada but Bill's wife. She came in looking around her, clearly not in the best of tempers, and catching sight of Bill hunched over his cards, she flew at him, whipping him round to face her.

'So this is where you are, drinking and playing cards, when I'm waitin' like an idiot for ma housekeeping money.'

'Ah wis comin', ah wis comin',' he stammered.

'When?'

She tugged at him, and he allowed himself to be pulled from the seat.

Towering above her he stood shamefaced as she berated him.

The men laughed, urging him to tell her to go away.

He threw his cards on the table, 'ah better go, see ye around.'

'Aw come oan, big man, we've still tae finish the game.'

The little woman pushed Bill before her.

'The game is over; he goes back tae sea tomorrow, so ye can forget it.'

Sheepishly he went out raising his hand in a final salute.

Aggie burst in on Eugene.

'What now?' he asked.

'He's away, his wife came and gave him a piece of her mind, she told him to go and he went.'

'Great!' Eugene heaved a sigh of relief.

'Ah can hardly believe it,' Aggie shook her head.

She went back to the counter; the three men had gone leaving only the cigarette stubs and empty beer bottles.

She was just clearing these up when Ada appeared. Aggie could not wait to tell her the whole story.

'Seems Hammy was right, who would have believed it,' Ada said.

'He is due back tae his ship, that means we will no' be seein' him for a while,' Aggie said.

'Good riddance. I wish Butcher was at sea too, come to think of it we haven't seen him since that attack.'

'He is probably scared of that big Bill,' Aggie suggested.

'I wonder if he knows big Bill is scared of his wife,' Ada smiled.

She went through to the back, Eugene was patiently stirring away.

'Heard you had some trouble,' Ada said.

'Och no, nae bother at a',' he said.

Word seemed to have reached Butcher that the coast was clear, and within days he was back again as mean and angry as ever.

'His face is a real mess,' Hammy said, as he reported the first sighting 'Well if he is looking for trouble, he will get what he deserves,' Ada warned.

The beat Bobby came in to tell Ada that there were several ships just docked at Finnieston. 'They are a mixed bunch so there might be trouble.'

'Thanks for the warning, I welcome the business, but I don't want trouble, I have had enough of that,' she said.

'There is a Russian ship in, I think it is the first we have had, at least for a long time. They like a good drink, and some may get a bit too merry, or worse,' the policeman said.

As the war wore on the number of foreign visitors to our shop grew.

Poles, Russians, Yugoslavs, men from New Zealand, Australia, Canada and America. There were men from the merchant fleet, and Indians and lascars.

With the English speakers there was little difficulty, but few if any of the others could manage to make themselves understood, resorting to hand gestures and facial expressions.

The Indians were delightful; they varied between fluency and pigeon English.

Eugene, like Tina and Da-dee believed in open house, he liked to feed people, show them hospitality. Often when summoned for his tea by Ada's banging on the floor, he would appear with five of six bemused young sailors in tow, 'poor lost lads' who he had invited to join him in a meal.

Ada would scuttle round trying to rustle up enough food, she would skim some from each of our already sparse plates, and we would shove up with good grace. We became quite used to seeing faces of all colours seated at our table.

Rarely did we see the same face twice, they really were, 'ships that pass in the night'.

One exception was Charlie, a ship's cook. He was a jolly rotund little Indian, whose ship had docked at Finnieston several times. He and Eugene had become fast friends, and would laugh uproariously at each other's jokes, even if they did not wholly understand them.

He appeared a week before my ninth birthday, bearing a gift for Ada, which was the most hideous Toby jug. Ada hated it on sight but to her credit received it with such grace, as if it was a rare pearl.

Eugene decided I should have a party. Ada was not pleased, where was she going to get enough food for a party, she complained.

'Och the family will chip in,' Eugene said complaisantly.

So it was arranged, the aunts told of the proposed event at their next visit. Charlie too, had been told by Eugene, who had obligingly held up nine fingers to tell my age.

'You have a 'jolly'?' asked Charlie.

'Eh? Oh aye, a wee party,' laughed Eugene.

'Ah this I see?' Charlie beamed.

'Oh aye, you are very welcome,' Eugene told him.

Charlie beamed again, leaning over to whisper in Eugene's ear, while he cast a wary eye on Aggie who made her disapproval plain.

Eugene clasped him on the shoulder, nodding and smiling.

Later, when Charlie had gone, Aggie asked what the whispering had been about.

'Och he just asked if he could bring his brother, I said OK, don't see a problem with that,' Eugene said easily.

'You better tell Eadie what you've done,' Aggie warned.

'Not at all, not at all, it will be fine, what difference will two more people make?' he told her.

Preparations for the party went ahead. Betty looking out the crepe paper to decorate the table. Ada bemoaning the fact that yet again there could be no birthday cake.

Once she had accepted the party idea, she was happy to try to make it a success. She sent off a letter to Mary and Jimmy, and her brother Glen and his wife Aggie. 'Granton' Aggie we called her to distinguish her from Aggie, or 'common or garden Aggie' as Betty impishly called her. The neighbours would be there too, and Eddie Gillan who was home on leave, looking very smart in his HLI kilt.

Every chair in the house, plus some borrowed from the Misses Murray who lived next door, was crowded into the big room.

Pride of place was given to Da-dee, as the esteemed head of the family.

Joe and Pat were there, their presence suffered by Ada for the sake of Tina and Famie.

Pat was not a drinker, one of his few virtues in Ada's eyes. Joe was a fairly moderate drinker but teamed with Eddie as he had been for most of that day, he was 'three sheets to the wind' by the time the party had got going. He and Eddie with much palaver and giggling had presented me with a bunch of artificial violets. They were dusty and faded and had, it transpired, been lifted from a cardboard box full of similar stuff outside Woolworth's back door.

I was unsure how to respond to this 'gift', but Ada was not. She was incensed that two grown men had been so silly, and had insulted me, and through me, her, in such a manner.

Eugene dismissed the episode by calling them 'daft buggers' and put it all down to the fact they had spent so much time in a pub, and had 'puggled' their brains.

Betty seeing my dilemma about what to do with the 'flowers' took them from me and put them in the ash can.

Famie gave me a hug and my real present of embroidered handkerchiefs.

Joe's reputation was not enhanced in Ada's eyes.

The family had contributed to the birthday tea just as Eugene said they would. The table though still somewhat sparse was looking very festive, thanks to Betty's ingenuity with various colours of crepe paper.

As I opened my presents under the indulgent eyes of the aunts, I found pencils, rubbers, rulers, a tin pencil case, ribbons and slides for my hair, fancy shaped soap, and colouring books. My delight in these was genuine. Suddenly there was a commotion at the door. Lena burst into the room where we all were, her face was a picture.

'Mammy!' was all she could say.

Behind her trooped Charlie and his 'brother', all ten of them, their brown faces wearing identical fixed grins, their frightened eyes darting round the room being met by a sea of astonished faces.

'Come in, come in,' Eugene pumped each hand in turn in a hearty welcome, Ada following suit as she quickly recovered from her shock.

'I bring my brother, Joe say it OK,' smiled Charlie.

Only then did we notice they all carried boxes, forming a circle in the middle of the throng, they opened each box in turn.

Out came tins of ham, salmon, fruit, boxes of dates, packets of raisins, chocolate, biscuits, jars of jam and marmalade, even bars of soap, tubes of toothpaste and bottles of shampoo.

The honour of opening the last box went to Charlie, knowing all eyes were on him he took off the lid with a flourish, and the sight of the birthday cake inside drew the response he wanted.

It really was a proper birthday cake, iced with pink and white icing, with the number nine picked out in sugar roses, and lying alongside were nine little candles, where he had got them goodness knows.

'This I bake for you,' he passed the box to me, eager to see my reaction. I was speechless, gazing in disbelief at a real birthday cake, it was so unexpected.

'Well say thank you,' chorused the aunts, and everybody laughed as I passed the box to Ada and gave Charlie a hug.

Ada insisted the box be paraded by Charlie round the room, so that everyone could get a proper look at it, before it was carried off to take pride of place on the table.

Da-dee pursed his lips and nodded vigorously when the cake reached him, 'Bene, Bene,' he said over and over, wiping a little tear from his eye. Ada led Aggie, Betty and Lena through to the kitchen followed shortly by Charlie and Eugene transporting all the goodies.

In the room there was much jostling around to try to find seats for the new visitors, but they squatted happily cross legged on the floor. Eugene produced his 'moothie' and launched into 'O Sole Mio', the aunts joining in, Da-dee keeping time tapping his stick on the floor. Uncle Glen was prevailed upon to give us something on the piano, till we were all called through for the birthday tea.

After tea, back in the room, the party pieces began in earnest. Famie with 'It's a Sin to Tell a Lie', Tina with 'Oi Marie', Ada with one of Da-dee's favourites, Funiculi, Funicula.

There was an unspoken understanding that each person had claim to a particular song. It just was not done for anyone else to sing it, and family parties followed a well established pattern. That night Joe chose to break the rule.

Standing by the door, his hand clasped to his ear, he began to sing in the traditional 'Glesca' pub singer nasal tones. The song he sang was Eugene's encore piece.

> *I don't care what you used to be*
> *I know what you are today*
> *If you love me as I love you*
> *who cares what the world may say?*
> *I was no angel in days gone by*
> *You ask no questions*
> *So why should I?*
> *I don't care what you used to be*
> *I know what you are today.*

The effect of this song was peculiar, usually the singer was encouraged by smiles or foot tapping, but as Joe sang on, the family kept their eyes on the floor, and a palpable unease was present in the room. The poor Indians, conscious of something, shifted uneasily.

It was not the fact that Joe had taken Eugene's song, it was the song itself. Often at family gatherings, when the hour was late and the singing had turned to sentimental ballads, Eugene would start to sing this song. Ada always became agitated, and she would sit hands gripping the sides of her chair eyes fixed firmly on the floor as if willing him to stop. At one point in the song he would reach for her hand, which she would snatch away. The atmosphere would be charged with tension, and a knot of fear would form in my stomach.

That night, as soon as Joe had finished and the smattering of applause died away, Tina was on her feet pretending to be Carmen Miranda and she gyrated across the floor, rolling her eyes.

> '*I, I, I, I, I, I like you very much,*
> *I, I, I, I, I, I think you grand.*'

The others joined in laughing at her antics, there was no stopping her.

> '*Oh I like your eyes*
> *and I like your lips*

I like your hips
to hyp-notize me.'

I watched Ada as she sang out louder than the rest; I knew she was pushing down the memory of that song.

I too was still bothered by the song, the echo of the words hung in the air, and the fear it engendered lingered, though I had no idea why.

Tina exhausted by her hip swivelling performance collapsed laughing into her chair.

Ada turned to Charlie.

'Do you sing or any of your brothers?'

Charlie consulted his brothers, there was much smiling and shaking of heads. He turned to Ada.

'We like Rabbie Burns,' he said.

Everyone laughed, Ada looked astonished.

'You know of Rabbie Burns?'

'Yes, yes, you sing, you say poem.'

Nothing could have pleased Ada more. She recited 'To a Mouse', leading the company stumbling through the immortal lines –

'The best-laid schemes o' mice and men
Gang aft agley.
An' lea'e us nought but grief an' pain
For promis'd joy!'

Charlie clapped his hands in delight, and then had the company in stitches as he tried to recite the lines on his own.

Ada sang 'Afton Water', followed by Uncle Glen in a surprising rich baritone, with 'My Love is Like a Red, Red Rose'.

Tina not to be outdone quoted the one line she knew, 'A man's a man for a' that.'

The whole company rose to join hands for 'Auld Lang Syne', Charlie and his 'brothers' grinning all over as they tried to cross hands for the last verse.

So after much bowing and shaking of hands, they smilingly took their leave, filing out of the door and down the stairs. We never saw them or the jolly little Charlie again.

It had been a birthday to remember. Mary and Jimmy, Glen and 'Granton' Aggie had missed the last train back to Edinburgh, so they stayed the night with us.

Eugene, Glen, and Jimmy slept on the floor, Mary shared with Aggie and me, me sleeping at the bottom of the bed, and Ada and 'Granton' Aggie shared the kitchen bed.

'Granton' Aggie was a bit put out. She lived in a council house, and had a bathroom, and had never slept in a kitchen in her life. Ada decanted Betty and Lena into the kitchen bed, and turned the big room over to 'Granton' Aggie and uncle Glen.

Jimmy and Mary looked put out, but Eugene shrugged and said it was only for one night, so what was the problem?

So far the influx of sailors had been good for business, with the unexpected bonus of Charlie and his gifts. Ada was well pleased the shop had a buzz about it that it had not had for a long time.

Eugene split his time between his business and working in the shop; he had still failed to make a profit, paying his workers and taking nothing for himself.

'I just thank the Lord we are getting money from somewhere,' she told Eugene.

'Eh, it takes time to build up a business, things will get better,' he assured her.

'It takes good common sense, and a person not being too pig headed to take advice,' Ada snapped.

He said nothing.

We were fairly used to all sorts of people coming into the shop, but from the moment he came through the door the Russian as we later found out he was, had something scary about him. He was big, bigger even than big Bill. He wore dark trousers and donkey jacket the pockets of which bulged, the material dragged and misshapen. His face was half obscured by a dark cap which seemed to tight for his huge head, and dark wiry hair stood out all round.

The shop was busy, and he walked up and down looking for a seat, squeezing in beside two men already seated on the bench behind the display shelves.

Breathing heavily he pulled a bottle of vodka from his pocket raised it to his lips and began to drink.

'You can't drink alcohol in here,' Ada said.

He grunted, but went on drinking. The two men stood up, forcing him to move to let them out.

He sat down heavily again, spread himself out and carried on drinking.

Ada stood arms folded across her chest looking at him.

'This is not a pub, you cannot drink alcohol in here,' she repeated.

He put down the bottle, stared at her, shook his head and, lifting the bottle again, began to drink.

'I will have to ask you to leave,' Ada said

He swivelled his eyes to look at her, and shook his head again.

Ada marched through to the back. We were all there coping with the dishes and helping Eugene.

'Either he does not understand English or he is playing me for a fool and he will not stop drinking,' she fumed.

Lena and I peered at the man through the net curtain.

Eugene came down from his stool to take a look.

'He's a big fella, wouldn't like to get on the wrong side of him,' he said, climbing back up on his stool.

'Well we might have to if he doesn't stop drinking that vodka,' Ada said grimly.

She marched out again, this time not speaking but miming her request.

She stood watching him.

He looked at her, put the bottle in his pocket and grinned a toothless grin.

She relaxed, 'would you like tea or Bovril?' she asked.

'Tea, tea, tea,' he laughed loudly.

Ada signalled to Aggie to fetch the tea.

Ada followed her through, casting a glance over her shoulder as she went, 'he could be trouble,' she said, twitching the curtain for another look.

Betty peered over her shoulder, 'I see what you mean. I wish I was staying to see what happens, but I'm meeting Ann.'

'I don't like the look of him,' said Aggie.

'He reminds me of Butcher,' Lena shuddered.

'For goodness sake give the man his tea, he is minding his own business so far,' Eugene protested.

Aggie took the tea reluctantly, placing it   before the man and waiting pointedly for the money.

He glowered at her and threw down some coins. She took the cost of the tea and pushed the rest back at him.

At that moment Butcher came thundering through the door, looking round wildly, and when he caught sight of the man, he lunged for his throat.

Ada was there in a flash, 'What's going on here?'

'This B**** is a bloody commie. He had a go at me in the pub. He's a commie, ah tell ye.'

'Be that as it may, you will do your fighting outside,' Ada gave Butcher a shove.

The big man swung a punch, but missed, and Butcher jumped on him.

'I told you take your fight outside,' Ada shouted.

'He's a bloody commie, ah telt ye,' Butcher persisted.

'I don't care what he is, you cannot attack my customers,' Ada persisted.

She stood defiantly between them.

Betty taking her chance flew past, head down.

Butcher aimed a punch catching the man on the jaw. He jumped up and soon the two were trading blows. Ada ran to the back shop for her shillelagh.

She began beating Butcher about the back, but to no avail. Customers began to make for the door, and soon the only people in the shop apart from ourselves were Butcher and the man.

'Get out! Get out now!' Ada shouted. She ran to the door, blowing three sharp notes on her whistle. Butcher straightened up, looking round him.

'I'll have you lifted if you don't move,' Ada told him.

He pushed the big man back into the seat and staggered towards the door. 'Ah'll be waitin' fur that bastard when he comes oot. Ah'm no finished wi' him, an' me an' the boys will sort him oot,' Butcher shouted, as Ada pushed him through the door and locked it after him.

The big man was looking round him in a bemused fashion; he got to his feet and made for the door. Ada pushed him back, shaking her head.

'You wait for the police, stay here,' she said.

He shook his head, and pushed her aside, but she was determined to keep him in the shop.

Mumbling to himself he slumped on a bench opposite the counter, pulled the vodka from his pocket and began to drink. Eugene came from the back shop, and grabbed Ada by the arm.

'You should have let him leave. What do we do with him now?'

Butcher will kill him, he's got a razor, I saw it,' she said.

'He looks like he can take care o' himsel',' said Eugene.

'He's drunk,' Ada said.

'He is no goin' tae get sober drinkin' more o' that stuff is he?' Eugene asked.

'No but I'm hoping the police will be here soon. I blew the whistle,' Ada said.

'Do ye think Butcher is away?' Aggie asked.

'Not for a minute; he said he would be waiting and he will be, unless the bobbies get here,' Ada said peering into the darkness through a chink in the door.

The big man took a last gulp from his bottle, shoved it into his pocket, and rose unsteadily to his feet.

'I go sh—ip, sh—ip,' he muttered.

'No! No! You must stay here,' Ada pointed to the bench.

'I go sh—ip,' he muttered again swaying, and holding on to the table.

'He's sozzled,' laughed Eugene.

Ada tried to push him down onto the bench.

'That man,' she pointed to the door, 'that man, very bad, he has razor,' she drew her fingers across her throat.

The big man gazed at her glassy eyed.

She pointed to the door again, drew her fingers across her throat in a more exaggerated gesture, 'A razor,' she mouthed.

I started to giggle, it reminded me of the cowboys films, when the white man was trying to talk to the Indians.

Lena dug me in the ribs and put her fingers to her lips.

'I wish the bobbies would come,' Ada said, placing her hands on the man's shoulders to keep him down.

As he struggled to get up again, Eugene shook his head and repeated the throat cutting gesture.

The man focused on Eugene for a moment, and then reaching into his inside pocket, produced a revolver.

Eugene and Ada stepped back as Aggie, Lena and I let out a scream. 'Oh my God! What do we do now?' Ada whispered.

'Open the door and let him go,' urged Eugene.

'Are you mad? There will be murder,' Ada was aghast.

'Let them fight it oot among themselves. One has a gun, one has a razor, it depends who's quickest, it is none o' our business,' Eugene insisted. Eugene moved towards the door, the man swung the gun round waving it drunkenly.

'Get back here. He can't even aim straight, and even if we did let him go, he could never defend himself. Butcher will have the gang, and they all have razors,' Ada argued.

'I say it is no' our problem, just get him oot o' here,' Eugene retreated behind the counter.

The big man fished in his other pocket and produced another bottle of vodka, took the top off with his teeth and began to gulp it down. Eugene pulled Ada aside.

'What are we goin' to do? If he was drunk before he is only goin' to get worse if we let him go on drinking.'

'You think we should try to take the bottle from him?' Ada asked, knowing the answer.

Eugene shook his head.

'I say let him drink himself cold, then we might be able to do something,' Ada said.

'Like what?' Eugene said.

'Wait and see,' Ada said, 'I just wish the Bobbies had answered my whistle.'

I daren't open the door to blow it again, Butcher will force his way in.'

Lena, Aggie and I stood huddled behind the counter watching the man gulp down the vodka. He paused now and then to run his hand across his mouth, brush the neck of the bottle with his sleeve and then start drinking again. Soon the bottle was empty. He stared at it for a moment or two, and then slumped forward, face down on the table, sending the two empty bottles crashing to the floor, the gun still firmly clasped in his great paw of a hand.

'We need to get that gun,' Ada whispered.

'What!' Eugene gasped.

'We need to get it, once that is out of the way we can move him,' Ada said decisively.

'Move him? To where?' Eugene asked.

'Into the window, it is the only place to hide him,' Ada said.

'Have you seen the size o' him?' Eugene argued.

'What else can we do?' Ada persisted.

'Mammy don't touch him,' Lena pleaded.

'It will be all right,' Ada assured her.

The man began to snore, so Ada edged forward and began gently tugging at his fingers to free the gun.

'Well help me!' she whispered twisting round to face Eugene.

The man grunted, and closed his fingers round the gun. Ada jerked her head at Eugene, urging him on.

Eugene moved nearer, his face white.

Ada motioned him to prize the man's fingers off the gun; Eugene shook his head.

'What now?' Ada hissed.

'We could get out and lock him in,' Eugene suggested hopefully.

'Don't talk rubbish, get his fingers loose while I tug on the gun,' Ada's patience was wearing thin.

We watched with baited breath as together they managed to free the gun. Ada moved behind the counter, Aggie let out a yelp of fear and vanished into the back shop.

Ada hid the gun behind a row of bottles, and straightened up, wiping her hands down the side of her apron, as if the gun had contaminated them. 'Right!' she said to Lena, 'get the window door open and prop some boxes against if to make sure it does not swing shut.'

Lena dragged a crate over and stood on it to reach the hidden catch on the door. The door was long and narrow with only a slight indent enough for two fingers to pull it open. As soon as Lena had the door propped open, Ada motioned to Eugene to grab the man by the shoulders while she took his legs. Lena rushed to help and together they pulled and tugged, stopping at every grunt and movement of the huge bulky frame. I had joined Aggie at the back shop, and we watched in terror as the man was half dragged half carried behind the counter.

Eugene waved us forward.

We advanced towards the counter with great reluctance.

'We need everybody to heave him up into the window,' Eugene whispered breathlessly.

Lena moved to the shoulders with Eugene, and Aggie and I helped Ada with the legs.

At last the big man lay on his back on the floor of the window, snoring gently on among the dust and bits of wood and torn paper. We heaved a sigh of relief as Eugene shut the door leaving the man in total darkness and completely hidden from view.

'It's an ill wind that blows no good right enough,' Ada said.

'Eh?' Eugene looked at her.

'Well the bombs lost us all the glass from the window, but if it had not been boarded up what would we have done tonight?'

'Aye, ah suppose, but now that he is in there what happens next?' Eugene queried.

Before Ada could answer Butcher began hammering on the door cursing and demanding to be let in.

'What will we do, mammy?' Lena whispered. For answer Ada went to the door. 'We are closed. What do you want?' she shouted.

'We want that commie bastard; he's gonny get whit's comin' tae him.' 'He's not here,' Ada shouted back.

'He f**** well is, we hiv been here a' the time an' he never came oot.' 'I'm telling you he is not here, you must have missed him,' Ada told him. 'Open the f**** door. We know he is in there'.

Ada fished the keys out of her pocket, and Eugene grabbed her hand shaking his head.

Ada shook him off, unlocked the door, and the gang burst in.

'Where is the bastard?'

'I told you he is not here. He left. You must have missed him in the dark,' Ada said calmly.

They spread out through the shop. Ada gave us all a warning look telling us to stay put.

Butcher was looking puzzled.

'I told you, he is not here, and you know we have no back door, so short of shinning down the drain pipe, there is only one way in and one way out of the shop.' Ada told him.

Butcher ignored her and went behind he counter. We held our breath. Ada remained calm.

'Ah know whit ye hiv done wi' him, the bastard is in the cellar.'

He grabbed Eugene by the neck and drew him round the counter.

'Open up!' he growled.

'He's no down there,' Eugene protested.

'Open the f*** up,' Butcher pushed him forward.

Eugene bent to pull up the trap door.

Ada walked round and stood with her back against the door of the window.

'You are wasting your time, he is long gone,' she said.

'That's whit you want us tae believe, ah know the bastard is hidin' doon there,' Butcher peered into the darkness of the cellar.

'It is just as well you missed him, he had a gun,' Ada said watching for the reaction on their faces.

Butcher shopped, his feet on the first step down to the cellar.

'Jamesy go doon an' see if he's there.'

'Go yersel' big man, ah don't want tae get shot dae ah?'

'Chick, you go doon,' Butcher ordered.

'Aye that will be right, it's no ma f**** fight,' Chick said backing away.

Butcher grabbed Eugene, pushing him onto the stairs.

Eugene went down to the foot of the stairs and looked up.

'There is nobody here,' he said.

'He's doon there ah know he is. Is there a f**** light in that place?'

Eugene obligingly switched on the light. Butcher drew a razor from his pocket, flipped open the blade and made his way cautiously down the stairs. He went through the cellar, pushing Eugene ahead of him, and kicking over boxes and crates, cursing all the while.

Satisfied that the big man was not there he climbed back up, leaving Eugene to put out the light and make his own way up.

Eugene replaced the trap door, dusting off his hands on his trousers.

'Satisfied?' Ada asked Butcher.

He stood scowling, looking carefully round the shop. We watched and held our breath.

'Come on big man, the B's no here,' urged the others.

'How the hell did that c*** get passed us?' Butcher growled.

'He was anxious to get back to his ship, he is long gone,' Ada said,

'He certainly had a gun, and he showed it to us, so we were glad to see the back of him,' Ada said.

'Ah'll find the B, gun or no gun. He is a dirty commie bastard, he had a go at me,' Butcher snarled.

'Gie it a bye, big man, furget aboot it, ah don't fancy bein' at the end o' a shooter,' Jamesy urged.

Butcher made towards the door, Ada held it wide and watched to see where they went. To her dismay Butcher grabbed the others by the sleeve.

'Naw, there is nae way that B could hiv got by us, he is still in there.'

'Aw fur Gawd's sake, gie it a rest, come oan,' Jamesy pulled him away.

Ada slammed the door shut and locked it. 'Well what now?' Eugene asked.

'We wait, we need to make sure that they have gone,' Ada said. 'Suppose Ivan wakes up?' Eugene said.

'Ivan?' Lena looked puzzled.

'Ivan the terrible in there,' Eugene jerked his thumb towards the window, 'he is a Russian, an' a big one at that.'

'What if he does wake up, mammy?' Lena asked.

'We will just have to hope we can get him away from here as soon as possible,' Ada said.

Aggie's eyes were dancing in her head and she was shaking. Ada patted her arm.

'Come on. Let's have a cup of tea, we all need it.'

We followed her through to the back.

'We need to get either him or us out of here. I still think we should go and leave him till morning,' Eugene argued.

'Suppose we do that and he wakes up, starts rampaging about in the window or breaks the door down and causes God knows what havoc. What do we do then?' Ada asked

'Well do you have a better idea?' Eugene sounded peeved.

'Yes I do, but let's have our tea, before I put the plan into action.'

We sat drinking our tea while Ada told us of her plan.

'We can't be sure that Butcher and the gang are really gone, so we have to listen for any sound they may make. If we can be reasonably sure they have gone, we show a little chink of light which will attract the warden. He usually passes around this time, and that way we will get the help.'

'It just might work,' Eugene agreed.

We followed Ada to the door, our ears straining to hear any sound of the gang, afraid to move too soon.

Aggie was pressing her ear to the window door, sure she could hear stirrings.

'Och he will just be movin' in his sleep,' Eugene reassured her.

'Shhhh!' Ada hissed.

We pressed harder to the door, no sound, nothing.

'I think we should risk it now,' Ada said.

'Don't show too much light. Gerry might be up there looking for a target,' Eugene laughed.

'Or Butcher might come back,' Lena said still very afraid.

'If we don't do it soon we will miss the warden and have to wait till he comes round again, and by that time our sleeping giant might be awake,' Ada warned.

'Right go for it!' Eugene urged.

Ada undid the lock, and opened the door cautiously, a thin stream of light lighting up the wet pavement.

She shut the door again, waited twenty seconds and opened it again; this she went on doing for a good five minutes.

We did not have to wait long before the warden was hammering on the door demanding to be let in.

Ada rushed to open the door, and dragged him in by the sleeve. He went red in the face brushing her off demanding to know what was going on.

'Whew!' he said as Ada finished her story.

'So where is this gun then?'

Ada produced the gun and the warden went pale.

He took the thing from her with his finger tips, then catching sight of our faces, cleared his throat and became very officious.

'It is my duty to disarm this weapon, and then inform the police of the situation,' he told us.

'That is exactly what we want you to do,' Ada told him.

'Aye and get rid o' Ivan as well,' Eugene added.

'This fellow is in your window you say?'

'Aye, and you will just have to take our word for that, and we are no' goin' to open that door till the polis is here,' Eugene told him.

'Right, leave it to me', said the warden.

He took the clip of bullets out of the gun and put them in his pocket slipping the gun itself into his haversack.

He made for the door, 'I'11 be back as soon as I can. I need to go to Cranston Street to get help.'

'Well let's hope you have more success than I did. Usually somebody comes when I blow the whistle,' Ada told him.

'Strictly speaking you should not blow a whistle, it can be confusing for the authorities,' he scolded.

'Sorry about that, but it can make the difference between averting trouble and clearing up the mess after it,' Ada said frostily.

'Maybe we should just let the man get on,' Eugene broke in, making to open the door.

The warden went off, promising to be a quick as he could.

We sat huddled on the benches counting the minutes.

He was as good as his word.

'I believe you have caught a Red Russian,' laughed the big highland Bobby as he and his mate squeezed through the door.

'He is all yours, we have him in cold storage,' Eugene said flippantly.

He opened the door gingerly, half expecting the man to burst out like a raging lion, but he was just as we left him, still snoring.

The two burly policemen shook him awake, hauling him into a sitting position. He stared at them then slumped down again, but they bundled him out of the window and dragged him out to their van.

Ada shut the door behind them with a sigh of relief.

'Well what a night, look at the time, nearly two in the morning and you have school in the morning,' she said, ruffling my hair.

We trooped wearily up the stairs and stumbled into bed.

As I went through, I heard Eugene say, 'you are no really goin' tae send her to school after all that?'

'Of course, it is not a good thing to miss school,' she answered.

I duly found myself huddled on the top deck of the tram as usual the next morning.

Butcher knew he had been duped, and made sure Ada knew of his anger by making more of a nuisance of himself than usual.

Ada got her revenge on him purely by accident, which nevertheless gave her much satisfaction.

Every tenant had to take a turn of washing the common stairs. Much pride was taken in getting them as white as possible, and each woman went to great lengths to outdo each other.

The best results were obtained by using pipe clay dissolved in really hot water and applied with first a scrubbing brush and then a rag.

As we were on the first landing it fell to us to wash the 'dunny' steps, which led down to the midden.

This was a really unpleasant job as the men would come out of the Breadalbane Arms and use the 'dunny' to relieve themselves.

This habit drove Ada mad, and she mounted a constant watch on the place to catch any offender with all the vigour of Betsy Trotwood in David Copperfield when she chased the donkeys from her precious grass.

A week or two after the Russian gunman, Ada was taking her turn of the stairs, finishing the main stair. She refilled her bucket with piping hot water and plenty of pipe clay, and then proceeded to the 'dunny' steps.

She heard the shuffle of foot steps, and glimpsed a dark figure with its back turned towards her.

Incensed she crept down the stair and getting behind the figure lifted the bucket and poured its contents over him, covering him from top to toe in scalding white water.

The man let out a roar of pain and a stream of oaths, turned and ran up the stairs pushing Ada aside.

She just had enough time to see the man was Butcher.

'Maybe that will teach you not to use this place as a toilet,' she shouted after him.

The reply was a string of obscenities, and threats to 'get her'.

'I'll be waiting for you,' she called back, and left him to his humiliating walk home.

CHAPTER 19

Da-dee was a man of simple habits and fewer wants. He had a daily routine which he kept whatever the weather. Every morning after his breakfast of gammon rolls and tea, he would don his heavy overcoat, make his way down the three flights of stairs, walk up the Gallowgate to Bain Street, down into Monteith Row which skirted Glasgow Green, up Charlotte Street to Ross Street where he would stop and chat with old neighbours and friends.

He was 'a well kent face', and the children would surround him waiting for the sweeties and bits of chocolate he always carried in his pockets. It did not matter to them that the sweets and chocolate was often covered in fluff, or even none too fresh, they danced around hands held out waiting for their share.

This was how he spent his sweet coupons, telling Tina with a twinkle in his eye that he did not want to ruin his teeth.

After his walk he would return home for a bite to eat and a little nap before setting out once more to walk from the Gallowgate to Lewis's in Argyle Street.

He had made a few friends there, one, a woman forty years his junior who would always buy him a cup of tea in the basement cafeteria.

Tina would tease him about his 'lady friend', rolling her eyes and saying she wouldn't put it past him. Eugene would laugh and say, 'Och it keeps me young.'

Da-dee would pretend to be angry with them, but he was secretly pleased to be thought to have a girlfriend.

As far as Tina knew he only went as far as Lewis's, had his cup of tea and walked back home, always in time for tea.

He kept the routine up all through the year, brushing aside Tina's pleas to stay home on days when there was ice or snow or fog. He was a man who had walked halfway across Europe, weather did not bother him. The winter of 1944 was severe. November brought dense fog and ice. Da-dee had set out as usual for his visit to Lewis's but had not returned at his usual time, he was at least two hours over due. Tina went looking for him, battling her way through the dense fog.

She had not gone far when she was forced to turn back, being totally unable to see where she was going.

The fog was just as dense in Sandyford and the shop was empty, even the Bath gang hadn't ventured out. Ada had taken a rare night off, and she sat by the fire reading, while I played at school with my teddies and dolls seated in rows.

Around ten o'clock there was a frantic knocking on the door. Ada rose, saying, 'who can this be at this time of night?'

I could hear by her tone the caller was not welcome, and was surprised to see Pat McCann follow her into the kitchen.

'You better sit down if you have something to say,' Ada said frostily.

'Ah think you better sit doon Eadie, it's bad news,' he said standing twisting his greasy cap in his hands.

'What is it? Is comar Tina ill?'

'Naw it's the auld man,' Pat said speaking barely above a whisper.

'Go through to the room and play,' Ada said to me.

'What's happened to Da-dee? I want to know,' I said.

'Go into the room till I call you,' Ada said.

I sat on the edge of my bed, furious at being banished, desperate to know what had happened.

After a few minutes I heard Pat leave, and not waiting to be called I confronted Ada in the lobby. She was putting on her coat and scarf. 'Where are you going Mammy?'

'I just have to go out.'

'Where to? Where is Uncle Pat? Has something happened to Da-dee?'

'Uncle Pat has gone to get your daddy, we have to go to the hospital, there's been an accident.'

'Can I come?'

'No, a hospital is no place for a child. I'11 send Lena up to look after you, so put all your things away and get ready for bed, and I'11 be as quick as I can.'

'I don't want to go to bed; I want to see Da-dee. Something has happened to him, hasn't it?'

'Just do as you are told, I'11 send Lena straight up.'

She went out.

In a few minutes Lena came upstairs. She was white faced and shaking.

'What's happened to Da-dee?' I pleaded.

'I don't know, some sort of accident, he is in the 'Royal'. Anyway mammy says you have to be in bed before she comes back.'

Lena could be just as infuriating as Ada in keeping things from me.

Ada and Eugene seemed to be gone for ages. Betty came home and went down to help Aggie close up. I lay awake listening to their voices, trying to make out what they were saying.

I heard the key turn in the lock and jumped out of bed.

Betty was making tea, Lena setting out the cups, and Ada was standing by the table still wearing her coat and scarf. She was looking down at Eugene, but saying nothing.

I stood just inside the door eager to hear the news but fearful of meeting Ada's eye.

She turned and saw me, and taking me by the hand, she led me back to bed, and went out closing the door after her all without uttering a word.

After a while Lena came in. She saw I was still awake and sat on the bed taking my hand.

'What is it?' I asked.

'It is bad, a really bad accident,' she said.

I jumped up, 'but what happened, he's my Da-dee too and I want to know.'

'You know how he always goes for a walk every day, how he always goes to Lewis's?'

I nodded, willing her to go on.

She sighed and took a deep breath, 'well-.'

'What? What happened?'

'Well we knew he went to Lewis's but we didn't know that he went on from there and sat for a while in St Enoch's,' she said.

'The railway station? Why did he go there?' I was puzzled.

'We don't know, maybe to have a rest before walking back home, or maybe he liked to see the trains, anyway, the porters knew him, he would buy a penny platform ticket and go on to the platform and watch the people getting on the train and then the train pulling out.'

'Da-dee went to watch trains?' I was amazed.

'That's what it looks like. He would buy his ticket get onto the platform and after a while pass through the barrier and walk home, only this time he made a mistake,' Lena finished.

'What kind of mistake, just tell me what happened,' I pleaded.

'It seems he walked the wrong way. He walked down the slope that leads to the line, must have been confused and tried to cross the line but --. She paused, squeezing my hand.

'What? What?'

'A train was coming, he fell across the track and it-it cut his feet off,' she finished in a whisper.

'Then he's dead, the train killed him,' I jumped out of bed, grabbing at my clothes. Lena gripped my two hands, pulling me towards her.

'He is not dead, but he is in a coma,' she said, hugging me.

'What is that?'

'He is unconscious. It's better that way, he can't feel any pain,' she said.

'He is going to die, isn't he?'

She nodded, 'I think so, there were other injuries too, and he is an old man.'

We hugged each other the tears coursing down our cheeks, and I could taste their saltiness on my lips.

Ada came through and looked at us, and then clasped our shoulders.

'Come and see daddie, he can't seem to take it in.'

We went through, going straight to him and giving him a hug.

'What's the matter? I'm fine. He is going to be all right, he is a strong man,' Eugene said, shrugging us off.

Eugene always found it hard to be demonstrative.

Da-dee lingered for a week, the family keeping a vigil at his bedside. I was not allowed to see him despite all my pleadings.

As a consolation Ada took me with her to Da-dee's to help Lena prepare the house for his funeral.

When our beloved Auntie Mary had died, I had been too young to fully appreciate the significance of the event, but with Da-dee I was conscious of a deep pain that claimed my mind and body. I could not believe I would never see him again, and deeply resented the fact that I had not been taken to see him in hospital.

I helped Tina to clean the house while Ada draped the windows and mirrors, and turned the family photographs to the wall.

Tina put a fresh cloth on the little alter and lit two nightlights just before the coffin arrived from the Royal Infirmary where he had died.

The knock on the door heralding the arrival of the coffin sent me into a panic. I loved Da-dee but I was afraid of death. What was it going to be like to sit in the kitchen knowing he was lying dead in the next room?

Ada had said she would be staying the night with Tina, and I was to stay too. I wanted to be where Ada was, even though I was afraid.

I sat in the kitchen listening to the muted noises and voices as they arranged the coffin on the trestles. After a time I heard the men going to the door, and Tina's murmur of thanks as she said goodbye.

Ada came through and filled the kettle, telling me to set out the cups and saucers.

We waited for the tea to brew, and for Tina to come through from the room.

She came, her eyes red with crying, her body shivering as if from extreme cold.

Ada sat her down and poured her some tea, spooning in two heaped spoonfuls of sugar.

I was so used to sugar being strictly rationed at the table, somehow seeing these heaped spoons brought home just how dreadful this occasion really was.

Tina sipped the tea, which seemed to restore her, and she looked up and smiled at me.

'It's ok hen, don't worry.'

I smiled back, not knowing what to say.

After a while, Tina stood up and stretched out her hand to take mine.

'Come and see him,' she said.

I drew back, looking to Ada for direction.

'I don't think she should,' Ada said.

'Tina looked puzzled.'

'Why no', he is her Da-dee, he loved her and she loved him.'

Ada looked at me.

'Do you want to?'

I hesitated; Tina smiled and gripped my hand, pulling me gently towards the door.

'Come on hen, he never hurt you when he was alive, so he is no' going to hurt you now.'

We went through, Ada following right behind.

I approached the coffin fearful of what I might see, then gazing down on my beloved Da-dee I saw he was peacefully asleep, his olive skin was smooth and unwrinkled, the familiar blush was there on his cheeks, and his dear gnarled hands clasped across his breast clutched his rosary beads which Tina had placed there.

Lizzie and Famie arrived, Famie inconsolable, Lizzie quiet and subdued.

The house began to fill up with friends and neighbours bringing flowers and Mass cards. The aunts and Ada dispensed tea and patiently told and re-told the story of the accident.

The Durkins who lived next door brought in extra dishes and chairs. The talking and praying went on all that night and for the next three nights till it was time to process the coffin on an open dray to St. Alphonsus, where it would lie, flanked by huge candles which would burn throughout the night till the requiem mass the next day.

Finally, as the coffin set out to Dalbeth Cemetery followed only by the men, I found myself back in Da-dee's with Betty, Lena, Ada and the aunts.

Soon the house was filled once more with the returning mourners, who seemed to shake off their solemn mood at the door, as they laughed and chattered. I looked around at Ada and the aunts expecting shock and disapproval, but they were busying themselves with making yet more sandwiches and tea and seemed not to notice.

How could they behave in such a way when someone so precious had gone forever? Not for the first time I realized I did not understand adults at all.

Rover was my refuge, it was into his soft fur my tears flowed, and he was the only thing to give me comfort.

The everyday life seemed to close over the vast chasm left by Da-dee's going, I went to school, the shop opened and closed, and the Bath gang still caused trouble. I overheard Eugene and Lizzie talk about Da-dee.

It was only once, and they seemed so accepting of Da-dee's death, so matter of fact that I was convinced they did not care.

'Nobody cares that Da-dee is dead,' I screamed at Betty.

'That's not true, we all care, but to speak about him hurts, we just get on with things,' she said.

I could not 'get on with things', I saw Da-dee everywhere. I would look up at the sky and he would be there, open my reader and his face would stare up from the page. I had nightmares in which he was trying to reach out to me, and I could not reach him. I would wake up screaming, rousing the whole house.

Ada was at her wits end, nothing she tried seemed to help me, and I would not eat and cried all the time.

She decided I should be seen by a doctor. I usually was in a good state of health and had seldom needed to visit the surgery across the street from the shop. Each visit cost seven shillings and sixpence and most-people including Ada tried home remedies first before resorting to a doctor.

Betty took me over early one morning, and I sat sullen and uncooperative as the doctor asked me questions.

Somehow my mouth would not work, the words just would not come and it was left to Betty to do all the explaining.

It was clear the doctor found me tiresome, shook his head and looked disapprovingly.

'Perhaps if she had a little holiday, get her away from the familiar places where her grandfather used to be,' he suggested.

'How long do you think she should stay away?' Betty asked him.

'It needs to be several weeks to be effective. Perhaps she could be sent to a relative?' he said.

'We do have relatives in Edinburgh,' said Betty.

I stiffened, I did not want to go to Jimmy and Mary, or to 'Granton' Aggie, and I wondered which one Ada would choose.

I could feel the tears pricking at my eyes, and dashed them away with my sleeve.

Betty fished in her purse for the seven and six and laid it on the desk.

The doctor was writing something in a file, looked up and scooped up the money, smiling his thanks.

As we rose to go, he stood up and patted my head.

'Children do not understand death, and the loss of a grandfather can be difficult for all concerned. Of course he was not your grandfather was he? This is your half-sister. Your name is Di Placido is it not?'

Betty looked startled, and she hurried me out the door, saying 'thank you doctor, I'll tell my mother what you advise'.

Outside I tugged at her coat.

'What did he mean we are not full sisters?'

'He didn't say that,' Betty said quickly.

'Yes he did, and he called you a funny name, what was it?'

'It was nothing he made a mistake that's all. He sees so many people, he gets confused.'

'But he said Da-dee was not your grandfather, I heard him,' I persisted.

'He was talking nonsense, forget it, don't say anything to mammy, we need to tell her what he said about you.'

'I don't want to go away,' I said.

'That will be up to mammy,' Betty said.

Ada received the doctor's advice with mixed feelings.

'Well, if he thinks that's best, I suppose we better do as he says. It will mean time off school, and I will have to send a note explaining the situation. I'll write to Glen and Aggie right away and see if it is possible for them to take her. Jimmy and Mary would never be able to cope.'

'She is better here with us, we are all grieving together, that way we will get over it quicker,' Eugene protested.

'She is just a child, it is different for her, she needs time to get over things, and she needs a change of scene,' Ada told him.

I did not want a change of scene, I wanted Da-dee back, but I knew that was impossible.

My miserable state grew worse as I mulled over what the doctor had said to Betty, and I remembered Betty's startled look and how she practically pushed me through the surgery door in her haste to get away. He had said Da-dee was not her grandfather, he had said we were not full sisters.

Betty had insisted he had made a mistake, and maybe he had, but I didn't think so, it was all part of the secrets that seemed to haunt our family, just like Mrs E Cocozza on all those hundreds of postal order stubs. I felt the ground beneath my feet was shifting sand, nothing was as it seemed. I was mortally afraid.

Now I was being sent away, having to leave Ada and my beloved Rover behind.

I had never stayed with 'Granton' Aggie before; I felt I hardly knew her. On the rare occasions she came through to St. Vincent Street I was always sent out to play, or into the room, while 'the big people talked'.

'Granton' Aggie lived in a four in a block council house. The scheme was still new and it was considered a relatively 'posh' place to live.

'Granton' Aggie certainly acted superior to us, who only lived in a Glasgow tenement.

Her pretensions were viewed with mild amusement by her son Glen and daughter Mima, Uncle Glen rarely troubled himself with petty 'womanly' concerns.

There existed a kind of rivalry between Ada and Aggie, both would seek to outdo the other in the latest household furnishings, both assumed a haughty demeanour when in each others company.

'Granton' Aggie did not approve of foreigners in general and Eugene in particular, she despaired too of Aggie and would hint at Ada's lack of judgement in letting her 'get away with things'.

I suspected that 'Granton' Aggie disapproved of me, but since I was rarely in her company it was only a feeling.

The village of Granton lay on the shores of the Firth of Forth, it was mostly a fishing village and though the huge housing scheme had been built on the hills above, the village itself had not changed.

Edinburgh's air was always bracing being a city built on hills and bordering the sea, but Granton air was even more so. There was a wildness in the wind that came off the sea and raced over the houses scouring their pebble dashed facades, and setting the lines of washing off in a mad dance.

The effect of the salt laden breeze did little for the health of garden plants and was the bane of Uncle Glen's life.

Filled with trepidation at the thought of being 'banished' to Granton I confided my fears in Lena.

She laughed them away, saying it was better then being sent to Mary and Jimmy, reminding me that Mary 'could no be daein' wi' a' that vegetarian nonsense.'

This sent me into a panic, as I had no idea what 'Granton' Aggie's attitude to vegetarianism was, or Uncle Glen's for that matter.

Betty, on hearing of my woe, consoled me by saying I could always slip any meat on my plate to Billy the dog.

Lena laughed and said Billy was too fat already, he had to be carried down the outdoor stairs for his walk and carried back up again.

Within days of Ada sending her letter off to Granton, Uncle Glen replied that they would be only too pleased to have me for a few weeks and help me get over the sad loss of Da-dee.

So it was settled. Ada decided I needed some decent clothes, as she did not want a 'showing up' in front of 'Granton' Aggie and her friends. She counted up the collective clothing coupons and decided some could be spared to get me two sets of underwear, long stockings and gloves. She had a coat of Lena's she could alter, which with my two thick woollen skirts and jumpers would see me through the cold winter days of Granton. We set out to Lewis's to buy what was needed.

The sales assistant spread out the regulation navy blue knickers and white liberty bodices with their laced up fronts. Ada rubbed the material between finger and thumb and frowned.

'They are all utility garments madam; it is all we have for the duration.'

'Hmmm,' murmured Ada, 'I don't think these are suitable. She is going to Edinburgh for a few weeks, and it is still winter.'

'Perhaps these would be better.' As the assistant pulled out a garment from a drawer and spread it over the counter, I winced.

'Combinations,' she said holding them up, 'they are very good for keeping children snug.'

Ada's eyes lit up, she liked to keep us snug.

'Yes, the very thing. Do you think we have enough coupons for two pairs?'

'I don't like those things,' I pulled a face.

'You need something to keep you warm. Granton is right on the coast.' Lena and I were no strangers to the dreaded combinations, she mercifully could now choose her own clothes, but we had joined forces in the past to do our best to get out of wearing these things.

Made of scratchy white material, they had long sleeves and long legs with buttons running from neck to crotch, and at the back there was a flap which could be let down when visiting the lavatory; this was the ultimate humiliation.

We hated them with a passion and would deny vehemently that we were wearing them if our classmates asked.

To my horror we had enough coupons not only for two pairs of combination but a dreadful brown woollen hat, scarf and mittens too. Ada watched well pleased as the assistant wrapped them up in brown paper and tied it with string.

I trudged alongside Ada to get the tram home, my heart in my boots. I knew Betty would have a giggle when she saw what we had bought, as she had, unknown to Ada, taken scissors to her combinations, preferring to shiver.

As we left Lewis's with the dreaded combinations, Ada glanced at my woebegone face and smiled.

'Come on, we'll go to Arnott Simpson's for a wee cup of tea.'

This really cheered me up, and we sat at a table covered in a snowy white cloth, on which lay delicate china cups and saucers, with heavy silver knives and teaspoons.

Ada ordered pot of tea and two currant buns.

The waitress in her smart black dress, pristine white apron and cap, brought the order, setting it out before us. She placed a little dish with two curls of margarine, and a little sugar bowl with two tiny cubes of sugar, glancing at Ada who smiled her approval.

The buns looked really inviting, but I knew I could not expect to eat the whole bun. Ada had strict rules on fairness, and if either Lena or I were out with her and had a 'treat', part of it had to be taken home to ensure the stay-at-home got her share.

Strangely these rules did not apply to trips to Edinburgh; these were considered 'days out' so a visit to a tearoom was essential.

Should an apple be bought from a stall on the street corner this had to be shared too, since to take half an apple home was impractical, as it would turn brown. Ada would take the little mirror from her handbag and hack away at the fruit till it was halved in two.

One half was duly fed to one of the many horses which stood patiently by the kerb while their drivers made deliveries.

So my bun was halved and wrapped in a serviette to take home to Lena. Most times she neglected to eat it, and it would be passed to Eugene, who would happily oblige, saying, 'waste not, want not.'

The day came when I was packed and ready to go. Tearfully I hugged Rover telling him I loved him and would miss him. He gazed at me with big soulful eyes, and wagging only the tip of his tail, offered a consoling paw.

Ada and I were frequent visitors to Edinburgh, usually confining our visit to Mary and Jimmy in the old town.

Ada loved her 'Athens of the North', telling me every stone had a story to tell, the place was steeped in history and each visit I was taught some more.

I secretly did not share her love of the place; to me the people were dour and Calvinistic, and there was very little humour to be found especially among the folk of the old town.

'Edinburgh folk are a' fur coat an' nae knickers,' Eugene would say, knowing he would rouse Ada's ire.

Like him I preferred the Glaswegians with their warmth and unfailing sense of fun.

As we got off the tram at George Square and crossed the road to Queen Street station to catch the train, my heart began to thud with a mixture of excitement and fear.

The station was always noisy and full of people, the trains coming and going with great plumes of belching stream and thunderous roars. Eugene had told me that the trains were pulled by great lions, whose bellows and roars could be heard as they strained to get free.

'The lion that pulls the Edinburgh train is the mightiest and the fiercest.'

I begged him to tell me it was not true, and he just looked at me in surprise.

'Och you know how hoity-toity the Edinburgh folk are, dae you no' think they would want the best lion tae pull the train, you know the lion that is on the flag?'

'You mean the Lion Rampant?'

'The very same.'

I was very impressed and very afraid.

I never ventured to ask Ada about the lion, fearing to repeat Eugene's slur about hoity-toity Edinburghers, instead I sounded out Betty and Lena who both confirmed the story.

So though I really loved travelling on the train, getting on and getting off were for me fraught with great danger.

Clinging tightly to Ada's hand, my eyes would strain through the steam to catch a glimpse of the great tortured beast bellowing out his misery.

Once in the carriage I could relax, settling into my seat as Ada swung the luggage up on to the rack above the brightly coloured posters of 'bracing Brighton' or 'Bonnie Loch Lomond.'

As soon as the guard slammed shut the doors and blew his whistle Ada would pull on the thick leather strap to close the window against the soot.

'We don't want the soot to spoil our best clothes, we must be clean and tidy to visit the capital, and we don't want people to think we are Glesca Keelies.'

The train had its own distinctive song, 'did-did-dee-dum-did-did-dee-dum.' Cows gazed unblinking from the fields rushing by, washing danced in the breeze in the back gardens of rows of houses. Now and then we would rumble to a stop, with the cry, 'Falkirk High — Haymarket.'

Soon we were skirting Princes Street Gardens and the huge bulk of Castle Rock came into view.

I hurried out the station after Ada, eager to leave the tormented lion behind. To my surprise Ada did not head for the blustery Waverley steps to take us to Princes Street where we could catch a bus to Granton, but took the more familiar route up Jeffrey Street and turned into the Royal Mile, past the Seaman's Mission, on down to the ancient Tollbooth, where the unfortunate Marquis of Montrose, who having failed to muster support for Charles the second had his head displayed on a spike after being hung at Edinburgh Castle.

Next to the Tollbooth stood the Canongate Kirk in whose graveyard lies buried the beautiful Nancy Mclehose (Clarinda), the fickle love of Robert Burns, and not far from Nancy's grave lies Robert Ferguson the poet, dead at twenty-four in the Edinburgh lunatic asylum. Burns who saluted him as 'my elder brother in the muse' was moved to pay for a gravestone when he found Ferguson lay in an unmarked grave.

Across the narrow cobbled street stood Moray House, where Cromwell is said to have stayed for several days, and where he took the decision that Charles 1sts life must be forfeit. It was from the balcony of Moray House that the aforementioned Montrose was pelted with missiles and reviled as he was driven past on his way to his execution that fateful day in May 1650.

Moray House had many other claims to fame; it was believed that at least three of the signatories to the union of parliaments put quill to paper in a room at the back of the house, and later still Daniel Defoe resided there for a short time.

Pulling my scarf over my mouth to cut the wind that threatened to take my breath I listened to these stories with only half an ear. At last we turned into a vaulted archway of rough hewn stone with cobbles underfoot.

'This is Dunbar's Close,' Ada told me. Your Uncle Jimmy and Auntie Mary have just moved here, and I want to see how they are.'

We climbed the unlit stairs, which were made of wood and well worn away. Up and up we went passing long dark passages with rows of doors on either side. There was a cacophony of sound and a medley of smells pervading the whole building. Finally reaching the top storey, we set off down the passageway, Ada peering at each door in turn till we came to the last door with the name James Miller scrawled on a piece of paper pinned to the door.

Ada knocked, and immediately the door was opened by Auntie Mary, who peered at us, before stepping back and exclaiming.

'It's Eadie and the bairn.'

'Weel bring them in, bring them in,' Uncle Jimmy's querulous voice answered. The passage door opened straight into the kitchen, and as we stepped in a cold blast of air struck us.

'You have your window opened on a day like this?' Ada said by way of greeting.

'Aye, fresh air ne'er harmed onybody,' Jimmy growled.

Mary stood looking at us, eyeing my suitcase obviously curious.

'Is the bairn goin' somewhere?'

'She is going to Glen and Aggie, just for a few weeks,' said Ada.

'She'll be missin' the school then,' Jimmy said staring into the half dead fire.

'I have written to the Mother Superior, and it is all arranged,' Ada told him.

'An' 'Granton' Aggie is expectin' her?' Mary queried.

'Yes that is all arranged too. I don't like her missing school but it is special circumstances,' Ada said.

'Aye weel, ah suppose there is enough brains in yon hoose tae make sure she keeps up wi' her lessons. Ah notice ye never asked me tae tak her,' Jimmy muttered.

'I knew you wouldn't, so what was the point?' Ada asked.

'Weel a penny or twa would hae been welcome ah'm sure,' Mary chipped in.

'Glen and Aggie are not looking for payment, they genuinely want to help,' Ada said, a hint of irritation creeping into her tone.

'It's a' right for them as can afford tae dae it,' Jimmy growled.

Ada looked around and I followed her gaze. The place was almost bare of furniture, and the cosiness of Waverley Buildings had been replaced by a well worn table and two simple chairs. A bed stood against the wall, and a coal bunker ran the length of the opposite wall, above which two shelves held china and pots.

Jimmy sat in a worn armchair, its faded upholstery burst, and, at the other side of the fireplace, stood a three legged stool covered by a cushion.

'What happened to the rest of your furniture?' Ada asked.

'We had tae sell it, no' that we got much fur it, ye ken. The Corporation gied Jimmy the sack, so we are on the Parish noo,' Mary said bitterly.

'Why didn't you let me know?' Ada asked.

'We kent ye would find oot soon enough. Jimmy is no wan fur sympathy seekin',' Mary told her.

She eyed the bag Ada had placed on the table. Ada emptied the contents, tea, sugar, butter, two rashers of ham, and a jar of meat paste.

Ada always skimmed our rations and the shop's allocation to bring something through to Mary and Jimmy.

They were always laid out without comment, and Mary would spirit them away just as silently, no word of thanks was ever given or expected.

I crossed to the open window and leaned out, as Ada came behind me.

The wind wafted the smell of hops from the nearby brewery. It was a smell that pervaded the whole of Edinburgh, but it was particularly strong in the Canongate.

'You have a fine view of the Salisbury Crags,' Ada said.

'We hiv an even better one in the lavvy,' Jimmy laughed.

Can we go and see?' I asked.

'Yer uncle Jimmy is tryin' tae be funny,' Mary said.

'Can we go, mammy?'

The lavatory at the end of the passage was set into a kind of turret-like tower, two steps down from the landing.

It was the usual wooden bench with a bowl set in, and newspaper squares hanging from a nail. The wind whistled in through a huge hole in the wall, which did indeed give a better view of the Crags and the Queen's road through Holyrood Park.

'Well nobody will hang around in there for longer than necessary,' Ada laughed.

'It's worse when the wind is behind the rain, and you get soaked as well,' Mary grumbled.

'The whole building is falling to bits,' Ada said shaking her head.

'Whit time is 'Granton Aggie' expectin' ye?' Mary asked.

'Well she said anytime, so get your coats on and we will go and get a bite somewhere,' Ada said, knowing they would expect it.

We made our way up the Canongate to the High Street. Normally we would cross George IV bridge to Crawford's tea rooms, but Ada decided to stay in the High Street to save time.

As we passed John Knox's house, Jimmy raised his walking stick to point at the lamppost.

'Ah mind we used tae swing roon and roon that pole, me wi' ma calliper, only bairns we were then, puir but happy.'

'I don't remember being happy,' Ada said.

'Happy is no' fur the likes o' us,' Mary scoffed.

'Dae ye ken the story o' yon place?' Jimmy asked me.

I looked at the entrance, one of the many closes in the High street, and shook my head.

'See whit it says above the close!' Jimmy said.

I screwed up my eyes, 'heave awa close'. What does that mean?'

'Weel a long time ago the buildin' collapsed, and a'body was killed, but as the workmen were trying tae clear the rubble a voice was heard tae say, 'heave awa lads ah'm no' deid yet.'

'Was he saved?'

'Aye, a young lad ca'd Jamie McIvor, sixteen or thereaboots,' Jimmy told me.

Ada smiled, 'Edinburgh is full of history.'

'I know,' I said.

'There is still a lot you don't know,' said Ada.

Leaving the tea rooms, we said our goodbyes, leaving Mary and Jimmy to make their way home while we headed across into Princes Street to catch a tram for Granton.

As the tram trundled along Ada reminded me of my manners, to go to bed when I was told, not to get under 'Granton Aggie's feet all day, and to help with the dishes and sweeping the floors.

'Remember your uncle Glen was wounded in the Great War and has a plate in his skull, so he may get irritable at times.'

'Why do they call it the Great War?' I queried.

'Because nations around the world were involved.'

'Is this a greater war then?'

'It is a dreadful war; some say it could never be as bad as the First World War.'

'I don't want to go to 'Granton Aggie' what if ...' Ada looked at me and smiled, 'what if?'

'You mustn't think about bad things. you are going here to make yourself better, so try not to think about the war.'

'But what if we lose and it is the end of civilization, like you said'?

'Whatever happens I would always come to find you,' she smiled.

I slipped my arm through hers, and she found my hand and slipped it into her pocket with her own.

CHAPTER 20

I sat clutching a cup of hot milk, while 'Granton Aggie' vigorously brushed my hair, pushing my head this way and that, and ignoring my yelps of pain as she tackled the tugs.

'This hair is far too long, still I suppose it is something that you don't have nits,' she complained.

I was shocked, 'I never have nits, Betty is always bone combing my hair to make sure, and when the nit nurse comes round I never get a yellow card,' I protested.

'I'd say your mother is lucky then, because long hair is just asking for nits. Your uncle Glen will take you to Edinburgh tomorrow to get it cut.'

'I don't want it cut!'

'You will do as you are told. While you are here you will do as I say.'

I came back shorn of most of my hair and feeling thoroughly miserable.

'Granton Aggie' gave me an appraising look and nodded her head, 'now it looks much better.'

My week long stay became two and then three, and I was miserable for most of the time.

'Granton Aggie' clearly did not know what to do with me. Her own son Glen and daughter Mima were considerably older, at work all day and invariably out at night. Uncle Glen was a man of habit and few words, and he too was out most days, or hidden behind a book or newspaper.

'Granton Aggie' sighed many a long suffering sigh at being the one who had to cope with me.

For the most part when they were around they were kind to me if 'Granton Aggie' was not within earshot. When she complained of my table manners, and refusal to eat meat, they stayed silent, except for uncle Glen's comment that since there was little meat to go around it should make things easier.

'Of course it doesn't. A simple rabbit stew can be stretched but I have to find different things to feed to her. This silly faddy vegetarianism is just a nuisance.'

'I don't think so, Ada doesn't eat meat,' Uncle Glen said mildly.

'Then she shouldn't force her ideas onto her children. You won't convince me the child thought it up by herself,' 'Granton Aggie' fumed.

'I did think it out for myself, I don't want the poor animals to be killed,' I said quietly.

'Speak only when you are spoken to,' she glared at me. I blushed and dropped my eyes, hearing Ada's voice in my ears telling me to mind my manners.

'I will never understand your sister, a clever woman like that, getting into such a situation,' 'Granton Aggie' muttered.

I looked up to see Uncle Glen flash her a warning look, just like the looks that passed between the aunts sometimes.

That strange feeling of something terrible lurking underneath all the ordinary things in my life came over me and made me shiver. I asked to be excused from the table and went to get ready for bed. I knew the routine; 'Granton Aggie' had established it from the first day. She had decided that I should be 'out in the fresh air all day', that way all my childish energy would be used and it was just a case of supper and bed.

So immediately after breakfast she would wrap some bread and margarine in a brown paper bag, fill a bottle with water and tell me to go out and play until tea time around five o'clock.

Since it was only after eight when I went out, I had a long day to fill.

Once on a visit with Ada, we had walked down to the old village with Uncle Glen to buy fish from the harbour. It was a fascinating place and I set out that first day to find it again.

Down the hill I went trying to remember the way. Across the road at the foot of the hill, I saw a flight of steps, Wardie Steps, leading to Granton Harbour, an old weather worn sign proclaimed.

I followed the steps down and found to my delight that I was indeed at the harbour. I amused myself watching the men mending their nets; they were old men, clay pipes clenched between their teeth, they took no notice of me, and I made sure I did not go too near, knowing they would chase me away if I did.

When the tide went out I scrambled over the rocks, searching the rock pools for strange little creatures I didn't know the name of.

After a while I would eat some of my bread and drink the water, careful to make sure it would last all day.

Day after day I would roam the seashore, returning tired and hungry, ready for bed.

I was lonely and longed for Ada to come and take me home, but she had never written so much as a note to me though she did write to 'Granton Aggie'.

Uncle Glen seemed to sense my loneliness, and he decided we would have a trip to Edinburgh. I soon found he was as keen on history as Ada and while I was able to tell him many historical facts, he had others up his sleeve. We trooped up to the castle, into the hall where the tattered colours of the regiments hung in memory of their past glories, into the tiny Queen Margaret chapel, and admired Mons Meg, whose booming signal for 1 o'clock was silenced for the duration. On our way down from the mound we climbed the steep winding stairs to the Camera Obscura, to me the most fascinating part of our day. Tired out I tried to hide the yawn that so wanted to come. He glanced at me and smiled.

'Maybe you have had enough history for today. Would you like to go to Arthur's seat?'

'Yes, I've only ever seen it from the train,' I said eagerly.

Soon we were standing high on the summit gazing down on the scene below. Edinburgh lay open to our view, the old town with its jumble of buildings and the new with elegant broad streets, lined with equally elegant houses.

Beyond lay the Firth of Forth and the coast of Fife.

It was magic to be so high, to have a bird's eye view.

'Had enough?' Uncle Glen asked

'Ye-es.'

'Right we will make our way down, we will take our time there is no rush.

Carefully we picked our way. To the left of us a flock of sheep grazed, their thick fleece impervious to the sharp wind. As we drew nearer we spotted a ram at the same moment as he spotted us.

He put his head down and charged.

'Run!' shouted Uncle Glen, trying to shoo the ram away.

I stumbled down over boulders, and glancing over my shoulder I could see Uncle Glen hot on my heels, the ram in hot pursuit.

On and on we ran, till at last the ram stood still shaking its head.

We breathed a sigh of relief and carried down the steep slope, not stopping till we reached the bottom.

Panting and holding my sides where a stabbing pain shot through I could see Uncle Glen was breathless to, his face grey, his hands clasping his head.

'I'm all right, don't look so worried,' he smiled at me.

I was thinking of the metal plate in his head, and Ada saying he was not supposed to get stressed.

We rested for a while, Uncle Glen sitting on the grass still holding his head but with colour in his face.

Back on the tram to Granton he turned to me a crooked smile on his lips.

'We won't say anything about the ram to your Auntie Aggie, she would just get upset.'

I nodded, feeling that if we did tell her somehow I would get the blame.

It was better from then on, Uncle Glen and I had a secret.

By the end of that week, Ada came to take me home.

She held me away from her and smiled, 'my you have roses in your cheeks,' she said.

'It is the good Granton air,' 'Granton Aggie' said, 'it seemed to tire her out, and she never had any trouble sleeping.'

I stood clutching my case, eager to leave.

Uncle Glen ruffled my hair, 'she can always come back during the school holidays, there will be other children to play with then, I think she was a wee bit lonely.'

'Well she seemed to be able to amuse herself, she was never in,' said 'Granton Aggie'.

I stared at her, but she met my gaze unflinching.

As the tram trundled its way to Waverley Station, Ada said she was well pleased with how I looked, and that I must have minded my manners as Uncle Glen had asked me back.

'The doctor was right, a change of scene has done you good,' she nodded. I fell asleep in the train on the way home, as I always did on visits to Edinburgh.

Eugene was at the station to meet us.

'She has slept all the way home, it is the good clean air and the healthy smell of the hops,' Ada told him.

Eugene grinned, 'if the air is so clean, why dae ye think they call the place 'Auld Reekie'?'

Ada gave him one of her looks.

I was delighted to be re-united with Rover, who followed me wherever I went. Betty was still her usual self, but Lena seemed subdued and moody.

'Is there something wrong with Lena?' I asked Betty.

She laughed, 'mammy has been going on at her about Big Bill Mathieson's young brother.'

'What about him?'

Mammy thinks he is after Lena, and she thinks Lena is interested in him.

'What is he like?' I asked.

'Very handsome, he is a bit older than Lena and mammy thinks he will lead her astray,' Betty laughed again.

'How do you mean?' I was puzzled.

'You don't need to know,' Betty played her infuriating 'too young' card.

I couldn't wait to see for myself and hung about the front shop in the hope he would come in. When he did it was easy to see that there was an attraction between Lena and him.

I followed her into the back shop.

'He's nice,' I said.

'What would you know? Mammy doesn't think much of him, she has warned me off sailors in general and this one in particular,' Lena grumbled.

'Is he really Big Bill's brother?'

'Yes, but he is nothing like him.'

'Has he asked you out?'

'Not yet, but mammy would never let me go,' Lena sighed.

He came in every night, sitting in the same seat.

Ada had warned that Aggie was to serve him, Lena had to kept away.

I'm not interested in him anyway,' Lena tossed her head.

'You better no' be, yer mammy said if he makes a move she wants to know, and she says he will have her tae answer tae,' Aggie regarded Lena over her glasses.

'Do you know his name?' I asked Lena.

'Of course I do, it's John.'

'Right!'

Having got nowhere with his efforts to speak to Lena, John decided to use me as a go-between. He caught my arm as I was passing, and thrust a note into my hand.

'Give that to your sister.'

'Which one?' I asked though I knew already.

'The one with the long hair. Give it to her make sure she reads it and bring me back her answer,' he said.

I watched as Lena unfolded the note, a blush rose from her neck to the roots of her hair.

'He wants me to go out with him,' she said.

'Will you go?'

Cocozza family group back row Tina, Tony, Eugene, Dominic (Tommy) front row
Mary, Granny, Famie, Dadee and Lizzie

Ada with Lena on her knee Benny between Eugene with Betty at his knee

Dadee looking slightly uncomfortable in a studio chair

Famie and my sister Benny aged three, Bennie died six weeks after the photograph was taken

Lizzie, Dora Ricardo and Famie

Lena on her first communion day

Eddie and Lizzie with Eddie's sister Betty who brought up her siblings
when their mother died

Betty (Domenica) aged 16

Tina, Benny and Famie

Lena, Myself, Lizzie and Eddie

Lena and Betty

Me outside our cafe with my faithful dog, Rover

'No, mammy would kill me,' she gasped.
'He says I have to bring him an answer,' I pleaded, 'will I say it is no?'
'You will say nothing,' she said.
'Do you want to go out with him?'
'Maybe.'
Next day he stopped me as I came in the door.
'Well?' he asked.
'Nothing!'
'What do you mean, nothing?'
'She said I was to say nothing,' I said.
'Och I'll speak to her myself,' he dismissed me with a shrug.
The next night Lena went dancing, she was still out at midnight.
Ada closed up the shop and came upstairs demanding to know where she was.
'Ah think she went to the Locarno,' Eugene said easily.
'She should be home by this time, no respectable girl stays out to this time,' Ada fretted.
'Och they will have missed the last tram,' Eugene said.
'Who is she with?' Ada was suspicious.
'Geena, the usual crowd, she will be fine, what are you worrying about?'
'Oh nothing ever worries you, there might be a raid, anything. She should be home.
Eugene sighed, 'Ah'll take the dog for a walk, see if ah can see her.'
I looked at Betty who narrowed her eyes and shook her head. We both knew Lena was out with John Mathieson.
Eugene was back within fifteen minutes, Lena at his heels.
'Where have you been?' Ada demanded.
'At the Locarno, we had to walk home,' Lena shrugged off her coat.
'Next time ,my lady, you make sure you are home at a decent time,' Ada warned.
Later, we three huddled on the bed, heads together talking in whispers as Aggie slept.
'I nearly died when I saw daddy walking towards us,' Lena said.
'What did daddy say?' I was eager to know.
Lena laughed, 'I expected him to be angry, but he just said your mammy is looking for you, he never even looked at John.'
'Will you go out with him again?' Betty asked.
'I don't know, anyway he is going back to sea tomorrow. I did promise to write, and so did he,' Lena said wistfully.
'Did you winch up a close?' I asked.
'You shouldn't ask things like that ,you are no' supposed to know about that,' Lena was shocked.
'Well, Mary Murray said she has seen people winch in her close, she has even seen them kissing,' I told her.
'You better no' let mammy hear you say things like that,' Lena warned. Betty grinned, 'never mind all that, did you winch?'

'That's my business,' Lena said loftily.

So John went back to sea, and before long a letter came saying he was due for posting somewhere far away and it may be difficult to write. 'That's an old excuse, they all say that,' Betty said.

'I believe him,' Lena said emphatically.

Ada caught sight of the letter, 'that is forces mail, who is writing to you?'

'Just somebody I know,' Lena said.

'Well I hope it isn't who I think it is,' Ada snapped.

'I would just go out and enjoy myself if I were you,' Betty said. 'Leave me alone!' Lena said stuffing the letter in her pocket.

'Just don't let mammy see you moping,' Betty warned.

'Who says I am moping?' Lena demanded.

Another letter came, this time containing a photograph, and Lena could not hide her pleasure.

'Maybe he is keen after all,' Betty told her, as she proudly passed round the snap.

'You better not let mammy see it,' I said. 'Don't worry; I am going to hide it.'

'Make sure it is somewhere Aggie won't find it, or you will be in trouble,' Betty said.

With no more letters Lena felt a little lost. She refused invitations to go out with Geena, instead she worked away in the shop night after night.

'Mammy will begin to wonder why you are not going out with Geena,' Betty warned.

I just don't want to,' Lena said.

Now and then she would leave the shop for a little while, then come back looking really guilty.

Betty decided to follow her, and found her in the close puffing away at a cigarette. On seeing Betty she stubbed it underfoot, frantically waving her hands around to disperse the smoke.

'You don't need to hide it from me, I smoke too, but I make sure I'm well away from the shop.'

Lena was caught out, Aggie finding cigarette butts in an apron pocket, she told Ada, who was absolutely furious. Lena was defiant when Ada challenged her.

'I won't stop, I like smoking,' she said.

'You watch your tongue lady, it is a filthy habit and not something a decent girl should do. I blame those dance halls. It's put ideas into your head,' Ada told her.

She repeated this to Eugene who placidly scraped away at his pipe before answering.

'Leave her alone. The more you get on to her, the more she will do it.' 'I don't know why I bother talking to you about these things,' Ada was exasperated.

The war between Lena and Ada got worse. Lena refused to talk to either Ada or Eugene, and she used me as a go-between which put me in Ada's black books.

Betty found the whole thing natural enough; she had gone through something similar.

'Mammy says if Lena doesn't behave she is going to wash her hands of her,' I said, a little confused.

'It will work out somehow, something else will take her mind off it,' Betty assured us.

She chucked me under the chin, 'can't wait to see if you go through this phase, you won't have the nerve,' she laughed.

It had been weeks since any letters from John had come. Lena said she wasn't bothered, but sat night after night looking at his picture, which was quite dog-eared.

Betty too was mooning over some new boy. I sighed a huge sigh.

'I wish I had a boyfriend,' I said.

'You're too wee!' they said in chorus, and aimed a cushion at me.

Betty's prediction that something else would distract from John Mathieson proved all too true.

Lena had seen nothing of her friend Morag McSween since the dreadful New Year incident. Now here she was in the shop asking if she could speak to Lena. She was clearly upset and Ada lost no time in calling Lena through from the back shop.

After a brief word the two left the shop.

Aggie's eyes danced in her head with excitement.

'Whit dae ye suppose has happened?' she asked Ada.

'Whatever it is, it is not good, she is very upset. I hope it is not bad news about her father,' Ada said.

Half an hour later Lena came home, very subdued.

'It's one of the twins, Hamish, he is in 'The Law',' Lena said.

We all knew what that meant.

'Tuberculosis!' Ada said.

'How bad is he?' Aggie asked.

'Really bad,' Lena said, 'it is so unfair, he is not even seventeen yet.'

'I'm really sorry to hear that,' Ada said, 'it was good of Morag to come to tell you.'

'I want to see him, he has asked to see me,' Lena said, near to tears.

'He may not be allowed visitors outside his family. They have probably been checked too, I suppose, it is a very contagious disease,' Ada warned.

'I don't care, I need to see him,' Lena was adamant.

She came back from her visit terribly upset.

'We could only talk through the window of the ward, he is too ill to have visitors near him.'

Ada patted her shoulder, 'well at least you went to see him.'

'I am going again, and I will keep going, he needs to know people care about him,' Lena said.

Ada nodded but said nothing more.

'She is going to get hurt through this, everyone knows going into the Law is practically a death sentence,' Ada told Eugene,

'It is a terrible thing to have happened,' he muttered.

'Yes, and I can't add to Mrs McSween's misery by turning up at her door, reminding her of things,' Ada said bitterly.

'Eadie, it is a' water under the bridge, it will be the last thing on her mind,' he said.

'Well maybe, but I for one am not going to remind her,' Ada told him.

'If you get the chance tell Mrs McSween how sorry we are,' she told Lena, thrusting a little parcel for Hamish into her hand.

Lena spent as much time as possible with Hamish, sometimes she was allowed to sit by his bed, helping him make the wire ear-rings which the patients were given as therapy.

Hamish was growing weaker by the day. When he was able he talked of things they would do when he got home. Lena would return from the visits totally wrecked by emotion.

The friendship between her and Morag was as strong as ever.

'It's an ill wind,' said Ada, 'thank God some good has come out of this.'

Hamish died just before his seventeenth birthday.

The whole family was devastated at his loss, especially his twin.

'There are men getting killed every day in this terrible war, yet somehow this young lad's passing is worse, because it is so near,' Ada said.

CHAPTER 21

The second visit to 'Granton Aggie' was much better, it was summer and the rain was warmer. I stayed for most of the summer holidays, and though I was still dispatched every morning, and told to amuse myself I was not alone, having made friends with the girl who lived downstairs, Sheila Farquarson. For me, coming as I did from a tenement, there was a special delight in a garden after rain, a wonder in the smell of the roses. It reminded me of Garrowhill and the happy time we spent there. As the summer wore on the bright faces of the nasturtiums staggered me with their profusion. Sheila laughed at my amazement, and happily pulled their leaves to chew, which I thought a sacrilege.

Sheila's father had a roomy garden shed, which we used when it rained, swapping scraps, dressing dolls, or drawing. Once we found a frog, who became our mascot.

Often I would join with the other children to go and explore the beach where I had spent so much time alone.

One of the children, a boy named Graham, lived in a very grand house on the corner at the bottom of the road. He was considered very posh and was not supposed to mix with the likes of us, but he was lonely and loved to join in our games.

He was the kindest boy I had ever met, and I soon developed a crush, when Sheila found out she teased me mercilessly.

Graham was having a birthday party, he persuaded his mother to invite some of the crowd. I was very nervous, and could hardly find my voice to answer the greeting of his very grand mother.

When she asked my surname I answered without thinking, Cocozza instead of Coutts, and she smiled thinly but said nothing.

Next day Sheila told me that Graham was not allowed to speak to me under any circumstances, as I was a foreigner and an enemy one at that.

'Why have you got two names anyway?' Sheila was curious.

I told her the whole sorry story.

'I suppose you won't want to play with me now?'

'Och no, we can still be friends, and I won't say anything to my mammy. She calls you a 'Glesca Keelie' anyway, so I suppose she thinks that's foreign.

I was almost more offended by being called a 'Glesca Keelie' than a foreigner, and Ada would have been horrified if she knew.

The ban on speaking to Graham hit me hard, not just because of the crush, which was all on my side in any case, but it brought again the feeling of inferiority, being something less, something different.

Heartbroken, I took to getting up at first light and slipping out of the house, walking down to Graham's house, pulling a leaf from the high hedge that surrounded it, and later pressing the leaf into a jotter.

1 felt like a romantic heroine in one of my stories, pining for my true love, a Cinderella to Graham's Prince Charming.

After a few times 'Granton Aggie' caught me as I was about to go out, and after demanding an explanation which I refused to give, grounded me for a week.

I told myself it was a sacrifice; it was what heroines did, after all and if I did tell her she just might tell Graham's mother, which would be the most awful thing.

My stay at Granton was lightened by the presence of Rosie; she was 'Granton Aggie's friend. Rosie was plump and jolly and when she laughed her two chins shook which fascinated me.

To my astonishment I discovered Rosie was German. I had never seen a German before and could not understand how she could be so lovely, when everybody knew that the Germans were evil.

I was curious to know why she was not locked up like the Italians and other Germans, but I knew 'Granton Aggie' would not answer my questions.

Uncle Glen let slip that Rosie had a son serving in the British Army.

Burning with curiosity I took the courage to ask my cousin Mima.

'Why do you want to know about Rosie?'

'Because she is a German and —.'

'And you thought all Germans were bad?'

'Well, mammy says they are our enemies.'

'Yes but your daddy is Italian and the Italians are our enemies, but that doesn't mean all Italians are bad, does it?'

'No, I really like Rosie, I was just surprised that's all,' I said.

'Well, Rosie is married to a Scotsman, she has two sons, one is in the army and the other will soon be called up, and she has to report to the police station every week, just like your daddy,' Mima said, in a voice that told me she had said enough and would say no more.

It was the longest conversation I had ever had with Mima, who came and went without even acknowledging that I was there.

My curiosity about Rosie was still not satisfied.

She was 'Granton Aggie's friend, and she was German, so why did 'Granton Aggie' approve of Rosie, when she didn't approve of Eugene? Rosie was often about the house and I warmed even more to her; she was like me, she knew what it was like to be different

Her son George came home on leave and Rosie invited us up for a celebration. He smiled at me when I was introduced, 'oh a wee 'Glesca Keelie',' he said.

I drew him a look which he ignored.

His younger brother Jim was lovely, full of mischief but really kind and considerate.

Rosie's eyes followed him wherever he went.

'If only he was still at school, I wouldn't lose him to the navy,' she whispered.

George decided to go through to Glasgow for the day, and he asked me if I would like to go along.

I jumped at the chance, as I was homesick, especially for Rover. 'Granton Aggie's dog Billy was like a fat spoiled child, and was quite jealous of me.

George and Betty got on really well that day, and it was the beginning of a real friendship, though not a romance.

Rosie liked to wear flowers in her rich dark hair; an ostentation frowned upon by the good Presbyterian folk of Granton. Rosie would turn up in her colourful shawl, a sprig of Mimosa or a rose in her hair, and waltz 'Granton Aggie' and I up the road to the pictures. If we had to wait in a queue Rosie would keep the queue entertained, singing in a sweet soprano voice-

Ramona, I miss you now at twilight fall
Ramona, I'll wait beside the garden wall.

'Granton Aggie' would smile indulgently even she loved Rosie too much to be embarrassed by her.

Just before the holidays were over Rosie's youngest son Jim was sent overseas.

'She has got it into her head that Jim will die young, she thinks she will never see him again,' 'Granton Aggie' told Ada when she came to pick me up.

'Oh the poor woman, it is a premonition, a mother knows these things,' Ada said.

A few weeks later a letter from 'Granton Aggie' told us Jim was missing presumed dead.

A light seems to have gone out of Rosie, you wouldn't recognize her,' the letter told us.

'Oh that poor woman, she knew, she knew from the beginning,' Ada said.

'Och you women wi' your premonitions, the boy is missing, he could still be alive,' Eugene said.

I wonder if she still wears flowers in her hair,' I said.

Not from what your Auntie Aggie says, she is totally changed,' Ada answered.

That night I included Rosie and Jim in the long list of people I prayed for every night.

When I did see her next I did not recognize her at all, she was thinner, and silent. Gone was the bright shawl, her dark hair scraped back in a severe bun.

Betty's romantic life was complicated. Eugene said she was like a sailor, except she had a man from every port.

The liaisons were kept on an innocent level, never going beyond the kissing and cuddling stage.

Even the rebellious Betty would not step over that line.

Nevertheless Ada was not happy. Betty would swear to be true as each one sailed away. She treated the whole thing as a joke, which infuriated Ada.

'It is a totally irresponsible way to behave,' Ada scolded.

'I'm never going to see them again am I? They don't take it seriously any more than I do,' Betty countered.

'Mark my words, chickens have a way of coming home to roost,' Ada told her.

'I don't know what you mean,' Betty laughed. 'We'll see, we'll see,' Ada said.

The news from the front was good, the allies were closing in on Germany,

Lord Haw-Haw's diatribes became more frantic, claiming Germany would be triumphant still. Ada shook her fist at the radio.

'It will be a sorry day for you my man when Germany loses. They'll stretch your neck for you, it's no more than you deserve. Italy broke away from Germany, paying a heavy price for her perceived betrayal. Eddie Gillan home on a brief leave told tales of the British soldiers being hailed as heroes as they entered Rome. Though he still cut a somewhat comic figure in his overlong kilt, his lean sunburnt face, dashing moustache and gleaming white teeth at last captured a female heart - Lizzie's.

Eugene was bemused, 'she cannae be serious, he is years younger than she is.'

Ada wagged a warning finger.

'Don't you dare say a word to either of them, Lizzie deserves this, she has never had as much as a date before.'

'Ah know, an' that's why ah don't think she is thinkin' straight. We a' know Eddie wants intae this family. Betty just laughed at him, Lena was mortified at the very idea, and now he has latched on to our Lizzie, an' she is gettin' carried away wi' hersel'.'

Seeing Lizzie blush and giggle every time Eddie was around convinced us that she was smitten. Eddie though was playing it cool, and went back to the front with nothing being said, except a promise to write to the family.

Lizzie went back to her quiet ways, working every day in the shop, or spending her evenings in the chapel.

She still devoted her day off to Lena and I, taking us to the pictures, using her coupons to buy us sweets, and making spaghetti on her little machine.

She never mentioned Eddie, but Lena whispered that she had seen her gazing at his photograph and smiling back at his smiling face.

Eugene complained to Tina.

'You need to talk tae her, get her tae see sense.'

'What's wrong wi' liken' somebody?' Tina demanded.

'He's no right fur her, he is too young for a start,' Eugene persisted.

'A man's a man for a' that,' Tina shrugged.

April 1945 was to prove a pivotal month. On the twelfth Roosevelt died of a cerebral haemorrhage while having his portrait painted. By the 28th the Italian people had meted out justice to 'Il Duce' who was shot and strung up by the heels alongside his mistress Clara Petacci. Two days later Adolph Hitler committed suicide.

I clung to Ada in delight, the arch enemies were dead.

'The war is not over yet,' Ada warned.

'Och Germany is finished, it is only a matter of time,' Eugene said with satisfaction.

By May 7th, the bells tolled the victory.

From the radio came the sound of the cheering crowds as they gathered in their thousands round the gates of Buckingham Palace to cheer the King and Queen, and roar their approval as Churchill gave the famous V for victory sign.

Everywhere people went wild.

At the crossroads where Breadalbane Street dissected Little Dover Street and Great Dover Street, small boys and grown men scurried to and fro, bringing old chairs, bits of wood, boxes, anything that would feed the huge bonfire they had built.

The laughing jostling crowd formed congas which snaked around the buildings, or strutted the 'Lambeth Walk'. As night fell they were still singing and dancing.

Any evening, any day,
When you stroll down Lambeth way,
You'll find them all,
Doing the Lambeth walk.

The rest of the crowd shouting a resounding Oy!

The firelight sent up grotesque shadows of leaping figures.

Few knew or cared where Lambeth was, it was good enough to be able to sing and dance, to kiss a sailor or soldier, to know the war was over.

I was determined to be in the thick of it. Rover, tongue lolling, prancing around my feet, and dogs barked furiously as they dodged the reeling dancers.

Even Ada who had cautioned restraint closed the shop and joined in the fun.

The night wore on, nobody wanted to sleep, and mothers calling to their children it was time for bed were shouted down by the crowd.

'Och leave the weans alane, the bloody war is ower!'

A group of boys arrived with a hastily constructed effigy of Hitler and threw it on the fire.

The crowd went wild.

The singing and dancing continued for three more days, crazy days when everybody was your friend, when mothers threatened to 'skelp the lug' of their offspring for running off with treasured pieces of furniture to feed the bonfire.

At last the crowds moved away, the fire was allowed to die, a huge ring of black ash moving in the breeze, all that was left.

It was an unforgettable time, the sheer relief mirrored on each face.

Happy and exhausted we sat round the table, as Ada dished up the dinner.

'So civilization didnae end, and the world is still standin,' Eugene said.

There is still Japan, they haven't defeated her,' Ada said.

By July the lights were on again in London if not 'all over the world' as Vera Lynn had promised all during the war. Tailors could indulge in the luxury of using more material.

By August two atomic bombs had been dropped on Hiroshima and Nagasaki, bringing the end of civilization and to the people of those cities, the end of the world.

'Oh my God!' Ada said, gazing at the report of the event in the newspaper. We have just come out of a devastating war, and now they have these horrendous bombs, the world will never be safe again.'

I cried myself to sleep that night, gone the wonderful feeling of happiness I had experienced; now there was the old familiar threat of the end of the world.

CHAPTER 22

Eugene stood gazing at the 'Try Our Blancmange' sign and mused how long it would be before we could get back to making real ice-cream.

'Huh!' Ada scoffed, 'we have more to worry us than that.'

'What?' asked Eugene.

'The war is over, Mr. DiMarco will want his shop back, and we will lose the shop and the house.'

'Not at all, not at all, we will be fine,' Eugene assured her.

'Well you tell me what we will live on, certainly not the proceeds of your Terrazzo business,' she snapped.

'We will think of something, we won't starve, we have never starved yet.'

'We have come pretty close,' Ada was not to be humoured.

'I'll see what I can do,' Eugene said.

'You need to work for a firm and have somebody else worry about the wages. A place like Toffolo Jackson, they know you, and you worked for years with them. You have to admit you don't have a business brain.'

'Eh what is there to know? I go out, I find the work, price it, do it get paid, and move on to the next one.'

'You don't take account of your overheads, and I have tried to tell you so many times. It is alright being straight with people and not over charging, but people know you are trying to make a living, and no one is going to complain if you make a modest profit,' Ada was losing patience. 'I know what I'm doing,' Eugene said stubbornly.

'You think you know what you are doing. We've got trouble, unless a miracle happens.'

Though Ada was exasperated with Eugene's stubbornness, she did recognize that he took great pride in his work and subsequently to his time to give a perfect finish.

Hour after hour he would be on his knees polishing the terrazzo. He would never consent to wearing a mask, and would come home covered in dust. It was in his nostrils, his eyelids, the folds of skin in his neck, and it would clog his ears.

Lena and I would soak cotton wool in olive oil, and clean every crease on his face and neck. Lena would polish the bare scalp, and I would gently brush the grey tinged fringe of hair.

We would compete with each other to see who could get the most dust removed.

While we worked the kettle would be on the boil so that he could wash.

He always insisted on the sweetest smelling soap, which drew caustic comments from Ada.

'Never mind how nice it smells, make sure you use it.'

This was a reference to his habit of lathering up the soap, dabbing it gingerly on the centre of his cheeks, then reaching for the towel.

Ada would hold the towel under his nose and say, 'look at the state of that. It is not you who has to wash it.'

He would feign surprise, 'Eh where did a' that dirt come from?'

Duly washed to his satisfaction if not Ada's, he would draw his chair up to the table, sit himself down, lay aside his pipe and await his tea.

Ada would cast a disapproving eye at the rolled up shirt sleeves showing a tidemark round his arms. He would sigh and roll them down, but leave them unbuttoned to flap around.

Eugene and Ada's seating arrangements at mealtimes were always unconventional. The fireside chair Eugene sat on caused him to be lower than the table. Due to his small stature this alone would have made eating difficult, but the fact that Ada, who was quite tall, sat on his knee complicated the situation.

Forced back into his seat, Eugene was left to stab blindly at his food. If he was successful he would shovel the food into the side of his mouth where, bereft of teeth, the rock hard gums did their best. He always took a long time to finish a meal, defending himself by saying food should be properly chewed.

I was always uneasy about the peculiar seating arrangement. Its origins were lost in the mists if time, but to me it seemed it had always been, nevertheless I could see no reason for it.

Even after they had had a blazing row they would sit down to eat in this fashion.

I would never have dared to voice my feelings on the matter, and consoled myself that they did sit properly when we had visitors.

Indeed it was a sign that a stranger was now viewed as a member of the family if Ada sat on Eugene's knee is his or her presence.

The expected letter telling of Mr. DiMarco's imminent return duly arrived. He said he was anxious to get back to his shop, asked Ada to have all the paperwork ready and thanked her for her services.

'At least we can stay on in the house, his wife doesn't want to leave that fancy flat,' Eugene said reading it over.

'Yes we can stay on in the house if we can pay the rent,' Ada said. 'That is easier said than done.'

Ill with the mumps, I lay in the recess bed in the kitchen listening to their muted voices going over the grim reality facing us.

It was back to the dark days of losing Garrowhill, back to facing the possibility of going back to Auntie Teeny.

Again that awful sense of loss, of constantly shifting sand, it seemed there was nothing that could be relied upon, and no one, not even Ada, could prevent terrible things happening to us.

I began to have hallucinations; a giant wheel spun faster and faster on the wall at the end of the bed, and as it spun it grew, bigger and bigger till it spun off the wall and engulfed me; black figures with contorted faces, nun like figures in flowing robes would reach out for me, their faces the demonic face of the devil above the sacristy door.

Night after night these figures appeared; night after night I sat bolt upright screaming. Ada was at her wits end.

'I think if you sponge her down with tepid water and dose her with ipecacuanha wine, syrup of squills and glycerine.'

This from the doctor who stood frowning down on me, 'she may be prone to hysteria,' he said packing his case and giving me a disapproving look. He turned to go, then as an afterthought said.

'Is there anything that is troubling her, something at school perhaps?'

'No nothing at all,' Ada said, 'she is happy at school and happy at home,' she added.

I wanted to tell her about how I felt about losing the house. I wanted to tell her about Molly and her gang who waited for me everyday and made my life such a misery, but I couldn't.

She would only tell me to stand up to the bullies, as she had done.

I sought consolation in my little books on the lives of the saints, reading again the story of St. Jude the patron saint of lost causes and last resort. I prayed to him morning and night, beseeching his help in finding a way out of our dilemma. He heard me.

Mr. DiMarco paced the length of the shop and back again. We stood watching as he inspected every nook and cranny. He lamented the beautiful plate glass counter now held together by tape, the boarded up window which had hidden the drunken Russian with the gun. He lamented the loss of the glass shelves and the graceful fluked bottles that had once held a bewildering variety of sweets.

Mrs. DiMarco stood, hands clasping her cheeks, murmuring over and over, 'Oi Madonna.'

The shop was clearly not as they expected to find it. The books were produced, Mr. DiMarco settling himself at a table to peruse them.

His eyes flickered over the columns, then back to the top, his finger tracing every line, resulting in much shaking of the head as if unable to believe what he saw.

Ada watched in silence, but she was struggling to keep her temper. Eventually she snatched the books away from him, snapping them shut and glaring at him defiantly.

'What happened?' he said, 'It used to be such a good business.'

'What happened?' Ada exploded, 'what happened was the war, which you should thank God you survived, a lot of good men didn't.'

She took the keys from her pocket, and thrust out her hand, 'you will be wanting these.'

He took them. As one we moved to the door, filing out without a backward glance at the place where so many dramas had taken place, and which had been our life for six long years.

We were not at home to witness the events that took place on the first day Mr. DiMarco opened for business.

By the time we returned at tea time, we were surprised to see the shop boarded up, and the pavement strewn with broken glass and bricks. As we sat down to our tea there was a sharp knock at the door. Eugene went to answer it and came back into the kitchen followed by Hammy. He was clearly agitated cracking his knuckles with more force than usual.

'What's wrong Hammy is somebody ill, is it your mother?' Ada asked. 'No, no, it's the wee man.'

'What wee man?' Ada was puzzled.

'The wee man that came back to the shop.'

'Oh Mr. DiMarco, aye he is back. The war is over and he has taken the shop back, so we don't have anything to do with it anymore,' Eugene told him.

'Aye, b-but it's no' that.'

'What happened? Sit down and tell us everything, take your time,' Ada said, pulling out a chair.

Hammy sat, his knees drawn up to his chin, the long thin fingers working.

'There was a mob, a big crowd, a' gathered round the shop as soon as it opened,' Hammy spluttered.

'They all started shouting and swearing, throwing bricks and bottles.' Hammy's words tripped over each other.

Ada's hands flew to her face, 'Oh my God!'

'Was the shop open?' asked Eugene.

'Aye, the wee man came to try to shut the door but they burst in, dragged him round the counter, turned him upside down and stuck his head in the freezer.'

'Was it the bath gang?' Betty asked.

'Aye, well they were there and it was mostly them that attacked the wee man, but there was a lot of ordinary folk there, folk I've seen in the shop,' Hammy's fingers worked overtime, his knuckles red and puffy with the pain.

'Oh my God! Oh my God!' Ada kept saying.

'They kept shouting, nae bloody Tallies here, nae Nazi bootlickers,' Hammy's hand flew to his mouth.

'Oh ah'm sorry for swearing but that's what they were shouting.'

'It's all right, it's all right,' Ada patted his shoulder.

'Did you go for the police?' Betty asked.

Hammy looked shamefaced, 'I was - I was really scared.'

Betty sighed.

'But - but somebody must have went to Cranston Street, because the two big Bobbies came flying down the hill blowing their whistles. A lot of the crowd ran away, but there was still a lot in the shop, still beating the wee man up, you could hear him screaming.'

'What about his family, where were they?' Ada asked.

'They were in the back shop, they were screaming, but all right I think.'

'This is just awful, I hope the police arrested the guilty ones,' Ada said.

'Aye well the Black Maria came as well and took a lot of the gang away. I saw the police leading the family out, the wee man was bleeding badly, he was shaking, and his wife and his wee boy were hysterical,' Hammy paused for breath.

'That big Bobby that always comes in for Bovril, he stood and waited till the men came to board the shop up. They nailed big bars across the door and it looks awful,' Hammy said.

'Aye we saw that, we were wondering what had happened,' Eugene said.

Our tea had been forgotten, nobody knew what to say, and as usual we waited for Ada to say something.

'Put the kettle on Betty, we need a good strong cup. No, no, sit where you are Hammy you need a cup too by the looks of you,' Ada said pressing him back down on his chair.

We sat sipping the hot tea, still finding it hard to make sense of it all.

'It is a bad business, I never thought that would happen, the war is over, and you would hope people can live and let live,' Ada said.

'Och it will blow over, things will settle down, people will have other things to worry about,' Eugene said placidly.

'You think so; do you honestly think the Di Marcos will ever feel safe in that shop again?' Ada asked.

'Aye of course, if they leave it for a week or two, it will be fine,' Eugene insisted.

For the next two weeks the shop stayed boarded up. It seemed so strange to see the place deserted and the empty space above the door where Ada's name had been.

On the third week a letter arrived addressed to Ada in a scrawling hand. As she read it her eyes widened, and conscious that my eyes were on her, she stuffed the envelope into the pocket of her apron and went on sweeping the floor.

Later when Eugene came home they held a whispered conversation in Italian, she looking concerned, he smiling and nodding.

This went on for days, as did their trips out during the day and evenings too. None of us knew what was going on not even Aggie. She sat hunched over her crochet, glasses on the end of her nose, complaining over and over that the rent was due in another week.

On the Tuesday of the last week Lena was suddenly given a month's rent money and told to pay it to the factor.

'I wonder where that money came from,' Betty said, 'I gave mammy my wages and so did Lena but it still wasn't enough for the rent.'

'Well at least we have a roof over our heads for another month. I don't know where it came from, but I'm glad it came,' Lena said.

Three weeks later as we finished our sparse Sunday dinner and waited for Ada to say the grace after meals, she told us she had some news.

'We are going to buy the shop,' she said watching our faces.

We gasped, Ada smiled.

'A bit of a surprise eh?' Eugene laughed.

'How can you buy it, we don't have any money,' Betty queried.

'We didn't have any money, but we do now,' Ada smiled.

'Aye in a kinda way,' laughed Eugene, who was clearly enjoying himself.

Ada held up her hand, 'I can see you are still puzzled, the true story is Mr. DiMarco is too scared to come back to the shop, so he wrote to me asking if we wanted to buy it. We thought it over, went to the bank for some help, and they agreed to give us the money.'

'So you pay Mr. DiMarco the money the bank gave you, and then pay back the bank?' Betty asked.

'Ye-es over time, but it does mean we will have to work very hard to be sure we are able to do that, it is a lot of money,' Ada warned.

'The business is in your mammy's name, it is safer that way,' Eugene said.

'Do you think it will be safe for us tae go back?' Aggie's eyes danced with anxiety.

'Och nae bother, the folk know us,' Eugene said.

'It will be fine, we have nothing to fear,' Ada said, but there was an edge of uncertainty in her voice.

It seemed no time till Eugene was balancing on the top of the ladder nailing up the familiar nameplate - Ada Coutts Proprietor, and he rubbed it with the sleeve of his jacket to give it a final polish.

Eugene went on a mission to replace the glass in the window and door, and we trooped out to have a look as soon as the glaziers finished.

The difference was amazing. While he pleaded and cajoled with the glazier to restore the plate glass counter, Betty busied herself dressing the window. She made cut-outs of bottles of Iron Brew, Vimto, ice-cream cones and tall glasses with straws. She made streamers of red, white and blue going from corner to corner, held together with paper rosettes, then she hung a banner proclaiming in huge red letters -

WE ARE BACK! BUSINESS AS USUAL.

'Well,' said Ada standing on the pavement surveying Betty's handiwork, 'we're certainly not sneaking in quietly, let's hope we get a better reception than the Di Marcos.

We did.

The people greeted us like old friends, they smiled with pleasure at the transformation in the shop, and they patted Eugene on the back and shook his hand.

'Whit did ah tell ye?' he beamed, 'nae bother, nae bother at a'.'

'So far so good, let's see what the rough elements do,' cautioned Ada. We did not have long to wait, soon they were back, chanting and singing at the door, intimidating customers, stubbing the butts of their cigarettes on the newly varnished door. Ada was having none of it, and she marched out to confront them.

'We are back to stay, you will not frighten us away, we stay whether you like it or not.'

'Whit will ye dae, bar us, call the polis?'

'If you cause trouble I will, just like before, I'm warning you.'

'Whit makes you think wee Joe will no get whit the other wee nyaff goat?'

'What makes you think I will stand for it?' Ada snapped.

'We ur no' feart o' you',' Butcher growled.

'And we are not afraid of you, so any funny business and you will be having a holiday as a guest of Her Majesty.'

So the lines were drawn. Ada determined the shop would prosper, it had to.

The re-acquisition of the shop gave Eugene a new impetus to get his terrazzo business up and running again. Already there was talk of the old slums of Glasgow being replaced, and people were moving out to new schemes on the outskirts of the city. Eugene was banking on the housewives thrilled by their new surroundings may just want a terrazzo doorstep to grace their new front doors.

With the approach of Christmas Betty allowed her imagination free reign when she decorated the window.

Cotton wool snow hung on thread, cut out snowmen held frosted glasses of lime and cola, Santa and his sleigh rode across a white cardboard moon, while sprigs of mistletoe and holly lay strewn across the floor. Though there was little fancy goods to be had, Ada decided to throw a party for the local children.

'The kiddies have had a hard time of it these past years, it would be nice to see them enjoying themselves,' she said, and set about hiring trestle tables, benches, cups, saucers, plates, serviettes and serviette rings that came in all colours of the rainbow. She ordered a six foot Christmas tree from Lewis's. When it was delivered, its branches bound together with twine, the smell of pine permeated the whole house. I could not wait to undo the ties and decorate it.

Betty and me were dispatched to Woolworth's to buy little gifts, which Santa would hand out to the children.

We bought pencils, rubbers, rulers, cut out dolls, scraps, soap in the shape of Snow White and the seven dwarfs, ribbons in all colours and comics.

I have always loved the preparation of a party better than the party itself, and the days running up to our party were wonderful.

Night after night we sat up making paper chains, which we hung on the tree once it was safely installed in a bucket of sand and weighed down with heavy stones.

Betty had bought some cheap beads which we took apart and restrung on long pieces of string which we hung on the branches.

The long tables were set down the centre of the room, flanked on either side by benches. Betty folded each serviette into a fan, tucked it into a serviette ring and slipped a silver sixpence inside which would tinkle on to each plate as the serviette was shaken out.

Ada persuaded 'Dusty Miller' one of our local Bobbies and the husband of Betty's friend to act as Santa Claus, only to have him unmasked by his three year old daughter.

We had dumpling and Lemonade, as many buns and cakes as Ada and Betty could muster. There was carol singing, pass the parcel, hunt the thimble, pin the tail on the donkey, and presents from Santa.

All the children came, even those whose mothers had disapproved of me.

The party was such a success that Ada decided to make it an annual event.

The Grove Stadium had reopened with twice weekly boxing matches. For a slice of the profits Eugene was given permission to sell soft drinks, cigarettes, and blancmange.

He also managed to get a small supply of pies which he heated up in the back room of the Stadium.

Lena was recruited to heat and sell the pies in the interval. I was given the job of going into the auditorium to sell the other items.

'We cannae pass up any chance of making money,' Eugene told Ada.

I was duly fitted out with a little frilly apron, a tray slung around my neck with a pyjama cord, on which the wares were set out, with a little tub for the money.

It had seemed an exciting thing to do when Eugene first told me about his plan, but on the first night I was petrified. The noise of the men shouting at the boxers was horrendous, and lights shone dimly through a dense haze of smoke that rose in curling twists to the ceiling. It was like a scene from Dante's Inferno that I had seen in my 'Lives of the Saints' books.

The men would hurl obscenities at the boxers, and sometimes a fight would break out among the spectators, which drew more attention than the official bout.

I would pick my way gingerly down the stairs, trying to balance my tray, make sure nobody stole my money and keep up with the demand. It was hard work for a ten year old.

Ada was not really happy about all this, but it did bring in much needed money. She suggested that Lena should take over from me and I should deal with the pies in the back room. It only lasted one night. Lena, young and pretty, attracted the wrong kind of attention, her fiery rebuffs caused a drop in sales, and so we were back to our first jobs.

After a while, the men realized I was very young, they became protective and tried not to swear when I was near.

Lena and I were totally exhausted by the end of each night.

The present day health and safety rules would not allow a child to do such a job, but then these rules did not apply. Eugene was only doing what Italian families had always done.

Though I did not enjoy the job, it never occurred to me to refuse or to Lena either.

There was one perk; I was the envy of all the boys and girls around who would have given their right arm to see inside 'The Grovey'.

CHAPTER 23

Betty's romantic chickens were coming home to roost. Within three weeks of each other she received four letters each professing love and devotion and hinting at marriage. All of them from sailors she had kissed goodbye, and thought she would never see again.

To further complicate the issue they were all different nationalities. English, French-Australian, Polish and Yugoslavian. All were blissfully unaware of each others existence.

She sat on her bed, the letters strewn around her, 'what am I going to do?' she giggled.

'Which one do you love?' Lena asked.

'I don't love any of them,' she added hastily as she caught the look of disapproval on Lena's face, 'I never actually TOLD any of them I LOVED them.'

'Can't you write and put them off?' Lena suggested.

'No I don't think so. Right now they are all at sea, a letter would never reach them before they dock, and they are all sailing into Finnieston at the same time. What can I do, tell me what to do?' she wailed.

'What you mean they are all on the same ship?' Lena was incredulous.

'No. Yes. Well I mean two of them are, the English one and the Polish one, but neither of them knows I was going out with the other, if you see what I mean.' 'What a mess', Lena said.

'I know,' Betty gathered up the letters and threw them in the air.

'You will be in serious trouble if mammy finds out,' Lena warned.

'Don't you dare tell her, she said this would happen and she was right,' Betty sighed.

'So what are you going to do,' I asked, really intrigued at all this.

'Oh I'll think of something,' Betty said.

'What?' Lena queried.

'Something-I—I don't know, do I?'

'You better be quick,' Lena said darkly.

'Oh go away and leave me alone, I need time to think,' she shoo-ed us out of the room.

'She is crazy', Lena said, 'She will get herself into so much trouble.'

'What do you think she will do?' I asked.

'Take to the hills, I would,' Lena laughed, 'whatever it is it will be something mad, you know what she is like.'

Betty loved to live on the edge; she loved excitement, kicking over the traces. The something she came up with was mad, crazy and all wrong but she was not to be talked out of it.

'You can't do that, it is the daftest thing I have ever heard,' Lena was aghast.

'No, it is perfect, it gets it over all at the same time,' Betty laughed.

'No, please you have to think again, you just can't do that,' Lena pleaded.

'It will be fun, it will work perfectly I have it all planned, and I can't believe any of them are serious anyway.'

'What - what is it, what are you going to do?' I begged.

Betty grinned, 'See them all on the same night.'

My jaw dropped, I was speechless.

'No wonder you are lost for words,' Lena shook her head.

'I will stagger the time they have to come, make sure one is away before the other one turns up, it will be exciting.'

She turned to me, 'I need you to be there to open the door, just in case they do overlap a minute or two, but it shouldn't happen, I will make enough time between each one,' she said.

'Me! I don't want to be there, I won't know what to say,' I protested.

'You can't ask her to do that, it isn't fair, she is only ten years old,' Lena said.

'It will be all right, it is better that she is young, they won't lose their temper with a little girl, like they might do with you if you did it,' Betty told us.

'Oh no, keep me out of it, the whole thing is crazy,' Lena said.

'Say you will do it, pleeze, pretty pl-eeze,' she got me in a bear hug.

'OK,' I said reluctantly, squirming out of her grasp.

'Great! Now both you goody-two-shoes leave me alone to work out my schedule.'

Nothing went according to plan. Each suitor unbeknown to him had been allotted exactly half an hour. Betty had convinced herself that this would be enough time for her to gently dash his hopes of romance or even marriage; she would simply kiss him goodbye and move on to the next one.

The Englishman was first. Betty opened the door to him herself, and with me hovering in the background (to see how it was done), she ushered him into the 'big' room she shared with Lena, giving me a wink as she closed the door. I went back to the kitchen carefully taking a note of the time.

I had the kettle on the boil and teacups at the ready should the worst happen and I needed to 'entertain' the would-be suitors till Betty was free.

The hands of the clock crept toward the half hour, and I listened for the outside door opening and the murmured goodbyes - nothing.

I tiptoed up the lobby, put my ear to the door and held my breath.

'I am sorry, really I am,' I heard Betty say.

'But- you gave me a promise,' the man said in a funny pleading voice I had never heard from a man before.

'People change, I'm sorry,' Betty said again. Her voice had risen a little and I knew she was getting worried.

I heard the scrape of a chair and knew he must have stood up; maybe he was going to leave. I sprinted back to the kitchen just as the doorbell rang.

I panicked, what did I do now?

The bell rang again, and I went to the door, opening it a few inches.

I saw a huge red face peering over a big bunch of red roses, obviously surprised to see me and not Betty the huge man stared at me for a moment or two.

'Bettee, I see my Bettee?' he grinned.

'Er yes come in,' I opened the door, praying that Betty had heard the bell and didn't come out.

I motioned to the man to follow me and ushered him into the kitchen, pulling out a chair for him to sit.

He looked around him, 'Bettee?'

'Yes, soon, would you like some tea?' I thrust the cup at him.

He ignored the tea and shifted his weight on the chair, which was much too small for him.

I glanced at the clock; the Englishman was ten minutes over his time. This was a disaster it would upset the whole plan. I wished fervently that Lena was there.

To my great relief I heard the front door slam, and the next minute 'Bettee' appeared all girlish and smiling, her hands stretched out in greeting.

'Bettee,' the jolly giant squeaked, lumbering to his feet.

She smiled again and gently steered him up the lobby to the 'big' room.

Within minutes anguished sounds came from the room, clearly the jolly giant was not taking things at all well.

Betty emerged to request two cups of tea, rolling her eyes and saying he wouldn't take no for an answer.

I quickly poured the tea with a wary eye on the clock and a silent prayer to any saint who may be listening, begging his intercession to delay number three, or else things would get really sticky.

Number two was digging his heels in, he just would not accept Betty's refusal to his proposal. He produced a brandy flask and laced the tea, saying she was obviously nervous and it would calm her down.

Nervous? She was near hysterics.

I left them to it and went back to top up the kettle.

I had no need to put my ear to the door to hear what was being said as the jolly giant had a voice to match his frame.

Time passed, his time was up, but suddenly things had gone quiet.

I feared Betty had brained him.

We were really running late and I was at my wits end.

The ring of the bell made me jump, number three was at the door and number two I was sure was lying comatose on the floor.

I opened the door; to the most handsome man I had ever seen, to my ten year old eyes he was like a film star.

He stood tall and erect in his navel officer's uniform, and under one arm he had the biggest box of chocolates I had ever seen.

I knew the box was real, nothing like the dummy boxes we displayed in our window.

He smiled, and entered at my bidding, following me into the kitchen.

This was the Polish Officer, but so far he had not spoken a word and I wondered if he could speak English.

I gestured to the tea cup, and he smiled and shook his head.

'I have come to see your sister Betty,' he said in perfect English and I felt ashamed at my thoughts.

I nodded.

'She is here?'

'Yes, yes, she — she is just speaking to someone - the insurance man,' I said lamely.

'Insurance man?'

'Yes, eh, she won't be long,' I smiled

'You will let her know I am here, please?'

'Yes, oh yes, right away.' I fled the kitchen, just as Betty opened the room door, her finger on her lips as she caught sight of me.

The jolly giant came lumbering at her heels.

She opened the front door wide steering him through it.

'Drazi is just going to get some cigarettes,' she said quietly, then through gritted teeth she muttered, 'and he is coming right back!'

I stared at her, 'what!'

'Yes,' she said, pushing him further out the door with a fixed smile on her face.

He clasped her hand, gazing at her soulfully.

'I will be back soon, and we will talk, my Bettee, it will be all right, you will see.'

She nodded her head and closed the door on him.

'What are we going to do?' I hissed.

1 don't know, I'll think of something.'

'The next one is already here,' I said.

'I know, I heard the door, I'm just coming. When he comes back try to keep him away from the room, I'11 try to get this over with as quick as I can,' she whispered.

'Oh, no this one is really nice, I like him,' I said.

'You are not supposed to like any of them, they all need to go,' she glared.

She swanned into the kitchen cool as a cucumber; the officer rose, clicked his heels and, raising her hand to his lips, brushed it with a light kiss.

I was captivated; it was just like the pictures.

'Would you like to come through,' Betty said with a winning smile.

They disappeared up the lobby, leaving me to cope with the jolly giant when he came back.

What was I to do? If I dashed down to the shop to get Lena, Aggie would get suspicious and she would tell Ada as soon as she got back from visiting Tina. Betty had chosen this night because she knew Ada was out.

The minutes ticked by, and I began to hope that the jolly giant had changed his mind and wandered off back to his ship.

Betty dashed in, grabbed two glasses out of the sideboard and vanished before I could say anything.

I was horrified. Ada would only allow alcohol at New Year, and if she knew Betty was not only having these men popping in and out like a French Farce but drinking alcohol too she would be furious and we all would suffer.

I was so upset by this that the sound of a sharp knock on the door made me jump out of my skin.

I glanced at the clock, number four, I had forgotten all about him.

Now he was at the door, the Polish Officer was still in the room, and the jolly giant might re-appear at any moment.

The knock came again and the doorbell rang.

He sounded impatient and I hurried to the door. Number four was the French-Australian and he was tall, tanned and handsome. He seemed surprised to see a little girl answer the door, but held out his hand and shook mine saying in a very formal tone, 'I have come to see your sister Betty,'

His formality rubbed off on me and I asked him in my most polite voice if he would please follow me to the kitchen. Not waiting to be asked he pulled out a chair and looked around him as the Polish officer had done.

I offered tea, he declined.

'Is your sister here?'

'Yes, yes, she is in the other room talking to the -insurance man.'

That was the second time I had lied and I made a mental note to remember it in my next confession.

Excusing my self I tiptoed to the 'big' room door. All I could hear was the low murmur of voices, and it didn't sound like farewells.

I knocked discreetly.

Betty called out brightly. 'Just coming.'

I knocked again, 'Can I come in?'

'I'm just coming, hold on,' her voice held a hysterical note.

I held on but she didn't come, so I made my way back to the kitchen. I smiled at the bewildered man and offered an apology; he shrugged and said he was in no hurry he would wait.

I busied myself with the kettle and teacups, at a loss as to what to do next.

'That is an unusual fireplace, I do not think I have ever seen such a piece before,' he said suddenly.

I spun round, why oh why had he homed in on the 'monstrosity' as Ada called it.

'Yes, my daddy made it,' I said trying to look proud of the massive slab of terrazzo in green and white with ebony edging. The design was the same as the doorsteps but three times bigger, and there was a huge chunk broken off one of the corners, which, every time I looked at it, filled me with guilt.

'Your father made it?'

'Yes, but it is my fault the corner is broken,' I said.

Breathlessly I launched into the whole sorry tale.

Eugene had wanted to have a sample of his work on display in the hope he could bring prospective buyers to view it.

Though he was a craftsman, Ada had not liked the design saying it was far too big for the house.

Eugene had paid no heed and went ahead with casting not only the huge single slab as the front piece but a solid mantle shelf and hearth too.

He chose a day Ada was off to Fazzi Bros. in Clyde Street where she bought her spaghetti, tomato puree and parmesan cheese.

He was determined to have the whole thing installed before she came back as a surprise. The only trouble was that I was the only other person in the house that day. He hauled the thing up the stairs by ropes, painstakingly negotiating the sharp bend. Once inside the house, he propped it against the wall while he prepared the sand and cement to fix it to the fireplace.

I stood watching his every move wondering how he was going to lift such a huge thing up high enough to get it in place.

When the time came he stood back and scratched his head, muttering to himself.

He placed two chairs a few feet apart, their backs to the fireplace, then stood back to judge the angle, giving a tweak here and there, then nodding with satisfaction.

'I need your help,' he said.

'Right daddy,' I stood awaiting instructions.

'I want you to lift that end of the slab while I lift the other, right?'

'Yes but it looks very heavy,'

'No, it is fine, just grab it like this,' he clasped one hand on the top and one at the bottom, 'see?'

I nodded.

'Now you do the same as me and we will lift on the count of three.'

I clasped the corners, feeling the rough back in sharp contrast to the smooth polished front.

'One, two, three, lift!'

I tried to lift but it was too heavy.

'Take a deep breath, right, now try again, 'one, two, three, lift!'

We both took a deep breath and raised it a few inches, then let it down again.

'Och you're not trying hard enough.'

'It is too heavy, daddy.'

'Not at all, it is all in the way you lift it, if you try hard enough you can do it. Now again, one, two, three!'

So it went on; we lifted and laid, lifted and laid, till my hands were red raw. Finally we managed to balance the thing on the backs of the chairs.

'Right! Now hold it while I try to get it closer.'

Suddenly I realized I was supporting this massive slab on my own. I felt my knees begin to buckle and felt the slab slip from my grasp.

There was a sickening thud, and looking down I saw a sizable chunk had broken off one corner, and closer inspection showed two or three cracks as well.

'Look what you've done, I told you to hold it.'

'I'm sorry daddy, I'm sorry, sorry,' I burst into tears.

He knelt by the slab, stroking it like a baby.

'Och don't cry, it happens, I will just have to fix it.'

Shooing me away he grappled with the thing himself and finally it was in place, but six months on and many rows later between him and Ada, the thing had still not been repaired.

All this I related to the rather bemused visitor who showed polite interest. He got up and ran his hand over the smooth surface, 'your father is very clever,' he said.

I detected a hint of sarcasm in his voice, and bristled, it was one thing Ada decrying Eugene's work but not this stranger.

'My daddy is very clever, he is a craftsman, this is not a good example of his work,' I told him, echoing Ada's words to another critic. He sensed he had offended me, and looked pointedly at his watch.

'Perhaps you could remind your sister that I am here and we did have an appointment this evening.'

'Yes, I will,' I said feeling guilty for showing my anger. 'Thank you.'

I stood unsure of what to do next and he smiled a little wearily. 'If you could tell her now?'

'Oh yes, I'm sorry,' I left the kitchen taking pains to close the door after me.

'Betty, Betty,' I rapped softly on the door.

She opened it so abruptly I almost fell in the room. 'What is it?'

'Your appointment!'

'Oh yes, right, I will be there shortly,' she said and closed the door.

What could I do now? I stood rooted to the spot, lacking the will to go back and face the austere man who seemed to be able to see right through me. I dived into the lavatory and bolted the door, it was all too much, I had had enough.

After a while I heard Betty come out of the room and make her way to the kitchen. I listened, hardly able to believe what I was hearing.

It seemed there were two male voices as well as hers. Sliding the bolt as quietly as I could I crept up to the half open kitchen door and peered inside.

The two men stood bolt upright facing each other across the table. Betty stood at one end, an amused expression on her face in sharp contrast to the stony expressions of the men.

'Oh no! What is she thinking of?' I thought.

Just then the bell rang; a prolonged ring as if someone was leaning on it.

Betty shifted her gaze and, catching sight of me, moved her head telling me to open the door. I shook mine emphatically.

The bell stopped and the thumping began.

'Bettee! Bettee! a voice wailed.

Betty's eyes flared at me to open the door.

I opened it and stood back, expecting to be pushed aside. The jolly giant stood swaying in front of me; clearly he had come back via the Breadalbane Arms.

'I come back, my Bettee,' he slurred, lumbering into the lobby and gazing around unsure where to go.

'They are all in the kitchen,' I sighed, giving him a gentle push in the right direction.

I followed him down determined to see the fun.

He pushed the door wide.

'Bettee, my Bettee, I come back,' he staggered forward. The Polish Officer hastily pushed a chair beneath the ample buttocks, as 'Drazi' collapsed in a heap, head on the table.

'Who is this?' asked the French-Australian.

'He-he had an appointment too,' Betty said.

230

'Like me?' the French-Australian asked.

'And me?' the Polish Officer echoed.

'Yes, yes, you were not supposed to meet each other,' Betty said.

'You planned this?' the Polish Officer seemed astonished.

'Yes, it wasn't meant to hurt anybody, it was fun, a joke—,' she finished lamely.

The silence and stern expressions told her they did not see the funny side of the situation.

'Drazi', sensing the silence, raised his head and looked around, 'Bettee?'

'Which one had you decided to choose?' the French-Australian asked in a hurt tone.

'I didn't intend to choose anybody, I just didn't take it seriously, and I thought all of you would feel the same,' Betty was sounding desperate.

They stared at her in silence. The jolly giant began to snore, and as Betty shook him awake, he peered through half shut eyes.

'Bettee, you come with Drazi?'

'No my friend I think not,' the Polish Officer hauled him to his feet and supported him.

I suggest we behave like gentlemen and bring an end to this matter,' he turned to Betty, 'if you will pour a drink for myself and my companions we will drink each others health then leave.'

Betty hurriedly set out glasses, and poured from the Officer's bottle.

'Your health,' he said. The others raised their glasses, Drazi spilling most of his on the table.

'Your health.'

'He-heelth.'

Betty stood looking on and they ignored her.

The Officer clicked his heels and bowed, making for the door. The French - Australian followed, pulling 'Drazi' behind him.

Betty opened the front door, and as they filed past, 'Drazi' clasped her hand and would not let go, hauling her over the doorstep. She unclasped his fingers and smartly closed the door on all three.

'Phew! I'm glad that's over,' she said leaning against the door.

'That was absolutely awful, how could you do that?' I said.

'What? Bring them together? What else could I do? The Pole would not take no for an answer and I couldn't keep the other one waiting any longer.'

'I liked the Polish Officer best, he seemed really nice.'

'He was nice, but not nice enough to marry, he actually wanted me to marry him and live in Poland. I don't want to live in Poland,' Betty laughed.

'Number four never got a chance to talk to you,' I reminded her.

'Yeah I'm sorry about that, I had forgotten how handsome he was,' Betty sighed.

'They were not very happy about what you had done,' I said.

'Yeah, really sniffy, didn't see the funny side at all.'

'There wasn't a funny side. The whole thing was scary, especially the jolly giant,' I shuddered.

'Oh no, he was funny, put on a lot of weight since I last saw him, and he never stood a chance in the first place. Anyway I will never do anything like that again. Thank God the Englishman didn't hang around it would have been too much.'

'It was too much,' I said.

CHAPTER 24

The national euphoria at the final declaration of peace in the Middle East began to evaporate as the grim reality of what lay ahead emerged. The nation was faced with the true cost of war, not only the loss of sons, fathers and husbands, or the six long years of privation, but the realization that the victory if not a pyrrhic one came very close. In common with the rest of Europe, Britain was in dire financial straights as a result of the abrupt ending of the Lend-Lease plan by the United States Government.

Mr. Atlee's newly elected labour Government, swept to power in a desire for change and new beginnings, found itself having to make some very unpopular decisions. In an effort to balance the books, food production had to go for export rather then home consumption. Germany, its capital and major cities bombed out of existence, faced an even greater disaster. With its agriculture in total ruin, 30,000,000 Germans faced certain starvation. So the victors found they had to rob the victorious Peter to feed the defeated Paul.

Britain went back on wartime rations, only worse. The 8oz allowance of butter, margarine and cooking fat was cut to 7oz. Bread became darker because of the cut in wheat content and joined potatoes and meat as rationed commodities. Tinned meat was allowed a modest increase, which after a few weeks was again reduced, and when rice imports were cut it meant all the 'fillers' and the 'staples' could no longer be relied upon to keep body and soul together.

For reasons which seemed to make no sense, the sugar and sweet ration was increased.

It was however some light relief as was the return of bananas. Some children born during the war had never seen a banana, others like me could scarcely remember what they looked like. The much anticipated treat proved something of a let down when Lena and I were presented with a strange black specimen with a pungent smell. Sadly the old adage 'too much of a good thing' proved true when a three year old girl died after being given and eating three bananas.

Men were being demobbed at the rate of 171,000 a month, at the same time as one million munitions workers, most of them women, were paid off. The 'Bevin Boys' conscripted into the mines were urged by Mr. Shinwell minister for fuel and power to boost production by 18 million tons. Returning fathers were viewed as strangers in the house, upsetting the familiar routine and demanding respect due a father. Wives found it hard to adjust as the hero in uniform became a disillusioned figure in an ill fitting demob suit, queuing up to sign on at the labour exchange. Wives who had held down a job, coped with air raids, rations, caring for children or enduring the separation of evacuation, found themselves relegated to the cooker and the sink.

Worse still were those who found the love so long professed in letters to the front had quietly died, and they were trapped in a union in which neither wanted to be.

Eddie Gillan wrote to tell his sisters he was coming home, and since he had proved himself in spite of his stature a valiant soldier, the neighbours literally hung out the flags.

Betty strung a 'Welcome Home Eddie' across the close mouth, and everybody turned out to hail the returning hero.

Eddie lived up to the occasion, dressed in his kilt and white spats, his tanned skin stretched tightly across his face, his moustache clipped and waxed.

The cheers were genuine, Rover running round in circles barking his greeting. Eugene called for three cheers for Eddie, and the loud hip! hip! could be heard two streets away.

Eddie was not the only returnee. Betty's French Australian wrote to say he had been denied his opportunity to say his piece on his last visit and was determined that she should hear what he had to say. Ada was not amused, having eventually got wind of the shenanigans on the night of the four suitors. She had left Betty in no doubt of her contempt for her conduct.

'I can hardly believe that a daughter of mine could treat decent men who have risked their lives in the cause of freedom in such an appalling fashion.

She was equally horrified that I, still in my tender years, should have been used in such a way.

'What do you intend to say to this man if he proposes?' she asked Betty.

'I — I don't really know, I like him well enough,' Betty said.

'Well enough is not a good basis for marriage, if that is what he has in mind,' Ada warned.

The letter had said he would be arriving within the week and Betty was on tenterhooks.

When he did appear, he was still in uniform, still as stiff and polite as before.

Ada was impressed, he was that most pleasing of all things in her eyes, 'distinguished'. She rolled out the red carpet, inviting him to tea. She set the table with the best damask cloth and matching napkins, took the best china from the back of the sideboard, unwrapped it from its protective newspaper, and washed it and polished it along with the cutlery. She felt sure such a refined man would be conscious of the honour. Only the scarcity of the food threatened to let the side down. Ada did the best with what was available, the meat eaters in the family resigning themselves to seeing most of their weekly ration ending up on the visitor's plate.

The meal was full of awkward silences. Betty was unduly quiet, her eyes rarely leaving her plate.

Ada asked polite questions of the visitor, who I was surprised to find was called John McIntyre.

She quizzed him as to his interests and hobbies, his ties with France and Australia, and which one he considered home.

He answered readily enough, saying he had been brought up in Australia, but had spent a lot of time in France. His father was a Scot who had settled in Australia, and his mother, born and bred in France, was the daughter of one of the oldest families in Le Havre.

He said he loved both countries and Scotland too.

He was interested in books, languages, trees and plants, and planned to go to college to study horticulture.

'How interesting,' said Ada and went on to tell him of her own mixed blood.

Eugene laughed, 'eh we are a' Jock Tamson's bairns.'

The talk turned to languages, Ada explaining she spoke the 'pure Italian' while Eugene spoke the dialect of the Neapolitan south.

'Och aye, ah'm a peasant ye see.'

Eugene was never afraid to own up to his roots.

'Tell me, do you speak Italian?' John said.

Lena dug me in the ribs; I blushed realizing he was talking to me.

'Er no,' I said.

'Oh but you must, it is your native tongue,' he looked around his eyes asking the unspoken question of us all.

'Only mammy and daddy speak Italian,' said Betty finding her voice.

'Then that is a great pity,' he said.

'Yes, it is,' I thought, 'but it is their secret language and they seem to have so many secrets they don't want us to know.

I looked at my family sitting round the table, and wondered again what had brought two people like Eugene and Ada together. Ada sat, not on Eugene's knee but on her own chair at the head of the table, her dark hair swept back from her face, and unusually for her she wore powder and lipstick. She looked regal, composed. Eugene sat at her side his tie slightly askew, a faint stubble on his chin, as he had forgotten to shave despite Ada's many reminders. Aggie sat nervously fingering her cup handle as if unsure of her ability to lift it to her lips. She darted glances from lowered eyes at the visitor, she was intimidated by him, clearly thinking him very grand. Lena was smiling and relaxed, and she seemed unaffected by the stiff formal tones of the visitor. It was to her that he turned his attention.

'What do you do? Are you at college?'

'No,' she said somewhat surprised by the question.

'She works in a clothing factory and helps out in the shop at night. People like us don't go to college,' Eugene answered for her.

'In France it is usual for most young people to go to college,' John McIntyre said.

'Aye but this is Scotland, we have tae work for a living,' Eugene laughed, dipping the crust of his bread in his tea.

Ada glared at him.

There was an awkward silence, then Lena said brightly, 'I like working in a clothing factory.'

'Yes, she is learning a good trade, she is very interested in making clothes,' Ada said.

John McIntyre smiled, 'perhaps some day she will go to college.'

'Not at all, she will get married and have babies, that's the way of things,' Eugene said easily.

I felt Lena stiffen, and saw a strange blank expression on her face.

The meal over, Betty and John excused themselves from the table, and went out for a walk to discuss matters, any suggestion that they should be alone in a room together being frowned upon by Ada.

Betty returned alone, saying John had a train to catch. When Ada asked how things went Betty smiled and said they would be writing to each other. He would be back but not until he had been demobbed and visited his mother in France.

Ada seemed well content, relieved Betty had not agreed to a proposal just yet. Eugene patted Betty's shoulder, 'remember there are plenty fish in the sea.'

Eugene's dream that he could return to making real ice-cream was not to be realized, at least not yet, though the slight increase in the sugar ration made the blancmange more palatable. The ongoing food rationing made it very hard to keep the cafe turning over. Ada was irritable and worried; the pressure to keep the bank happy was becoming unbearable.

Eugene did begin to have more success with his terrazzo business, but he still had not learned how to cost jobs effectively, and he and Ada had the old familiar arguments about how to run a business, over and over again.

One Saturday morning he arrived at the door of the shop pushing a rather ramshackle ice-cream cart.

He was grinning from ear to ear, clearly pleased with himself.

'Well what do you think?' he asked Ada.

She walked round it, 'it has seen better days.'

'Aye, but what do you think?' he said, still upbeat.

'It needs a good coat of paint. Where did you get it? Don't tell me you spent good money on it.'

'It was a bargain.'

'How much?'

'Enough,' he said avoiding the question.

'What do you intend doing with it?'

'Sell ice-cream, eh blancmange at the park, it will be a wee goldmine.'

'A very wee goldmine,' Ada sniffed.

'Och you'll no' know it by the time ah'm finished wi' it,' Eugene chuckled.

He went to work restoring the thing in his workshop. It sat shrouded in a blanket till the school holidays, when on the first day he trundled it to the shop still shrouded in its blanket for the great unveiling.

There it stood gleaming with red and gold paint, totally transformed from the broken down thing he had first shown us.

'Well?' he grinned.

'Oh it's great daddy!' Lena and I told him.

Ada stood arms folded across her chest taking it in. Eugene rested the long handles on the ground and lifted the shining chrome lid of the little freezer compartment. He pointed out the chrome tray with slots for tongs, and the tool to make the sliders, the little compartment for water to wash his hands, and the tiny towel rail alongside.

Ada unfolded her arms and inspected all these things for herself. She smiled, 'I will give you your due, you have made it looks really splendid.'

Eugene grinned at us, 'yer mammy likes it.'

We grinned back, knowing what her approval meant to him.

He rubbed his hands, 'well let's get it loaded up.'

'You are going up to the park to-day?' Ada seemed surprised.

'Aye, the sooner the better,' he turned to Lena and me, 'come on, you lassies can give me a hand.'

We went at it with a will and soon we were walking with him as he pushed the cart all the way to Kelvingrove Park.

He chose a spot at the gates of the swing park, positioning the cart where all the children would be sure to see it.

'How long will you stay here?' Lena asked.

'Oh ah'm here for the day,' he said.

'But what about something to eat? You can't stand here all day without eating,' Lena said.

'Och ah'll be fine, you know me, no eatin' disnae bother me.'

He shoo-ed us away as a crowd of children gathered round eager to spend their pennies.

Kelvingrove Park was a place of wonder for me, and ever since we had come to stay in Sandyford I had loved the place. I knew every nook and cranny, every season. In spring I would go searching for that first faint greening of the trees, for the sight of yellow and purple crocuses, peeping up through the bare earth under the trees. The drifts of daffodils, huge golden trumpets of 'King Alfred', the delicate white Narcissus, stretching as far as the eye could see along the banks of the slow moving river Kelvin.

As spring gave way to summer, the formal flower path would teem with carefully cultivated blooms, each one flowering in rotation, while beyond in the less formal parts of the park, buttercups, daisies and dandelions were allowed to flourish for little hands to pick and make daisy chains, or gifts for mammy.

Summer brought the bands to the band stand, and you could walk the ridge of the modest hills, listen to the music and see courting couples entwined oblivious of passers-by.

By autumn the ducklings who had swam in line behind their watchful parents had grown fat and self sufficient, and the leaves went sailing on the water swirling round and round at the mercy of the wind. The park took on a sad dying whisper, as the trees shrugged off their heavy summer splendour and settled down for their winter sleep.

On short winter days when the light was fading and the snow lay thick on the grass and bent the boughs, I would go wandering far into the park to stand in awe at the beauty and the majesty of the scene. I had tried to convey how I felt about nature to Mary and the other children who were my friends, but they never seemed to understand, and though I enjoyed the summer ramblings when we would find a den among the trees to eat our picnic of bread and jam and drink our water, and enjoy too the snowball fights and building snowmen, I liked it best when I was alone to hold a silent conversation with the trees.

One magical evening I had stayed behind when my friends had gone home for their tea. The park was deserted deep in snow, the sky groaning with the weight of snow laden clouds.

I stood in a glade of fir trees, every branch an exquisite tracery of pristine snow, every blade of grass covered by a blanket untouched by footfall. The silence was overwhelming; it was as if I had become part of it all, as if the trees were welcoming me in, inviting me to partake of the magic.

I stood on the edge of it all, so that no footprint of mine should spoil the beauty, and gazed and gazed unable to get my fill of such a scene. I could not tear myself away, and having no watch I had no idea how long I had been there, or how late it was. Only a bird suddenly alighting on a branch and the soft plop of snow showering down broke the spell, and made me glance up at the sky, from which all the light had vanished. I turned for home, though my feet moved swiftly the spell of the snow and the trees still wrapped itself around me.

Opening the door, Ada greeted me angrily, 'where on earth have you been? Betty is out looking for you, have you any idea what time it is?'

'No,' I said, which was true.

Now that Eugene was stationed at the gate of the swing park my happy wanderings were curtailed, as it was my job to keep him supplied with all he needed. On his instruction I never went further than the 'floral path', which led to the fountain where children sailed their paper boats, or jumped in fully clothed laughing and splashing each other.

I had to listen out for the blast of the whistle that told me Eugene needed me. Off I would race, my plimsolls giving my feet wings, and arrive breathless and panting back at the shop to gather the supplies. It was heavy work. The wafers, cones and cardboard tubs were tucked into a satchel strapped on my back, and a bucket filled to the brim with blancmange and covered by a gingham towel tied round with string was the biggest burden. I would set off on the fifteen minute walk back to the park, stopping every now and then to change hands. However hard I tried to cut the time it took to get to Eugene it was never short enough. As soon as I came within sight of him he would be waving frantically for me to hurry.

Sometimes one of the boys I played with in the street would offer to help me carry the bucket, and the difference this made was amazing. Tommy was always rewarded with a slider, but I got nothing as it was regarded as a duty for me. It went on all summer long, day after day. At weekends Betty or Lena would sometimes take over if Ada could spare them from the shop, and this gave me a chance to go out to play.

The boys liked to challenge the girls to races, but all the boys were good runners and one boy, Alex Gordon, was a superb runner and no one could ever beat him. We nicknamed him 'Flash' Gordon after the popular space hero we saw on Saturday morning trips to the cinema.

I found to my delight that the sprinting from the park to collect supplies had increased my speed, but I was no match for 'Flash' or any other boy. All the girls had crushes on 'Flash' and I was no exception. The races got longer and longer, and the 'super' race involved several blocks. We always ran in pairs which I hated as I felt duty bound not to let my partner down.

I would push myself to the very limit always arriving totally spent, my chest heaving, my throat on fire.

'Flash' of course was already past the post and timing us all as we came in. He never took any notice of me, but one memorable day, as I staggered to the finishing line bent over in agony, I looked up to find him at my side looking down on me.

'You should always keep your mouth closed when you are running, that way you won't get that burning feeling in your throat,' he said.

'Eh- thanks,' I stammered, but he was already gone.

When we were not running races we would spend our hard earned pocket money in the little shops round about. In Kent road at the top of Breadalbane Street you could buy a penny drink of Iron-Bru and a halfpenny sticky bun which we devoured greedily even though it had sat on the counter all day exposed to flies.

At the foot of Little Dover Street there was a 'Jenny A' Things' shop, run by an old woman we were convinced was a witch. We would dare each other to go in. As you pushed the door the bell would clang noisily bringing the old woman shuffling through, her stick tap tapping on the grimy linoleum.

She would emerge through the heavy chenille curtain that served for a door, her bent figure swathed in layers of drab clothes, her rheumy eyes peering through thick glasses.

'Well?' she would rasp.

You had to have your answer ready, because if she thought you were a time waster she would chase you from the shop brandishing her stick. We would ask for cinnamon sticks, or penny chews.

The interior of the shop was very dark; it smelled of wax polish, stale cigarette smoke, paraffin and carbolic. Every surface was covered in boxes and jars, buckets jostled for space with sweeping brushes, mops, carpet beaters and fly papers. The window must have been at sometime clean but now it was grim, flyblown and strung with cobwebs, the glass thick with grime.

Grown-ups would wonder aloud how she made a living, but we knew she didn't need to make a living as she was a witch and could magic up anything she wanted.

We all knew there was a young girl somewhere in that shop. We had caught sight of her peering from behind the curtain. She had long blonde hair that hung to her waist and swung as she jerked her head away from view.

If the old woman caught her looking out she would lift her stick and scream at her to go inside.

We convinced ourselves that the girl was being held prisoner. Was she we wondered really a princess or the daughter of a very rich family that the old woman was holding to ransom?

We set up surveillance on the shop front and back, but we never saw anything, indeed never saw the girl come out or go in. After a while we gave up, leaving the 'princess' to her fate.

It was many years later the truth was known. The girl was the old woman's daughter, born to her late in life, and rather than keep her prisoner she had scrimped and saved to have her educated at a private school, keeping her away from the 'riff-raff' round about. The girl eventually qualified as a doctor.

Across the street from the 'Jenny A'thing' there was a woman who made toffee apples and sold them from her ground floor window, and sometimes she would sell Sherbet Dabs and Lucky Bags as well.

There was always a queue at her window.

Besides the witch, who scared yet intrigued us there were other people who were different.

People, who in those days when little or nothing was known of mental health problems, were considered 'daft'. One such woman lived above us and she would come down the stairs talking to herself, or let out ear-shattering screams for no apparent reason.

Other times she would appear quite rational and bid you good morning with a bright smile.

Ada would shake her head sorrowfully and say she was a poor soul, and wonder what had happened to her to make her so strange.

The 'daft' woman had two daughters and a son all of whom went on to become professional people.

In Breadalbane Street lived a family whose youngest child was retarded. He had a growth problem and though he was in his teens, he looked and behaved like a little child. This poor boy was the butt of cruel jokes and name-calling. It upset me to see and hear it, and I would try to defend him along with his two older sisters who would let fly both verbally and physically. Though the boy was judged an imbecile and could not speak there was a look in his eyes that made me think he was aware of the taunting and jibes.

Ada deplored the treatment of the boy and said the tormentors would answer to God for their cruelty.

'They should give thanks to their Maker that they have their wits about them, though little do they use them,' she stormed.

The plight of the boy touched me deeply, but I had no way of knowing that in the years to come I would have personal cause to champion the cause of people like him.

I had hoped my 'bucket duty' would spare me my annual visit to 'Granton Aggie', but it was not to be.

Ada declared that I needed the fresh sea air, and so I was duly collected by my cousin Glen, and found myself once again under 'Granton Aggie's eagle eye.

Sheila and I resumed our easy friendship, organising back-green concerts where memorably on one occasion I sat cross legged on a bed of leaves and warbled, 'I'll Get By As Long As I Have You'. The reaction of the audience was enthusiastic, mainly because they had to ensure support for their own efforts.

Even though the light lingered on in the long summer nights 'Granton Aggie' still insisted on an early bedtime. I would snuggle down and feign sleep as she looked in to see all was well, then scramble up to the window where down below Sheila was waiting in dressing gown and slippers, and we would conduct whispered conversations while exchanging scraps by means of a little basket lowered and raised by string.

I loved these clandestine meetings with the smell of the dew soaked grass, and the moon a shining sliver of silver in the soft grey twilight with Venus shining like a jewel.

I shared the room with cousin Mima, by then just turned twenty. She was a plump attractive girl with shining coal black curls and a creamy complexion. As we had got to know each other she was really nice to me though still treating me as a child.

One night there was a sudden eruption of raised voices, and minutes later Mima dashed into the room and threw herself on the bed in floods of tears. I was really anxious to find out what the matter was, and asked if I could do anything.

She refused to answer and just went on sobbing wildly into the pillow.

The scene was repeated night after night. I made clumsy efforts to comfort her but she pushed me away saying I was too young to understand.

Ada turned up to take me home early, having received a letter from 'Granton Aggie' saying she was under a great strain and I was just an irritation she could do without.

I was banished to the bedroom by Ada as she and 'Granton Aggie' had things to talk about which were not for 'young ears'.

As I sat on the bed thumbing through a picture book nursing my annoyance at always being banished when something interesting was going on, I heard Ada ask after Rosie, 'Granton Aggie's' German friend.

'Oh she is not the woman she was, and even though her oldest son George came back safe and sound from the war, she has never got over losing young Jim.' 'Granton Aggie' said. 'So they never found him?' Ada asked.

'Oh no, missing presumed dead, just like they said, but she won't accept it, she still believes he will come back some day, but it is as if she has vowed never to smile till that day comes. Honestly Eadie you wouldn't know her,' 'Granton Aggie' said.

'It is a terrible burden to bear the loss of a child,' Ada said. 'Aye, well you will know that, I'm sure, but it is also a terrible thing to see your child defy you, fly in the face of all our good advice,' 'Granton Aggie' said.

I wondered if they knew I could hear every word. My conscience pricked me and I got up to tell them when I heard Mima's name mentioned. I let my curiosity get the better of me.

'I have told her it just can't happen. I'm sick of repeating myself, but he is her cousin it is not right,' 'Granton Aggie' said wearily.

'No, I suppose you are right,' Ada answered.

'Of course I'm right, she can't marry her cousin, you know the risks, it just can't be.'

'It is a pity, he is such a nice lad, he would make a good husband for any girl, and they do seem to care a lot for each other,' Ada said. 'Well, I can hardly expect you to understand, in your situation,' 'Granton Aggie's' tone was scathing.

'My situation has nothing to do with this, it is an entirely different matter,' Ada said sharply.

'Och I'm sorry, it is just that I am so upset. They have to part, there is no other way, but she won't hear of it,' 'Granton Aggie' said.

'After all it is the law, God knows how many times her father has pointed THAT out.'

'Yes that's true,' Ada said.

I was really surprised to hear by Ada's tone that she was really on Mima's side, and so was I now that I knew what the trouble was, Mima was in love with her cousin. I knew him, he was tall and handsome with the whitest teeth I had ever seen. He had been coming about 'Granton Aggie's house for a long time, and we had all gone out together on picnics and to the pictures. I had not realised there was anything between him and Mima, but now I knew, I thought it was so romantic, like something out of a story, two young lovers who were forced to part. No wonder then at the river of tears Mima shed every night.

I felt reluctant to go home, eager to find out if there would be a happy ending to this romance.

I shared the news with Lena, swearing her to secrecy because I was not supposed to know. She, like me, was on Mima's side, and we hoped against hope that all would be well.

It was not to be. Soon word came that the couple had vanished and 'Granton Aggie' was distraught. Ada hurried through, as Eugene shrugged and said that if they were left alone it would have all blown over.

They had been gone a week before they were tracked down in the Borders. Mima was confined to the house, her cousin persuaded to go overseas. They would never see each other again.

Lena and I wanted to write to Mima telling her how sorry we were, but we couldn't as we were not supposed to know anything about the affair.

Everything went quiet, till some weeks later a letter with an Edinburgh postmark lay on the mat.

It was from Jimmy and Mary, to say that they were both ill and needed help. Betty and Lena were working, Eugene was out with the cart, Ada could not be spared from the shop, so it was decided to send Aggie.

'She canny look after hersel' never mind other folk,' Eugene scoffed.

'Well they will just have to make the best of it,' Ada said.

By the end of the following week Jimmy wrote asking Ada to take her back.

Ada arrived to find the invalids almost recovered and Aggie in a state of high excitement, eyes dancing in her head as she could not wait to tell Ada the news. Mima was dead.

Ada deeply shocked tried to find the truth of this, it did not make sense that a young healthy woman should die. She quizzed Aggie trying to find the source of the news. Aggie refused to tell her.

'What do you make of it?' Ada asked Jimmy.

'Ah dinnae believe her, you ken whit she is like fur makin' up stories.'

'I find it hard to believe myself, and I can't understand why Glen has not been in touch, surely he would tell us such a thing,' Ada shook her head in bewilderment.

'Aye weel he would hae telt you, surely,' Mary put in.

'I need to go to Granton,' Ada said.

'I think I should go on my own,' she told Aggie.

She said nothing to 'Granton Aggie' when she arrived, merely saying she was through in Edinburgh and had been anxious to know how things were.

Certainly both 'Granton Aggie' and Uncle Glen were distraught and Ada began to fear the worst. She was relieved to hear their anxious state was due to Mima's disappearance, though she said nothing of this to them. Mima going missing was serious enough, and they were clearly thinking the worst.

Ada stayed an extra day to help in the search but was forced to return for the shop. She begged to be told as soon as possible if there was any news. Back home she quizzed Aggie again and again about the story that Mima was dead, hoping to find a clue to her whereabouts. Aggie could only say somebody had told her, somebody that knew the family.

It was another three weeks before news came that Mima had been found in Edinburgh, staying with a workmate. Everyone breathed a sigh of relief.

None of us were prepared for the news six months later that Mima was indeed dead from a rare blood disorder.

Superstitious as ever Ada blamed Aggie's gossip for bringing about Mima's demise. Aggie was crushed by the accusation, and she repeated over and over that she had got the original story from a reliable source.

'You have to tell us who it is,' Eugene urged, eager to put the whole thing to rest.

But she wouldn't and never did.

Mima's death put an end to my Granton holidays. 'Granton Aggie' could never cope with any strain.

Ada felt it was better for me too, afraid I would get depression again.

CHAPTER 25

I was due to sit the 'Quali', the dreaded exam that could seal your fate if you failed. According to my teachers I was not expected to do well, every report had the same refrain 'could do better'.

Truth was that Molly and her gang of bullies had undermined my self esteem to such a degree that I felt worthless and could scarcely apply myself to class work.

Ada who was unaware of the bullying had high hopes for me; if the teachers said I could do better she took it upon herself to make me.

She monitored my homework, bombarding me with questions on verbs, nouns, adjectives and adverbs. She set mental arithmetic posers, quizzed me on decimal points. Made me draw maps, and chant dates of battles, and names of Kings.

On the day of the exam I had a sick feeling in the pit of my stomach, and kept breaking out in cold sweats. I desperately wanted to get into the 'big school', which in reality meant crossing the playground to the main building, but I was haunted by the fact that Molly would still be there and things were not likely to get any better.

The results were something of a surprise. I passed, Molly didn't, and I could hardly believe my luck. Even if she resat I would still be a year ahead.

She vanished, and I never knew what happened to her, and could only suppose she went to another school.

I looked forward to entering Secondary school with real confidence.

My joy was short lived, I soon found out that bullying had many forms, and the less overt kind could be just as hurtful. The protocol of the first form was soon established, an elite group of four girls with refined accents and obviously from well-to-do parents sought out a target for their torture, and that target was me. They would roll their eyes and snigger behind their hands when my name was called at register. In the playground they would walk towards me linked arm in arm smiling broadly, then drop the smile as they passed grimacing as if smelling something unpleasant.

I resorted to my old routine of hiding away in a remote part of the playground.

Yet even the subtle bullying could not dim my delight in being in the Secondary school. I loved lining up when the bell rang and waiting for the signal to march up the broad marble stairway to the stirring marches played on the piano by Sister Celeste. She had three favourites, Colonel Bogey, Blaze Away, and the Radetsky March. I loved the precision of the girls moving up the stairs wheeling round without command into their respective corridors, or marching on up to the second and third floors without missing a beat.

I loved the constant change of class, as the bell rang for end of period, gathering my books, filing out, upstairs for science, along the corridor for needlework, downstairs for gym.

Halfway through the term a new girl joined the class. She was tall and stick thin with frizzy red hair and perched on her long nose the same awful wire spectacles as I wore myself. I just knew she would be a target for the snooty quartet.

I watched her to see how she would react. She was very intimidated, and I decided to try to befriend her.

She was English with a Northern accent that sent the four bullies into peals of laughter every time she opened her mouth. We soon became friends bonded by our misery.

Lena had left school, but her reputation for mischief lingered on. French was taken by Miss Duff, her diminutive figure dwarfed by her flowing robe. She wore her dark hair in thick plaits wound round her ears, and on her nose perched a pair of pince-nez. To me she looked as if she had stepped out of 'The School Friend'. I was delighted with her and followed her little figure with approving eyes as she wafted across the playground.

Lena had been very good at French, but her prowess in the language was not what she was remembered for. She had been a mischief maker, passing notes, whispering under her desk, reading comics inside her French Grammar, and given to fits of giggling. All of these earned her the belt, which Miss Duff delivered rising up on her toes with every stroke, causing Lena to stifle her amusement in spite of the stinging blow. On the day of my first French period, Miss Duff regarded me over her pince-nez with obvious disapproval.

'I feel I must warn you that I remember your older sister very well, and warn you that I will not tolerate the same unruly behaviour from you, which is no doubt your intention.'

She soon found my behaviour was better but my French was worse. Ada enlisted the help of John McIntyre, now engaged to Betty and studying horticulture as he had planned.

He kept me captive hour after weary hour, learning French verbs, perfecting my pronunciation and translating endless passages.

I would emerge totally exhausted, and beg Ada to cut the lessons down, but my pleas fell on deaf ears.

It would be nice to record that his persistence paid off and today finds me fluent in the language, sadly it is not so.

Being in Secondary school had other advantages, I could join the school library, and joy of joys also join the Corporation library in Anderson Cross.

I stepped gingerly through the heavy glass doors, glancing up at the motto carved above, 'let there be light'.

Ada had told me that most of the libraries in Scotland were gifts to the community from the great Andrew Carnegie, who, born into poverty, had become one of the richest men in the world.

While still a youth Carnegie had seen these words carved on an impressive mantelpiece in the home of one America's richest men, when delivering some bonds. The millionaire had told Carnegie that the 'light' was education - the key to prosperity for people and nations alike. Carnegie had never forgotten and made it his concern when he had prospered to offer the 'light' of education to all, through the gift of access to books.

I for one was deeply grateful to the enlightened Carnegie. There was reverential hush in the library; it was like entering a church. The voice of the librarian was muted as she bent over her counter to ask why I was there. My voice came out in a squeak strangled by nervousness and awe.

'I would like to join please.'

She pushed a green form across the counter and pointed to a table where an inkwell and pen stood on a large sheet of blotting paper. I carefully dipped the pen in the ink praying I would not blot the form, and carefully I scratched my name, address and age on the dotted lines, then turned it face down to blot up the surplus ink before returning it to the watchful librarian.

She jotted the information down in a huge ledger, wrote a number in the top right hand corner of the form, and then the same number on a green cardboard ticket which she handed to me.

Bending far over the counter to see me, she fixed me sternly through her spectacles.

'You may go and choose a book after you have read and understood the rules on the back of your ticket, and—' she pointed to large sign above her, 'always remember.' I nodded. It said 'Silence Please'.

I sat down on a bench to read the rules.

1. This book is the property of Glasgow Corporation Libraries, and must not be defaced.

2. This book must not be loaned to any unauthorised person.

3. A fine of one penny will be charged for every week the book is overdue.

4. Infringement of any of the above may result in withdrawal of membership.

There was no question that I would obey the rules; I had no indention of surrendering what was to me a passport to a magical world. I skipped off to lose myself among rows and rows of books.

There on the shelves were familiar friends. The Adventures of Tom Sawyer, The Water Babies, Black Beauty, Gulliver's Travels and many more. Even as I ran my hand over them I knew the library was not really silent, it was full to bursting with the voices of the characters trapped between the covers, all of them waiting for someone to turn the page. I was spoiled for choice, but my heart sang because I knew I could come back again and again and take them home with me. I chose my first book, it was Lorna Doone.

The success of the sales at the Grove Stadium had fired Eugene's imagination. He decided to supply cinemas with ices, and he rubbed his hands with anticipation, certain he was on to a winner.

Ada as always was cautious and she warned it might be too much to take on, it would need careful thought and some research.

Eugene made the rounds of the local cinemas to sound them out. He came back well pleased that they were open enough to the idea, but they wanted individually wrapped ices, and little tubs. They were not prepared to have him stand and dispense cones from a bucket.

'Then you can forget it, we would need machines, workers, suppliers of tubs and wrapping paper and we just can't do it,' Ada told him.

'Aye we can, we need to do it before somebody else gets the idea,' said Eugene.

They already have the idea in the big cinemas in town,' Ada pointed out.

'Aye, but we are local, supplying local places, our stuff would be fresh and we would be cheaper.'

'It will have to be costed properly with a decent profit margin; I am not having you doing your usual mess of estimating the true cost.'

'You can check the figures then if it will keep you happy.'

'I'm not sure I'm happy about the whole thing.'

'Och it will be fine, a real money spinner. What is it you always say? Small profit quick return.'

'As long as the profit is not too small,' Ada said sourly.

So the venture began. Soon a huge freezer was delivered that took up most of one of the walls in the back shop.

Ada stood looking at it shaking her head, 'I have a bad feeling about this.'

'Och woman ye see disasters around every corner, it will be fine.'

The 'workforce' consisted of Lizzie on her day off, Betty, Lena and me in the evenings and weekends, oft en working late into the night.

The deliveries were made by tram, Eugene and me sitting hugging boxes of frozen ices. At first he only targeted the cinemas round about, the two or three in Partick, Maryhill, and Argyle Street. While Eugene conducted business I was allowed to slip into the back row to see the film, and this way I saw snatches of many films but never a full one.

The venture was proving a good one. Eugene, fired up with the success, set his sights further afield. He succeeded in securing new orders but the pressure to have production meet demand was too much.

All of us were working flat out and there was little time for anything else. My homework suffered and the late nights meant turning up late for school.

'We need to do something. Everyone is worn out,' Ada acknowledged.

Without consulting her, Eugene went out and bought a car, a little Ford Prefect, which cost £275 on hire purchase. Ada was furious, 'this will eat into any profits we make.'

'It will pay for itself, I can deliver the stuff to the cinemas in half the time,' Eugene explained.

We girls were delighted by the car. No one around had a car and our stock in the neighbourhood rose considerably.

Eugene knew he had to win Ada over or the car would go back to where it came from, so he proposed a trip to Dundee.

To earn the trip we had to work flat out to make enough ices to tide us over the loss of a days work. Lizzie would look after the shop with the help of Eddie who was finding it hard to settle back into civvy life.

Eugene wanted an early start and by nine o'clock we all piled into the car, Ada in the front passenger seat, Aggie, Lena, Betty me and Rover complete with a bottle full of water and his bowl, crushed into the back seat without an inch to spare. So novel was the experience not one of us complained or moaned at Rover's constant turning and squirming to get comfortable and breaking wind in our faces.

There were few cars on the road just after the war, which given Eugene's erratic driving (two lessons and no test) was something of a blessing. No jaunt in a car since could ever match that wonderful feeling of wheeling along stopping where and whenever we chose, sitting on the grass our backs against the car eating our sandwiches and drinking our stewed tea from the flasks.

By the end of the day Ada was a fan, at least of the car if not Eugene's driving. The coming years would see many an argument between them, resulting in Ada storming out of the car and Eugene crawling along beside her pleading, 'don't be daft woman, get in the car, it is perfectly safe.'

'I'd rather walk than risk my life,' she would snap.

Aggie always quit the car with Ada on Ada's instruction, but as they made their weary way home the look on her face said she would willingly take her chances for the comfort of the car.

Ada was always too proud to give in.

With the new orders Ada knew we needed at least another pair of hands, and Eddie seemed the obvious choice. He readily agreed to come in on the venture. It was not long before he and Eugene had put their heads together on another money making scheme. Eddie had spotted a second hand ice-cream van for sale, and he persuaded Eugene to buy it, the plan being they could both deliver to the cinemas, and on Saturdays park outside the football grounds selling pies, Bovril, soft drinks and ices. Here again Lena and I were pressed into service, and we would work a morning shift wrapping ices and in the afternoons go to Hampden or Ibrox with Eugene and the van.

At half-time Eugene would be at the gate shouting 'Pies and Bovril for sale', and Lena and I would brace ourselves for the rush. We heated the pies on a Heath Robinson contraption based on a primus stove. The Health and Safety Executive were still in the far distant future and it was more by luck than good fortune the whole thing did not go up in flames. The hard work was bringing its reward, Ada was well pleased and she splashed out on some second hand furniture from an antique shop that had opened just round the corner.

She bought what the man in the shop called a chiffonier - a tall bookcase with a writing desk attached - a standard lamp and a Persian carpet big enough to cover the whole floor of the 'big' room. Aggie loved to spend her money on things to please Ada or us and she bought a little table lamp, two brass candlesticks and lace antimacassar for the arms of the settee.

Lena and I set the room to rights, polished the furniture, arranged the table lamp on the occasional table, set the candlesticks on the mantelpiece and lit the candles. Lena drew up another little table by the chair near the fire, set out tea things and a plate of biscuits, and then hurried off to fetch Ada, while I settled myself on the piano stool and began playing very softly.

Lena was guiding Ada by the arm.

'Keep your eyes closed till I tell you to open them,' she said.

'What is going on?' Ada asked smiling, her eyes tight shut.

Lena stood her in the middle of the room.

'Open your eyes,' she said, letting go of Ada's arm.

Ada opened her eyes and looked around her. The firelight sent shadows dancing on the walls, and the flickering candles reflected in the mirror above the fireplace sent a pool of light onto the little table where the tea cups waited.

'Oh how lovely,' Ada said.

Lena caught my eye and we beamed at each other, it was our delight to please her.

'Come and have some tea,' Lena said, already pouring it out. Ada settled herself into the chair and watched as Lena added the milk and sugar then took the cup and selected a biscuit, smiling broadly.

I launched into my specially prepared rendering of 'Russian Rose', a song I had spent many rainy afternoons practising on Sheila McPherson's piano in Granton.

After Ada had had her tea we went searching for books to fill the bookcase, and admiring the little drawers in the writing desk. Ada said there should be a secret drawer, but we tried in vain to find it.

'It must be there, these things always have a secret drawer,' she said.

We found it eventually. It suddenly swung out at a touch so suddenly that Lena could not remember how she had done it, but after a while we could open and close it at will.

'So much for the secret drawer, we all know about it now,' Ada laughed.

She stood back and surveyed the room, 'very elegant, you have done well girls, thank you.'

Eugene, too busy to work at his terrazzo business but reluctant to wind it up, hired a 'wee man' to fulfil the orders which truth to tell were not very many. Glasgow has always been full of 'wee men' who could turn their hand to anything and would work conscientiously. The 'wee man' felt he needed a boy to labour for him and so it was arranged. Eugene still insisted on scouting for business himself and so because he was so busy the 'wee man' and the boy were often hanging about in the workshop waiting for the next job.

'It doesn't make much sense paying men for doing nothing,' Ada scolded.

'Eh ah need to have them ready to work if an order does come in. I know what I'm doing.'

'Well, don't say I didn't warn you,' Ada said.

Ada had inherited a chartered accountant from the previous owners the DiMarco's. Mr Nicol lived in Knightswood, then a very superior area of Glasgow. The Nicol's became friends as well as business acquaintances, and soon we were invited to genteel tea parties where Mrs Nicol introduced us to 'influential' friends.

We drove to these soirees in the little Ford. On winter nights I would be kitted out in thick woollens and dark tights, but to my delight I was allowed to change into a posh frock, ankle socks and black patent shoes. The company was an adult one and I was the only child, expected to be seen but not heard. I would spend the entire evening seated on a little stool at Ada's feet, taking on a cloak of invisibility, except for being handed a plate with a small triangle sandwich and a cream cracker. I was painfully shy and would squirm in agony rather than draw attention to my self by asking to be excused to visit the lavatory. Finally the last cup of tea would be served and people would stand up to leave, taking an age to say their goodbyes. Ada would tell me to follow her upstairs to change into my woollies.

'You better visit the lavatory before we go,' she would say, and I would rush to obey with great relief.

So ingrained was this habit of being wallpaper in adult company that I found even into my teens and twenties I could not rise from a seat until someone signalled it was all right for me to do so.

CHAPTER 26

It was the start of the school holidays, and on the first day I went down with chickenpox, which meant one less pair of hands in the shop, and nobody to keep Eugene supplied when he was up at the park. Tina was brought in, her health somewhat restored, though she still tired easily and had lost a lot of weight. Teeny, on hearing Tina had lost pounds, wondered aloud where she had got them in the first place. Ada said she would not even bother to explain.

Tina worked really hard and I felt really guilty sitting at the window all day playing with dolls or writing in my secret journal. It was shaping up to be a good summer; the breeze that drifted in through the open window of the 'big' room was gentle and called to me. Rover lay at my feet eyes gazing soulfully, occasionally thumping his tail, making me feel even more guilty for not taking him out. I bent to pat his head telling him I knew the breeze called to him too. Down in the street the shopkeepers washed their windows and swept the pavement ready for business. Trams came and went rattling and clanging their old familiar song, delivery carts came clopping along, the horses head down, neck muscles bulging at the strain of the load. Often they knew each stopping place and would lumber to a halt, turning their heads to catch the drover's eye, in the hope of getting the hay bag, while he delivered the goods.

Our first caller was always the ice-man. Jumping down from his perch he would sling the hay bag round his horse's neck, then roll out the little two wheeled trolley.

Then stabbing into the huge ice block, he would grapple it off the lorry onto the cart, securing it with ropes, before wheeling it into the shop. These days we needed two or three blocks and while one was broken immediately and packed into the freezer the other two were slid down the cellar steps, the ice-man, carefully guiding it down by playing out the rope and pulling it back till the thing rested on the floor. He would then follow it down and ease it aside covering it with hessian to keep it cool.

No sooner would the ice-man depart than the 'lemonade' man took his place. He would jump from the lorry and pull the crates of Vimto, Iron-Bru, American Cream Soda and Cola on to the pavement, dumping them so hard the bottles rattled and chinked in protest. Once he had three or four stacked he would swing them up effortlessly and carry them into the shop.

Emptying the crates and refilling them with empty bottles returned by small boys for three half-pennies or penny chews, was one of my jobs on a Saturday morning. You had to be quick as the delivery man was always grumpy and would scowl and mutter under his breath if you held him back.

Sitting by the window watching him carry in the crates I noted the time and if Tina or Aggie had him out and away within ten minutes I would silently applaud them.

I longed to be able to answer the call of that soft summer breeze. The city has its seasons too, and city children responded subconsciously, one day we would be playing skipping ropes, the next the mood had changed and we would be playing rounders, our coats rolled up against the wall as the batting area. We would play 'kick the can' or 'release', and as twilight descended a daring game of 'KDRF' (kick door run fast). I was always a reluctant participant in this as I never felt comfortable upsetting grown-ups, but I was also scared of being branded a 'scaredy gowk', so I would take my turn tying two door handles together then kicking each door and hiding to watch the as the neighbours tried to open their doors. Fear of being a 'scaredy gowk' also led me to climb onto the roofs of middens, though I had no head for heights and was very scared.

The first time I managed to climb up I was elated, and soon found I loved being up there, but the boys were never content to climb up on one midden they had to jump from one to the other and dared the girls to do it too. I was terrified but I managed it and joined the gang searching for higher middens to climb.

Rover would stand barking furiously because he could not get up beside me, and often his constant barking would cause a window to be thrown up and an irate housewife bellow, 'You weans don't belong here. Away an' climb yer ain middens an' take that bliddy dug wi' ye.'

So my happy midden climbing was over, as the gang would not let me join them. Sitting by the window itching from head to toe, covered in Calamine Lotion and looking according to Ada 'like Pepper's Ghost', I felt sorry for myself, longing to go out.

Betty took pity on me, and she announced we would go for a walk to Charing Cross to see Lizzie, who none of us held seen or heard of for several days.

It was Sunday, and few people were about, still at mass or church as it was early.

I wanted to go up Breadalbane Street, to Kent Road, up Claremont Street and on to Sauchiehall Street. This was my favourite route and I always took it on the first Sunday in May when we all went out to show off our new spring dresses and shoes, which had been laid out on a chair ready, and which kept us from sleeping in excited anticipation. Sauchiehall Street was the 'Parade' and Lena and I would mince along eyes down admiring our shoes, and then taking in all the other 'rig-outs' on show.

We always ended up at Charing Cross and got an ice-cream from Auntie Lizzie.

Betty preferred to go the 'low' road, along St. Vincent Street to North Street up past the Mitchell Library, where aged eight I had sallied up to the desk and asked in all seriousness for a book on Robert Burns.

The Librarian had regarded me with disdain and said icily, 'we have a whole room devoted to Robert Burns, which you are too young to access, so please come back when you are older.'

Red faced and chastened I never returned.

On the sunny Sunday we strolled up North Street, Rover bounding on ahead. We stopped to look at a shop window, Betty stretched out her hand to point something out and suddenly the whole window collapsed on top of us. Our screams sent Rover off at a tangent disappearing from sight, and we stood shaken and covered in cuts. People appeared from nowhere and took us upstairs offering tea and towels, somebody called an ambulance and we were whisked away to the Royal Infirmary.

I was in a panic about Rover fearing we would never see him again, but Betty felt sure he would find his own way home.

Duly bandaged we were discharged and left to catch the tram home.

There was Rover, sitting at Ada's feet as she scanned the street obviously looking for us. Lucky for us our cuts were mostly superficial but we felt pretty sorry for ourselves and for the next few days Betty joined me sitting by the window. Ada daubed us 'the wally dugs'.

Compensation had never been heard of as far as we were concerned, we resigned ourselves to what had happened and waited for the cuts to heal.

Because of the accident we had never reached Lizzie, so the reason for her self imposed silence was still unclear. Ada and Tina theorized that she was pining for Eddie, who appeared unaware of her feelings. Eugene would not give approval to any idea of a union between Lizzie and Eddie, insisting that Lizzie was 'not the marrying kind'. It was rare for him to interfere in any of his sisters affairs, but he really was against this match.

'It looks as if you won't have to worry, Eddie either has no idea or he is playing dumb,' Ada commented.

'He knows it is just not on,' Eugene said.

'Och, love will find a way,' Tina said.

We girls were on Lizzie's side, we knew she was older than Eddie, but she was so sweet-natured and so undemanding, we wanted her to be happy.

Lena in particular was sympathetic for Lizzie's plight. She still had a hankering for her handsome sailor, who had not been home on leave for such a long time.

'I thought once the war was over he would come back, but he has signed on for a long time,' she sighed.

Betty would finger her engagement ring and say nothing.

Eugene bought a radiogram. 'It's the latest thing,' he told Ada. She sighed and asked for the receipt. Soon we had a sizable collection of 78s, and Betty hit upon the idea of playing requests for the customers. She pinned a list of all the records, each one allocated a number, and the choice was relayed to her via the speaking tube Eugene had devised.

Inserted through the ceiling of the shop to emerge in the kitchen upstairs, it was an improvement on banging with the sweeping brush to attract attention. The 'request programme' proved very popular with customers, even Ada was impressed. Within a year Eugene had persuaded Ada to have the latest from America, a juke-box, a massive thing all flashing lights and chrome.

The honour of choosing the first record went to Hammy, and he chose Twelfth Street Rag.

The records were changed every two weeks, but when Perry Como's version of 'Temptation' came along Lena liked it so much she asked the man to leave it for another two weeks.

One night alone in the shop she slipped the coins into the machine, selected 'Temptation' and stood by the machine to listen. As the first few words were sung, 'you came, I was alone', a huge rat appeared from behind the machine. Lena screamed and jumped up on a bench, her skirt gathered close round her legs, and she was still there when Eugene turned up fifteen minutes later.

Eugene scoffed at the story of the rat, 'Och you've been imagining things, get down and don't be daft.'

To Lena's horror the rat appeared almost every time she played that particular record, and witnessed by Aggie.

'Why does it always turn up when I play that record?' Lena complained. Eugene shrugged and smiled, 'it's simple, it's a Perry Como fan.' The record was removed the next time the man called to change the selection.

We were still working flat out to keep things going, and getting a bite to eat or answering the call of nature could be a problem. One very busy summer day, Aggie was taken short; she ran through the back and jammed a chair against the door then climbed on a stool and balanced herself over the sink. The window of the back shop overlooked a rectangular court which housed the middens, a favourite place for children to play and for back court singers, who would sing for pennies thrown from the windows.

Not only was Aggie's desperation witnessed by the back court singers, but Ada, demanding to know why the door was blocked, forced the chair away just as Aggie was in full flow. Aggie let out a yell, tried to get down, lost her footing and ended up legs in the air her bloomers round her ankles. The episode became a standing joke, and Ada did not help matters by penning a few verses recounting Aggie's embarrassment.

Ada was fond of reading tea leaves, and we would turn our cups upside down, turn them three times anti-clockwise and sit with bated breach to see what the leaves foretold.

We never questioned her gift as she had often been proved right. Tina was very anxious to see if the leaves had anything to say about Lizzie, who still had not been in touch

The leaves had little to say, so Aggie offered her cup.

'There is a birth in your cup,' Ada said. We all laughed and Aggie blushed.

Ada smiled, 'it is news of a birth; there is a bird here which means news.

'Ah dinnae know onybody who is having a bairn,' Aggie said.

'Well it is in the leaves, time will tell,' Ada said.

She rarely read her own cup, at least not in front of us, but this time she give it the three turns and studied it for a moment or two. A glance at her face told us the happy mood had deserted her.

'What do you see?' Tina asked.

Ada shook her head, 'I don't want to say.'

'Is it trouble?' Tina said.

'Trouble — and sorrow,' Ada said after a pause.

'What kind of sorrow? What kind of trouble?' Tina pressed.

'The leaves only warn they never tell exactly what will happen, but there is trouble and sorrow ahead, and we will just have to wait and see.'

She stood up gathering the cups, signalling the reading was over.

Mary and Jimmy arrived unannounced for a visit, and they had surprising news. Mary was expecting a baby. The general astonishment this news created puzzled me, as I was totally ignorant of sex and childbearing. I did not know what Tina meant when I overheard her say to Ada that it was such a shock as Mary was 'past it'.

Ada made a great fuss about Mary and Jimmy, and she confided to Tina that she felt she had been neglecting them because the business was so demanding. She decided Mary needed a holiday, and booked a holiday flat in Rothesay in the Kyles of Bute.

Ada was too busy to go with them, so Betty was recruited to do the 'honours', and I was also to go along to cheer me up after the chickenpox and getting cut by the glass.

'I can't think of anything worse than a week with Mary and Jimmy,' Betty moaned.

'I want to go, but I want Rover to come too,' I said.

'Yeh good idea, it will give us an excuse to take him walks and maybe get some peace,' Betty laughed.

Ada was not sure taking Rover was a good idea.

'Your uncle Jimmy is not very fond of dogs.'

'But we will look after him, we will take him for walks,' I pleaded.

'Well I don't suppose it will do any harm,' Ada gave in.

Everyone went to Rothesay at Glasgow Fair. On Fair Friday the works would close early, women would be waiting at the works gate to make sure their men came home with the wages and didn't make for the first pub to celebrate the holiday.

Glasgow became a ghost town as everyone headed for either the Central Station or the Broomielaw where you could catch one of the Paddle Steamers. We had our own 'Queen Mary', a much more modest version than her illustrious namesake, the 'Waverley' and the 'Jeanie Deans' named after Walter Scott's intrepid heroine in 'The Heart of Midlothian'. Mary was wary of sailing, so we headed for the Central Station to join the crowds waiting patiently for the trains to take them to Wemyss Bay to catch the Steamer.

The holiday atmosphere was infectious, especially once we were on the boat. Children squirmed from mother's hands, racing to the rail to watch the boat pull away from the quay. Girls in bright summer dresses held hands with shirt sleeved young men, swaying in time to the accordion music being played on deck. We squeezed into the little cafeteria for tea and scones, then, tying Rover to Jimmy's chair, I clambered down the iron stairs behind Betty to see the giant pistons of the engine rising up and down pushing the Steamer through the water. The smell of engine oil caught my throat making me feel queasy. Though the engine was huge it had a beauty all its own; the brass was burnished to shine like gold, and every part sparkled and shone in the sunlight slanting down from the open gangway.

Up on deck sitting back to back, grannies in shawls and boots patted fretful babies, while mothers chased after toddlers getting lost among the forest of legs.

Dad, freed at last from the daily grind in the shipyard or railway sidings, sat, handkerchief-wrapped head slumped on chest, quietly snoozing.

Even if the rain came, which being Glasgow Fair it usually did, people were happy.

The little flat, really a 'but and ben' was above a shop in the Main Street. Opening the window filled the room with fresh sea air, and down below there was hustle and bustle, as the crowds in their bright summer clothes filled the shops and queued for ice-cream.

Betty, inspecting the cupboards before storing our food, found mice dirt and at Jimmy's insistence had to go out to buy traps.

Jimmy directed operations declaring war on 'the bliddy menaces', and he was to spend most of the holiday inspecting the traps and grinning with grim satisfaction if one contained an unfortunate mouse.

Though nothing was actually said it was understood that Betty would be the one to provide and cook the food, Mary being in a 'delicate' condition.

The forthcoming event which was supposed to bring them joy seemed to make them moan and complain even more than normal. Betty coped good-naturedly. She tried to chivvy them out of their morose mood, but to no avail. She and I would romp about the beach with Rover while they sat like two crows on a bench, stone faced and moaning about the weather.

Halfway through the week, Tina appeared on a surprise visit, and she succeeded in enticing the expectant parents to a show at the Winter Gardens; she even had them walking along the prom eating ice-cream and sporting hats with 'kiss me quick' on the front.

Leaving a sad-faced Rover to the mercy of the mice Betty and I escaped to see The Dolly Sisters showing at the local cinema.

I loved the film, admiring the beautiful clothes worn by Betty Grable. The life they lived in the film was light years away from mine, and as always I accepted that such things were not for me.

'I wonder what it is like to be rich.' I asked Betty.

'Very nice, I suppose,' she said.

'Well we'll never know, we are just ordinary folk,' I said.

'We are just as good as 'the next one', in fact I want to be even better than the next one, I want the good things in life, and I am going to get them,' Betty said.

'Daddy is always trying to get rich, but he never manages it,' I said.

Daddy's away with the fairies, his head is full of daft ideas,' Betty laughed.

'That's not a very nice thing to say,' I protested.

'Maybe not, but it's true,' she was unrepentant.

It was with some relief we returned from Rothesay and after a cup of tea saw Mary and Jimmy off on the train to Edinburgh.

'Well, since both of you have had a wee holiday I think it is Lena's turn,' Ada said, 'she has been invited to go to Skye for a week with the McSweens. She deserves it, she works hard.'

As we said our goodbyes to Lena, Betty said under her breath, 'lucky you - no Mary and Jimmy.'

Ada, Aggie and Eugene never took a holiday save for runs in the car, which always ended in a quarrel. We did take a day off and drive to Hawick in search of Ada's sister and we succeeded in finding her. My recollection of the trip is sitting under a tree with a book till summoned in for tea. The grown-ups had things to discuss which were not for my ears.

Sadly the contact with her sister Mary got lost again over time.

CHAPTER 27

I woke to the sound of raised voices. Ada and Eugene were arguing, nothing unusual about that as over the weeks the strain of meeting delivery deadlines had grown. Ada was near to breaking point already but this row had a new edge, her voice had a hysterical note that made me shiver.

Aggie lay gently snoring; she always had a good night often at my expense as she took up most of the bed.

I sleepily dragged on my clothes and crept to the kitchen door to listen.

'We're finished, done for,' Ada shouted.

'Not at all, not at all,' Eugene's placid tone only inflamed her anger.

'When are you going to see sense, we can never afford this, it's the end.'

'It can be an opportunity, we move into the big time.'

'Huh! If you believe that you are a bigger fool than I took you for.'

The big room door creaked and Lena and Betty joined me, Lena taking my hand and squeezing it reassuringly.

'What are they arguing about?' I whispered to Lena.

'The new regulations,' she whispered back.

This meant nothing to me.

Betty looked at me and shrugged, 'I don't know what it is all about either.'

She pushed open the door and we filed in.

'What's up?' Betty asked.

'Nothing, go back to bed, the three of you,' Ada waved her hand in dismissal.

'The Lasses need to know,' Eugene said.

'Tell us, what is the matter, you woke us up with all your shouting,' Betty said, sitting down at the table.

'Since you are all so keen to know, this is the matter!' Ada threw down a letter in front of us.

Lena grabbed it and scanned in before handing it to Betty. 'What does it say?' I asked.

'It says that unless we spend thousands of pounds we will have to shut up shop. Your father in his usual airy-fairy way thinks it is a wonderful opportunity,' Ada said bitterly.

'Your mammy always sees disaster she never sees the bright side.'

'That is because there is no "bright side",' Ada was scathing.

'Ah keep tellin' you it could be the makings of us.'

'Huh! The breaking of us more like.' Betty picked up the letter.

Dear Madam,

I refer to my recent visit to inspect your premises under the new regulations under which food can be manufactured (Sanitary Act 1946). I have to inform you that your premises do not meet the requirements of the Act. In order to meet the regulations you will be required to make the changes listed below:-

1. Production area to be completely tiled.
2. Persons engaged in food preparation must wear head covering and white overalls.
3. Toilet facilities and access to hot water for the purpose of hand washing must be available.
4. All machinery, utensils and storage must meet the standards set out in the Act.
5, Failure to meet any of these requirements will result in a substantial fine and closure of premises.

'Whew!' Lena sighed, 'it will cost a fortune.'
'Huh! I'm glad somebody sees that,' Ada sighed.
'Aye but don't you see, if we do this we can really compete with the big boys, play them at their own game,' Eugene stressed.
Ada threw up her hands and turned away.
'It will mean borrowing more from the bank,' Betty said.
'Exactly, money it will take years to pay back, that is supposing the bank will help,' Ada said.
'We don't need to go near the bank. We deal with the suppliers, get the machines on hire-purchase, as for the tiling I can do that myself, no need to pay anybody else,' Eugene argued.
'NO, NO!' Ada said.
Maybe it is the only way mammy,' Betty said, 'think about it, and sleep on it.'
'Sleep on it! I have hardly had a wink since this damn letter arrived.'
'Aye, Betty is right, sleep on it and think it over. I'll bring you some tile samples tomorrow,' Eugene said well pleased. He winked at Lena, 'put the kettle on for a nice cup o' tea.'
Ada sat down heavily, 'tea, the answer to everything.'
Lena put the kettle on but she kept a wary eye on Ada.
The following week a notice was pinned to the shop door, 'Closed for Refurbishment'.
'Not only do we have to put ourselves in massive debt, but we lose two weeks business as well,' Ada complained.
'Well look at it like this, even if we were not supplying cinemas, we would still have to tile the shop and make the other changes just to stay open for ordinary business,' Eugene said easily. Ada just nodded glumly.
'Look, I'll be as quick as I can but we need to rip out a few booths and knock down the wall to extend the back area. The machines are big brutes,' Eugene said, rubbing his hands, relishing the challenge.
He worked day and night, doing most things on his own, even installing the tiny toilet, on which Betty in her usual flippant mood pinned 'Aggie's relief'.
The difference in the shop was amazing, and all done at cost due to Eugene's contacts. He surveyed the result tired but happy. Ada gave him the credit due for a job well done, but she was not happy at all about the situation.
A week later the two machines arrived, even with the extension one of them took nearly all the available space.

Ada stood hands on hips gazing at the thing, her face dark with thunder. 'What is this doing here? It says dipping machine, we don't need a dipping machine.'

'Aye, we do, for chocolate ices, it's the latest thing, the cinemas are demanding them,' Eugene told her.

'We don't know the first thing about making chocolate ices, more importantly just how much does this thing cost?'

'We can learn, the machine does most of the work and it will pay for itself in no time.'

We lined up in our white overalls and hats, to be instructed in the finer points of getting the chocolate to the right temperature and the right consistency, to load and operate the carousel and catch the dipped bars as they came off the assembly line, where they were wrapped, boxed and stored ready for delivery.

'We really need a wrapping machine,' Eugene complained. 'If we had that we wouldn't need so many workers.'

'No more machines, we are overstretched as it is.' Ada snapped.

After a few false starts we finally produced a decent choc ice, and a sample was prepared for Eugene to take around the cinemas. He came back well pleased, a fistful of orders in his hand.

In all the flurry of excitement Eugene forgot to apply for the actual licence which had to be granted and displayed on the wall for all to see.

The grim faced inspector came to inspect, stalking round the huge machines, poking his nose into every nook and cranny and testing the temperature of the water, before pronouncing himself satisfied.

Eugene had secured orders from the 'Savoy' in Sauchiehall Street, and the 'Regent' in Renfield Street. We waited with fingers crossed for the verdict.

The sales had been disappointing. While the product was good, they were being left on the usherette's tray in favour of the fancy wrapped Lyons ices.

Eugene set out to find a supplier and within the week boxes of small, medium and large tubs, adorned by a jolly little Eskimo, were delivered along with Eskimo wrapping paper.

'This just gets worse and worse,' Ada frowned studying the figure on the invoice.

'We need this stuff; it will make all the difference you'll see,' Eugene told her.

The orders picked up and we had to work well into the night. Each day I would arrive home from school, dump my schoolbag, grab a quick sandwich, and take Rover for a short walk, steeling myself against his accusing eyes when I slipped him back through the door and rushed downstairs.

My white overall was too big for me and had to be secured by a broad belt wound round my waist several times, and my long hair would be pinned up under a turban, secured by Betty's deft hands. I was now ready to help at the machine. Hour after hour we dipped and wrapped, stacking the product to one side for the others to pack and store ready for delivery. We became very adept at wrapping, getting faster and faster and vying with each other in friendly rivalry.

We would work well into the sma' hours, and at weekends the pace was even more hectic. I missed mass time after time and found myself hauled up before Mother Philippa several times. She grew weary of me and dispatched me to St. Alphonsus to face Father Malone, who would shrive my soul in the confessional by the penance of two Our Fathers and three Hail Marys.

Fearing for my immortal soul Famie, in her role of Godmother, took Ada to task, demanding that I be given time off to go to mass.

Ada, her nerves as taut as violin strings, snapped that we were trying to make a living, trying to keep body and soul together and there was little time to think of other things.

Father Malone would sigh with resignation when he recognized my voice confessing once more to missing mass. He took Famie aside as she left the chapel one Sunday and enquired if she was fulfilling her duties as a Godmother on my behalf.

She told him all, pleading that she had tried everything and perhaps it needed his intervention.

'My brother has never attended mass as you know Father, but even he would listen if a priest visited him.'

'If you think it will help I will go.'

Famie alerted Eugene to the forthcoming visit, and he shrugged and said he didn't see what difference it would make.

'But you can't turn a priest away, you have to listen to him,' Famie said.

'Aye fine, let him come but it will be a wasted visit.'

Father Malone refused the offer of tea and got right down to business.

'Are you aware that you are living a Godless life, putting your immortal soul in danger of damnation?'

'Aye well, ah don't really think aboot it,' Eugene muttered.

'If you don't care about yourself surely you must care about your child, your youngest child who is missing mass and thereby putting herself in danger of eternal torment in Hell.'

'She is only a wee lassie, she disnae sin.'

'We are born in sin and shapen in iniquity,' Father Malone fixed him with a look.

'Well, if you say so, but honestly that wee lassie doesnae sin, she is a good wee lassie,' Eugene assured him.

'She is in a constant state of sin by missing mass and the blame lies on your shoulders as her father.'

'You see it is like this. We are trying to build up a business here and we need to use the girls to help us, otherwise we would have to hire workers and we cannae afford that,' Eugene explained.

Father Malone sighed and stood up, 'I can see I am wasting my time here, I'll bid you good day.' He went off shaking his head sorrowfully leaving us to our fate.

I watched him go with a heavy heart, the sin of missing mass lying heavily on my conscience. After all I was still striving to learn how to be a virgin like

Our Lady and having a soul black with sin was not going to help. My prayers became more earnest each night as I assured God I had not forgotten my promise to emulate Mary, and I would be a virgin no matter how long it took.

Word came that Mary had given birth to a baby boy; the news was not good, the birth had been difficult and the baby was weak.

Ada went through to see the baby and give Mary and Jimmy a bit of support. She came back despondent, both Mary and the baby were far from well.

'I doubt if it will survive,' I heard her tell Tina.

'Aye well she was too old; it is a terrible shame poor wee thing.'

I tried to think what it would be like to have Mary and Jimmy for parents. They were so dour and solemn, so set in their ways, yet I did not like to think the little baby would die, it just seemed so unfair.

'Whit is Jimmy saying aboot it?' Aggie asked Ada.

'He just sat and stared at the wee thing. He never said a word. I don't think he knows what to do,' Ada sighed.

'Whit will happen tae the bairn if anything happens tae Mary?' Aggie asked.

'Well Jimmy can't look after it that is for sure,' Ada said.

'Eh qui sera, sera, nature has a way of solving these things,' Eugene said.

'What do you mean, daddy?'

'Never you mind, just say a prayer for them all,' Ada said quickly.

After a few weeks both were allowed home, and Ada went through laden with gifts. All the aunts had sent something.

She came back as worried as ever, 'Mary is at her wits end, the wee thing is nor feeding as well as he should, and Jimmy can't get used to the upheaval in his routine.'

After a while a letter containing a photograph of the baby arrived saying that he was a little better and Mary was coping well enough.

It was the first photograph and the last, the little thing died at four months.

Ada, Aggie and me went through for the funeral, Ada saying that it was fitting that such a young infant should have someone young there to say goodbye.

Mary and Jimmy stood silent, hot tears spilling from their eyes. As the little coffin was lowered, Jimmy dashed away the tears with a large handkerchief.

'He was a bonny wee bairn, aye a bonnie wee bairn,' he said.

As I prayed that night I asked God to explain why a tiny little child should die so young, but I received no answer.

Back at the shop there was a back log of work to catch up on.

Ada said she was pleased to have it as it helped to take her mind off the sad event.

'God knows what they will do, how they will cope, but maybe we should leave them alone for a while to grieve in their own way,' she said.

'Nature will deal wi' that too,' Eugene said philosophically.

Betty was to be married and preparations went ahead despite the drawbacks. The aunts were canvassed for coupons not just for food but for material for a wedding dress.

'It just isn't fair!' Betty moaned, when it was announced that the Princess Elizabeth who was soon to marry her Greek Prince had been allocated extra coupons for her dress.

Press reports on the Royal tour of South Africa told of the King's wish that his loyal subjects should know of his concern and sympathy for the privations they were suffering at home in Britain.

The warm feelings these sentiments engendered in the 'loyal subjects' were somewhat cooled by the pictures on Pathe News of the apparent luxury of the Royal Tour.

'It's a' right for them, lappin' up the sun and everything,' Tina said.

'Ah now I won't hear anything against the Royal Family. They are the backbone of Britain, the glue that keeps this great Nation together, and I especially won't hear a word against his Majesty. He did not ask to be King, he had that thrust upon him by his feckless brother,' Ada scolded.

'Well that's ma nose on a plate,' Tina laughed.

The King was right on one thing. His subjects had no end of privations.

Severe rationing, strikes, the use of coal or gas fires banned from April to September, electricity supply cut to four hours a day and Government snoopers wrinkling out transgressors. It was not a good time to plan a wedding.

Ada harboured other concerns. Though she liked John McIntyre, she felt he and Betty were not suited.

John was of a serious turn of mind and he had definite ideas of how a wife should behave and took every opportunity to expound his ideas to both Ada and Betty. He possessed a certain 'old world courtesy' which Ada admired but which Betty referred to as his 'Southern Plantation' mode.

Though Betty made her flippant comments when John was not around, Ada feared once they were married if would only be a matter of time before the cracks began to show.

She tried to talk to Betty but to no avail.

'I want the good things in Life and I believe he can give me them,' Betty snapped.

'Do you love the man?' Ada demanded.

'Of course - well enough. I know what I'm doing,' Betty flounced from the room, slamming the door behind her.

'There is trouble ahead, mark my words, that man is too serious for her,' Ada told Eugene.

'Och you worry too much, it is their business, and they are old enough to know what they are doing. She will settle down, you'll see,' Eugene said from behind his newspaper.

The wedding went ahead, complete with cardboard wedding cake hired from the City Bakeries. It was all any bride not of Royal blood could expect in 1947.

The honeymoon was to be in Le Havre, getting to know John's mother and other relatives.

'I hope to God she behaves herself,' Ada said.

'Och love will find a way,' Tina ever the romantic smiled.

'Hmmm,' Ada muttered.

On their return they set up home in the 'wee room', Aggie and me being decanted to share with Lena. It was not the life Betty had envisaged, but with John still at college and Betty working in our 'factory' as Eugene liked to call it, money was tight.

When the college broke for holidays Ada suggested they spend a few days with 'Granton' Aggie, who had written that she would welcome the visit to help her get over Mima's untimely death which was proving very difficult for her and Uncle Glen.

John had been on visits to Edinburgh with Betty and they had taken me along. He had been impressed by my knowledge of the old town, and all those history lessons from Ada had paid off.

He had visited Mary and Jimmy at Dunbar's Close, professing himself charmed by its 'quaintness'.

'It's a dump,' Betty said. 'It needs pulled down and decent houses built in its place.'

He had never been to Granton, as all the family had stayed away to avoid upsetting 'Granton' Aggie.

As they got down from the tram to climb the hill to Granton Terrace, John stood as if rooted to the spot.

'What's up?' Betty asked.

'I feel I have been here before. There is a big house at the top of the hill and it has iron gates flanked by two stone pillars, which have carved Scotch Thistles on top. At the end of the drive there is a double door painted dark blue, and there is a large tree - an oak or elm - on one side of the door.

'How can you know that? You have never been here before.'

'I have seen this place many times in a dream. It is as I say, isn't it?'

'Yes, exactly as you say, I just can't believe it,' Betty said.

'Surely it means it was my destiny to come to Scotland, to find you, to marry you,' John said earnestly.

'Well yes, but it's sort of spooky,' Betty laughed.

'There are more things in heaven and earth —' Ada smiled leaving John to finish the quotation, but clearly delighted at this 'proof' of the power of dreams.

Sadly the harmony they had achieved at Granton was short lived. Back in St. Vincent Street lack of money and space caused tempers to fray, and their raised voices filled the house.

So it was with mixed feelings Ada greeted the news that Betty was pregnant.

'Great news! It will make a' the difference, you'll see,' Eugene assured her.

'It will make a difference, but what kind of difference? Honestly there are times when I could knock their silly heads together.'

She took Betty aside to tell her a 'few home truths', and related the conversation to Eugene and Aggie, for once forgetting that I was still seated at the table.

'I have warned her to stop goading that man with her flippant remarks; he is too seriously minded to take it. I told her that now there is a baby on the way she needs to act like an adult and not like a silly girl.'

'Eh, let them sort it out, they are man and wife, a' the adults they will ever be,' Eugene advised.

The pregnancy was relatively uneventful except for Betty's craving for oranges which were still fairly hard to come by.

Word got round and soon the aunts and neighbours were handing in contributions, and in the end Betty ate so many of them the baby was born with an all over tan which caused much amused comment.

Home from the hospital we soon got used to that special new born cry which is like no other sound on earth. We all became the baby's willing slaves.

John was eager to show off his beautiful daughter to his mother, and when the baby was six weeks old a letter containing a cheque and a summons to visit for a week arrived.

The arrival of the letter broke the truce that had held throughout the pregnancy.

'I think the baby is too young to travel,' Betty said.

'Nonsense, it is the perfect time, the beginning of June, what could be better?' John said.

'I still think she is too young.'

'Her grandmother has a right to see her, we are going, we cannot ignore her kindness in sending the fare, and it is unthinkable.'

'You don't want to hurt your mother's feelings but you are quite happy to hurt mine and put the baby at risk,' Betty snapped.

'The child being too young is just an excuse, you don't want to go to France because you do not like my mother,' John shouted.

Ada had kept out of it, but now she sat opposite Betty as she rehearsed the reasons why they should not go.

'I think John is right, you are looking for an excuse not to go, his mother does have a right to see the baby,' she told her.

'I don't like the woman, she doesn't like me and thinks I'm not good enough for her precious son,' Betty burst out.

'Most mothers think like that, but it is up to you to show her you are a fit wife. For goodness sake act as she would want you to. You will not be there forever, you married her son not her and once back home you make your own way.'

'I am dreading the whole thing, I never felt comfortable when I went there before, and now all the relatives and friends will be snooping around to see the latest edition to this so called great family.'

'I warn you now, if you go with that attitude John will never forgive you, and remember these people matter to him just as we matter to you,' Ada was stern.

We waved them goodbye, Betty promising to be on her best behaviour.

Greeting them on their return, one look at John's face told us all was not well.

Betty had, despite John's warning, gone over her duty free limit and he had warned her that if she was caught he would not support her.

At the time, everyone was searched going through customs, and she had stood calmly watching as the customs officer went through her suitcase.

'Can I see your shoulder bag madam?'

She handed it over with a smile, 'it is really only the baby's things that are in there.'

She smiled apologetically as the man was about to plunge his hand in the bag. 'I am sorry there are two soiled nappies in there, I had nowhere else to put them.'

The officer hastily withdrew his hand, gave her back the bag and waved her through.

Safely out of earshot she laughed, 'little does he know what is underneath those nappies.'

They arrived home in frosty silence.

Ada was not amused, 'John is right to be angry. What would it have looked like if you had been detained? You are in the wrong and you have broken the law.'

'Oh just for once I wish people around here could learn to take a joke. Anyway I needed something to cheer me up after a week with HIS relatives,' she scooped up the baby and slammed the door behind her.

'Things didnae go too well then?' Eugene observed mildly.

Ada got the whole story over the next few days.

'They are so grand and la-de-dah; I just felt so out of place.'

'Did you behave yourself?' Ada asked.

'What does that mean? I was just as I always am but buggerlugs would scold me as if I was a little kid when we were upstairs on our own.'

'Which you didn't take kindly?'

'No, too damn right, I'm his wife; he was the one who came chasing after me.'

Later it was John's turn to complain to Ada.

'My mother is not used to someone so — so....'

'Devil-may-care? Flippant?' Ada suggested.

'You know what I mean?'

'You knew what she was like when you married her,' Ada reminded him.

'Yes, it was what attracted me to her, she was different from any other girl I had known and she was really fun, like a breath of fresh air.'

'So what is the problem?'

'Well, you know, now that we are married—.'

'You mean the cocky flippant girl was all right as a girlfriend but not as a wife?'

He put his hands to his head for a moment then spread them wide.

'I don't know what else to say.'

'I think I understand very well.'

'What am I to do?'

'You work it out together. There is a little child to consider, and if Betty is to change perhaps you will have to change too and meet each other halfway.'

Things were quiet for a while, till one day coming home from college John heard the latest songs being played on the radiogram.

He stormed into the wee room where Betty was changing the baby.

'I don't want my child to get used to that rubbish; I want her to hear classical music.'

'Don't be daft, what difference does it make, she is only a baby.'

The argument grew and grew till John stormed out of the house.

It was the first of many, culminating in him slapping her face and her hurling a heavy tobacco jar at his head.

Hearing of the fracas Ada give them a severe talking to, but things only got worse.

On Ada's instructions, whoever was around when the quarrels started had to knock on the door, go in, lift the baby and go out again without saying a word.

'You know if he had any sense he would realize that modern music will do less harm to the wee one than all this rowing,' Ada told Eugene.

'They need a place of their own, the room is too wee especially now that the kiddie is here,' Eugene answered.

'That is exactly what they need, but she still has not learned her lesson with these smart remarks. Only last week Famie was asking her how she was getting on. Oh, she said, we have a bit of a tight squeeze in that room, nowhere to hang our clothes, so I stick John in the corner and use him as a tallboy.'

'Eugene laughed.

'It's not funny,' Ada snapped.

'Och, it is just her way, she doesn't mean any harm.'

'Well I am glad you can see the joke because John certainly didn't and neither did Famie,' Ada said.

It was with some relief that Ada heard of John's plan to go to England to find work and a place to live. 'Now that I have qualified I think there will be more chance of work in England,' he said.

'Where were you thinking of?' Ada asked.

'I thought Southampton for several reasons, the climate is quite constant, it is near the coast, will be handy for France and it has suffered a lot of bombing in the war so many people will be looking to restore their gardens.'

We were grateful for the peace that descended on the house, but Rover was inconsolable. John had made such a fuss about him, taking him and me on long walks very early in the morning, John being as concerned for the health of my body as Famie was for my soul.

We would rise long before the others, Rover and I skipping out to the Clark's Dairy to get the big galvanized pitcher filled with milk. I loved to watch the girl dip the long handled ladle into the churn and then pour it into the pitcher, I would buy half a dozen rolls and cold ham always asking the girl to put on an extra slice for Rover. John would have the tea ready when I got back and after a hasty bite to eat we would head for Kelvingrove park, always choosing the wild parts so that Rover could run wild.

As we made our way home down Claremont Street to Kent Road we kept a look out for Laddie, Rover's mortal enemy. Every other canine was met by a friendly wag of the tail, but for some reason Rover hated Laddie, a black and white collie cross, and as far as Laddie was concerned the feeling was mutual. If they did meet John would slip Rover's lead and let him fend for himself. He always cautioned me not to interfere, but occasionally things would really get out of hand and fearful that they would do themselves a real injury, John would request a pail of water from one of the shops and pour it over the two snarling twisting forms. They would yelp in surprise and back off from each other shaking a shower of water over the onlookers, and at a word from John, Rover would stand, tail between his legs, drops of water dripping from his ruff and allow his lead to be clipped to his collar.

Now Rover lay across the doorway of Betty's room sighing and rolling his eyes in despair. I hugged him and promised that just because John had gone it didn't mean we couldn't have our walks, so the routine went on.

Word came that John had found a job and a place for Betty and the baby. Ada said the letter was a bit short on information, no real description of the living accommodation, but Betty was excited she was missing John.

'Can't live with him and can't live without him,' Ada observed.

We all went with her to the station. It was a dreadful feeling hugging her and the baby and not knowing when we would see them again.

'If you don't like the place just come home,' Ada told her.

'Eadie her place is with her man, so let her go,' Eugene urged.

The train pulled out, Betty leaning far out the window waving and waving till she disappeared altogether.

There is no feeling like loss of presence, and we were adrift in pain and sorrow. The baby had been the hub of the whole house and we had stretched ourselves to the limit to help look after her and still cope with the work in hand.

'Och it's a' for the best. Her place is with him, they can start a new life, we all have enough to be gettin' on wi', and before we know it something else will happen to fill the gap.'

'My, it is not like you to prophesy,' laughed Ada.

'Aye maybe no, but ah'm right,' he said. And he was.

Lizzie announced she and Eddie were to be married.

'Well what a surprise, and we all believed nothing was happening,' Ada smiled.

The happy pair came to visit, full of plans for the wedding. Lena was to be bridesmaid, I a flower girl.

Lizzie was dizzy with delight and her eyes shone like diamonds, her happiness infectious. Eugene pecked her on the cheek and wished her well, his opposition vanishing before her dazzling smile.

'You're a dark horse, never a hint of what was going on,' Ada shook Eddie by the hand.

'Aye well I didn't want to count my chickens,' he laughed.

'You are getting a gem, see you take care of her,' Ada warned.

'I will, don't worry.'

With three musical brothers there was no shortage of music at the wedding and everyone had a wonderful time. Lizzie danced the night away, her smile never faltering.

CHAPTER 28

I was due to make my confirmation in St. Mary's Cathedral on Clyde Street. There was a lot of discussion as to what name I should take, but I knew only one was expected of me - Philomena, after my Godmother Famie, though she had chosen to spell it differently. She was very pleased and I felt it made up a little for all her concern about my missing mass so much.

All of that had got much better with the aunts taking it in turns to escort me there and back.

It meant I could kneel at the alter rail before the Bishop with a clear conscience.

To my great surprise Auntie Teeny offered to knit me a cloak for the great day, and Ada decided the dress I had worn to Lizzie's wedding would have to do, but she did buy me a pair of new shoes.

The cloak when it came took my breath away. It was exquisite, so fine it could be passed through a wedding ring, and it was the most beautiful Madonna blue. I couldn't wait to wear it.

The day dawned fair and reasonably warm. As I filed through the great doors of the Cathedral I felt sure all eyes were on my wonderful cloak. I didn't want the day to end and insisted on wearing it all through the family tea afterwards.

'Well at least everything went right this time, not like the day you were to make your first communion,' Tina laughed.

I remembered it so vividly, at first too excited to sleep I lay gazing at my white communion dress hanging behind the door, and on a chair by my bed my new shoes lay wrapped in tissue paper in their box with the white ankle socks on top.

I clutched the pillow trying to ignore the fever and headache that had plagued me all day, and finally I must have fallen asleep because the next thing I knew Ada was standing by the bed her hand on my forehead a frown between her eyes.

'You feel very warm and you are flushed, I don't think you will be going anywhere today, and I think you have the measles.'

'But I need to go, I want to go,' I pleaded.

'You can't and that is that. We can arrange to have you make your communion another time,' she said.

Later, though complaining that I needed to stay in bed in a darkened room, she relented long enough to let me watch at the window as the procession of children went by on their way to St. Alphonsus. Tina had told me that on your first communion you became a Bride of Christ, I wasn't sure what that meant and wasn't at all sure I wanted to a Bride of Christ or anyone else's bride.

'Maybe it was better to let the others do it then I could ask them what it was like,' I thought.

It was weeks before I was well enough to think about making my communion. I dearly wanted to wear my white dress even though it was an ordinary Sunday, and I stood out like a sore thumb. Molly had mocked me next day at school, saying I was just a show-off.

At least for my Confirmation I had been one of the crowd.

With everything that had been going on Ada had quite forgotten about John Mathieson, but Lena had not. Egged on by Betty, Lena had taken her advice and went dancing with her friends Morag and Geena, to the Locarno, Dennistoun Palais and Barrowland, but while her friends would fall in and out of 'love', their broken hearts quick to mend as the next handsome sailor or soldier came along, Lena's heart was already given and once given she would never take it back.

Geena confided in her that she had found true love, a young sailor, Ricky, had stolen her heart as they danced the night away to 'A Nightingale Sang in Berkeley Square'. Later he had walked her home and as they stood in the cold draughty close he had proposed, drawing her into his arms and singing 'their tune' as they danced.

He had sailed the next day, promising to leave the navy after this last voyage. The news that two ships had docked sent both girls searching the newspapers to see the names of the ships.

Geena, full of excitement, had rushed home to get herself ready to meet Ricky. She placed the record on the turntable and the familiar song filled the room,

> *I may be right, and I may be wrong*
> *But I'm certainly willing to swear*
> *That when you turned and smiled at me*
> *A Nightingale sang in Berkeley Square.*

The sound of the doorbell sent her rushing to open it. On the mat stood a young sailor, nervously twisting his cap round and round.

One look at his face told Geena all she needed to know.

Bursting into tears she flew to the record player, sending the needle scraping across the disc with a whine.

'Why? How could it happen when the war is over?'

'Accidents happen even in peacetime,' the young sailor said, 'I volunteered to come and tell you, he was my mate.'

'He was my life,' Geena whispered.

I hung on Lena's every word as she told me this, part of me ached for Geena, but part of me exulted in the fact that Lena had opened the door into a grown up world, and that for once she had not hidden it from me saying I was 'too wee'.

She fumbled under her pillow and drew out the dog-eared photograph of John Mathieson, holding it up to the light to see it more clearly.

'I had hoped one of those ships that came in was John's but it wasn't,' she said

I hugged her not knowing what to say.

'What if something happens to him?'

'Nothing is going to happen to him,' I said.

'How do you know?' she said against my hair.

She was right, I didn't.

A letter came the following week from John saying his ship would be docking soon.

Lena danced around the room with glee, stopping suddenly to point at me and say, 'not a word to Mammy, promise?'

'I promise.'

She hugged the letter, and then tossed her head defiantly.

'It doesn't matter if you do say something. I have decided I am going to be with John whether Mammy likes it or no'.'

By the time John came home her courage failed her and they met in secret. My lips were sealed.

The secret did not last long as Aggie, ever on the lookout for gossip, heard a rumour the John was back. She knew Lena had been taking time out from the dipping machine, ten minutes here, five minutes there, and she put two and two together and told Ada.

There was an almighty row.

'I warned you about seeing that young man. You know his background as well as I do and you will have nothing more to do with him.'

Lena stood eyes blazing, cheeks flushed.

'He is nothing like his brother, he has nothing to do with the Bath gang, and you can't stop me seeing him.'

'I can and I will. You are far too young to get serious about any man, let alone him,' Ada shouted.

'I am not, I can do what I want, and if you don't let me see him I will leave the house.'

'Don't you dare.'

'You can't stop me.'

'Basta, basta,' Eugene said coming between them, 'what is all this aboot, what are ye gettin' het up aboot?'

They glared at him.

Eugene gently pressed Lena into a chair, then turned to Ada.

'Can we no' talk aboot this?'

'I've said all I have to say, she knows what I think, and if you have any sense you will see I am right,' ,Ada fumed.

'It's not fair, you don't know him, won't give him a chance.'

Eugene looked at Lena fondly. He loved her dearly and would always take her side in any argument.

'You like this man, eh?'

'Yes.'

'You think he is the one for you?'

'Yes'.

'Huh, over my dead body,' Ada muttered.

'Then maybe we should meet him, talk to him, and see what he is like, eh?'

There was stony silence. Lizzie, Tina and I worked on at the dipping, our heads down listening but saying nothing.

Eugene looked at Ada, 'what dae ye think?'

'Maybe,' she said.

We looked at each other, then at Lena, her head had come up and she was staring at Ada in disbelief.

'I won't have you saying I am unfair, I am only thinking of what is best for you, but maybe it is the only thing to do, to meet this man and talk to him. You can tell him is invited for a meal on Sunday.'

'Yes Mammy,' Lena smiled broadly.

We grinned at each other as Eugene put a hand on Lena's shoulder and smiled.

'Right now that's sorted lets get on wi' the work.'

A rather bemused John found himself seated at our table staring at a huge plate of spaghetti.

'Mange, mange,' Eugene urged.

John reluctantly picked up his fork.

'You don't like spaghetti?' Ada asked.

'I was waiting for the chips,' John said.

Lena and I suppressed a giggle then looked at Ada's stony face.

Eugene burst out laughing, 'you don't eat chips wi' spaghetti, here have some parmesan,' and he grated a liberal helping over John's plate.

The rest of the meal was eaten in silence and Lena and John escaped as soon as decently possible.

Later when we were all ready for bed, Ada called Lena into the kitchen. I followed knowing the verdict was about to be pronounced on John.

Lena jumped in before Ada could speak.

'I'm really sorry Mammy. John didn't mean to offend you, he is just not used to spaghetti.'

'I know!' Ada said grimly, then looking up she burst out laughing, 'chips indeed! He won't live that down in a hurry.'

We all laughed, Lena hardly daring to believe what was happening.

As we said our goodnights, Ada called Lena back.

'He can come again but next time we will just send down to the chip shop for a fish supper.'

Back in the big room Lena hugged me and much to Aggie's surprise hugged her too.

As time passed we grew to know and like John so much that when Lena was engaged it was a real cause for celebration. John was eager to marry and it was agreed the wedding would be on March 11th a few weeks before Lena's nineteenth birthday.

'Aye a wise man, marrying before the end of the tax year,' Eugene teased.

'Well it shows good judgement,' Ada said, by now quite a fan of her prospective son-in-law.

To the aunts' dismay Lena was to be married in a Protestant church which was just across the road from the cafe, and when the bans were called it was our neighbours who heard them.

Young Tommy, who helped me ferry the supplies to the park, told me the neighbours were talking.

'What do you mean?' I asked.

'Well they say that the minister keeps gettin' your sister's name wrong, he keeps sayin' a funny name instead of Coutts.'

'Och it won't matter,' I said quickly.

'You should tell your Mammy, she could sort it,' he persisted. 'Ok,' I said, but I didn't.

Ada had written to Betty inviting them all to the wedding. To her joy Betty was coming with the baby but John could not get time off work. We were all looking forward to seeing them, letters had been few and far between.

Lena had decided not to take up Ada's offer of the wee room, opting instead for two rooms in Elderslie Street which was not too far away.

'Aye, it is the right thing to do, she has always been a sensible lassie,' Eugene said.

'That's true,' Ada agreed.

On the day of the wedding Eugene could not be found anywhere.

Ada was frantic and she swore to kill him if he made Lena late.

He had taken the car and though he had not been missed at first, Tina said he had been away for hours.

He finally turned up, amazed at all the fuss his absence had caused.

'Eh what's the problem, the church is just across the road,' he said.

'You still have to change, look at you, where on earth have you been?' Ada demanded.

'I went for petrol.'

'Where did you go, the moon?'

'Anderson Cross.'

'There are places nearer than that, did you go to the workshop?'

'Aye.'

'On your daughter's wedding day?'

'Aye, well ah wanted to see if any more orders had come in, and there was a row of doorsteps needing to be turned oot o' their moulds.'

'You were playing about with doorsteps on a day like this?'

'Aye well, it is all business.'

'Had you no idea of the time?'

'You know how it is you get engrossed.'

He was struggling with his tie and Ada took over.

He stretched his neck, waggling his head this way and that as she tightened the knot.

'As ah say ah got engrossed then realized the time, ah jumped into the car reversed oot the pend and......'

'What?'

'Ah bumped intae another car,' his eyes were on the ceiling.

'You hit another car, you damaged the car?' she tugged at the knot.

'And the other one,' he croaked as she pulled at the tie.

He backed away rubbing at his neck.

'It's no' too bad, and the other one only has a wee dent. I tried to get our car fixed right away, but ah'11 need to wait to next week.'

'How much?' Ada said.

He shrugged 'well ah don't know yet an' then there is the other fellows car as well.'

Betty pushed open the door, 'Ready?'

'Aye just aboot,' Eugene spluttered.

'He has crashed the car,' Ada announced as they emerged from the room.

'Just as well you are insured,' Betty said.

Eugene turned away, but Ada saw the look and spun him round. 'Don't tell me we are not insured.'

He spread his hands helplessly.

'Just wait till this wedding is over,' she hissed.

After the reception the house was full, the aunts came back for tea, and Mary and Jimmy, still in funereal black, sat silently watching and saying nothing.

Eugene was the life and soul of the party, eager to postpone the hour of reckoning.

Betty went back to Southampton still with many of Ada's questions unanswered.

I missed Lena so much and now that Betty had gone back I felt really alone.

I had hoped that Ada would move Aggie into the other room and I could have a room of my own, but she opted to keep the 'big' room for visitors. At fourteen I needed my own space. Aggie pried into all my activities, and if she saw me writing she would peer over my shoulder. No budding writer likes anyone peering over their shoulder; it made me want to scream. Most of my scribblings were fantasies, fairy stories, or modelled on the stories in the 'School Friend', full of midnight feasts and tuck boxes.

Now that I was thrown on my own resources any spare time I got, which was very little, I spent writing or visiting the library.

Ada was not settled in her mind about Betty.

'There is something she has not told me, I feel it in my bones.'

'Eh, when are you going to stop worrying aboot thae lassies? Thae are grown women noo, wi' husbands tae look after them,' Eugene puffed away at his pipe.

'Husbands to look after them? That is what is supposed to happen, Lena and John are fine, but Betty, no, a mother's instinct is never wrong.'

Eugene sighed but said no more.

CHAPTER 29

Unable to rid herself of the nagging worry about Betty's situation, Ada decided that she and I would pay a surprise visit. Eugene assured her that everything would keep ticking over, though it meant only Tina, Lizzie and Eddie would man the machines, with Aggie doing her best to cope with the shop, and he would do all the deliveries.

Our journey to Southampton would be by sleeper to London, then on by train to the town.

Ada felt it was unlikely that Betty would have a spare room so we would sleep in a guesthouse. I was thrilled by the whole thing and looked forward to the trip.

The journey was much longer than we expected and we emerged a little weary from the train at Southampton.

Ada took the last letter from Betty which was a few months old from her bag and approached a ticket collector to ask directions.

He shook his head, saying he had never heard of the place. Several others gave the same answer, but eventually a taxi driver said he had an idea it may be near a rather remote village.'

'Never had call to take anyone there but I believe the army had a camp there,' he told us.

Ada asked about a bus service and he obligingly pointed out where we could get a bus that he thought would take us near the place. We thanked him and, dragging our cases to the stance, stood waiting for what seemed an age before the bus came.

Ada showed the driver the address, but he shook his head, saying he would take us to the terminus.

As we got down from the bus, the driver pointed vaguely to a rutted path, 'you probably want to go in that direction.'

We thanked him, and set off, lifting and laying the cases as we went along. There was nothing to see but stubbly fields, and after a while we rested on a grassy bank. The silence closed in on us, and in the distance a bird flapped its wings and wobbled on the post of a gate.

'I think we are lost, there is nothing here, maybe we should retrace our steps to where the bus left us and catch the next one back to town,' Ada said.

I stood up, climbing higher up the bank.

'There are some buildings a few fields away,' I said helpfully.

'Houses?' Ada asked.

'Barns I think.'

'Well, maybe it is a farm and there may be people there we could ask, let's go.'

It took another twenty minutes or more before we neared the buildings. They looked deserted, broken down, and Ada sat down wearily on the grass verge.

'We are on a wild goose chase, we'll rest a while than go back,' she said.

Suddenly I caught a movement in one of the buildings.

'There is somebody there,' I said excitedly, 'a woman and she is carrying a child.'

Ada stood up, 'My God, it's Betty, I swear that is Betty.' She had spied us at the same time as we saw her, but instead of running towards us she hurried away and disappeared into an old barn.

We grabbed our cases, half running, half staggering across the stubble till we reached the buildings and Ada marched into the barn calling Betty's name. She emerged out of the gloom and stood looking at us.

'What in the name of God are you doing here?' Ada demanded. Betty burst into tears but said nothing.

'Do you LIVE here?'

She nodded, then through her sobs, 'it is only till we can find another place.'

Ada looked around, 'where exactly do you live?'

Betty led us through the barn to a small two storey building at the back, and we climbed after her up a flight of broken stairs along a narrow passage to a room with peeling plaster and fungus growing out of the walls.

'My God!' Ada breathed.

I looked around. There was a little window with two missing panes covered with cardboard, two sagging armchairs with stuffing hanging out, a couple of orange boxes with a piece of wood on top that served as a table, and in the corner a little cot draped with a tartan shawl, pressed against a bed which in turn pressed against the stained damp wall.

'This is where you live with this little mite?' Ada said, shaking her head.

'The kitchen is downstairs,' Betty said in a low voice.

'And what is THAT like I wonder,' Ada was scathing.

We went down to the kitchen. It had no door, no running water, a one ring gas cooker, and through the broken window I could see a small lavatory, the door sagging on its hinges. All around what had once been a garden was overgrown and choked with weeds.

Ada was shaking her head in disbelief, and she turned to Betty who stood with her face buried in the neck of the baby.

'Pack your things, you are coming home with us,' Ada said.

'1 c-can't just go like that,' Betty said into the baby's neck.

'You want to stay here?'

Betty raised her head, her eyes red with sobbing, 'I can't leave, not without saying anything.'

'Leave a note. I'll leave a note, give him a piece of my mind,' Ada snapped.

'No!'

'When will he be home?'

'Not until six, he works in the town.'

'And leaves you and his daughter to rot all day in this place.'

'Go pack your bags, and be ready to leave as soon as he returns.'

She looked around, 'is there a kettle? We all need a cup of tea.'

As we sat clutching the warm teacups, Ada pressed Betty to explain how they came to be in such a place.

'It is not really his fault, good places are hard to find, and everybody is looking for somewhere to live. Southampton was badly bombed and a lot of the houses in town were lost,' Betty said.

'Maybe, but what I can't understand is that a man like that, so refined and correct, should bring you and that little soul to a place like this. Eugene has taken me to some places in the past, but never anything as bad as this.'

'He really did try, he told me, and I believe him,' Betty said.

'He should have left you where you were till things got better.'

I watched the hands of the clock creep round to six and I was dreading the coming confrontation.

Betty was feeding the baby as we heard the sound of John's footsteps on the stair. He pushed open the door and took a step back in surprise.

'Did you know about this?' he asked Betty.

'No, they came to surprise us,' Betty said.

'It was us who got the surprise, the shock more like,' Ada's tone was acid.

'You are shocked,' he said. It wasn't a question, merely an observation.

'You are surprised? How could you bring your wife and child to this?'

'I am sure my wife has explained the situation.'

'She has tried to make excuses for you, but they do not wash with me. You should be ashamed of yourself.'

'What would you have me do?'

'Leave them in Scotland until you really did find a decent place. This place is a health hazard,' she said as she punched the walls and a shower of spores drifted down.

'A family should be together, if there are rough times we should all experience them together,' he said.

'You think so?' Ada said.

'Yes it can bring them closer,' he said.

'Or drive them apart,' she pointed to Betty, 'look at her, she has lost weight, see how pale she is, and the baby's health is in danger too.'

All this time Betty sat with her head bowed, and the baby began to cry as the voices grew louder. I had said nothing as I knew only silence was expected of me, but I was shocked at the pathetic figure Betty made. She was nothing like the bright bouncy, smart-mouthed girl I knew.

Outside the light was fading and my heart sank as I realized we would probably have to spend the night here. Ada would not leave without Betty and that had still to be resolved.

The baby's distress caused both Ada and John to mellow their tone, and though the harsh words still hung in the air, the body language was different, and for a while no one spoke.

'I expect you will want your evening meal,' Ada said.

John looked at Betty, who jumped up placing the baby in the cot, where she started to scream her annoyance.

'Go pick up the baby,' Ada said to me, 'I'll help with the meal.'

She and Betty went downstairs, and to my relief John followed them, saying he would go and draw water from the well in the garden.

It was obvious there was little to eat in the house. Ada had found some potatoes, which she mashed with a little butter and milk. This and suffced for us, John got two rashers of bacon with his, and there was bread and some jam.

As Betty cleared away Ada said in an even tone, 'I want Betty to come home with us, in fact I insist on it, She will only come back when you have found a decent place to live, and by the livin' Harry, it had better be a decent place before you think of asking her back.'

Silence.

He cleared his throat and looked Betty in the eye. 'Is this what you want?'

She was about to speak, but he held up his hand.

'Before you answer, let me tell you that if you do go, you will not be welcomed back.'

She stared at her hands.

'You may go, but it will mean the end for us and for you the loss of your daughter. I will insist the child stays with me.'

Ada bristled, but to my great relief she held her tongue.

'Now,' he said, 'do you want to go back to Scotland?'

'I want my baby,' Betty said.

'It is your choice. Do you want to go or stay?'

'Don't let him intimidate you, there are courts of law you know,' Ada said.

'Betty?'

'I want to go,' she said.

He stood up, 'very well, you have made your choice. I will permit the child to go with you for now, but I have told you my decision.'

He turned to Ada, 'you may share the bed with Betty tonight and I will make my own arrangements. You will understand if I am not around to say good-bye in the morning.'

He collected a few things and went downstairs.

'Where will he go?' I asked Betty.

'Probably one of the barns,' she said.

She pulled a rather frayed camp bed from beneath her bed and smiled apologetically.

'This is the best I can do.'

'That will suit her fine,' Ada said briskly.

Later as we settled for the night I feared the camp bed would split right through. Gingerly I tried to distribute my weight holding on to the metal sides, but I found it difficult to sleep. Shadows danced on the walls, distant barking which I thought was a dog but later Betty told me was probably a fox and owls hooting in the surrounding woodland were all unfamiliar sounds filling me with fear. On the makeshift mantel shelf a clock that I recognized as one of Betty's wedding presents ticked loudly and struck every quarter, half and hour. As it struck three I heard a ripping sound as the canvas parted company and deposited me on the floor.

I lay there, pulled the blanket over me and free from the fear of the thing ripping, fell asleep at last.

The morning dawned grey and chill, and Ada, always an early riser, shook me awake, anxious to get rid of the camp bed as it took up all the floor space. She had little concern that I had spent most of the night on the floor, as her mind was set on quitting the place as soon as possible. Stiff and sore I followed her downstairs out to the well with two buckets, and despite the cold water she turned me away while she had her usual strip wash, then when she was finished instructed me to do the same, using the second bucket of water. I knew I had no option but to comply. Ada meanwhile busied herself making tea and the baby's feed. Of course our first port of call had been the privy at the end of the garden. It was all right in the daylight, but the night before when I had expressed fear of going down in the dark, Ada had told me not to be so silly, and half pushed me out the door. Upstairs, Betty was writing a farewell letter, which she propped behind the clock.

Taking a last look around we set off lugging the cases over the field to the road and making our way slowly but steadily back to the bus terminus. Southampton was a revelation. It had indeed suffered badly in the war and everywhere buildings lay in ruins, the ugly piles softened by rosebay willow herb and buttercup. Small children scrambled over the bricks and mortar making dens, playing cowboys and Indians. Ada winced as they dared to climb broken walls ready to collapse. The heart of the town showed signs of regeneration, with Woolworth, Marks and Spencer, and British Home Stores, which we didn't have in Scotland then. It was to this store we went for tea, and I thought it was so modern and bright, so full of life and bustle.

Eugene accepted Betty's return without question, though Aggie sensing some drama was keen to find out what had happened. She quizzed me at night, but I feigned sleep, afraid to say anything that Ada would disapprove of.

In time everything was out in the open, because the saga was repeated time and time again over the next few years. John's threat to refuse to have Betty back never really materialized, and he did find a suitable place, but always there were bitter rows, and a letter from Betty appealing to Ada would have Ada going to the post office buying postal orders to pay her fare home.

We became used to meeting her at the station one week and waving her good-bye the next.

Ada's fear that they were not suited was certainly realized.

Even Eugene was growing weary of the constant coming and going.

'Ah don't think it is a good idea to let her come back every time.'

'You want me to let my daughter suffer?' Ada snapped.

Eugene looked shamefaced, 'ah was only sayin'.'

A thought stirred in my mind, the doctor saying Betty was not my full sister. Ada had said 'my daughter'. Eugene was not Betty's father, it was true, it must be true.

Lena and John had no such troubles. Theirs was a marriage made in heaven, Ada gratefully acknowledged.

The business was running into difficulties, Ada was finding it hard to meet the high hire purchase payments, and even the modest wages for Tina, Lizzie and Eddie were a drain on resources. Eugene tried to revive his terrazzo business, Eddie taking over deliveries. Lizzie went back to the Rossis in Charing Cross, putting a heavier burden on Ada, Aggie, Tina and me.

Ada was often distracted by Betty's troubles, but she could not afford to keep baling her out. This preyed on her mind and she became snappy and easily roused.

I felt isolated, still considered a child. I was still excluded by the conversations in Italian, the whispered conversations between Tina and Ada. I turned to my little books on the lives of the saints for solace, and scribbled away at my stories which next day would be torn up and binned.

Aggie bought me the Pollyanna stories, and soon I was a devotee of the 'Glad Game'. Since the sobbing letters were still coming from Betty and Ada was unable to respond as she used to, it occurred to me that perhaps the 'Glad Game' may be the answer to all Betty's ills.

I wrote to her telling her how to play it.

At first she wrote back with upbeat letters, saying she was playing it, and it was a good idea.

Soon however she was home again after one of their bust-ups, and I tried to console her but she suddenly turned on me screaming that she was sick and tired of me and my bloody glad game, I was only a silly little girl who knew nothing, and believed all the problems in life could be solved by a silly bloody game.

I fled from her anger, Rover at my heels and it was to him I poured out my misery, sobbing into his soft fur.

Of course as I write now I can see the reason for her outburst.

I had continued the early morning walks with Rover after John had left, but now I rose even earlier, and each morning at five am I would slip from the bed taking care not to wake Aggie, quieten the exuberant Rover, gripping him by the collar and clipping his lead on once we were out the door, and we would make straight for the park to University Avenue, where I would gaze in awe at that dear familiar building and dream of going there someday to immerse myself in study.

Round the duck pond we would go, Rover making mock runs at the silly ducks who would rise up and run into the water their outstretched wings flapping.

There among the trees sat the brooding figure of Thomas Carlyle, a man who had laboured over a manuscript for some years only to lend it to a friend whose maid mistook it for paper to light the fire.

It was not only the misfortune which was truly remarkable, but Carlyle's response which drew the admiration.

He held no grudge and set to rewriting his work.

I dared to identify with the great man, feeling that many if not all of my efforts turned to ashes. Betty's outburst brought home to me how little I knew about life, there seemed to be rules that no one had told me, and I ended hurting the very people I loved most. I sent up fervent prayers to the Blessed Virgin, feeling that I needed to get her on my side if I was ever going to be a virgin like her. I pledged my intention over and over again, but here a cruel awakening lay in wait for me.

On a visit to Lena, in a rush of sisterly exchanges of confidences, I told her my confusion about life.

She smiled kindly and said 'you will learn, you are too young to understand.'

'But Betty is so miserable; I really wanted to help her.'

'She is just going through a bad patch, it will work itself out.'

As we sipped our tea I told her about school and the snooty girls who looked down on me and my friend, and she told me to ignore them as they were not worth my concern.

In a rush of gratitude knowing she was on my side I told her of my secret ambition to be a virgin like Mary.

She put her cup down and stared at me for a moment.

'You already are a virgin,' she said.

Seeing my astonishment she went on, 'every girl is a virgin to start with. I used to be a virgin too, until I got married.'

'What do you mean?'

'Every girl is a virgin till she has been with a man,' she said patiently.

'I don't believe you. How can being with a man change you? I don't understand.' I was tormented by what she had said.

It's true and you will find out when you are grown. I can't tell you everything, Mammy would be angry, so you will just have to wait.'

No amount of pleading would change her mind.

That night I lay alongside Aggie staring into the darkness. I was more confused than ever and suddenly I thought of Aggie. Was she a virgin? Did she know if she was or not?

'Aggie. Agg-ie. Are you awake?'

'Aye whit is it?'

'Do you know what a virgin is? Are you one?'

She was shocked, 'ye shouldnae ask things like that.'

'I need to know. I wanted to be a virgin like Mary but Lena says I am one already. She says she used to be one but now she isn't.'

'She's right. That's a' you need to know.'

'No, I need to know. What did she mean? She said it was something to do with being with a man, but I don't see how that can change anything.'

'You know mair than ye should, and yer Mammy would be angry if she could hear you.'

'But I don't know anything, honestly. I need to know. Tell me.'

'You are just a daft wee lassie. It is a' aboot sex, an' that is a' am sayin, so get tae sleep,' she turned her back to me.

Sex! That mysterious thing that Ada would not have mentioned in my presence. I remembered a day I had been watching Eugene rewire an electric plug. He had held the two pronged plug up and then inserted it into the socket, 'you see it's simple, male to female.'

I had no idea what he was talking about.

Ada covered her eyes with her hands speaking low in Italian.

Eugene looked up and answered in English, 'she will need to know sometime.'

'But not now, not yet,' she snapped.

So now I lay next to Aggie, staring wide eyed into the darkness feeling as if the bottom had dropped out of my world.

If I had been a virgin all along it meant that my offering to God was worthless, and maybe he had been laughing at me. He, St. Francis, St. Jude all of them, laughing at a silly wee girl who knew nothing. The world was not as I believed it to be, all the things that I depended on were not solid, they floated on a sea of deceit, mocking me at every turn. Ada and Eugene with their secrets, the aunts with their furtive glances, Father Malone in the confessional hearing me say I was striving to be a virgin, and he knew, he knew I was already a virgin, and he said nothing only giving that funny choking cough, he had been laughing just like all the others.

For days I could not pray. God had been in on the joke. I moped about keeping myself to myself, still turning up after school for work at the dipping and wrapping, but saying nothing. I was adrift on an island of ignorance and despair.

Who could I speak to? No one, there was no one.

Lena had meant it when she said she would say no more.

I sank to my knees in the end. God was almighty and who was I to turn my back on Him?

As I prayed I thought of St. Francis, the gentle one, I needed him, perhaps he had not really laughed, only smiled at my ignorance.

Here then was something I could do, I could be like him and offer that to God in repentance for my foolishness and all the times a mortal sin had stained my soul.

I read and reread the account of his life. 'If you have two cloaks give one away to your needy brother'.

I had a cloak, the beautiful Madonna blue that Teeny had knitted for me. Should I give that away?

Night after night I took the cloak from its protective wrapper, imagining myself without it. Did I have the strength to give it away?

I would wrap it up again and put it away, saying I would do it but not yet.

Christmas was coming and preparations for the party had begun. The list of names of the local children had to be drawn up. A new family had moved into the ground floor flat in Mary Murray's close, and we found out that the five children had no mother or father only an old granny to look after them. They were younger than us and very poor. I asked Ada if they could come to the party, and she agreed. When the invitations were ready I plucked up the courage to go to their door. The close was always dark and the lobby to their door even darker, and I was a little scared as I knocked on the door.

I could hear shuffling footsteps and then a bolt being drawn. Slowly the door opened and the old woman peered out, behind her a dim gas light spilled onto the floor, and we stood peering at each other without speaking.

'What is it hen?' she asked.

'I've come to invite the children to my Christmas party.'

I held out the invitation, but she didn't take it, instead she opened the door wider saying, 'Come ben hen, ah cannae see anything in this light.' She shuffled off and I followed.

The room had little furniture, everywhere clothes lay in bundles, a ginger tom licked at an unwashed plate, the tap dripped a staccato beat into the sink and torn net curtains covered the window.

There was a stale smell that caught at the throat.

I offered the card again. She took it, turned it over and over, held it close to her eyes and then shook her head.

'Ah cannae see tae read wi'oot ma specs, but for the life o' me ah don't know where ah've put them,' she said.

'Will I read it to you?'

She handed me the card straight away, 'aye hen that wid be best.'

I read the card, realising she couldn't read.

'That is awfy good o' yer mammy tae invite the weans, ah don't think they hiv ever been tae a pairty afore.'

I told her of the tree and the presents, of Santa Claus and the jelly and buns.

'Oh that will be grand, wi' things the way thae ur, thae will be lucky tae get an orange an' a penny.'

As I looked at the cloak that night I thought of the children in that house and how little they had, and I fingered the cloak lovingly, wondering if giving them my cloak would really help? In my mind's eye I could see them falling on it, fighting over it, dragging it across that dirty linoleum. I held the soft material to my cheek; it was so beautiful that I longed to keep it. Ada would be absolutely furious if I gave it away. While St. Francis had urged sacrifice, and said that if you had two cloaks you should give one away, I only had one, and that had been a gift. Quickly I put the cloak back in the wardrobe and shut the door. I felt happy that the cloak was still mine, but guilty too. I had only one cloak, but I did have lots of other clothes, and I began pulling things out of drawers, skirts, jerseys, dresses, underwear, socks, and then on to books, toys, fancy soap, all my treasures. I sat back on my heels surveying the jumble strewn across the floor. I remembered reading that if you parted with only that which you had grown tired of it was no sacrifice at all, and since I had given in to the temptation of holding on to my cloak I decided I would give my favourite things away. Maybe I should share things around, find others who were needy too, and I spent the next few days scouting around for likely candidates. In Little Dover Street there was a 'wild' bunch - an unruly mob of five boys and four girls, all with freckles and flaming red hair - the Corrigans.

They never seemed to catch any of the common children's ailments; they would romp around in all weathers, matted jerseys full of holes, seats out of their pants, the girls in thin worn dresses.

They lived on the ground floor and came and went through the kitchen window. Though regarded as the poorest of the poor, they neither seemed to know or care.

Neither did they care about or heed the constant threats to 'tan their hide' their mother made when the truant officer called. All of us were a little scared of them.

The women round about would gather at the close mouth and gossip, shaking their heads in disapproval as the Corrigans spilled out of the window, the brothers brawling among themselves, the girls cat-fighting over thick bread crusts.

One summer, news got round that the mother of the fighting Corrigans had been rushed to hospital, leaving the children with no one to care for them, as no one could remember ever seeing a man about the place.

As one, the women took the squabbling bunch under their wing. The first two to enter the house reported it was in a foul state, and an army of willing helpers appeared with mops, scrubbing brushes and bottles of 'Jeyes Fluid'.

I joined in with some of the bigger girls, and the first thing that hit us was the stench from chamber pots full to overflowing with urine and excrement. As we emerged from the house carrying the pots at arms length, the crowd of onlookers held their noses and ran.

The volunteers went through the place like an unstoppable tide.

Protesting children were stripped of their tattered clothes, dumped squealing into tin baths. Dressed in clean clothes with shining faces and tamed hair, they stared at their reflections in amazement.

A rota was formed to care for them until their mother's return. When she did it took only a day or two for the whole rumbustious crew to return to 'normal'.

Ada had never included the Corrigans in the party list, but now as I looked for needy children I felt they were the ideal candidates.

There was a problem however; I could only help the girls, having only girl's clothes and toys.

I made a few parcels of the things I intended to give away, and hid them under the bed till I could think of a way to get them to my chosen few, without them knowing where the things came from, and more importantly without Ada knowing.

I asked Ada if I could go to midnight mass with Lizzie. In years past Lena and I had gone with her, but now Lena was married she had given up Catholicism, which I knew had hurt the aunts very much.

Ada said that I could go if Lizzie was willing to take me, which she was. My next hurdle was to get the parcels out of the house and delivered without involving Lizzie, who would immediately tell Ada.

I decided under the circumstances a white lie was permissible.

I told Lizzie that the parcels belonged to Mrs Murray, who had been hiding them from Mary and her sister till Christmas time. Lizzie nodded and said she would wait on the corner for me till I delivered them.

I hurried as fast as I could first to the family in Mary's close, and stumbling into the dark lobby, I placed two of my bundles at the door and fled without knocking.

Next I dodged round the corner to the Corrigans. As I entered the close I thought I heard someone moving in the dunny, but told myself it was probably a rat, which was reason enough for me to get out of there as quickly as possible.

I dumped the parcels and ran back to where Lizzie was waiting, rubbing her gloveless hands to keep them warm.

All through mass I wondered what the reaction to the parcels would be. I could hardly wait for the exchange of presents to be over on Christmas morning, as I was eager to see if there was any reaction to the gifts I had left. Rover gave me the excuse I needed. As I turned into Breadalbane Street I met Mary Murray on her way to find me.

'The wee lassies that live in ma close say Santa left presents at their door last night.'

'Oh that's nice.'

She stared at me in surprise.

'What do you mean? How could Santa leave presents? He isn't real.'

'Do they really have presents, you've seen them?'

'Aye, toys, books, dresses, skirts and jumpers, they're nice but they are no' new, and it's funny cos some things look like things you have.'

'Well, even if the things are not new at least they got something. Do they like them?'

'Aye they think it was really Santa.'

'Let's go for a walk with Rover,' I said trying to change the subject.

I hadn't bargained on the little girls wearing the clothes to the party, and although some things were too long and others too big they were as proud as punch. Ada's eyes followed them as they danced around the room, and I knew she would have something to say to me after the party. Calling me into the wee room I shared with Aggie she began opening drawers and then the wardrobe, where the empty hangers told their own story.

'I think you have some explaining to do,' she was furious.

I tried to tell her about St. Francis, and how he set an example of giving to the poor, but she cut me short and marched me through to the kitchen, to let Eugene and Aggie know what I had done.

Eugene laughed, 'that's Famie puttin' daft ideas in her head.'

'It is no laughing matter; she has hardly left herself with a thing to put on her back,' Ada snapped.

'Och it's hardly a sin, she was tryin' to do something good,' Eugene said.

I don't need a lot of clothes. St. Francis......'

'I don't want to hear another thing about your blessed St. Francis.'

'Yer mammy has tae buy a' thae things fur ye,' Aggie chipped in.

'I'm sorry mammy, I only wanted to give them some presents, because they don't have anything.'

'Is that the only place you left things?'

I looked at her, trying to judge her reaction.

'I can see it wasn't, you better tell me.'

'The Corrigans,' I said quietly.

'The Corrigans! Talk about casting pearls before swine. I'll bet you won't see them wearing your stuff. It will end up on a stall in the Barrows,' Ada said.

'Well, what's done is done, the intention was good enough,' Eugene said.

'Don't you ever, ever, do anything like that again, do you hear me?'
'Yes mammy.'
Later as I was getting ready for bed, Ada came into the room, her mood had changed and I could tell she was no longer angry.
'I have been thinking about what happened. I know you were trying to think of others and that has to be a good thing to do, but there are ways of going about things. If you had come and asked me first it would have been better.'
She turned to go, and then said, 'I will be watching you, remember that.'
Aggie was Ada's eyes and ears and she watched me like a hawk, which made what happened some months later all the more mysterious.
Our neighbour, Mrs. McCormack from upstairs, came to ask Ada if she could borrow the Madonna blue cloak for her youngest daughter's confirmation.
Ada had gone to get it from the wardrobe but it had vanished.
As soon as I came through the door from school she pounced on me.
'You have been up to your old tricks trying to follow that - that saint.'
'I don't know what you mean.'
'Playing lady bountiful again giving away that beautiful cloak.'
'I didn't.'
'Don't lie to me. It is not in the wardrobe where it should be.'
'I didn't give it away. Honestly, I thought about it but I couldn't because I loved it too much.'
'I told you not to lie to me,' she gripped me, 'come with me.'
She pulled me into the room. The door of the wardrobe was wide open, the cloak was not there and I frantically rummaged through the clothes.
It was not there.
'Stop this nonsense. It is not there and you know it because you gave it away.'
'I didn't, honestly I didn't.'
She slapped me hard across the face the stinging blow bringing tears to my eyes, and gripping me again by the shoulders, she shook me.
'Who did you give it to? I want to know, and, whoever it was, you will go round there at once and get it back.'
'I didn't give it away,' I sobbed.
'I don't believe you. Where is it then?'
She pushed me on to the bed, 'You can stay there till you decide to tell me the truth.' She stormed out banging the door behind her.
I was trembling with rage at the injustice of it all, as I had not given the cloak away but it really was not to be found. How was I ever going to get Ada to believe me? I was devastated at the loss of the cloak. Who could have taken it? I thought of the night that I had agonized over giving it away and had given in to my selfish desire to keep it. Was I being punished for that? Had I offended St. Francis so much that he had somehow taken the cloak? No, that was a daft fancy, yet the cloak had gone, so it was a punishment nevertheless.
I slid to my knees and asked forgiveness for my selfishness in keeping the cloak for myself. I accepted that maybe I deserved to lose it but I still needed

to know what had happened to it. I prayed to St. Anthony, patron saint of all lost things. He would surely find it for me.

He didn't.

I never did find out what happened to the cloak, though in later years I was to have my own theory.

Ada never forgave me, not only for supposedly giving away the cloak but for lying and defying her by not telling her where it was.

She was to return to the subject time and time again over the years convinced I was still lying.

CHAPTER 30

The cinema orders were drying up. The big suppliers were squeezing us out. Ada was at her wits end trying to meet the hire purchase costs every month. Eugene was trying to find new outlets but with no success. He turned his attention to the terrazzo work but this only worried Ada more knowing he was running it at a loss.

'Things are going to change around here, mark my words, or else you will all wake up and I will be gone,' she threatened.

She and Eugene rowed all the time, he placid but stubborn in his belief that things would get better, she screaming at him that he was a fool, a dreamer who would not face the truth.

I was afraid to go to school in case she would not be there when I came home. Tina was no longer needed in the shop, and Lizzie and Eddie were gone too. Tina and Famie came for a visit every Thursday, always with a bar of chocolate for me. They would sit chatting while at Ada's request I made the tea, then she would send me out of the kitchen, a signal that they would be talking of things that were not for my ears.

I longed for Ada to recognize that I was growing up and that she could trust me, but she still saw me as a child, and she was so used to having secrets that nothing changed.

Of course I knew things were bad, but there was something else that was in the air, in the looks that passed between Ada and the aunts, in the set of Ada's face whenever Eugene was around.

Aggie as usual could not keep things to herself when I challenged her that 'something was up' and she could not resist telling me.

'Yer mammy thinks that yer daddy is havin' an affair.'

'What does that mean?'

Her eyes danced in her head with excitement, 'he is goin' with another woman.'

'That's not true, it can't be true.'

'It's what yer mammy thinks, yer mammy is always right, she can always tell.'

'What do you mean always tell? Has he done this before?'

She ignored that, 'Well yer mammy thinks he is that's a' I know.'

I began to watch Eugene closely, even to follow him if he went out without taking the car.

Most days he went to his workshop at Anderson Cross, he walked trying to save the petrol for any deliveries.

One Saturday he took a different route and as I watched I saw him meet up with a woman at the corner of the street behind his workshop. I felt a shiver go through me as I recognized the woman. She came into the shop all the time and she lived in Great Dover Street. She was small with light brown hair and a coarse face and she was much younger than Eugene. They walked off arm in arm and I shrank into the shadows as they walked towards me.

I watched as they boarded a tram that was heading into town. I went home my mind in a whirl. So Ada was right. How could he do what he was doing? I began to wonder if he suspected I was following him and so took the different route. I was not going to follow him again; I had seen all I wanted to see. How could I look him in the face when he came home? How could I act as if nothing had happened, not only to him but to Ada?

I knew the woman was a regular customer in the shop; she would sit with a Bovril making it spin out as long as she could. Often she would laugh and joke with Eugene, calling him 'Tally Joe'. I had thought nothing much of it as he always joked with customers, both men and women, but now little things came back to mind that if I had been looking would have given clues to their real relationship.

Ada had not confronted him with her suspicions, but her face was stony her tone icy. He constantly asked her what was the matter but she never replied. As we sat down to tea one night he produced a lovely wooden musical box, winding the little key round and round till the 'Blue Danube' tinkled sweetly through the room, and he set the box at Ada's place.

With an unspoken agreement she had stopped sitting on his knee at table and now sat facing Aggie.

He looked at her expectantly as the little golden drum of the box moved slowly round.

'What's this?' she said dryly.

'A present for you,' he said.

She drew him a look then swept the box to the floor, the music jangled out of tune then stopped.

Aggie was staring at them both, I felt my heart pound.

'I don't want your gifts, you can give that to your lady friend,' Ada snapped.

'Eh what are you talking about?'

'You know damn well, now pick that thing up before I stamp on it.'

He said nothing but getting up he picked up the box and left the kitchen, and a moment or two later we heard the front door close behind him.

Ada picked up the teapot, 'do you want more tea?' she asked Aggie.

Aggie held out her cup, 'a wee drop on tap o' there.'

It was her standard reply that we girls had often mimicked. Ada was signalling that the episode of the music box was not for discussion.

A few days later a box tied with red ribbon lay on the table, Ada's name was scrawled in bold letters on one corner. It lay there ignored for two or three days, Ada setting and clearing the table around it as if it was invisible.

I watched eagerly as she eventually pulled at the ribbon and lifted off the lid. Under a layer of tissue lay a peach silk slip and matching cami-knickers, and she held them up staring at them her face set in stone. Letting them fall back into the box she went to the cutlery drawer and took out a pair of scissors, began to cut the slip and knickers into tiny pieces and when she had finished she heaped them on to a plate and set it at Eugene's place. I watched the whole thing in silence, tears running down my face. She seemed unaware that I was even in the room. Calmly she returned the scissors to the drawer, lifted the box with its tissue and ribbon and threw it on the fire.

By tea-time the table was set as usual, Eugene's knife and fork placed either side of the heap of cut silk.

Aggie and I sat our eyes downcast waiting nervously for Eugene to come in. When he did, he went immediately to the plate, and lifting the pieces he let them drift back through his fingers.

'Who did this?'

'Who do you think?' said Ada from the door.

'Eh what for, what is this a' aboot?'

'You think you can buy me off with paltry things like that? It is an insult, I'm not stupid, and I won't fall for your tricks.'

'What are ye goin' on aboot woman, ah bought you a present, what's wrong wi' that?'

'You bought me a present to salve your guilty conscience. I told you already to keep your cheap presents for your lady friend, the slut.'

'What lady friend? What are ye talkin' aboot?'

'Don't lie to me!' she grabbed plate after plate and let them fly, as he dodged the plates he shouted over her screaming for her to calm down.

The dishes kept coming, there was a pile of broken crockery on the floor.

'Get yer mammy a glass of water,' he shouted to me.

'Don't bother. I'll throw it about him.'

Aggie sat spellbound like a rabbit caught in a headlight and I ran from the room. I could not believe Eugene could lie so blatantly.

I stood in the lobby listening as the screaming went on.

'I tell you there is no affair. If you don't believe me I will get her to come round and tell you hersel,' Eugene shouted.

'So there is somebody. I never said her name but you seem to know who I am talking about.'

'Eadie, listen to me, ah swear.....'

The kitchen door flew open and Eugene stumbled out, Ada pushing him from behind.

'If she comes near this house I will kill her.'

She punctuated each word with a further push towards the front door, and grabbing his jacket from the peg she opened the door, threw him out and the jacket after him.

Days later I answered the door to find 'the slut' on the door step, I felt myself go weak at the knees unable to speak. She asked to speak to Ada, who appeared like a flash from the kitchen having recognized the voice. Ada launched herself at the startled woman, slamming her up against the wall.

'Get aff me, ah hiv something tae say tae you,' yelled the woman.

'I'm not interested in anything you have to say,' Ada hissed.

'Ah well wait tae you hear it first. Wee Joe wanted me tae come here tae tell you there wis naethin' goin' oan, but whatever else ah might be ah'm no a liar. We hiv bin goin' thegither fur months. If you want tae know he has bought me rare presents see!'

She produced a box from a shopping bag that was identical to the box that had held the peach slip and knickers Ada had cut up.

Ada snatched at the box screaming abuse, words I had never heard her say before. The woman squirmed in her grasp trying to get away, and made a grab for the box but Ada was too quick for her.

'This will end up like the other lot!' Ada tossed the box aside and marched the trembling woman to the top of the stairs. She gave her a hefty shove and down she went tumbling over and over.

She managed to pick herself up grimacing with pain.

'I'll get you fur this; ah'11 get the boys ontae you.'

Ada ignored her and slammed the door, resting against it, her chest heaving.

I ran to comfort her, but she pushed me away.

'I'm fine, just fine; it takes more than the likes of her to frighten me.'

She picked up the box, 'this will do for your father's tea to-night.'

The pile of cut silk was waiting for him at tea-time, but he was very late. I wondered if he was ever coming home though I dreaded what would happen when he did.

He came in smiling broadly, 'I've been trampin' all over Newton Mearns knocking on doors to try to get work and I did, an order for a garage, good eh?'

There was total silence, Aggie and I held our breath. Eugene looked around then spotted the pile of silk on his plate.

'Is that stuff still there, ah thought we had sorted a' this oot.'

Ada lifted the plate and hurled it at him, and the shreds of silk floated around him some landing on his bald head.

He put his hand up to brush them away and looked puzzled.

'We had a visitor to-day. Your slut had the nerve to come to this door.'

'Eadie ah....'

She raised a hand stopping him in mid sentence.

'I thought I would not be interested in what she had to say, but actually it was very enlightening. She told me that this sordid affair has been going on for months, and she said you bought her, as she said, rare presents.'

'She's lyin'.'

'No she isn't. She said she was not a liar and I believe her, in any case she brought some proof, your rare present which I have just thrown at you and which was exactly the same tawdry stuff you gave to me!'

He fished in his pocket for a hanky and wiped it over his face again and again.

'So who's lying now?' Ada said.

Ada turned to me, 'you will be sleeping with me in the kitchen tonight. ur father can sleep on the floor or down in the shop.' She threw the keys of the shop at his feet.

He picked them up and placed them on the table.

'This is daft. Ah'm sorry, ah'm really sorry.'

'Sorry doesn't wash with me; you have gone too far this time.'

I climbed into the recess bed and pulled the covers over my head. It cut me off from the light and cocooned me from the horrible oppressive atmosphere that filled the room.

Eugene made a bed on the floor that night and was up and away before the rest of us in the morning.

The next day was Thursday, Tina and Famie due for their weekly visit. Ada gave me a note to take round to Tina on my school dinner hour. Tina read it with a puzzled frown, and then looked at me.

'Is everything OK at home?'

I hesitated not knowing what to say and she read my face.

'Your mammy is asking us no' to come the night.'

'Oh!'

'So you don't know the reason she has put us off?'

'Er no, at least I don't think so.'

'OK hen, tell her it will be a' right.'

I was feverish and had a pounding headache, and I put it down to worry about Ada and Eugene and lack of sleep. By the time I got home from school I was feeling really ill and Ada took one look at me and put me to bed in the recess bed.

'I think you might have German Measles. That's all we need,' she said.

I woke bathed in sweat, not knowing where I was. There was a low murmur of voices and a soft flickering light. I pushed the bed clothes down and struggled up on one elbow. Ada, Aggie and Tina sat huddled round the table heads close together clutching teacups, their faces lit by the light of a flickering candle.

Aggie was sniffing as if she had been crying. I tried to see the clock face on the mantelpiece but it was deep in shadow. What, I wondered, was Tina doing here after I had given her the note to say she was not to come.

Tina sat up and stretched, and I lay back down not wanting them to know I was awake.

'What time is it?' Tina asked. Ada looked at her watch, 'half past five.'

'We have been sittin' here a' night. We need to get some rest,' Tina said.

'I'm too angry to sleep but you should have a lie down,' Ada said. 'Maybe another cup o' tea,' Tina collected the cups and rose to rinse them at the sink. 'He will be back,' she said.

'I don't want him back. I don't care if I never see him again,' Ada said. Tina filled the kettle and lit the gas ring, 'Och he is ma brother but he is a daft bugger.'

'A daft bugger that has left me in a pretty mess. I will kill him if he ever darkens this door again,' Ada said.

'Will ye no try to find him?' Tina said spooning tea into the pot from the caddy.

'Why should I?' Ada snapped.

My head spun. Eugene had gone, he had been gone all night, and Ada didn't think he was coming back. Tina set out the cups and poured the tea, while Ada sat spooning sugar into her cup not paying attention to what she was doing. She doesn't take sugar I thought as she lifted the cup to her lips and pulled a face.

'Here take this wan',' Tina swapped cups, 'you need tae get tae yer bed.'

They sipped at their tea in silence, the clock ticked on, and through the shutters a weak ray of light shone down on the brass tap at the sink.

'Why did you come up when I told you not to?' Ada broke the silence.

'Ah jist put two an' two the gither. The excuse you gave - well it wisnae really an excuse - an' when ah asked the wean if everything was OK she looked as if the world wis fallin' roon her shoulders, so ah thought tae masel ' Tina there is somethin' up, ye better go and see whit it is.'

'Well I'm glad you did come, it has helped to talk to you,' Ada said.

Aggie's cup slopped tea over the cloth and she sat up with a start.

'You are done in, the two of you, get through to bed. I'll be fine,' Ada said.

'Aye ah think ah will, if ye don't mind,' Tina rose.

Aggie shifted in her seat.

'You too, off you go, leave the cups. I'll see to them,' Ada said.

They went through and Ada sat on staring at the wall for a while, then she rose, gathered the cups and put them in the sink. She emptied the tea pot and then stood hands covering her mouth. I slid deeper under the clothes not wanting her to see me, but though she was looking straight at the bed she did not seem to be seeing it at all.

Hands still covering her mouth she began to pace up and down. The warmth of the kitchen and the hypnotic tick of the clock lulled me back to sleep. I woke to find Ada still pacing up and down. The light filtering through the shutters was stronger now, it was morning. Ada noticed I was awake and she came to the bed and put her hand on my forehead.

'How do you feel?'

'OK.' Funny thing was I did feel physically all right but there was a heavy feeling of gloom, I felt I should be worrying about something, and then I remembered Eugene had gone away.

Ada examined me for spots, 'hmmm there's no rash, and maybe you were just overtired. I think you should be able to go to school today.'

'Do I need to mammy?'

'Of course if you are well enough as I think you are.'

She looked at me sharply, 'why do you not want to go to school?'

'Where's daddy?'

'Out, why do you ask?'

'Out where?'

'He is just out, on some business or other, anyway your Auntie Tina is here, she stayed the night, and she can chum you down on the tram to school.'

She was not going to tell me about Eugene and I was angry. Why did she keep treating me like a child? I got up and got ready for school. Tina and Aggie both looked tired, and Ada looked really exhausted. I wanted to say that I knew what had happened but I knew Ada would get angry.

As Tina and I were about to leave for the tram Ada drew Tina aside and spoke quietly to her in Italian. Tina nodded.

Tina and I boarded the tram and sat in silence.

She was usually so chatty her silence scared me, and finally I could bear it no longer.

'Daddy has run away hasn't he?'

She looked at me in surprise, 'you are no' supposed to know.'

'Why not, he has run away hasn't he?'

'Aye he's a daft - a daft so – and - so, your daddy.'

'I heard you talking during the night, and I know mammy is upset. She is always threatening to run away, now he has done it.'

Tina patted my hand, 'yer mammy says more than her prayers, you know what she is like. She gets het up aboot things.'

'I know why he went,' I said.

'No ah don't think ye do.'

'I do, there is another woman, I've seen her, and she isn't nice.'

'So ye do know, but it's no just that...'

'It's money as well, I know.'

'You know a lot, yer mammy would be as well tellin' ye wouldn't she?'

'Yes, but she still treats me like a little girl.'

'Aye well ye are a little girl as far as we're concerned. Don't be angry wi' yer mammy, she is only tryin' to protect ye, we a' are.'

'What will happen, Auntie Tina?'

'Ah don't know hen, honestly ah don't, but don't you worry you will always hiv me and yer other aunties.'

'What did mammy say to you before we left? She is always speaking in Italian so I won't know.'

'She said if your daddy gets in touch wi' me ah have tae tell her.'

'Do you think he will?'

'No, if he gets in touch wi' anybody it will be Lena, you know how close they are.'

'Yes, she doesn't know, maybe mammy will go round to-day to tell her.'

Lena was there when I got home. She took my hand and told me everything would be all right, but I didn't believe it.

'I'm going to stay here for now,' Lena said. I hugged her, glad to have her beside me.

The next morning's post brought two long white envelopes addressed to Ada, and inside each was a postal order for five pounds. There was no address, no note and no signature. We sat staring at them in silence. We knew they had come from Eugene. The next morning brought two more, each containing a five pound postal order.

'What is he playing at, where is this money coming from?' Ada asked. When Ada went down to the shop, Lena took the envelopes from the drawer and spread them out on the table.

'What are you doing?' I asked.

'Checking out the postmark.'

She held each in turn up to the light, 'Glasgow, it is definitely Glasgow.'

The next day only one envelope came, no postal order, and just a note saying, 'I have sold the car'. There was no signature.

It was now Tuesday and he had been gone five days. That morning's post had brought two envelopes with postal orders for twenty pounds in each. 'I think he is enjoying this. He is doing this to annoy me and he is succeeding,' Ada fumed.

'Do you think that is all he got for the car - £60?' Lena said.

'I wouldn't be surprised, he is daft enough to settle for that,' Ada sighed.

'It is a funny way of sending the money, it is costing him every time he buys a postal order,' Lena said.

'It's typical of your father. Anyone with any sense would buy one postal order and put the damn thing in an envelope and be done with it, but not him,' Ada was scathing.

The next two weeks brought more postal orders each in its own envelope, and the final total was £150. The last envelope bore an English postmark.

When Lena came round that night Ada threw the envelope on the table saying, 'he has gone to England, probably taken the slut with him.'

It was a great comfort to both Lena and I when a few days later Aggie reported that she had seen the slut passing by on the other side of the road. Though I had been in on all the postal order business and all that had happened since, Ada had not actually told me anything, there was just a mutual understanding that I knew and could be included in discussions.

Eddie offered to come back and do the football crowds again and Ada accepted gratefully as we needed all the money we could get.

Mr. Nicol the accountant was a frequent visitor, he and Ada pouring over the books. Ada's mood was super sensitive and she snapped at everyone, even Rover would slink under the table to escape her wrath. Aggie, summoned up for her tea, would stand halfway in the kitchen door, the shop keys dangling from the tip of one extended finger, her eyes darting from the table to Ada's face fearful that she was either too early or too late.

The aunts came for a family conference and they urged Ada to try to track Eugene down, Famie declaring that Eugene must be brought home to face the music.

Betty going through another 'rough patch' came home unexpectedly. She too felt that Eugene should be tracked down and it was decided that Betty would take over in the shop to free Ada to go with Tina to England to find him. The baby, now a toddler, needed looking after and the decision was made (without consulting me) that I should look after her. Ada gave me a note for the Mother Superior requesting that I be excused from school on urgent family business.

I stood nervously shifting from foot to foot as Mother Superior read the note her lips pursed in disapproval. I did not know what Ada had actually written but I was sure she had not said that my father had run away and deserted the family.

Mother Superior looked up from the note and regarded me over her spectacles for a moment or two. I felt the blood rush to my face and cast my eyes to the floor. She set the note down very deliberately on her desk smoothing it out with her gnarled fingers. She dipped her head till the spectacles slipped down her nose and magnified her eyes, they were as cold as steel.

'Your mother writes that she is required to go to England to care for a sick relative and that your help is required at home to look after a child during this family crisis.'

'Yes, Reverend Mother.'

'I do not approve of a child's education being interrupted during term time. However the matter seems to be of some urgency, so I will permit you to be absent for one week without informing the school board.'

'Thank you Reverend Mother.'

'One week only do you understand?'

'Yes Reverend Mother, thank you Reverend Mother.'

'Very well you may go,' she waved her hand.

'Thank you Reverend Mother.' I fled from her office fearful she would change her mind.

Ada and Tina decided to head for Newcastle, Eugene had worked there before and Ada had a 'feeling' that he might be there, but for once her hunch was wrong. They travelled on to Liverpool crossing the Mersey to the docks at Birkenhead, intending to keep watch on the dock gates. The weather was miserable and they had been at their posts for two days before they spotted him, a small lonely figure swept along by the stream of men pouring out of the gates. He was dressed in stained overalls and a metal 'Piecebox' was tucked under one arm. Tina wanted to rush forward and confront him, but Ada held her back.

'We'll follow him. I want to see if that woman is with him.'

'She's no'. Aggie saw her, remember?'

'That was days ago, she could have come down since then,' Ada argued. They followed at a safe distance, dodging into a doorway as he stopped suddenly to light his pipe. At last he turned into a street lined on either side by identical two up and two down houses, each with a shiny brass knocker and pipe clay white doorstep.

'Ada gripped Tina's arm, 'Wait. We don't know which one he is going into.'

'Aye, OK. But as soon as we know ah'm fur speakin' tae him.'

He let himself into one of the houses, closing the door without looking up or down the street.

'Come on,' Tina urged.

They crossed the street and knocked on the door, the woman who answered eyeing them suspiciously.

She shook her head when Ada asked for Eugene by name saying her only lodger was called Joe.

'That is him, I know it's him. We saw him let himself into this house,' Ada said.

'I don't allow female visitors,' the woman said.

'I'm his wife, this is his sister and we need to speak to him.'

'Wait here I'll call him,' she said and closed the door.

When it opened again Eugene stood blinking at them in surprise.

'So this is where you are, you have some explaining to do,' Ada snapped.

'You should be ashamed of yoursel',' Tina burst out.

'Ah'm sorry,' he said.

'Sorry! So that's it, that's all you have to say?'

'Eadie ah'm sorry. What else can ah say?'

'You need to came home and face the music.'

He shrugged, 'it's a mess.'

'You're telling me, a mess you seem happy to leave me to sort out,' Ada's voice rose.

'You are ma brother but ah'm ashamed o' ye'.'

He spread his hands, 'Ah'm sorry.'

'So you keep saying but what are you going to do about it?'

'Ah don't know, that's why ah came here. Ah couldnae face you, you have always been better than me at a' that stuff, and it just got such a mess.'

'And you took the cowards way out,' Ada said.

'Aye well — ye know.'

'Ye need to come back wi' us,' Tina said.

'Ah will come, but no' the noo, ah'm workin'.'

'Another excuse!' Ada said.

'Naw, ah have a weeks lying time and ah need tae work at least another week tae get some wages. Ye know how these things work.'

'Then you'll come back?' Tina said.

'Aye.'

The landlady came downstairs and looked from one to the other, 'is everything all right? I won't have any trouble.'

'Aye, everything is fine,' Eugene told her.

'Well if you are sure, otherwise I would have to ask you to leave,' she looked at Eugene.

'No, no everything is fine,' he said.

She sniffed and went away and Eugene gave a wry grin.

'She has a good reputation, keeps a good house, and she tells me that every night.'

'Maybe just as well she doesn't know what you've been up to,' Ada said dryly.

'So will ye go back the night?' he asked.

Doesn't seem much use in staying,' Ada said.

As they turned to go, Tina came back and prodded a finger in his chest, 'you better come back and sort this oot or else......' she left the words hanging in mid air not really sure what threat she was making.

'Ah've said I would come an' ah will.'

Ada walked off and Tina went after her. She turned to see him looking after them, then go in and close the door.

She took Ada's arm, 'whit dae ye say tae a wee cup o' tea before we catch the train?'

We were all gathered round the table listening to this account, Betty, Lena, Aggie, Famie, Lizzie and me. I was near to tears and I could see Lena was too. We knew we could not show any sympathy for Eugene for fear of upsetting Ada, but he sounded so alone, so lonely. Betty asked the question we all wanted to ask, 'do you think he really will come back?'

Ada shrugged her shoulders, 'who knows? Personally I don't want him to darken this door again. It is only because he has to answer for what he has done and somehow resolve this problem. Yet I swear before my maker that once things are settled I want nothing more to do with him.'

Lena and I exchanged glances; Lizzie squeezed my hand under the table.

'We a' make mistakes,' Lizzie said gruffly.

Ada rounded on her, 'what's that supposed to mean, that I should welcome him back with open arms?'

'It's no' our business, it is between Eadie and Eugene,' Famie put in hastily.

Tina nodded, "ah told him ah was ashamed o' him, and ah am, but at the end o' the day he is still ma brother an...'

'A man's a man for a' that!' Ada said icily.

Tina shook her head, 'ah wisnae goin' to say that, Eadie, it's just that if he had nowhere to go ah would take him in.'

'Famie and ma would do the same,' Lizzie said.

'Well that is up to you, it isn't your life he has ruined. I for one will never forgive him,' Ada said.

She turned to Betty, 'how have things been while I was away?'

Betty avoided her gaze and Lena and I stared at the table.

Ada sighed, 'well?'

'The men daddy took on to finish that garage came looking for their wages and there are bills for sand and cement and other stuff,' Betty said.

'So he has left them in the lurch as well. I am sorry for them but that business is in his name and I have no responsibility for any debt there. God knows how he is going to settle that.'

'Write to him, right now and remind him he is responsible,' Lizzie said. Tina shifted uneasily in her chair.

Ada smiled grimly and nodded, 'yes that thought had occurred to me too. He might run off to somewhere else if he gets reminded just how much he owes.'

Tina looked sheepish, 'ah never said that.'

'You didn't have to,' Ada said.

'Do you want me to write to him mammy?' Betty asked.

'It is between yer mammy and Eugene, as I say,' Famie butted in.

'He said he will come back, give him a chance,' Lena said.

'Ah would get him here as quick as possible. You don't want to have to go chasin' all over the countryside after him again,' Lizzie said.

'We will wait a day or two,' Ada said, her tone final.

It was three days before the note arrived to say he would be home the following day.

I lost no time in running up to Lena's lodgings to tell her, she hugged me and we cried a little.

'We need to try to get mammy and daddy together again. I know she swears blind she will have nothing to do with him, but I think she only says that in the heat of the moment,' Lena said.

'Do you really think so', I said doubtfully.

'I'm sure of it, so what we need to do is plan a nice homecoming, a nice tea so that we can all sit down together and start again,' Lena said.

'I don't know. What if mammy gets angry?' I said.

'We won't tell her till the last minute. We'll set the table and buy the things for the tea. We need to give it a try,' Lena insisted.

'The two of you are off your heads!' Betty said when I told her of the plan.

'We are trying to make things better,' I said.

'You will only make things worse. Well count me out. I'll take the baby for a very long walk while all that is going on,' Betty said.

We hurriedly went ahead with the plan; Lena had made a 'welcome home daddy' banner, she bought an ashet pie from the butcher's and cream horns, (Eugene's favourite) from Bilsland's bakery.

We left the banner draped over a chair in full view trying to judge Ada's reaction, but she totally ignored it.

Lena strung it above the mantelpiece, and set the table with the best china and serviettes.

Betty looked in and shaking her head quickly disappeared.

Ada and Aggie were down in the shop and I waited with Lena upstairs on tenterhooks for the key turning in the lock.

To our surprise Ada came up first. She surveyed the table but said nothing only the tightly pursed lips betraying her feelings.

At last we heard the key turn and next minute Eugene was standing in the kitchen doorway clutching his cardboard case.

'Welcome back daddy,' Lena hugged him, and he kissed both her cheeks. He cupped my face between his rough hands and kissed my cheeks. Ada sat motionless saying nothing. Lena filled the kettle and lit the gas.

'Call Aggie up for her tea,' she said to me.

I lifted the speaking tube and said quickly, 'tea's ready.'

'Comin',' Aggie's voice was nervous.

She came up, Betty at her heels.

I knew Betty's curiosity would get the better of her.

Eugene shook her hand and tickled the baby under the chin. He made no attempt to acknowledge Ada or Aggie.

He glanced up at the 'welcome home' banner and took in the festive table.

'This is nice,' he said, and then placing his suitcase on a chair he opened it and began handing out brown paper parcels, one for each of us. When he came to Ada she flinched turning her head away, and he put the parcel on the sideboard.

Each parcel contained a frilly apron, all identical.

'I see you took a lot of care choosing them,' Ada said with heavy sarcasm.

'No, they are all the same,' Eugene answered. He never understood sarcasm.

Lena poured the tea, 'sit down everybody,' she said.

Ada rose, she walked to the door, 'the girls may have killed the fatted calf for their prodigal father, but I for one will not be joining in the feast.'

She went out Aggie scrambling after her. Eugene shrugged and took his place at the table.

The rest of us ate in silence, grateful for the antics of the baby to break the ice.

The frosty reception from Ada did not affect his appetite and he tucked into the ashet pie and the cream cakes with gusto.

When he had finished he stood up and put on his coat, snapped shut the suitcase and stood looking at us.

'You're not leaving? You can't. There are things that need sorted,' Lena said.

'Aye, ah know, but your mammy doesnae want me here, a blind man could see that, so ah better go,' he said.

'Go where? You can't go back to England,' Lena persisted.

He shrugged, 'eh, who knows what is best.'

'You better stay here and try to sort things out. Mammy will go mad if you run away again,' Betty said.

'Auntie Tina said she would take you in,' I said.

'Aye, right then, ah'll go to Tina's.'

'Just for tonight,' Lena said.

'Aye, maybe.'

We hugged him again and watched as he went slowly down the stairs.

As soon as he was gone we cleared all signs of celebration away.

'I told you this was a bad idea,' Betty said as she helped with the dishes.

'Somebody had to do something,' Lena said.

'Don't tell me the bird has flown the coup again,' Ada said when she came in.

'He's away to Auntie Tina's,' Lena said.

"Is he now, then I will speak to him there,' Ada said.

She took her brown paper parcel from the sideboard and threw it on the fire.

He came home the next day, saying he was going to work in the workshop to see if he could salvage anything from the mess.

At night he and Ada sat talking into the sma' hours, the account books spread across the table, with a pile of bills on one side, their red 'final demand' headings clamouring for attention.

Ada set me to spy on him in the workshop, on pretence of taking Rover for a walk. She told me to watch to see if the 'slut' was around. I hated doing it, it had been bad enough the first time, but how could I face telling her if I did see the 'slut'.

To my great relief she was nowhere to be seen.

'I'm not surprised she hasn't been around, she was only after money,' Ada said when I assured her the 'slut' was gone.

The hoped for solution was not to be found and the arguments were long and bitter. Try as he might Eugene could not raise the money to pay the wages due to the men.

Though the accountant, Mr. Nicol, was not involved with Eugene's business, Ada asked his advice.

'He has no option than to be declared bankrupt,' Nicol said bluntly. Ada told Eugene, trying to convince him it was the only solution. He sat staring ahead his hand rubbing his chin.

'So what are you going to do?' Ada pressed.

'Ah'm damned if ah know,' he said.

'You better do as Nicol says. What else is there?' Ada said bitterly.

'Ah'll think o' something,' he said.

The something he thought of was to run away again.

This time the suitcase was left behind, he took only dungarees and his piece tin.

Ada had been preoccupied with Betty, trying to persuade her not to go back to Southampton even though John had written assuring her he had found a decent place.

'Tell him to come up here and tell you about it, I don't trust him,' Ada urged.

Betty wanted to go. It was the old story over again, when she was away she wanted home, when she was home she wanted to go away again.

In the end Ada decided to let her make up her own mind. We helped her pack and once again waved her farewell from the Central Station.

When we got home Aggie was agitated, clearly eager to tell Ada something.

'He just came into the shop and said 'tell Eadie ah'm sorry.'

'What! Did you ask him what he meant?'

'He just went away,' Aggie said.

'The silly clown has done it again. Oh my God I can't believe it,' Ada fumed.

She hurried up to the house, me at her heels. We looked in vain for a letter of explanation but there was nothing. The cardboard suitcase was still in its place beside the washing machine and all his clothes were still in the trunk under the bed.

The only things I can see missing are his dungarees and that piecebox of his that he never parts with,' Ada said, sitting down on the bed worn out with searching high and low.

I ran to Lena. She was really upset, and John got angry and said she had her own concerns to worry about and all this nonsense was causing her strain when she needed to be well.

She smiled through her tears and whispered, 'I'm pregnant.'

The morning post brought letters with red tops, warning that the hire purchase payments on the machines were in arrears. Ada sat head in hands looking at them.

'If it wasn't for the two or three orders we still have I would send them back even though I would lose out on the deal. I do have a wee bit put away, and it will buy me a wee bit of time,' she said.

She went through to the big room and a moment or two later I heard her scream. Aggie and I rushed through. She was holding the little strong box. It sagged in her hand its lid open. The box was empty.

'He's taken the money, he's taken the money,' she repeated over and over.

I took the box from her and sat her down, 'what money mammy?'

'The bit I told you about, the money I had put away. I didn't want it in the bank, I had to make sure I could get my hands on it, and it was to tide us over, at least this time, for those blasted machines. He has taken it; your daddy is a thief.'

I wanted to run to Lena but stopped myself. I hadn't told Ada the news and now did not seem a good time.

Instead I made Ada a cup of tea; it was all I could think of doing.

Once she had calmed down a little she set about writing to Mr. Nicol saying she needed to see him right away.

I still had to go to school, after being off for a week I knew I dare not stay away. I hated having to leave Ada in the state she was in. Mr. Nicol had listened to Ada's story, and he made it his business to find out what he could.

Eugene had used the money to pay his workmen, settle the rent for the workshop, and pay one or two smaller bills, but there were still some bills outstanding.

Tina and Famie came for their Thursday visit.

'You should have told us right away, sent the wean roon after school,' Tina said.

'I should have never listened to you, to any of you, taking him back here, believing he was going to do the right thing,' Ada said bitterly.

'Eadie we need to try tae find him,' Tina said.

'No! No! It is better for him that we don't; I would only kill him,' Ada warned.

'Do you think that Mammy meant what she said?' I asked Aggie as we lay side by side that night.

'Aye, ah believe she did, and ah believe she would,' Aggie said with relish.

The men had come to take away the dipping machine, it was being repossessed, and we watched it go with mixed feelings.

'Well, that puts paid to our last cinema orders, the other machines are no use to us now, they are under another company so it will just be a matter of time I suppose,' Ada said despondently.

Some nights later, Uncle Eddie and Uncle Pat turned up. It was late, very late, and soon clear that it was no social visit.

Ada draped an old blanket over the sideboard, ignoring my questions as Eddie and Pat carried it down the stairs.

They came back for the piano and the writing desk. Ada whispered her thanks and closed the door after them, still saying nothing to me. I went to school the next morning with a heavy heart, something was terribly wrong, and I was afraid of what I might find when I got home.

I could not wait for the school day to end.

Swinging down from the tram I looked across at the shop, it was closed, and there was some sort of notice pinned to the door. I hurried across. The notice said in bold black letters 'WARRANT SALE', and in smaller print it said that the business had been declared bankrupt and a sale of goods and chattels would be held the next day in a bid to recover debt.

I flew up the stairs.

'What does a warrant sale mean?' I asked as soon as Ada opened the door.

'Nothing for you to worry about,' she said.

'But it says bankrupt, a sale of goods and chattels, what's that?'

'It is about the machinery, the machinery,' she repeated giving Aggie a sharp look which was not lost on me.

After tea I took Rover for a walk. He was down, dejected as if he sensed something, and no amount of fussing could get his tail wagging. He just Slunk along close to my leg.

When we got back Hammy was helping Ada put Smokey and her five kittens into a cardboard box. Hammy was punching air holes into the lid and trying to keep the kittens from climbing out at the same time.

'Where are the cats going.'

Hammy looked embarrassed and busied himself with closing the lid of the box with sticky tape.

'Hammy is just looking after them for a day or two and he is going to take Rover too,' Ada said.

'No!' I hugged Rover to me and he pressed close to me.

Ada stroked Rover and looked at me, 'it's better this way,' she said.

'Why does he need to take them away? What is going on?'

'It's OK, I'll bring them back after,' Hammy said.

'After what?'

'You know—,' his voice trailed off.

'That's fine Hammy, you can take them now. I know you will take good care of them,' Ada ushered him to the door, clipping Rover's lead back on and dragging him after her.

'I don't understand. Why does Rover need to go? I want him to stay.'

'You have to trust me it is for the best. He will be back just as soon as everything is over,' Ada said.

'Tell me what is going on. Will we be all right after this sale thing?'

'It is nothing for you to concern yourself with. Leave everything to me, it will be all right,' Ada said in a voice that brooked no more questions.

I looked at Aggie, but she refused to meet my eye.

Next morning Ada could not wait to get me out of the house, and I knew it was useless to plead to stay off.

I sat on the top deck of the bus gazing gloomily through the window at the people going about their business. I wanted to stand up and shout to them, 'something awful is happening in my house to-day.'

Even my wild imaginings had not prepared me for what I found when I did get home. All the furniture had gone. I ran from room to room, each one as bare as the last.

'You said it was the shop,' I screamed at Ada.

'When you are declared bankrupt they take everything,' she said.

'What will we do?'

We try to survive. We will get by somehow. We still have the cooker and a bed, they have to leave you that. It is the law,' she laughed bitterly.

'Does it mean all the debts are settled?'

'If only that were true. No they take what they can get, but we still owe a few Thousand,' Ada said.

'Will you open the shop again?'

'No, we can't, not ever, the business is gone, just like everything else,' she sighed. 'Oh it was horrible, the humiliation, having people pawing over your things, all the things you treasure going for a pittance, even the brush and shovel, could you believe that?'

'Was that why you asked Uncle Eddie and Uncle Pat to move the other things?'

'Yes, I was determined they were not getting my sideboard. The piano and the bookcase were an after thought. It was Pat who suggested they take those too. Pat McCann, who would have believed that I would have cause to be grateful to him.'

'Where did they take them to?'

'The cellar of the cafe in Charing Cross, Lizzie will keep an eye on them for me, and if we ever get another place to live at least we will have something.'

'So we can't have them back here now that the sale is over?'

'Good God no! They would sell them if they found out.'

'What about Rover and the cats, would they have sold them?'

Ada smiled, 'no, they were in no danger of being sold, I only wanted them out of the way. They would have got under people's feet, especially the kittens.'

'Then Hammy really will bring them back?'

'Of course, either to-night or tomorrow.'

'We have a kettle and tea and sugar, and we'll buy some chips.'

Throughout all this Aggie had been quietly sobbing, sitting on a box, leaning into the dying fire.

Ada fished in her pocket, 'here get some chips. I'll see if I can bring her round with a cup of strong tea.'

By bedtime we were emotionally exhausted and we lay huddled in the one remaining bed, Ada and Aggie at the top and me at the bottom, my toes up round their ears. As we lay in the darkness, I could hear Ada sobbing. I wanted to comfort her but I knew she would push me away. Aggie totally exhausted by all her crying was now snoring gently. I just could not get to sleep, my mind was in a turmoil, and I missed Rover, missed the comfort of knowing he was lying alongside the bed.

I needed to do something to help. We needed money, not just to clear the debt but for day-to-day living. A chill ran through me as remembered Ada saying, 'if we ever get another place to live', that meant we couldn't stay in this house. We wouldn't have the rent for a start, but even if we did Ada would not want to stay where she had been so humiliated.

I realised I needed to get a job, I needed to leave school, and satisfied at last that I had a plan of action, I fell into a fitful sleep.

'No! I won't hear of it, I totally forbid it,' Ada shouted at me when I told her my plan.

'I want to help, we need money, I know I won't earn much for a first wage but it will be better than nothing,' I protested.

'It is not what I wanted for you. I wanted you to stay on to sixth year, I wanted you to go to university. I really thought it could happen. If you leave now, you will be stuck in some dead end job.'

'It can't happen now, any of those things, it just can't happen,' I said.

'You could still stay till sixth year, it would be something. You can't leave, I will not let you,' she said.

'How can I stay on? From what you said last night we won't even be living here in this house,' I said.

'We will have to move to God knows where,' she said.

'Then I will leave on my next birthday, it is only two weeks away. I will ask to speak to Mother Superior to-day after school.

'I never wanted this, I never wanted this,' Ada said over and over.

'I know.'

She looked up sharply, 'you mustn't tell her the real reason you want to leave. There are enough people who know of our shame.'

'I won't,' I said, realizing how difficult it was going to be to think of a reason that would not bring the Reverend Mother's wrath upon my head.

I watched the clock creep round to four o' clock, dreading the long walk down the corridor to that office.

Sooner than I wished I was standing before Mother Superior's desk, shifting uneasily under her stern gaze.

'So you wish to leave school?'

'Yes Reverend Mother.'

'I do not approve of girls leaving such a school as this at fifteen, to my mind you are squandering your opportunities and showing little regard for the privilege you have enjoyed being educated at this school. Do you understand my point of view?'

'Yes Reverend Mother.'

'What is not clear is your actual reason for leaving.'

She rifled through some papers on her desk and found what she was looking for. I recognized Ada's handwriting.

She adjusted her spectacles, 'family circumstances which are not fully explained.'

I stood dumb.

'You do not seem to want to enlighten me.'

'No, Reverend Mother, I'm sorry.'

'You plan to work no doubt. What kind of employment will you seek? In a shop or factory? Is this what you want in life?'

She regarded me over her spectacles and grimaced with distaste.

'No Reverend Mother — I mean -,' I gave up.

She skimmed through the papers again and selected one with a flourish, reading it with pursed lips, 'your record shows you are a well behaved pupil, not brilliant, but diligent nevertheless. You do however have an appalling time keeping record,' she fixed me with a look, 'something that will not be tolerated in the world of work, and your record of attending mass is even more deplorable. Indeed Father Malone has on several occasions brought the matter to my attention. He also explained to me that at the request of your Godmother who feared for your immortal soul, he visited your parents to remind them of their duties to Holy Mother Church.'

'My mother is not a Catholic, Reverend Mother,' I knew she would not be pleased to be reminded of this but I felt Ada had enough to contend with without being blamed for dereliction of duty to a religion she did not espouse.

'I am aware your mother is not of our faith, your father on the other hand is but neglects his duties shamefully.'

It is not just his spiritual duties he has neglected shamefully I thought, and tried to imagine her reaction if she knew the truth.

'I am sorry Reverend Mother.'

'So you should be my child because you are losing out. I recall a similar situation with your sister, who also quit at fifteen, giving equally obscure reasons for doing so.'

I was minded to withhold permission for you to leave, though in the eyes of the law you can legally do so. I feel so strongly that you are casting aside what this school offers with blatant disregard. However I have decided to let you go. I fear for your immortal soul and will intercede for you with the Blessed Virgin and St. Francis.'

'Thank you Reverend Mother.'

'You shall go to confession the day before you leave, it is my duty to send you out into the world with a shriven soul. Father Malone will no doubt impress upon you the burden you carry as a Catholic girl in the world.'

'Yes Reverend Mother, thank you Reverend Mother.'

'Very well you may go, and may God have mercy on you.'

'Thank you Reverend Mother.'

She waved me away as if I was a fly she was swatting and I turned to the door.

'Please close the door behind you,' she said.

CHAPTER 31

'Bless me father for I have sinned, it is two weeks since my last confession.'
'What are your sins my child?'
'Please father I am leaving school.'
'You think this is a sin, my child?'
'It displeases my mother and Reverend Mother, Father.'
'You are disobeying their instructions?'
'Yes father.'
'Why do you wish to leave school, my child?'
'I need to earn money to help my family father.'
'Your family has financial difficulties?'
'Severe difficulties, Father.'
'Your wage will be very small as a beginner.'
'Yes Father.'
'Are you guilty of the sin of pride child, thinking that you and you alone can resolve these financial difficulties of which you speak?'
'I don't know father, I want to help.'
'You are the Cocozza girl?'
'Yes father.'
'Your immortal soul has been placed in grave danger many times when you have missed mass.'
'Yes Father.'
'Your mother is not of our faith, your father does not perform his duties to Holy Mother Church and seems totally unrepentant, is this not so?'
'Yes Father.'
'Both your sisters have married outside the Faith, I have no doubt you will do the same.'
'No Father, I mean I don't know Father, I hope not.'
'You must permit me to claim superior knowledge in these matters. There is no hope for you my child. You will go to hell, as will your family; I have no doubt about it.'
'Ye-es Father.'
'Say three Hail Marys and one Our Father as a penance go in peace.'
'Th-Thank you Father.'
I was shocked. Hell was very real to me and I was terrified of the prospect. It seemed that Mother Superior's intervention for me to the Blessed Virgin and St. Francis would not be enough, my wickedness would need the whole company of saints interceding on my behalf. I genuflected before the alter and knelt in a pew to say my penance, and when I finished I looked up to find the devil face above the sacristy fixing me with a baleful stare.
That night as we prepared for bed, on the spur of the moment I asked Ada if she believed in hell.
'Yes,' she said, 'I'm in it.'
My last day at school found me full of regret that I was leaving. Despite all that had happened, Molly's bullying, poor Marian Cuthbertson dying, the

teacher holding me to ridicule before the whole class over the 'Mussolini heel', I knew I loved the place and did not want to go. There had been happy times too, the trip with the school to see the film 'The Song of Bernadette', the joy of finally being selected for the choir to sing in the Bi-Centenary concert, the thrill of being back-stage in the noisy hubbub of girls, brushing their hair, jostling each other to stare in wonder at young faces suddenly transformed by make-up, admiring legs clothed in silken nylon. For a whole week we performed to sell out audiences, singing 'Dream Angus', 'The Creation Anthem' and a frothy little piece 'A Fairy Went A-Marketing', it gave me a taste for the theatre, for performance. I would miss the marching up the stairs to the stirring notes of the piano, the hopeless (in my case) attempts at scoring in netball, at the end of the day I would lose the right to walk the corridors, to sit in assembly. I would be out in the world and, if the priest was right, on the slippery slope to hell.

The next morning I inched myself out of bed. Hushing an excited Rover, grabbing my clothes and dressing as quickly as I could, I slipped out the house, making sure Rover's lead was attached to stop him scampering down the stairs and barking his delight at being out.

We made our way to the park, to the walk by the river from where you could see the imposing pile of Glasgow 'Uni'; this too was now denied me though if I was honest with myself it is unlikely I could ever have afforded to go there. The seated figure of Carlyle, bespattered by bird droppings looked broodingly out on the scene as always. He had overcome disappointment and risen to better things, so could I. Rover sitting patiently at my feet looked up with soulful eyes that seemed to say 'I'm always here, I understand'. I patted his head and turned for home, no longer a schoolgirl, but a jobseeker. Later that day I would go searching for my first job. I had little idea what it would be at this point I was not seeking to start a career. It was very easy to find a job, merely a case of taking the tram into town where every store had a vacancy for beginners. I chose Woolworth; it was a place that had figured large in my life, indeed in every Glaswegian's life. Argyle Street without Woolworth or 'Woolworse' as Eugene called it was unthinkable.

I stood nervously on that first day behind the counter which sold light bulbs, batteries and torches. The elderly assistant looked me up and down and did not seem too impressed by what she saw.

'Ye'll need tae learn tae use the till, an' test the bulbs before ye sell them. She placed a clear bulb on top of a socket - twisting it until it engaged the 'Lugs', it lit up for a second, before she expertly whipped it off and returned it to its place on the counter. The bulbs were unwrapped so care had to be taken when placing them in the brown paper bag for the customer.

'Mind ye don't dunt it, or ye will hiv the cost taken oot o' yer wages.'

This made me extremely nervous, the wage was very small, and I could not afford to have money taken off.

I dreaded the tea break, which was spent in the company of many other sales assistants up stairs in the canteen. I didn't know what I liked least, the women who talked to you usually asking probing questions, or the ones who ignored you leaving you to gulp down the scalding tea as quickly as you could and escape back to the stern faced fellow counter assistant.

At the half hour dinner break I would scurry from the store, hot footing it along to the Trongate where in the huge National Restaurant you could get a bowl of soup, a plate of custard and a cup of tea for sixpence. Each night as we left the store we had our bags and pockets searched by a supervisor who stood at the bottom of the stairs leading down from the cloakroom. I was faintly shocked by this as the idea of stealing anything from the store would never have entered my head. When I expressed my shock to my mentor on the bulb counter she sniffed and said, 'No' everybody is as honest or as daft as you, it would surprise ye the things they can smuggle oot.'

'Even past the supervisor?'

She sniffed again and tapped her nose, 'aye even past 'Hawkeye'.

'But where do they hide the things?'

She smiled grimly, 'ye don't want tae know.'

I found I liked working. I loved coming into the city early in the morning and see it waking up, the steady stream of workers coming off and boarding the trams, the night workers tired and weary after their shift, the day workers sometimes equally tired and sourly anticipating the day ahead, the ever cheerful delivery boys whistling as they ferried boards of cakes and buns to the baker, or slung bloody carcasses over their shoulders to deliver to the butcher and the clip clop of the dray horses pulling the heavy carts laden with barrels of beer. Glasgow was busy, bustling and cheerful even in the rain and the unfailing cheerfulness of the Glaswegian shone through.

There were always the poor old men and women who shuffled about waiting for the stores to open so they could get in the warm, and they would wander from counter to counter rarely if ever buying anything. These 'worthies' were known to all, most assistants asking after their health, even my partner on the bulb counter would occasionally allow herself to pass the time of day, or grimace in what passed for a smile. I became quite confident talking to customers and testing bulbs; I loved the buzz of the place and helping to keep our counter sparkling and tidy, which endeared me to my mentor as she conducted a fierce rivalry with the other assistants. The buyers would come around and ask about sales, which lines were moving and which were not, but as a junior my opinion was not sought of course until the day my mentor was off sick and being the start of the week when it was quiet I was left in charge of the counter. The buyer looked over the display and asked me what was selling best. I told him the lines which I thought were top sellers, and he asked about a new style torch which had been introduced. I told him it was a winner, lots of people had shown interest and many had bought it. He seemed impressed and noted my comments down on his pad. The next week we received boxes and boxes of the torches, for which despite a promotion not only on our stall but in the window, the fickle public had gone off and the things lay unsold. I had sleepless night about that and dreaded meeting the buyer face to face again. I was spared this by the news that I had to hand

310

in my notice as we were moving to Edinburgh to stay with Mary and Jimmy. I felt on balance I would have rather faced the buyer.

'Why do we need to go there?' I wailed to Ada.

'Do you have any better ideas?'

'But the place is so small, there is no room and uncle Jimmy doesn't like dogs. I'm not going without Rover, I can't.'

'We have no choice, beggars can't be choosers. Rover will be coming. Jimmy says it is OK. I think they are hoping we will not be there for long.'

'So do I.'

'Well, that's as maybe but we need a roof over our head. We won't be staying there for free. You will need to get a job and I will be doing the cooking and cleaning for my keep,' Ada said.

'What will happen to this house?'

'With luck your sister will move in here. You know she is pregnant. Of course you do, everyone does. I it seems was the last to know.'

'Mammy I'm sorry it was just that you had a lot on your mind.' I said.

'Oh it is all right, it wasn't your place to tell me anyway, it was hers and she was worried it just was not the right time with all that was going on.'

'But you are pleased?'

'Delighted, that marriage is the one good thing I can think of at the moment. This house will suit them fine; the rooms they are in now are too small for three of them and all the baby stuff. They just need to find the 'key' money and it will be settled.

So it was settled, we moved to Edinburgh, after a tearful farewell to Lena and my friends and to my beloved Glasgow.

We were to have Jimmy's room, which could only be reached by walking through the kitchen. We stared in dismay at the 'accommodation'. Ada had hoped to take our bed through but it proved to be too big for the room. Jimmy had found two singles, one he placed on the floor the other he had propped on two chairs and the wall.

Our clothes would remain in boxes around us. Ada was right, beggars could not be choosers.

From the first we had to conform to their spartan routine.

They rose at 5am and went to bed at 8pm, though neither worked. They did not have a radio, did not own books and their sole pastime was playing dominoes. At the stroke of eight Jimmy would begin to stack the dominoes back in the box and say, 'time we went tae our beds, it'll no' be this in the mornin'.'

We had no option but to retire too as burning gas was out of the question. Rover was miserable; he somehow managed to get under Jimmy's feet and as Jimmy cursed would scramble under the table head on paws eyes swivelling to see if he was still in the black books.

The early bedtime meant Rover was desperate to relieve himself by 5am. He and I would take off to Holyrood park which was a short walk away at the end of the Canongate. We had the park to ourselves save for rabbits and birds, the stillness was balm to the soul, even the city was half asleep at that hour and the day to day rumble of traffic was silent.

Within a week I had a job. Ada decided that I should be apprenticed as a bookbinder to McNiven and Cameron's in the High Street. She had served her apprenticeship there as a girl. It was an old established firm, highly respected, housed in a grey Victorian building and across the front in large letters an advertisement declared, 'They come as a boon and a blessing to men, The Pickwick, The Owl and the Waverley Pen'.

I was slightly puzzled that a bookbinder should advertise pens, but the ways of Edinburgh folk were strange to me and I put it down to that.

Ada insisted on coming with me to the interview.

'This is no ordinary firm, they do things in a special way,' she said.

It seemed to be the case, her presence was not remarked on and indeed it seemed expected.

Ada proudly volunteered the information that she had learned the trade and risen to 'journeywoman' which meant she got piece work and taught apprentices.

The interviewer seemed impressed by this and the fact that Ada was eager for her daughter to follow her footsteps. Sadly they did not have a vacancy in the bookbinding but there was an opening in the box making department. Ada agreed, I was not consulted and she signed the form committing me to three years apprenticeship starting the following Monday. She was well pleased, 'it is good money, and you will be learning a trade. You have been very lucky; they only take a good class of girl.'

From the first day it was clear that things had changed since Ada's day. The girls soon realized just how 'green' I was especially in the matter of sex.

A young lad had started on the same day and had been sent by his new workmates into the box making section on a pretext. The girls wrestled him to the floor, divested him of his trousers and underpants with much shrieking and giggling, and as the red faced youngster struggled to get free, they hauled him to his feet and paraded him up and down the isles to be pointed at and catcalled.

My face must have shown my discomfort, and soon I was being cajoled to give the boy a kiss. As I slunk away in embarrassment resolutely refusing to comply I marked myself as a sacrificial lamb for every future joke. I went home convinced that I was in for a repeat of Molly McKay's bullying only this time there was no escaping my tormentors. Ada was eager to hear how my day had gone. I told her what she wanted to hear and mentioned in passing that a young lad had been given a rough time at the hands of the girls, though I was careful not to give precise details. Ada smiled, 'yes they did get up to tricks in my day too, I suppose they sent him for a tool that didn't exist, tartan paint was a favourite, or a long stand, which meant the poor thing stood for a good half hour before somebody put him out of his misery. I expect they ribbed him about his sweetheart too.'

'Yes,' I said, 'something like that.'

The girls spoke a language I did not understand, everything seemed to have a double meaning, and the most innocent remark would set them off in peals of laughter. A radio played all day and everyday and the girls would have their own words to the songs.

I'm going to bed with Harry Lauder
I'm going to let him turn me over.

I can never hear the rune of 'Whispering' without hearing the lewd words sung at the tops of their voices.

I worked on wedding cake boxes, Melody and Rhapsody, they were completely hand made, with many nips and tucks and trimming with an extremely sharp lance like tool.

I found I had a natural aptitude for the work. All the hours spent shaping and wrapping chocolate ices had made my fingers quick and deft and I found I was able to turn out many more boxes than the other girls at my bench. The journeywoman on the shift was impressed and I was put on piece work which meant more money. Ada was delighted and said it was the best thing she had ever done to get me that job.

The girls at my bench were not so impressed.

Accidents would happen to my work, the stacked trays of boxes would be 'bumped' into accidentally, the boxes would spill out on to the floor where someone would accidentally tread on them and I would have to make more.

Toilet breaks were strictly timed and if I went I would be followed by someone who would swear that I had been there too long. I would be splashed with water (accidentally) and return to find my glue tray had been upended over my supply of paper. All of this was hard to complain about as the girls would look the picture of innocence either claiming it was an accident or denying any knowledge of how such a thing could have happened. Even my innocence regarding sex was called into question.

She is no' as green as she's cabbage lookin'. She just thinks she is better than us, too stuck up tae laugh wi' the likes o' us'. I was miserable. I hated to have to face those sneering girls every day, hated the sound of 'McNeevin's horn' as it summoned me to work every morning, hated the all pervading smell of the hops from the brewery at the foot of the Canongate, hated living with Mary and Jimmy and their dour Calvinistic mode of life, and hated Edinburgh.

It went without saying Ada was miserable too. I at least could get out of the house for several hours but she was stuck with them. It went against her proud nature to be beholden to Mary and Jimmy when it had always been the other way around. Having to cook on the coal range, having the gaslight turned off at eight o' clock brought back all the memories of that other period of humiliation when we lived as lodgers in Teeny's house in the Gallowgate.

There had been a few rows since we had been there but Ada had always swallowed her pride knowing we needed a roof over our head. Aggie was a bone of contention, being nervous and acting helpless, causing Mary in particular to mumble under her breath that Ada had spoiled her. Aggie spent her days wandering round the old town as before.

Tensions had been mounting over the weeks. It was there every evening as Ada and I sat reading the few books we had brought with us while Aggie played dominoes with Mary and Jimmy, the steady tick of the mantel clock, the click of the dominoes as they were moved, and the low murmur of the players voices seemed to add to the repressed resentment that hung in the air. One fateful Friday things came to a head. As I climbed the rickety stairs to the top landing and turned into the corridor that led to the little but and ben I could hear raised voices, and as I drew nearer I realized that Ada and Mary were having an almighty row. I stretched my hand out to open the door then hesitated as I heard Mary screech, 'Ye ca' yersel' Mrs Cocozza and put on a' the airs an' graces, when ye are a liar, a sinner, livin' in sin. Yon wedding ring is a sham, that Lassie is a bastard bairn an' she has a right tae ken that, an' ah'm fur tellin' her.'

There was a scuffle and a scream and I imagined Ada had gone for her. Rover was barking, they were screaming and it would be only a matter of minutes before the neighbours were out wanting to know what was going on. I turned and fled down the stairs tripping over my feet, down and down, out through the pend, on and on down the Canongate to Holyrood park, and even then I kept going till a stitch in my side forced me to the ground. It was October, already dark, the biting east wind cut through my clothes making me shiver and down the path I could see the lamplighter going from post to post igniting the lanterns, leaving pools of yellow light as he passed. My mind was in turmoil. Mary's harsh words echoing in my head. What did she mean? Could it be true that the wedding ring was a sham, that Ada and Eugene were not really married? It couldn't be. I could not believe it yet I had always known there was some secret. I thought of all the conversations in Italian, the furtive glances that passed between the aunts, the doctor saying Betty and I were not full sisters, and a mental picture of the bundles of postal order counterfoils made out to Mrs E Cocozza. What did it all mean? Was I really a bastard bairn? The thought came that if that were true then Lena was too. Did she know? Was this another thing that had only been kept from me?

So many questions crammed my mind. I knew about bastard bairns, they were despised, objects of scorn and derision. Were we really like that, Lena and I?

What about Eugene? He was gone so why should he come back if the wedding ring really was a sham? Would I ever see him again?

I sat on rocking myself back and forth, my arms clasped tightly round my body. The cold gripped my cheeks, it numbed my fingers and toes and the tears fell from my eyes and dripped off my nose.

In the distance the Tron clock chimed seven and I realized I had been there for over two hours. I rose stiffly. I had to go back as Ada would wonder where I had got to. I needed an excuse for being late. I could not let her know that I had heard what Mary said.

There was an even greater shock in store for me. As I opened the door, Rover launched himself at me tail wagging, tongue lolling, and as I bent to stroke him I realized the figure with its back to me staring into the fire was not as I expected Jimmy but Eugene.

'Daddy?'

He turned, 'Aye, it's me, the prodigal returned,' he smiled.

Ada got up, 'where have you been? Your tea is ruined. Do you see the time?'

'I'm sorry I am late. We had a rush order.'

She asked no more but drew a plate of dried up spaghetti from the range and set it on the table. Rover had brought his lead and was begging to go out. I looked at the meal. I couldn't eat it not least as they all sat in gloomy silence like spectres at the feast.

'Maybe I'll just take Rover for his walk first,' I said.

'You will sit and eat your tea, we can't afford to waste food. Anyway I was just about to take the dog out. I will do it now,' Ada said grabbing her coat from behind the door.

I ate slowly, my mind racing. What would happen now? Did Eugene have any idea that Mary and Ada had had that row?

Jimmy began to fidget, 'come on eat up. It's gettin' late and we'll soon be wantin' oor bed.'

I stole a glance at Eugene but he was still staring into the fire and Aggie's eyes were downcast studying the buttons on her cardigan.

The mantel clock grunted and prepared itself to strike eight o'clock. Ada had not returned. Jimmy heaved himself up from his chair and turning his back on us began to undress, the gnarled fingers of his good hand struggling with the buttons of his shirt. After what seemed an age he finally shrugged off the shirt and began to tug at the belt of his trousers, and as he finally clamoured into bed in his long combinations he grunted to Mary to put out the gaslight. She tilted Eugene from the chair and climbed up snuffing out the gas.

'What time of night is this to go to your bed,' Eugene asked.

'We hae an early rise,' Jimmy said from under the blankets.

'An early rise. Where dae ye have to go?' Eugene asked.

'It's whit we dae, it is oor hoose,' Mary said sourly closing the shutters over the window and plunging us into complete darkness.

'It's best ye wait in the room fur Eadie, as fur sleepin' arrangements that is up tae you.'

We sat in relative darkness the only light a pale sliver from the moon. Eugene laughed, 'ah always thought they two were a funny pair.'

I could stay silent no longer, 'where have you been daddy?'

'Granton.'

'Granton! With 'Granton Aggie'?'

'No, no fear of going near them. I was working in a boat yard but ah've been laid off. The work dried up.'

'How did you know we were here?'

'Ah wrote to Lena at her lodgings and the landlady took the letter to her. It was a bit o' a surprise hearing that she has the hoose.'

'How could we stay there efter a' that business?' Aggie said suddenly roused into anger.

'Aye, ah suppose,' he said.

'Are you going to stay with us?' I wasn't sure what answer I wanted from him.

'Yer mammy is still awfu' angry,' Aggie said before he could answer.

'Aye well she has a right tae be ah suppose,' he said.

We fell silent. I was worried that Ada had not come back, and as if reading my mind, Eugene said, 'yer mammy is no' the type tae run away, though she threatens it.'

'Do you not think we should go and look for her?'

'No. She needs tae be by hersel' for a while,' he said.

At last we heard Ada's footsteps at the door as Rover burst through into the room bringing a burst of warm air from the dying fire in the kitchen. Ada threw down the lead, crossed to the window and drew aside the thin curtain but it made little difference.

'Are you still here?' she said dryly.

'I have nowhere else to go,' Eugene said.

'And you think there is room here? There is no room to swing a cat, no light, no fire, no beds,' her tone was icy.

'If ah could stay the night, ah'11 sort something oot in the mornin'.'

'With no money? That won't be easy. If you are staying you will need to sleep on the floor and you can use the coats for cover, it is the best we can do, and more than you deserve.'

'Aye fine,' Eugene said unfazed.

I fell asleep to their muted voices trying to conduct a clearly frosty argument. I woke to the sound of heated voices. Ada and Aggie were both lambasting Eugene and he was getting heated too, all pretence at whispered tones forgotten.

The clock struck the half hour and I peered at Ada's watch holding it to the window. The clock was striking half past two in the morning.

The room door flew open and Mary stood, her tiny figure swamped by a long nightgown. She was quivering with rage.

'Whit in God's name is a' this racket aboot?'

'Dae ye ken the time?' Jimmy shouted.

Ada and Eugene ignored them, their anger blotting out everything else.

I sat hands over ears as Rover put his nose on my lap and offered a consoling paw. Before long Jimmy too had struggled from his bed and joined in the row.

He gripped his useless arm by his good hand and stumped his way between Ada and Eugene. They looked surprised and stopped shouting.

'Mary an' me hiv had enough o' this nonsense, ah want ye tae go.'

'What!' Ada said.

'Ah want ye oot, oot, oot, oot, the lot o' ye and that damn dug as weel.'

'What now?' Ada said.

'Aye noo. We hiv had enough, get yer things an' go, noo.'

'Don't be daft man it's the middle o' the night,' Eugene said.

'Makes nae difference tae me. Ah want ye a' tae go and the quicker the better,' Jimmy' s cheek had gone red and the veins stood out on his brow.

'Right! If that is what you want, you two get your clothes on and get your things together,' Ada said to Aggie and me.

'Calm down, nobody puts people out in the middle o' the night, have you heard the rain oot there?' Eugene said.

'It's nane o' ma concern whit the weather is like, ah want ye oot o' here in the next ten minutes,' Jimmy was adamant.

'Suits me, I will not stay where I am not wanted,' Ada said, tugging at the bed covers and rolling them up.

'The least you can do is let us light the gas to see what we are doing,' Ada said.

Mary handed Eugene matches, he lit the gas.

We dressed in silence, and then stuffed everything we had into the pillowcases.

'We can't take everything, we have nowhere to go,' Ada said.

'They can bide where they are fur noo, but ye mind and tak them away as soon as,' Jimmy said.

We trooped out, no words, no goodbyes, and lugged the stuffed pillowcases down all the stairs, shrinking back from the driving rain when we reached the bottom.

'What now?' Eugene said.

'The only place I can think of is the railway station, there will be a fire in the waiting room,' Ada said.

'Right come on,' Eugene urged.

We set out for Jeffrey Street, trying to shield the pillowcases under our coats.

The waiting room was deserted and there had been a fire but it was now in its dying embers, but we sat huddled round it glad to be out of the rain.

A porter came by and looked at us but moved on without saying anything.

'This is all your fault, why did you have to come back?' Ada railed at Eugene.

'Ah'm sorry. Ah didn't think yer half brother would put you oot in the middle o' the night. Ma idea was to go in the mornin' but keep in touch. Ah didn't want tae stay wi' them,' Eugene said.

'Oh and you think we do? You think I liked going cap in hand to them and have them humiliated us?' Ada snapped.

'Aye, OK, ah'm sorry.'

'You are good at saying sorry, pity you never manage to put things right!' Ada said.

'What are we going to do now?' I asked. 'We can't stay here all night.'

'She's right,' Eugene said. How much money have ye got?'

'What business is that of yours?' Ada snapped.

'Ah've got about three pounds,' he said ignoring the jibe.

'All we have is Madalena's wages, God knows that is not a lot,' Ada said.

Aggie sniffed wiping her eyes with the sleeve of her coat. The porter went by again looking at us a little more closely. He moved to come into the waiting room, changed his mind and went away.

'He'll be in here asking questions in a minute or two, we need to get going, though God knows where to,' Ada said.

'We might just have enough for a lodging house,' Eugene said.

'And use up all the money we have in one night? Besides what lodging house would take in a group of half drowned bleary eyed tinkers, carrying all their worldly goods in pillowcases and dragging a bedraggled dog as well?' Ada said.

We laughed in spite of ourselves.

We sat on gazing into the fire which had lost its glow.

Ada stood up and we looked at her, 'We will go to someone I used to know,' she said.

'Who?' I was astonished.

'Someone I went to school with, we always got on,' she said.

'You went to school with? How long is it since you have seen her?'

'Him, seen him,' she corrected.

'Him!' That's worse I thought.

I tried to calculate how long it had been since Ada left school. I couldn't but I knew it was a considerable time, and turning up at an old

school friend's door in the middle of a stormy October night did not seem like a good idea.

I haven't seen him since we left school, but I do know where he lives. Jimmy bumped into him just the other day, it was an omen, it's fate.' 'Yer a great one fir the omens,' Eugene said.

'Aye, only it is a pity they let me down where you were concerned,' Ada said.

'Aye,' he sighed, 'Well this friend, dae ye think he would take us in?'

I couldn't believe what they were contemplating.

'We just can't turn up at this man's door in the middle of the night and expect him to take us in,' I protested.

'Do you have a better idea?' Ada snapped.

'Well no but -.'

'Well nothing, desperate situations call for desperate measures. I think he will take us in, but I don't really know,' Ada said.

'If ye don't ask ye don't get,' Eugene said.

'Right the quicker we start the quicker we will be there. It means walking as there are no trams running,' Ada said.

'Where does he live?' I asked.

'Niddrie Mains, it is a new scheme, on the outskirts,' Ada said.

'How far out?'

'Far enough, now come on, lets go,' she urged.

We set out. Rover slunk along tail down against the rain; we had no hats no umbrellas and in no time we were- soaked.

Ada was out in front, striding ahead like a warrior queen leading her troops. Eugene tagged a few steps behind, Aggie, Rover and me bringing up the rear. Aggie was crying openly now and she clung to my arm like a drowning man. As I peered at Eugene and Ada through the rain I suddenly felt they were strangers, they were not who I had always thought they were. We trudged on and after a while we left the city and found ourselves skirting fields, stumbling along in the dark, having left the street lighting behind. Rover grew excited by the smell of the damp grass and trees and he pulled away anxious to explore.

'Keep up, we mustn't get separated,' Ada called out.

She kept up a gruelling pace, but once or twice she seemed to get lost and we found ourselves back where we were ten minutes ago.

We seemed to have walked for hours. At last ghostly shapes of buildings loomed into view, gas lit lanterns pierced the gloom.

'I think this is Niddrie Mains,' Ada announced.

'What street does this man live in?' Eugene asked.

Ada thought for a moment.

'You know his address, right?' Eugene asked.

'Well I know the street. I think it is Niddrie Mains Terrace,' she said. 'What number?'

'Well I don't really know the number. I never really paid close attention to Jimmy when he told me about meeting Tom,' she said.

'If you don't know the number and you are not sure of the name of the street we don't have much of a chance of finding him, especially not in the dark,' Eugene said.

'I wish I had a torch,' Ada said ignoring his comments.

'It would be a great help,' agreed Eugene.

Part of me was relieved that she was doubtful about the address as I did not want to meet this man, especially in the middle of the night, but Ada was determined.

'We haven't walked all that way for nothing,' she said.

'Well I suppose we better start looking,' said Eugene.

'We will need to split up,' Ada decided.

'Right, what name are we looking for?' Eugene asked.

'Reynolds, and the more I think about it the more I am sure Jimmy said Niddrie Mains Terrace.

We split up. Ada marched off, Eugene darted up a close and I was left to trail Aggie behind me. She looked exhausted and I handed her Rover's lead.

'Here, hold on to Rover and stay down here while I go up the stairs and look at the name plates,' I told her.

She seemed happy with that, so I dashed off, peering at each name plate as I went but I drew a blank. Coming back down stairs I asked Aggie if she knew the man we were looking for.

'Aye, a funny sort o' fellow,' she said.

'Funny? Funny peculiar, or funny ha ha?'

'He's nae joke,' she said darkly.

'I don't want to find this man,' I said.

'Och, he's no' that bad,' she said quickly; clearly feeling she had let the side down.

It was Ada who finally found him. She gathered us together telling us to wait at the foot of the stairs, while she climbed up to the third floor and made the first approach.

We waited, huddled miserably together, straining to hear what was being said. Ada's voice was clear enough, it echoed in the wide stair well, the man's voice was muffled but sounded hesitant.

'Poor bugger has been wrenched oot his bed,' Eugene said.

Minutes later, Ada's head appeared over the banister and she called us up. Wearily we climbed the stairs. I hung back very reluctant to face this man. He stood framed in the doorway in the low light from the gas lamp on the landing, clutching the waistband of his pyjama trousers, which looked in danger of falling down.

'Come in,' he said a bemused expression on his face.

We trooped into the lobby uncertain what would happen next.

He looked down at Rover.

'A dog,' he said.

'Yes, didn't I say,' Ada said.

'No, but I suppose it will be a'right,' he dragged each word out as if it was a real effort to speak.

He thinks he is dreaming, I thought suddenly wanting to giggle.

Ada turned to us, 'Tom has very kindly agreed to put us up for the night, or what is left of it.'

We smiled our thanks shaking his hand in turn as Ada introduced us.

We were cold, damp and tired, longing to sit down. Tom looked cold too, his bare feet long and thin with dirt encrusted toe nails that were turning blue.

'In here,' he said opening a door.

The room was reasonably large; it held a double bed with a bare mattress, but there was no sign of pillows. A table stood against the wall, half of each front leg was missing and propped up by a pile of tatty books, next to the table, a soot blackened fireplace flanked by a three legged stool and an old kitchen chair. The streetlamp filtered light through the grubby curtainless window, and lit up the rough bare floorboards.

Eugene dropped the bundle he carried and his haversack and nodded.

'Fine, fine, this will be fine,' he said.

Tom looked at Aggie, 'You and the lassie can hae the other room.' He led the way across the lobby, opening the door to a much smaller room, same bare floorboards, same curtainless window, a single bed pushed against the wall, the bare mattress badly stained.

Aggie stared but said nothing, and I smiled our thanks.

Tom's pale blue eyes blinked sleepily as he yawned, and as he turned to go Ada came from the other room.

'It is very good of you. I hope we have not disturbed your family.'

He shrugged, 'Och no, the wife is a deaf mute and the bairn ay' sleeps sound.'

'That's good,' Ada said a little uncertainly. She touched his arm as he turned to go.

'Where is the lavatory?'

'Just there,' he yawned again, and pointed with a long bony finger down the lobby.

'Thanks, thanks again, we chorused.

'Night,' he said and disappeared through a door.

Eugene came back from the bathroom smiling, 'They keep their coal in the bath.'

'None of our business,' snapped Ada.

Rover gave himself a good shake, showering us with cold water.

Eugene bounced on the mattress, 'Made o' bricks.'

'We are lucky to be in out the rain,' Ada said.

'Aye, ah wis just makin' a comment,' Eugene said easily.

'Better get our heads down, and you two get through and take your coats off before you catch a chill,' Ada said.

She tugged at the pillowcases, pulling out the bedclothes, 'These are damp.'

Aggie wandered through to the room, Rover and me followed, and I wondered fleetingly whether Ada would insist Eugene slept on the floor, but I was too tired to bother finding out.

'Ah'll sleep nearest the wall,' Aggie said handing me her glasses.

'Fine,' I said, 'it is only for one night anyway. I slipped her glasses under the bed so as not to tread on them.

We lay cold and miserable, but fell asleep nevertheless.

The morning sky through the dirt encrusted window was grey to match our mood. I became conscious of a pair of curious eyes staring at me; a child of around three or four stood in the doorway, her hand on the handle, her eyes widened and she drew back a little as Rover emerged from under the bed.

'Don't be scared, he won't bite,' I said.

The little girl said nothing but continued to stare.

Aggie sat up peering around for her glasses, and I reached down and found them.

'Whit's yer name?' Aggie asked the girl.

There was no answer.

'Maybe she is deaf and dumb too,' I whispered to Aggie.

'Ah'm no,' the child shook her head.

'Oh, well maybe if you go back to your mammy for a little while till we get up and then you can come and see the doggie,' I said.

She turned on her heels, and we heard her go through to Ada who asked her to come back later.

Braving the bathroom Aggie and I had a quick cold wash and joined Ada and Eugene. Ada looked ill, my heart went out to her and the night had taken its toll.

Tom knocked on the door then entered.

'The wife will be through the noo, but she says if ye want a cup o' tea it will be a shillin' fur the four o' ye.'

'Oh!' Ada looked slightly taken aback, 'a shilling. Right, well I think we would like a cup of tea.'

'Right!' said Tom, 'ah'll come through an' tell ye when ye can make it.' He left closing the door behind him.

Eugene laughed, 'his wife drives a hard bargain.'

'Shush!' Ada hissed, 'beggars can't be choosers.'

It was the wife who came to sign to us that the kettle was at our disposal. She was a tiny wizened woman with wispy straw coloured hair. She wore an old smock held together by a safety pin and on her bare feet a pair of plimsolls burst at the toes.

Ada proffered her hand but the woman ignored it, instead she counted invisible money into her hand. Ada nodded and drew a shilling from her purse. The woman motioned Ada to follow her, Ada touched my arm and we both followed the woman to the kitchen.

The sink was full of dirty dishes and Ada looked around signing for clean cups. The woman shrugged and indicated we would have to wash some. Making the tea took some time, but at last we carried the cups through to Aggie and Eugene.

We sat gratefully clutching the warm cups, Ada on the chair, Aggie and I on the bed and Eugene on the stool. We sipped in silence each of us alone with our thoughts.

His tea finished Eugene put down the cup and lifted Rover's lead. Rover jumped up excitedly running back and forth to the door.

'Come on,' Eugene said to me, 'we'll see if we can find a shop in this miserable place.'

In the daylight the place was dismal indeed, grey uniform blocks marched up the hill as far as the eye could see, here and there a skinny dog rooted about in overgrown gardens.

'I don't like this place,' I shivered.

'Well it must be better than these folk left behind, at least they have a bathroom to store their coal,' Eugene said tongue in cheek. We trailed up and down identical streets but there was not a shop in sight.

'The planners need their heids examined,' Eugene said, 'it's the same story in the new estates in Glasgow. Plenty hooses, nae shops.' We walked on till at last we spotted a cafe and it was open.

'Wait here.' Eugene went in and was gone for ten minutes or so. He emerged carrying a cardboard box, his face split in a huge grin.

'I got tea, sugar, milk and a loaf. It is from their own stuff but we Italians stick thegither.'

'Great!' I said.

'Oh an' they say there is a chip shop no' far frae here, an' it opens at six o'clock,' Eugene added.

'Is the cafe open on Sundays?' I asked.

'Of course, the Italians serve God first thing in the mornin' an' make money the rest o' the day,' he laughed.

'Thank goodness we got something,' I said.

'Aye we don't hiv much money an wi' the price that wee women charges fur the tea we'll soon run oot, and who knows, she might charge us fur the cups as well. Let Rover off the lead. There are some trees back there and we need to try to find some wood so we can make a fire, the rooms are freezin',' Eugene said.

'But we are not staying there,' I said.

'Aye ah know but we need another cup o' tea and a heat, and we need to try to dry oot our things, before we go stravagin' again.'

We trudged back laden with the wood and provisions well pleased with ourselves. Ada watched as Eugene set the groceries on the table, then started to arrange the wood in the grate and tear up the box to get the fire going.

'I have arranged with Tom to rent these rooms for a few weeks,' she said.

I was horrified, 'You mean we are going to stay here?'

'Where else is there?'

'But we can't stay in this awful place, anyway how am I going to get to work?' I asked

'There must be buses and trams, I'm sure other people travel to work from here,' Ada said.

'We should have a cup of tea and think it over.' Eugene blew gently on the fire, a little flame flickered then died and he started again.

'We don't need to think about it, we are staying, you are going,' Ada's voice was firm.

Eugene looked up in surprise. 'You want me to go?'

'Of course I do. You are the reason we are in this mess. I swore to my maker that I would not have you back and I meant it. As soon as you have had your cup of tea I want you to go.'

'But you will need money coming in, I can get a job, we could find somewhere to live, we need to stick together,' Eugene told her.

'We needed to stick together before, but you decided otherwise. I have made up my mind and I won't go back on it.'

'Mammy please!'

'It is nothing to do with you. It is between your father and me. Now if you can get the fire going I will offer a shilling for the gas and boil some water for a cup of tea,' Ada said calmly.

The fire stuttered into life and we drank the tea and ate the dry bread, even Rover gobbled it, it had been so long since he had eaten.

I watched Ada and Eugene sitting side by side on the bed. They were locked in their own private struggle and Aggie and I were merely onlookers, with a stake in the outcome but powerless to influence it.

I knew they were both hurting. What had kept them together all these years? Was it love, duty, habit or merely convenience? I knew now they were not legally bound together, so if Eugene went away again what was there to bring him back? I flinched as he drained his cup and laid it on the table, stood up and gathered his things.

'If you want me to go it is better I go while it is daylight,' he said, looking at Ada and obviously hoping she would change her mind.

'I want you to go, don't let me keep you,' she said coldly.

He drew two pound notes from his pocket, setting them by the empty cup. Ada looked at them and pushed them towards him.

'I don't want your money.'

'Don't be daft woman, take it, you'll need it.'

'I don't want it, we will manage, take it back. If you leave it there I will put it on the fire.' Eugene sighed and stuffed the notes back in his pocket. I rushed to hug him and he pinched my cheeks and smiled.

Rover nuzzled his nose under Eugene's hand; he patted the dog on the head and pushed him away.

He went from the room and I ran after him, whispering in his ear to let me know where he was. He nodded.

I went back to the room as the front door closed behind him. Ada's head came up, 'Well now we can get on with the rest of our lives.'

CHAPTER 32

After Eugene had gone Ada decided we should make our way back to Jimmy's to collect the rest of our things. The atmosphere was still frosty, they did not ask where we had gone and Ada did not tell them. We took the tram to the terminus and walked with some difficulty back to Niddrie Mains Terrace. Ada had come to what she thought was a fair agreement with Tom for the two rooms, after all it was the barest of accommodation, we would pay for any gas we used and would have to supply our own coal. This would prove to be difficult as coal was still rationed and it would be hard to get registered as only householders were accepted.

Tom supplied us with a bucket of coal to tide us over, but when his wife found out she came and demanded extra payment. She communicated by a mixture of facial gestures, hand movements and a scribble pad. Ada preferred to answer her by writing too.

We found that there was indeed a bus that went into town. It was a fair walk to the bus stop from the terrace and it meant a very early start.

Each morning I joined the queue of shivering souls at the bus stop which was flanked by open fields, leaving us at the mercy of the howling north wind that invariably brought rain and sleet.

Above us the crows wheeled and screeched, jostling for space on the bare branches of the tall gaunt trees.

In that first week Ada took Aggie into Edinburgh to try to find her work. Within the week she had secured a position in Crawford's Tea Rooms in the New Town, where she would help out as a kitchen hand. The first morning she joined me at the bus stop she could not stop shaking, all the way into town she sat nervously twisting the belt of her coat round and round her hand. My heart went out to her. She had never worked for anyone but Ada, it was as if she was attached to Ada by an invisible cord and now that cord was broken and she was on her own. I could not help her either. I had my own cross to bear and there was nothing for it but for both of us to get on as best we could.

At least we were out of that dreadful house while Ada was stuck there with that awful woman.

Tom left early for work, and it soon became clear that his wife was no early riser. The child would roam around the house, unwashed and unfed, till her mother rose at around eleven to make a meagre breakfast of tea with bread and jam. Neither she nor the child would have anything more until six o'clock when she would heat up the tea and give the child a cup and have one herself. The meal such as it was would be eaten when Tom returned at ten o'clock.

To Ada's horror she found the little girl was beaten with a buckled belt for the slightest cause of annoyance.

The first time Ada heard her screams she flew into the kitchen and threatened to call the police. Hetty scowled and mouthed abuse; her face contorted, her hands gesticulating wildly.

Ada began to notice that things were going missing from our store of provisions which we kept in the cupboard in Ada's room.

She went to Hetty and complained, writing her concerns in capitol letters on her pad. Hetty erupted in fury when she read the note, she shook her head and mouthed the word MICE!

'Clever mice that can carry tins away and open packets of biscuits,' Ada scrawled.

Not long after this, returning from walking Rover Ada surprised the culprit. It was the little girl. She was so thin and undernourished; her wrists like that of a tiny infant rather than a child of almost five years old and Ada could only pity her as she munched hungrily on the biscuits. Ada told her she had no need to steal, she could come and ask for bread or biscuits and she would get them.

More and more things began to disappear, things the little girl would not want, tea, sugar, tins of soup. Ada suspected Hetty was using the child to steal for her and she penned an angry note, left it for Hetty to see and waited for the response.

The note was ignored, but a padlock was fitted to the kitchen door and a note couched politely in Tom's hand requested Ada to draw water from the bathroom and cook on the fire.

'Well two can play at that game,' Ada fumed and fitted a padlock to our room door. Things were now very difficult; we needed a supply of coal to get heat, hot water and hot meals.

Ada came into town to meet me and we bought a tin bath from a general store and took it home on the bus perched awkwardly on our knees.

A neighbour had told us that you could get coal from the coal merchant's yard if you went along and collected it yourself, so we decided it was the only thing to do. As soon as I arrived home on the Friday of that week Ada and I set out again with the bath and a stout piece of rope to walk the two miles to the coal yard. We soon found that the coal he was prepared to let us have for a price was the waste material that lay scattered across the yard. We set to work gathering as much as we could with our bare hands. It was poor quality, but pricey nevertheless. Ada watched anxiously as it was weighed and priced, she paid without question and we set off pulling the bath behind us. Once back at the flat we carried load after load up the three flights of stairs and stored it under Ada's bed.

This ritual was repeated every Friday in snow, sleet, or driving rain.

Money was tight and we survived on a very meagre diet. Aggie was allowed to bring home 'cutting' loaves and buns which would have otherwise been thrown away or sent to the zoo.

We would devour these gratefully, Ada always making sure the little girl got her share.

Evenings were spent huddled round the fire in Ada's room. She had tacked some netting across the window but it did little to dispel the chill.

Draughts whistled through the bare floorboards and under the door, and eager to preserve the coal, Aggie and I would undress in Ada's room and scuttle through to our bed, and on very bitter nights Ada would carry through a shovel of burning coals from her fire and pop it onto the grate of our fireplace where it sent out a little cheer before dying out.

There was little to do but listen to Aggie's gossip about the women in the tearoom, and through the wall we could hear the mumble of Tom's radio which he switched on in the evening as soon as he came home.

Ada and I would sit staring into the fire letting Aggie's lurid tales wash over us.

Rover would drag his lead from the nail and drop it hopefully at my feet, I was always glad of the excuse to take him out.

We would wander through the little wood where Eugene and I had gathered wood on that first day. I longed to know where he was, but there had been no word not even from Lena, though I felt sure he would have written to her.

Ada was becoming more and more depressed and she took to pacing back and forth, going over and over the events that had led her to this awful place. She would scream at me and warn that some day I would come home and she would be gone, and on really bad nights she would hint that she would end her life and then we would all be sorry. I became very worried about her, if she wasn't screaming she would sit on her bed rocking to and fro.

'Why has this happened? What sin have I committed? Why does God punish me. Why won't He answer my prayers?' she would mumble.

I was fearful of leaving her to go to work. I could hear her crying in the night, but if I went to her she would turn her back on me and say she wished she was dead.

I sought solace in keeping a journal, recounting all that had happened and was happening. I wrapped the exercise book in newspaper and hid it under the mattress of the bed I shared with Aggie.

Coming home one night I found Ada grim faced, poking at something in the fire. She looked up as I came in pointed to the stool and said, 'sit down.'

I sat on the little stool staring into the fire as the pages of my exercise book curled, flared crimson, then fluttered to ashes.

'So YOU are unhappy? YOU miss your father!' she snarled.

I said nothing.

'You think I am losing my mind! She slapped me across the face, 'is it any wonder?' she screamed.

Aggie sat hunched over the fire, her hands clasped in a tight ball.

'Well have you nothing to say?' I couldn't speak.

'You had plenty to say in that book.'

'I'm sorry, I just get afraid, afraid of what might happen.'

'What might happen is that I might not be here much longer, I would be better off dead, then you wouldn't have to worry any more.'

'No mammy, don't say that please.'

'What I can't understand is that you could care a damn for that feckless father of yours who betrayed us all. It is he we have to thank for being in this horrible place, yet you don't give a damn for me, when I have looked after you and always tried to do my best for you.'

'I know that mammy, I'm sorry.'

'Sorry! You are as bad as your father, he is good at saying sorry, it is easy to say sorry, but sorry does not put things right. I am the one he has betrayed the most, I am the one who should have run away and left all the mess behind, but I have a conscience which is more than your father has. I don't shirk my responsibilities.

'Yes, I know mammy, I'm sorry, I didn't mean to hurt you, I love you,' I was sobbing now.

She shook me, 'don't let me catch you writing anything like that again, it is bad enough that we are in this state without you recording everything for all and sundry to see.'

'It was only for me, I wouldn't show it to anyone else.'

'I don't believe you, half of that stuff isn't even true, it is only as you think you see it, you are only a child and you don't understand.'

I jumped up.

'I'm not a child, I'm sixteen, you won't let me grow up,' I screamed. We stared at each other for a moment.

'Oh I'm sorry mammy. I didn't mean to shout at you,' I stammered.

'So that is what you think, I won't let you grow up, well if you are so anxious to grow up I will start treating you like an adult, but I will expect you to behave like one, and not scribble nonsense in some exercise book like a little schoolgirl.'

'I'm sorry mammy.'

She gripped me again shaking me like a rag doll, 'I mean what I say, do you hear? From now on I will be watching you like a hawk. You will get rid of any paper you have.'

'Mammy please!'

I couldn't be without paper, I needed it around me, and I was always scribbling stories and poems.

'I mean it,' she said pushing me away.

Rover brought his lead, sitting at my feet, his eyes on my face. I hugged him and clipped on the lead, grabbed my coat and made for the door.

I kept going over the whole scene in my mind. How could I have hurt her like that? I knew it would be a long time if ever before she forgave me, and I cursed myself for being so stupid. The rain blew in my face, slanting silver in the gas light, I let Rover off the lead and followed wherever he went. After an hour I let myself back into the house, the fire was still burning brightly, the room full of a strange odour. Ada looked round at me, picked up the poker and stirred something in the heart of the fire, it was my best platform shoes, tan and green lace ups that I loved so much.

'Maybe that will teach you what it is like to lose something you care about,' Ada said.

I wrote to Lena telling her of my misery. She wrote to reassure me that Ada was just upset and it would all blow over. It did not feel like that from where I was, Ada was cold, she only spoke if she had to, and the long trek to the coal yard was taken in silence. I decided not to bother Lena again, she had her own concerns. A letter came from Tina, saying she was coming to visit, it sent Ada into a panic, and she wrote to Lena begging her to put Tina off.

'I can't stand the shame of anybody seeing what we are reduced to,' Ada said breaking her silence.

Tina was determined to come. It was clear she was shocked at what she found, though she tried her best to hide it.

Ada was blunt, 'I didn't want you to come and I don't want anybody else to come,' she swore Tina to secrecy.

The shame put a barrier between them, but gradually Tina's genuine nature got through and she put a gentle hand of Ada's arm.

'Comar, you an' me hiv always got on.'

'Yes, I know,' Ada said.

When Tina took her leave they hugged briefly.

Ada said earnestly, 'give my regards to people but tell them nothing, not even Lena. She knows we don't live in a palace, but she had no real idea.'

'It's no' your fault comar, that brother o' mine...'

'Yes well, least said about that the better,' Ada said.

We stood and watched the bus till we could see it no more, taking Tina's tearstained face from our sight. Things got worse after Tina's visit. Ada withdrew into herself and refused to wash or get dressed. I would come home from work to find her in her nightdress, hair in disarray and Rover desperately needing to get out.

Our stock of groceries dwindled, and Aggie and I had to bring things home with us. The weekly coal run became my sole responsibility and I took Rover along for company, he really needed the exercise.

Ada sat arms tight round her body weeping silently. She seemed back in her childhood, crying for her father, cowering from James Miller, talking to the young Aggie, asking where Elizabeth was.

Sometimes she would cry out that Waverley buildings was 'not her destiny', 'I shouldn't be here', she would cry.

Aggie became more and more agitated as the 'rock' that was Ada crumbled before our eyes.

I wrote to Lena, not spelling things out but only that Ada was depressed and not very well. Lena begged me to call a doctor, but mention of this roused Ada from her trance-like state to cry out and push me away.

Tom would look shocked and try to be supportive and Hetty would screw up her face and twist her finger at her forehead to show she thought she was mad.

At work I told them that my mother was really ill and they allowed me time off, but as the weeks went on I had to leave, I needed to be with Ada all the time. The days were long and difficulty and I was so glad to have Rover he was my only comfort. I made soup in a pot hung over the fire and this I spooned into Ada as if feeding a child and I scraped some money to give to Tom to buy Guinness, remembering Ada had always believed in its goodness. This too I fed her one spoon at a time. She allowed herself to be washed and dressed like a little child, and seemed unaware of the tears that rolled down my cheeks as I worked with her.

She lost so much weight, and though I knew the trouble was in her mind I prayed the Guinness would give her strength.

Gradually she seemed to come back to us, talking of Benny, blaming Eugene for letting her near the Granny's coffin, railing at Da-dee for his cold remark about not losing the breadwinner. Now and then she would look at me and seem to remember who I was and she would ask why I was not at work. I would make some excuse, sit beside her taking her hand and talking of happier times.

'One morning she looked at me with concern, 'you will lose that job if you stay off any longer,' she said.

I felt a great sense of relief. She was coming back to us and I knew I needed to be careful about what to tell her. It was not the time to let her know I had no job to go to.

Aggie had been as big a concern as Ada on occasions, but now that Ada was recovering her mood lightened.

'Maybe ah could look efter Eadie and you could try to get your job back,' she suggested.

I was afraid to risk it. Ada was better but still delicate, yet we needed the money, we were behind with the rent and Tom had been very good.

Christmas was coming. McNiven and Cameron worked over Christmas which shocked me and made them in my opinion heathens, but Christmas in Scotland was not really a big thing and to many people it was just another day.

I longed to go back to Glasgow and see Lena and all my friends, but I knew Ada would never go back there especially not to St. Vincent Street.

Ada was much better but very upset that I had given up the job so I decided to try to go back for a while at least, truth was I had not missed the place at all. As it was a busy time for them they took me back, but I knew that I wouldn't stay.

We spent a miserable Christmas and on Hogmanay we agreed we would go to bed early; there did not seem much of reason to celebrate.

Tom and Hetty had been invited out, the little girl was in bed and I had agreed to look after her if she woke.

Tom had brought in his radio for us to hear the bells ring in the New Year. At the last minute we decided to stay up and listen in.

As the strokes of midnight rang out there was a loud knock at the door. Rover got up and stood with his tail wagging slowly, he didn't bark.

'Don't answer it,' Ada whispered, 'it will be somebody for Tom and he is out anyway.'

The knocking persisted and Rover pawed at the door to get into the lobby. He put his nose down, snuffled at the front door and I opened it just a little. Eugene stood grinning on the doorstep, a lump of coal in one hand, a bottle of whisky in the other.

'Happy New Year,' he said.

I stared at him.

'Well can ah come in? Ye cannae turn away a first foot.'
He walked past me into the room before I could warn Ada.
'Happy New Year,' he said proffering the gifts.
'You!' Ada said.
'Aye, ah'm back, turnin' up just like the bad penny,' he grinned.
Aggie was looking at Ada as if waiting for her to explode. Ada eyed Eugene coldly.
'What are you doing here?'
'I heard you were ill, so ah've come back.'
'I'll be the judge of that,' Ada snapped.
He shrugged, 'eh, ah suppose.'
'Who told you I was Ill?' she asked.
She glared at me suspecting I was the culprit.
'Lena. We kept in touch,' he said easily, then laughed, 'are ye no' goin' tae wish me a happy New Year, the bells are still ringing.'
'You waltz in here because it is New Year and you expect to be welcomed with open arms. Nobody asked you to come here,' Ada said.
'Eadie,' he pleaded, 'look ah heard things were bad, and ah thought it was time to come an' offer some help.'
'Very generous I'm sure, but we are fine thank you very much, things are back to normal now, or as normal as they could ever be in this place.'
'Aye, but it is time to get oot o' here, ye cannae stay here forever, ah can help, bring in some money.'
'Huh, what makes you think I want your money?' Ada scoffed.
'Come on Eadie, it's a New Year, it could be a new start, life has to go on.'
He looked at me, 'what dae you say?'
I was too scared to answer; if I said the wrong thing the fragile relationship Ada and I had re-established could break down.
'Oh I'm sure she would welcome you back with open arms,' Ada said.
Eugene opened the bottle of whisky and looked around for something to pour it into. I gathered up the cups and went to rinse them in the bathroom. He smiled and poured tiny amounts into each cup.
'None of us are whisky drinkers ah know, but this is a special occasion.'
He handed round the cups and held his aloft, 'to better times.'
We all looked at Ada as she sat clutching the cup, her face blank.
'To better times,' Eugene repeated as he reached out and clinked Aggie's cup and mine, then turned to Ada, cup extended, slowly she raised her cup and touched his briefly.
'To better times,' she said quietly.
Eugene turned to me, 'maybe yer mammy would like a drop o' tea in her whisky.'
We all laughed a little self-consciously.
As we drank our whisky-laced tea he told us that Tina had tracked him down in Birkenhead. He had work but it had been intermittent, and to save money he had rented a room but cooked for himself.

'You cooked?' Ada was sceptical.

'Aye well kinda, ye know. Ah lived on porridge and boiled eggs. Ah just made a lot o' porridge and poured it intae a drawer an' cut a bit as ah needed it. Ah made polenta and did the same wi' that but it did get a bit monotonous after a while.'

'I should think it would,' Ada said dryly.

'Aye well, Tina said she had seen ye an' things wernae sae good and she told me tae come back but ah thought ah better check wi' Lena first.' 'Lena has enough to do with the baby, I don't want her bothered,' Ada said. The night wore on, revellers could be heard singing in the street. Eugene took Rover's lead from its nail and said, 'Ah'll take the dog for his walk. It is better you stay with your mammy.'

I knew he wanted me to talk to Ada to let him stay.

I did not know where to start, but she spoke first.

'Can you imagine the cheek of him coming back here as if nothing has happened. Happy New Year! It won't be very happy if he is around, we are better off as we are.'

'Mammy it would be better for all of us if we could leave here, you know you are not happy here,' I ventured.

'You want me to rely on that man who has let me down so badly?'

'He was worried about you mammy. He came back when he heard you were ill.' I said.

'He has come back for his own ends, the job has dried up and he thinks he can worm his way back in here.'

'Can he at least stay the night?' I asked.

'He can sleep on the floor on the coats the way he did before. It is up to him, I won't beg him to stay,' she said.

I detected a softening in her tone, but didn't dare hope she was coming round.

Eugene came back and looked at me, trying to judge the mood. I shrugged and spread my hands to say I did not know what would happen.

He stayed the night. He stayed many nights, sleeping without a grumble on the floor.

'Does your back not hurt?' I asked.

'Ach a bit, but it disnae bother me,' he said.

We were going to Glasgow just for the day. Carol and Tommy's son was to be Christened.

I could hardly contain my excitement, but Ada was moody and noncommittal as we sat opposite each other in the train each preoccupied with our own thoughts. Eugene as usual seemed unaware that Ada's heart was not in the trip. He puffed contentedly at his pipe and read his newspaper as Aggie was quietly dozing.

I had never seen Tommy and Carol's flat, and was deeply curious.

Later as we sat clutching delicate china cups filled with expensive coffee, I gazed in wonder at the sumptuous trappings, comparing them mentally with our hovel in Niddrie Mains.

Ada was ill at ease. Being back in the bosom of the family seemed to unnerve her and she gazed at Carol who sat with elegant poise framed in the bay window which was swathed in delicate tulle, her silk clad legs neatly crossed at the ankles, her feet in pink velvet slippers with mink pom-poms while beside her dressed in a satin christening gown the baby lay in an opulently padded Moses basket. Tommy was doing the rounds with a tray of sherry in preparation for a toast to the baby's health.

Tina had been chosen as Godmother, and earlier that day had carried the child proudly to the chapel, giving the 'chittering piece' as was the custom to the first female she met.

'A boy for a girl, and a girl for a boy,' she explained to me, the usual 'chittering piece' was a piece of cake and a silver sixpence.

As we toasted the baby's health Famie came up to Ada and took her hand.

'Comar, you don't look well. Livin' in that awful place is going for your health. Why don't you come and stay with me?'

Ada withdrew her hand, 'I don't know what you mean, we are fine where we are,' she said.

'Comar, Tina told us. She is worried about you, about all of you,' Famie persisted, 'if you don't want to come maybe you could let Madalena come, it is not a life for a young girl.'

Ada stood up and beckoned me over, 'we are leaving, get the coats,' she said.

I did as I was told, smiling apologetically at Famie who stood awkwardly looking on.

We clattered down the stairs after Ada, Eugene bringing up the rear and asking over and over , 'what happened?'

'Your sister Tina just could not keep her mouth shut. I swore her to secrecy, instead I am humiliated, having the whole family feeling sorry for me,' her voice came breathlessly as she stormed on into the street.

'But what happened?' Eugene persisted still none the wiser.

'Auntie Famie said something to mammy,' I flung over my shoulder trying to catch up with Ada who was striding towards the tram stop.

They argued all the way back on the tram and on the train, Ada repeating how humiliated she felt being offered a room in Famie's house.

'What's wrong wi' that?' Eugene said in his usual tactless fashion, 'it can hardly be worse than where we are noo an' we would be shot o' that awful biddy.'

'I do not want to be beholden to THAT Joe McCann,' snapped Ada.

'Well at least he is family, he's no that bad,' Eugene argued.

'I won't hear of it, there is no more to be said.'

They lapsed into injured silence. That night I quizzed Aggie as we lay in the darkness.

'What did Auntie Famie actually say to mammy?'

'She said Tina had told her aboot the 'awful place', an that if she didnae want to come she should send you because it wisnae the place fur a lassie.'

'Did mammy say I could go?'

'Whit dae you think?' Aggie scoffed.

The weeks dragged on and having Eugene there did make a difference. He took over the coal run and walked the streets of Edinburgh looking for work. I grew more and more depressed. I tried to find the courage to ask Ada if I could go to live with Famie, but I knew she would see it as a betrayal.

Hetty's abuse of the little girl was getting worse. We could hear her screams and it became unbearable. Ada took Tom aside and told him of her concerns. He was a mild and placid man but she had touched a nerve and he rounded on her saying it was only proper discipline and none of her business. Ada, loathe to abandon the child, told him he did not understand what was going on as he was never present when the beatings went on.

'Look at the little thing, her body must be full of bruises under those thin clothes,' Ada pleaded.

'You have to let my wife and I bring up our child as we see fit,' Tom said and turned away.

Hetty's response was to demand more money for the rooms.

I was finding it harder and harder to forgive Ada for not agreeing to let me go to Famie. Night after night we sat huddled round the miserable little fire, Ada and Eugene rehashing all the problems that had led to losing the business, Aggie getting a gibe or two when she could get the chance. Aggie always brought home magazines that customers left behind in the tea room and most nights I buried my nose in them trying to blot out the arguments. I always read the problem pages and realized that you could write for advice and receive a personal reply. I poured my heart out in a letter to Ruth Martin of Woman's Own, begging her to reply and giving Lena's address. Next I wrote to Lena asking her to look out for it and send it on to me as I knew Ada would recognise Lena's hand and not open it. It seemed such a long time before the answer came and I hurried off to the room I shared with Aggie to read it nervously, alert to Aggie or Ada approaching. .he tone of the letter was not what I had expected, It was hectoring, taking me to task for interfering in the relationship between my mother and father. I was, said the writer, too young to understand the relationship between adults, and had no business making judgements on things I knew nothing about.

I tore the letter into a thousand tiny pieces and put them in my coat pocket, then saying I was taking Rover for a walk I dropped them down a drain as soon as I was out of sight.

I was a ship without a rudder, there was nowhere to turn, no one to turn to, this adult world was so strange, and I did not feel a child yet clearly this woman regarded me as one, just as Ada did. Eugene went his own sweet way almost wrapped in a bubble that shielded him from knowing the pain those around him suffered. Aggie took her cue from Ada, having no real opinion of her own but knowing how to pour coals on the fires of contention. Lena had her own concerns, as had Betty who seemed so far and remote from us now as we had not heard from her for so long. My only real friend was Rover, his love was unconditional and unchanging. A few days before my birthday Ada surprised me by saying as a treat I could spend the weekend in Glasgow at Famie's.

I was overjoyed, each night I lay thinking of all the things I would do while I was there. Through the wall came the sound of Tom's record player and the one scratchy record he played over and over again. Usually it drove me crazy, but now it seemed to be in tune with my mood.

Pack up all my care and woe
Here I go singing low
Bye, bye, Blackbird.
Where somebody waits for me
Sugar sweet, so is he
Bye, bye Blackbird.

No one here can love or understand me
Oh what hard luck stories they all hand me
Make my bed, light the light,
I'll arrive late tonight
Blackbird bye bye.

At last I was on the train, leaning out of the carriage window, getting last minute instructions on minding my manners from Ada. Rover stretched his full height to get to me, gazing wistfully, his tail down. I hugged him and told him I would soon be back.

The guard was slamming doors, raising the whistle to his lips when Ada suddenly blurted out, 'if you can find a job during the weekend you can stay in Glasgow.'

The whistle blew, the train shuddered to life, and already Ada, Aggie and Rover were slipping away.

'Do you mean that?' I yelled.

'Yes,' she mouthed. I couldn't hear her but I saw the nod and the movement of her lips. I slid down in the seat breathless. She said I could stay in Glasgow if I could get a job and all the plans I had made vanished. I knew I would have to spend all the time I could visiting shops and offices. I had only one day, that day, Saturday as everything was closed on Sundays. Before I knew it we were pulling into Queen Street Station. I tumbled excitedly from the train, half running toward the ticket collector, eager to get out into my beloved Glasgow.

The dear familiar sights and smells were all around me as I hoisted my little bag up and set off across George's Square, revelling in the wonderful City Chambers and the General Post Office, each of which took up two sides of the square. I made my way down towards Argyle Street to catch the tram to Bridgeton. I had forgotten how busy Argyle Street was on a Saturday, crowds swayed this way and that even though it was January and bitterly cold. Each corner had a stall, the vendor calling their wares, with that wonderful Glasgow banter. Edinburgh could boast nothing like this I thought, not even its fine buildings, its broad streets and mounted statues could compete with this gallus Glasgow in your face optimism.

I watched the trams come and go, their green and cream Glasgow Corporation livery a welcome relief from Edinburgh's genteel maroon.

The Bridgeton tram trundled towards me and when it stopped I scrambled up the stairs making straight for the little cabin above the driver, slid open the door and, sliding it shut again behind me, dropped gratefully onto the red leather bench.

I was in heaven.

The 'clippie' came clattering up the stairs, stomped along the passage and flung open the door of the cabin, her face like thunder. She stood before me eyebrows raised as I fumbled for coins to pay my fare. She took the coins and dropped them deftly into the bag at her waist, tapped in the amount and expertly snipped off the thin white stream of paper that pumped from her machine.

Shoving the ticket at me she left the cabin neglecting to close the door.

With a broad grin I jumped up and slammed it shut. Nothing had changed, 'clippies' had always resented having to march the whole length of the tram past rows of empty seats to get to the fare of some smart alec who chose to sit in solitary splendour.

The only thing they hated more was a noisy bunch of children in the cabin jostling and jumping around and making enough noise to wake the dead. I knew because I had been part of such a mob many times. It had always been the proud boast of the City Fathers that a short tram ride would let you leave the dust and fumes of the city behind and find yourself surrounded by tranquil natural beauty.

It was no idle boast and thousands of Glaswegians demonstrated its truth every weekend. For children of school age the parks were fine on early spring or fine autumn evenings, but in the summer holidays the call of the wild drew them further afield.

Harassed Glasgow mammies still tied to the sink and cooker, with a cigarette hanging from her lips and the youngest on her hip, would rouse her brood early, fill used 'ginger' bottles with water, slap jam between two slices of bread, tie a sixpence in a paper bag and pin it to trousers or dress and tell them to get lost in 'Mulguy' for the day. When ever I could I would beg off from my shop duties to take off with the crowd.

As soon as Ada gave her consent I was out of the house before she could change her mind. We would set off, a group about five or six to begin with, being joined by others on the way, jostling and laughing we made our way to Charing Cross to catch the tram. Hopping impatiently from foot to foot we would watch the tram slowly trundle towards us straining to see if the cabins were occupied. If they were we would groan and wait for the next one. The trams had cabins at either end, being built on a push me/pull me design, the driver simply going to the other end, jumping out to change the points and 'hey presto' he was off in the opposite direction.

Once on board we would argue about what games we would play, and how far into the woods we would go.

The woods were full of massive trees and giant ferns that grew thick and impenetrable. In late May and early June the bluebells carpeted the whole floor of the wood with a magical lavender blue drift that caught the breath with their beauty.

When the tram reached the terminus, we would scramble down the stairs and gather in a subdued group on the pavement. There was something about the stillness of the village, the smart bungalows with their manicured lawns and weed free flower beds that hushed our mouths and put us in awe.

We knew we were being observed behind twitching lace curtains and adults put the fear of God into us.

None of us lived in anything so grand as these houses, these were rich people, a different species.

Quickly we made for the woods, to run free and wild, and there we knew no fear. Nature had always stirred me, trees in particular, and in 'Mulguy' or Milngavie to give it its proper name, the trees were magnificent. Where the wood thinned and finally ended the surrounding meadows stretched as far as the eye could see, bright with wild flowers and tall swaying grasses. Here, tired of battling our way through the giant ferns, we would sink down among the grass gazing up at the deep azure sky and doze off to the lazy humming of the bees, and sometimes a lark would rise soaring into the heavens in full song. I tried to convey to the other children how all this beauty had such a profound affect on me, but they never understood, perhaps like me they thought it had always been there and always would be. The future was not something we thought about or at least only as far as the next day, or the next treat.

On one of our jaunts I spied a large horse standing motionless in a field. From where I was standing it looked to me as if the horse had five legs, one being much shorter than the others. I became concerned thinking the horse was ill and I called to the boys.

They took one look and fell about laughing.

'That's no' a leg, that's his thing,' they giggled.

'What thing?' I asked truly puzzled.

'You know! His thing!' they were convulsed.

'I don't know what you mean,' I said, exasperated.

'The THING he uses to...' they trailed off, too overcome with mirth to go on.

'Well I think he is ill and we should tell the farmer,' I insisted.

'He will think you're daft, or havin' him on,' they ran off still giggling.

'Come on. We're goin' tae play rounders.'

Later at home I told Betty about the horse and she fell about laughing just as the boys had.

'You mean it really was that THING they said?'

'Yes he was male horse, a stallion, he was just excited.'

'What was he excited about?'

'Pr-pr-probably a female horse,' she giggled.

'I didn't see any other horse.'

She held her hand to her mouth, 'then maybe it was just wishful thinking.'

'I don't understand what you mean,' I was annoyed.
'I know!' she said and left the room.

CHAPTER 33

Famie and Joe were waiting to greet me, the table set and a cheery fire burning in the grate.

As I ate I told them of Ada's surprise suggestion and they were delighted.

'You don't have much time. Your best bet is to see if any of the shops in Dalmarnock Road are looking for somebody,' Joe said.

'She doesn't want just any job though,' Famie said.

'Well she cannae afford tae be fussy, can she?' Joe reminded her.

I excused myself as quick as I could and set off for Dalmarnock Road which was only a few minutes away.

It was lined with shops of all kinds and there were lots of people about. One shop in particular looked really busy and the queue, housewives with message bags and squirming complaining children hanging on to their coat tails, came right out the door.

I looked up at the sign, 'Cochrane Ltd, Grocer and Purveyor of fine meats'.

Through the window I could see the assistants scurrying up and down, pouring sugar into blue bags, slicing cold meat on a wicked looking contraption and cutting great round cheeses with fine wire. Over in the far corner, totally engrossed in his work, a man in a white coat was expertly boning a huge side of ham and I watched him in fascination. My gaze seemed to get to him as suddenly he looked up, straight at me.

I shrunk back, and then chanced another peek. He had gone back to his work.

Could there, I wonder, be any vacancies. They certainly seemed rushed off their feet. I looked the whole scene over again and again, trying to imagine myself working behind that counter, and then I caught sight of a small notice low down on one of the windows, 'GIRL WANTED'.

I squeezed past the waiting queue answering the muttered protests with whispered apologies and nervously I stood before the man in the white coat. He knew I was there but chose to ignore me for a while.

Without looking up he said, 'I suppose you have come about the job?' 'Yes.'

He gripped the end of a rib and slid the knife beneath it, slicing it out in one easy movement.

'Think you can do that?'

'I don't know.'

He put the knife down on the counter, wiped his hands on his coat, and beckoned me to follow him.

'Right, come through and we'll talk.' I followed him into a gloomy storeroom with shelf after shelf of packets and tins, sacks of flour and oatmeal sagged against the walls and above, the ceiling was festooned with salami sausages and boned ham wrapped in netting.

'So tell me about yourself,' he said ripping a sheet of paper from a pad, and settling himself on a high stool. I told him, not everything but enough.

'Box making. A bit different from serving groceries,' he said scribbling away.

'I am used to serving the public,' I said. I worked in Woolworth and in my mother's café.'

'Right,' he said, and scribbled some more.

I waited.

'Ok, the job is yours. You say you live in Edinburgh, so how about you start next Wednesday, that's the half day. It will give you a chance to find your feet. How does that sound?'

'That will be fine, thank you,' I said.

'Right, we'll see you on Wednesday,' he offered his hand.

I shook it briefly, and thanked him again and he ushered back through to the shop. Though they were busy, I could feel the eyes of the assistants on me. I gained the door and sighed with relief.

AS I walked home the interview played over in my head, the smell of the storeroom, the clipped precise tones of the man, the thick stubby fingers gripping the pencil so hard the blood drained from his ragged nails. My heart gave a little skip of joy. I had a job. I could stay in Glasgow.

'Well how did you get on?' Famie asked pouring boiling water into the teapot, and carefully covering it with a knitted tea cosy.

'I start next Wednesday in Cochrane's,' I said excitedly.

'That's great. What's the wage?' she asked.

I stared at her. I didn't know. I had forgotten to ask.

'Yer mammy will no' be happy about that,' Famie warned.

'I know, but I can't go back and ask. I'm too scared.'

'Well it is either that or facin' yer mammy.'

'I'll leave it. She said if I got a job I could stay. I've got a job.'

'Oh well, it is up to you. Pass me your cup and we'll have some tea,' Famie said.

'I think I'll go and see Lena. She must be wondering where I am and she doesn't know about the job thing.'

'Well make sure you're back before it gets dark,' Famie said offering a plate of scones.

I nodded and selected one with plump raisins. It was fresh from the oven.

As I jumped off at the old familiar bus stop Lena spotted me from the window, and by the time I had crossed the street she was at the close mouth.

'Where have you been? I expected you ages ago,' she said.

I poured out the whole story as we climbed the stairs.

'Mammy really said you could stay in Glasgow?'

'Yes, it was a big surprise to me too.'

'I know she has been very worried about you.'

'Worried about me? Are you sure?'

'Of course, that place sounds awful.'

'You don't know just how awful,' I said.

The table was set for tea; it had the air of waiting, the sandwiches beginning to curl at the edges, the jam roll drying.

'I'm sorry I kept you waiting.'

'Doesn't matter you're here now, tell me all your news,' Lena lit the gas under the kettle.

'Have you heard from Betty?' I asked.

'No, she has written to mammy, but not to me.'

'I didn't know she had written to mammy. Recently?'

'Yes, I thought mammy might have said,' Lena poured the tea.

'She tells me nothing, they treat me like a little girl.'

'Maybe she doesn't want to worry you.'

'Is there something to worry about? Has something happened to Betty?'

'Everything is fine,' Lena smiled.

'See you won't tell me either,' I protested.

'There is nothing to know,' Lena said, 'why don't you go round and see your old pals. I am sure they would be pleased to see you.'

As I climbed the stairs to Mary Murray's house I wondered what I would find. We were all older now, things had changed for me and they would have changed for them too.

It was Mary who answered my knock and she stood back in surprise, 'Oh it's you,' she said, 'Come in.'

'I just thought I would see you while I was through,' I felt strangely uncomfortable.

I followed her into the kitchen. Nothing had changed; it was still dirty and untidy. She nodded towards the saggy settee and I sat down, watching her. She wore a flowery silk dressing gown, her hair was caught up in a scarlet scarf whose long fringed ends reached to her feet, her face was heavily made up with some deep bronze foundation, the scarlet of her lips matched the scarlet of the scarf and her eyes were outlined in dark khol.

She stood on tip-toe and peered into the smeared mirror above the mantelpiece, touched her eyebrows briefly and frowned.

'You look different,' I said.

'Ah've joined Scottish Ballet and changed ma name,' she peered closer, bared her teeth and rubbed away a smudge of lipstick.

She looked at me, 'Ah always wanted to be a dancer, remember?'

'Yes, and you made it, so what's your name now?'

'Miranda.'

'Miranda! So is that only for the Ballet or do you use it all the time?'

'A' the time, well ma mammy an' daddy still call me Mary, so does Jenny.'

'Right, so how is Jenny?'

'Still tryin' tae be a singer. She is in some choir, don't know the name.'

'That's nice,' I said.

'Want a cup o' tea?'

'Eh, yes, OK.'

'Right ah'll put the kettle on.'

I watched her fill the kettle and light the gas, the long scarf swung dangerously close to the flame, and suddenly I remembered the time years ago when the house really did go on fire, and the neighbour downstairs had rescued them.

Mary's dad had arrived just as the emergency was over, had been interviewed by a reporter and appeared on the front page as a hero.

It was my first experience of how a news reporter could twist the truth to make a better story.

Mary and Jennifer had been in the house alone when somehow the fire had broken out. Their screams had alerted the neighbours, one dashing upstairs fighting his way into the house, first bringing out Jennifer, handing her over to willing hands and then going back in for Mary. It took some time to carry the frightened girls down the three flights of stairs, but as they emerged from the close the waiting crowd cheered, clustering round as the girls were swaddled in blankets. I saw again in my mind's eye the harrowing photograph of the two next day. Both were suffering from Impetigo at the time and had their heads shaved, so it was a heartrending picture as they stood swathed in blankets, hairless and black faced. The story told how Mr. Murray had ranted and fought with the firemen to get to his girls, the brave father ready to sacrifice his life for his children. The real hero of the hour was mentioned as someone who helped.

The kettle boiled and Mary reached over to lift it from the gas.

'Careful!' I shouted.

'It's a' right!' she laughed.

As we drank our tea she filled me in about the others. Alex 'Flash' Gordon was that very week about to set sail for a new life in Philadelphia. The news was no real surprise as he had always wanted to live in America. Tommy who had helped me carry the buckets of Blancmange to Eugene had gone to live in Easterhouse, one of the new housing schemes which were springing up around the city.

There was news of others too, all either gone away, or working in the city.

'So, are you happy in the Ballet, have you performed on stage?'

'Oh aye, maistly in the chorus. They say ah still need tae lose a bit o' weight,' Mary said.

'Well as long as you are happy,' I said lamely.

I told her about getting the job in Cochrane's the Grocer; it seemed very tame compared to the Ballet.

'You were gonnae go tae the Uni,' Mary said.

'That was a long time ago, things happen.'

'Aye like yer faither havin' a fling wi' yon wummin.'

I stared at her.

She shrugged, 'Och it wis a long time ago, as ye say.'

I stood up knowing I no longer belonged here. We had been close as little girls, but that time was gone.

As we stood at the door saying our goodbyes, Mary swung the scarf behind her and clutched her dressing gown.

'Well, see ye again sometime.'

'Yes, see you again,' I said.

I arrived back at Niddrie Mains in the dark; Ada was not expecting me and immediately thought something dreadful had happened.

'Is Lena ill? What's wrong?' she asked.

'Gie the lassie a chance tae tell ye,' Eugene said.

I told them what had happened.

'So you really did get a job,' Ada said.

'Mammy you said I could,' I watched her face and I knew she had expected me to fail.

'Fine, fine, it's the best thing that could happen. We a' hiv tae move on,' Eugene said.

'So you are leaving tomorrow morning and that is that,' Ada said.

'Auntie Famie says she will have my room ready,' I said.

'I see,' Ada said.

'Mammy? It is all right isn't it?'

'Aye, aye, of course,' Eugene said.

My eyes were on Ada.

'Yes it is fine, it is not the kind of job I would want for you, but it will do for now,' Ada said.

I felt I had let her down.

As I packed my things, Eugene followed me into the room and sat on the bed.

'Ah mean tae work on yer mammy tae try to get her tae move tae Famie's, fur us a' tae move tae Famie's,' he said.

'Oh daddy, I don't think she will.'

'Well we cannae stay here fur ever. That wee wummin will drive us a' tae drink.'

I laughed.

I loved the job. There was never a dull moment, shinning up and down the short ladder to fetch what the customer wanted, weighing out the sugar and tipping the huge scoop of the scale into blue paper bags, blue for sugar and brown for eggs. These were the same bags Da-dee had smoothed and folded so carefully to save. Behind the counter at eye level row upon row of biscuit tins sat open to display the layers of biscuits.

These were sold by quarter and half pound weights and the tin at the end was reserved for broken biscuits sold to children in penny and half-penny bags. Just before closing women would come asking for cracked eggs, or ends of ham. These, always at a knock down price, would provide a meal for a family. On Fridays the ham bones were sold, ham hough which would make soup and then sandwiches.

The women fought over these, jockeying for a place in the queue. It was first come first served and children would be sent to book a place as early as five or six o'clock in the morning.

All the sides of ham had to be boned and rolled. I found to my horror that I was expected to learn how to do this. Pulling a face I told the manager that I was a vegetarian and could not touch a dead animal.

He gave a look and said, 'don't be daft lassie, there is no such thing in Bridgeton.'

Soon I became an expert at boning and rolling, and found I liked doing it, it was bearable because there was no blood.

Once boned and rolled, I would hoist the thing over my shoulder, carry it through the back and climb the ladder to hang it with the others. It became second nature.

One thing I didn't like was the smell that lingered on my skin.

The relationship between Joe and Famie was more like mother and son than husband and wife. She waited on him hand and foot granting his every wish. He would thank her in a little baby voice, which startled me the first time I heard it, but mindful of the stern advice from agony aunt 'Ruth Martin' I decided the way they behaved towards each other was none of my business. I said nothing of all this to Eugene and Ada when I visited, but could not help wondering what they would make of it if they came to stay with Famie.

Famie seem to regard my living under her roof as a God given opportunity to ensure I booked my place in heaven by going to devotions twice a week and regular confession. On Sundays we would attend mass at The Sacred Heart and then walk to Dalbeth Cemetery where Famie would tend the family grave, trimming the grass and placing fresh flowers. She would talk as she worked telling all the family news, saying I was present and inviting me to speak. On the way home we would have hot peas and vinegar, and buy a carton of ice cream to take away to have later with tinned peaches. Joe was often absent from these outings. Famie would find a note propped against the teapot saying he would be late and 'wee mammy' should not wait up.

Often it would be late evening the next day before he would return. He would offer no explanation and Famie would never ask for one, and would place a meal before him with a sweet smile, clearly only too pleased to have him home. He would stretch and yawn, asking her to ease off his boots and bring a stool for his feet.

I would excuse myself and vanish into the room to listen to the radio. Later Famie would bring me tea and say fondly that Joe had nodded off. It was a tiny little house with a square kitchen and a long narrow room. Famie kept it like a new pin, even though she worked full time. She was fussy about her clothes and personal hygiene, as was I and there was much boiling of kettles and carrying of basins of hot water into the room where we would take it in turns to wash. Famie had a full set of false teeth, which she placed each night in a tumbler of water to which she added a generous helping of household bleach. In the morning after much rinsing with cold water she would turn from the sink and flash a brilliant smile. Joe did not approve of the bleach, he would warn that she was damaging her 'innards' but she would shrug and bare her teeth to show how white they were.

He was fussy about his own teeth and would scrub them day and night with Colgate toothpaste swearing it was the finest of them all.

He liked clean smart clothes, and Famie kept up an unending supply of crisply laundered shirts and well pressed trousers.

Joe was corpulent and spent much time in the Turkish baths.

I missed Rover very much and tried to get through every other weekend. Ada had written that she was concerned about him and I wondered what to expect as the train chugged its way to Waverley.

Eugene would usually bring Rover to meet me from the train, but on this occasion Eugene was alone.

'Where's Rover?'

'Ach he's no that great. Yer mammy thought it better tae leave him.'

He gave me a sharp look then took my bag from me and led the way out to Princes Street to the tram stop.

Eugene sat hugging my bag on his lap and stared out the window all the way. Rover was at the door to greet me and he seemed animated enough but when I got him into the light I was shocked at how thin he was, his eyes had a sadness in them and his coat had lost its lustre.

'What has happened to him?'

'I don't know. He is not the dog he was that's for sure. We have had him to the vet, but they didn't give any real answers,' Ada said.

'Did they give him anything?'

'Yes some pills, but they don't seem to be doing much good,' Ada said. 'Cost a bob or two, as well,' Eugene said.

'He is worth it, though God knows we don't have much,' Ada said.

I fussed over him but after a while he lay down, head on paws, looking really exhausted.

'Ah think he is just missin' you,' Eugene said.

'I miss him too. I need to take him back with me.'

'You better ask Famie and Joe first,' Ada said.

'It will only delay things, it will be fine and Famie knows I love him.'

'Well if you are sure,' Ada said.

Famie and Joe accepted the dog without comment and for a while Rover seemed to rally. I spent all the time I could with him, but as the weeks went by he began to fail, his appetite was gone and with it his strength.

Soon I had to carry him up and down the stairs when we went out. A further visit to the vet confirmed cancer.

'It would be kinder to let him go,' the vet advised.

I shook my head. I couldn't do it. Two weeks later Eugene, through on a visit, took one look at Rover and said, 'he needs puttin' oot o' his misery.'

He hoisted Rover onto his shoulders.

'Come on,' Eugene said to me.

'Daddy no, I can't.'

'Eh you want him to suffer like this? You are no' bein' kind. It's cruel tae let him go on like this.'

'Yer daddy is right,' Famie said.

'Ye can stay or come, it's up tae you, but ah'm takin' him now,' Eugene said.

We walked all the way to the vet. Rover lay unmoving, only his eyes told that he knew what was happening.

I held him close, his soft brown eyes on my face, full of trust. The vet took over laying him gently down on the table. He undid the collar and handed it to Eugene who passed it to me. Rover sighed. I kissed him and turned away.

We walked home in silence. I clutched the collar that was still warm from Rover's body.

'Eh it was for the best. Ye can get another dog, they say that is the best thing,'

Eugene said.
I couldn't answer.

CHAPTER 34

I recognized Ada's handwriting on the envelope as I handed the letter to Famie. She stood reading it carefully then looked up with a smile.
'They want to move through here. Eadie's asking if the offer is still open.'
'It is a lot to ask of you Auntie Famie.'
'It is what families do, anyway it was me that made the offer, though ah didn't think Eadie would ever agree. We a' know how proud she is,' Famie spoke without malice.
'When are they coming?'
'If your daddy gets this job he is after, they could be here within the week.'
'Good,' I said, though my heart sank. I wanted my family around me, but I had got used to solitude. It was going to be so crowded in that narrow room. Famie read my thoughts.
'It will be a tight squeeze but Eadie says Eugene is trying to find a house for them, so we will all have to make the best of things meanwhile.'
Eugene had gone back to Toffolo Jackson the firm he had worked for so long ago. They took him on to lay a floor at the Savoy Cinema in Glasgow, one of the cinemas he had supplied with choc ices. He was hoping there would be more work to come.
The day Ada moved in, she sat on the soft upholstered couch and wept. It was such a contrast from the bare floorboards, broken down chairs and curtainless windows of Niddrie Mains.
'Eh what's the matter noo?' asked the ever tactless Eugene. It was impossible for tempers not to fray in that overcrowded space, we were literally climbing over each other.
Ada's repeated resolve not to complain deserted her and soon she was begging Eugene to go with her to find somewhere to live. Though she tried to avoid Joe as much as possible it was clear neither of them had any love for the other. It took over a month before a house was found; the only snag was it was not for rent but for sale. It was unheard of for a tenement flat to be for sale but it seemed it was a growing trend. Eugene bargained with the factor to rent the flat with the option to buy once finances were a bit more secure. So we moved to Garfield Street in Dennistoun, a room and kitchen with a tiny but very welcome inside lavatory.
Once again Ada and Eugene had the recess bed in the kitchen and Aggie and I shared the bed settee in the little room. Ada could not wait to be reunited with her precious sideboard again which had stood swathed in blankets in the cafe cellar in Charing cross and its arrival along with the piano and the writing desk was a real cause for celebration. The bad old days were behind us, this was a new start. Eugene put his fingers to his lips and tip-toed out the door and I followed to watch as he screwed the nameplate to the door which honestly proclaimed Cocozza.
'Well, here we are, settled,' he beamed as we sat at our first meal in the house.
'Well so far so good,' Ada said, suspicious of good fortune.
'Eh what can go wrong?' asked Eugene, 'what is the use of worrying. If you

worry you die and if you don't worry you die, so why worry?'
Ada threw her hands up in despair, and shook her head.

Aggie signed on at the Labour Exchange and was found a job at the grandly named Bellgrove Hotel, which was in effect a hostel for homeless men. She was in her element as the place was a hotbed of gossip. Soon she was regaling us with accounts of the sins and intrigues of her workmates, her vivid imagination embroidering the facts.

She had made a friend of one woman in particular who seemed a cross between a seer and a saint and Aggie hung on her every word, till Ada demanded to know if this woman jumped off the Central Bridge would Aggie follow suit.

Aggie's eyes would dance and a slight blush would stain her cheeks, but she would say nothing.

It seemed, besides being the fount of all wisdom, that this woman's standard of cleanliness was of the highest order and hers were the whitest tea towels in the kitchen. Soon Aggie was bringing tea towels home to wash, whether in a desire to flatter her friend by copying her example, or as Eugene insisted, to rival her.

Whatever it was the ritual washing of the tea towels began and took place every night. First they would be steeped in cold water, after an hour they were wrung out and scrubbed on the washing board with Sunlight soap, rinsed and then steeped in bleach, where they would lie until just before bedtime, when they were rinsed in cold running water for what seemed an age.

The sink was right behind Eugene's fireside chair and he would sit puffing on his pipe reading his newspaper, now and then swatting at the water droplets that landed on his bald pate.

'For God sake woman, put that damn water off, ye'll rub the damn things away.'

The tea towels finally hung on the pulley to dry, Aggie would come to bed, her hands red raw, reeking of bleach and icy cold. I would cling to the edge of the bed in an effort to escape not only the frozen hands but the equally frozen feet she insisted on planting on my back each night.

I longed for a room of my own, space to experiment with make-up, to read magazines without Aggie peering over my shoulder and sniggering at the latest styles, or warning me, 'yer mammy wouldnae be pleased if she knew you were readin' thae agony letters.'

To please Ada I had left Cochrane's for an office job in the Coliseum Department Store in Jamaica Street. I worked in a little glass walled office with a rather severe spinster, who was a stickler for good timekeeping, which was not one of my strong points. However as we got to know each other and my timekeeping improved we became if not friends at least amiable colleagues.

Lena came to visit every week. She and Ada had grown very close, marriage and motherhood had blown away all the rebellion in Lena and she was a model housewife and mother. After one visit as we said our goodbyes and

Ada closed the door behind them, she came back into the kitchen and said, 'Lena is pregnant again.'
'How do you know?' I asked. Lena had looked exactly the same to me.
'I just know,' Ada said.
'Get away,' Eugene said from behind his paper.
'You mark my words, a mother knows these things,' Ada said.
'I'll get some wool the morn. What colour should ah get, pink or blue, or maybe yellow would be best?' Aggie was agog.
'Better wait till she tells us,' smiled Ada.
Ada was right, Lena was pregnant, and soon Aggie was busy with her crochet hook fashioning bootees and little cardigans.
We all looked forward to the new addition to the family.
Eugene never let up on his quest for work and once again he decided to be his own boss, a decision that filled Ada with trepidation.
'What are ye worryin' aboot woman? Ah finish a job, ah get another. You know me if there is work ah'll find it.'
'It is better to work for somebody else, that way you can put your hand out at the end of the week for a wage.'
'It'll be fine, ah know what ah'm doin'.'
I don't want to lose this house; I could never go through that again.'
'That's no goin' tae happen; I'll make sure of that.'
'I'M saying no more,' Ada waved a hand in dismissal.
To show how serious he was he got some business cards printed and spent many hours on tram journeys to the new housing estates putting his card through letter boxes with little response. He visited firm after firm offering freelance work and here he did meet with some success. He came home one day an impish grin on his face obviously very pleased about something. Ada gave him a sceptical look and we waited for him to tell us the news, instead he produced a piece of grey material and laid it proudly on the table.
'What is that?' Ada asked.
'It is magic stuff, fire proof, a' the builders are using it. It's called asbestos. Ye can stand a hot iron on that and it won't burn the table.'
'Where did you get it?' Ada asked inspecting it closely.
'I managed to get some work wi' a builder for a month or two.'
He would arrive home covered in asbestos dust and as he took off his overalls in the tiny hall, the dust would rise and settle on every surface.
'My God, you look like Pepper's ghost,' Ada would exclaim, 'I don't think that stuff can be doing you any good, you should wear a mask.'
'Not at all, it is harmless. I've brought a bit to go on the wall at the cooker, it is fine stuff. The asbestos you can get,' he would say, chuckling at his own joke.
I would sit him down and start cleaning the dust from his head. It was everywhere, in the eye sockets, clogging his nostrils, his ears and the creases of his mouth and neck. I would clean away with cotton wool and olive oil just as Lena and I used to when we were children.
He continued to work with asbestos, installing it in cafe's and chip shops. He

would put money on the table without a word, and only if Ada asked would he say if he had more work lined up. He would leave the house each morning and be out till dusk. If he was successful in gaining a job that would bring in more than usual he would rub his hands and say 'ah've seen a nice brooch, and ah'll be able tae buy it for you after this job.'

'I'm not interested in brooches, it's food on the table and the rent paid I worry about,' Ada would say dryly.

He was installing an asbestos ceiling and painting all the walls in the cafe in Glasgow Cross, the one he and I had walked to that foggy November night so long ago.

'I need to work through the night. He disnae want the shop closed for too long,' he told Ada.

The shop had a very high ceiling, so Eugene built a scaffold and set to work and once he started he worked on without a break of any kind. He seemed to forget to eat and drink; it had always been his way. On this occasion nature got the better of him and he was caught short. He was forced to climb down from the scaffold to try to clean himself up, but despite his best efforts he was still left with a tell tale brown stain on the seat of his trousers. He worked on, only coming down when he had finished. The problem was how to get home. He could not go on the tram in the state he was in and it was a long walk from Glasgow Cross to Garfield Street. He searched around and found two fairly large cardboard advertisements for Tizer and Barr's Irn-Bru, so tying one on front and one on his back he walked home, no one any the wiser, providing they did not come too close.

We heard the key in the lock and then he stuck his head round the door, saying 'don't laugh'.

We did.

Gradually life settled into a pattern, Aggie happy with her tea towels and her gossip, Ada mellowing in her attitude to Eugene, he working, or searching for work, sometimes putting two hundred pounds on the table then nothing more for six or eight weeks. With the coming of summer he went out to the affluent suburbs he had worked so many years before, and he was successful in gaining orders for patios, garages and driveways, but just as before he under-priced his work and only ever made a modest profit. Nevertheless Ada tried to squirrel away as much as she could, so when an insurance policy matured she was able to add enough to go to the landlord and ask if he would sell, and she was able to put three quarters of the asking price on the table and arrange to pay off the balance within the year.

'If we have to live off bread and cheese we will, but there will always be a roof over our heads.'

I would watch them sometimes, all three of them their lives so entwined, and a little knot of fear would form in my stomach. What did the future hold? What if something happened to Ada, how would Aggie cope? Ada was her rock. Aggie herself with all her foibles was woven into the fabric of our lives, and though I longed to be free of her constant prying I was fond of her. She loved to spend her wages buying little gifts for everyone and the house was full of little trinkets, sewing kits for Lena, and books for me. She seemed so helpless, so dependant, I could not imagine her surviving without Ada.

Lena's baby duly arrived - a boy. Aggie promptly went out to buy blue wool, and had a gift ready even before the little mite arrived home.

Garfield Street was full of ordinary people just like ourselves, but word got around that a near neighbour had broken the mould and was on her way to fame and fortune. The McLaughlin family lived only two closes away and their oldest girl Marie had changed her name to Lulu and made a record that had taken the music world by storm. Everybody was talking about Lulu and the Luvvers, and their record 'Shout'.

I did not really know Marie, but she did come to our house on one occasion, for what reason I can't remember. I remember her leaning against the sideboard her vivacious face framed by flaming red hair. Eugene, never one to miss an opportunity, tried to interest her in some songs written by an Italian acquaintance. She smiled a non-committal smile and took her leave and we never saw her again as Marie, she went on to greater things.

'Come and see what I have bought,' Eugene urged us and we followed him down the stairs and out of the close.

'What are we looking for?' Ada asked.

'This!' He stood beside a huge grey car, 'It's mine.'

'Yours?'

'Aye, ah bought it - well ah'm payin' it up. You put so much down for a deposit and....'

'I know how it works, but how are you going to pay for it?'

'It will pay for itsel'. It means ah can get round ma jobs easier an' ah'll be able tae take on more work. It is the best thing.'

'Hmm,' Ada said.

The car was a Standard Vanguard, big and roomy and soon we were being persuaded to go runs to Loch Lomond and other beauty spots. Eugene's driving was erratic and he blithely ignored the fact that the roads were much busier than the last time he had driven. As for the Highway Code - that was for other drivers - it did not apply to him. Ada was the classic back seat driver, and arming herself with a tube of Spangles, she would issue warnings of pedestrians about to step into the road, or the car behind threatening to overtake.

Eugene would dodge and weave over the road, saying testily, 'Quiet woman, ah know what ah'm doin'.'

Arriving home nerves shattered, Ada would swear she would never ride in the car again, only to set out at the weekend on another jaunt.

'Why don't we go to Hawick and look up your sister again?' persuaded Eugene.

It was late summer, but the weather was foul. We set out for Hawick but it soon became clear that we had lost our way in the driving rain. Eugene was reluctant to turn for home, 'we came for a day oot and we should make the best o' it.'

'Well we could go and visit Tammy Norrie and his wife; they live quite near here down by the river. The river was the Tweed, and it was in spate. Eugene pressed on under Ada's nervous direction and we arrived to find the quaintly named Tammy Norrie trying to keep the water at bay with sandbags round his door. When Ada said they lived near the river she was right, it ran only feet from their door. Tammy and his wife were lovely people and insisted we stay for a cup of tea. While we sat chatting, Eugene set to helping Tammy pile the sandbags. As a precaution the car was parked some distance away, safe according to Eugene from any threat from the rising water. It was dusk before we rose to go, finding to our horror we had to wade through inches of water to reach the car, Ada was all for leaving it and splashing our way to the nearest bus stop and then to find a B&B. Eugene would have none of it, and they stood arguing the point, and as the heavens suddenly opened we quickly piled into the car.

Eugene began to creep cautiously along the river bank, but it was hard to tell where the bank ended and the river began. As the waters swirled and rose higher and higher, Ada began to panic.

'Stop the car, stop the car, we'll all be drowned.'

'Don't be daft woman, where are you going to go?'

'Just stop the car. We will end up in the river. Stop right now!'

He stopped, 'Now what?' he asked.

'Get out, we all need to get out,' she grabbed Eugene and tried to pull him over to the passenger side but he refused to move.

'I'm fine, leave me be.'

Ada leaned over and released the back door, 'Get out as quick as you can,' she urged and Aggie and I scrambled out.

The water reached almost to our knees and Ada splashed out after us staring in consternation at Eugene still crouched over the wheel.

'Will you come out?' she shouted, her voice rising in panic.

For answer Eugene started up the engine and crawled along the riverbank disappearing into the gloom.

'Mammy he'll drown,' I screamed.

'Hell mend him,' she snapped.

By now he had really disappeared. We were wet through, the rain unrelenting.

Ada splashed forward in the direction Eugene had taken.

'Are we going to find him, mammy?'

'Of course, we need to make the old fool see sense,' she flung over her shoulder.

We caught up with him, the car stalled.

'Well are you coming out now?'

'No fear, ah'm no leavin' the car, we'll never get another one.'

'You would put that thing before your own life?'

'Ma life isnae in any danger. Ye always see disasters women, away ye a' go and find somewhere dry, ah'm stayin' right here.'

We trailed miserably away, finding shelter where we could, and at last reaching the town, we found a B&B.

The morning brought a brighter day, a weak sun shone in a patchy blue sky. We set out to find Eugene not knowing what to expect. The car had not moved very far from where we left him and he was stretched out on the back seat fast asleep.

As we drove home, Ada reminded him of the risk he had taken and she swore she would never let him drive her on a trip again.

Eugene hunched over the wheel told her not to be daft, anyway he was not responsible for the rain.

Ada's threats were just that, within days Eugene had persuaded her to let him drive her to Southampton in answer to a tearful letter from Betty that all was not well.

Aggie declined to go with them, and she, Lena and I stood hearts in mouth waving them off.

Ada armed with her thermos flask and packets of Spangles sat tense and white-knuckled in the passenger seat.

Three days later a postcard arrived saying Ada would be returning by train and requesting that someone meet her at the station.

We felt sure there was a tale to tell and we were right.

Ada had acted as map reader, but Eugene had never agreed with her reading. They had got hopelessly lost and exhausted by the long journey, had stopped for the night, having no real idea where they were. Next morning Ada woke with a strange smell in her nostrils and something rough licking her face. She opened her eyes to stare into the large brown eyes of a cow, the rough tongue sandpapering her cheek.

Her yells of alarm failed to rouse Eugene who snored blissfully on.

Pushing with all her might she tried to get the cow out of the window, but it gazed back at her completely unfazed.

She dug Eugene in the ribs, yelling in his ear. He sat up, gazed about him and lay back again.

'Help me get this thing out of here,' Ada shouted.

'Eh?'

'This cow, I woke up with it licking my face.'

'Get away,' he stumbled out of the car and pushed the cow away, 'there it's away, nae bother.'

'It was your fault for leaving the window down.'

'Eh, we needed a bit o' air.'

Eugene arrived home in solitary splendour, beaming all over his face.

'So you found you way back,' Ada said dryly.

'Aye, nae bother, nae bother at a',' he grinned.

For many months the health of King George VI has been a real cause for concern. The King had cancer and had undergone a lung operation. By the end of January he was pictured saying farewell to Princess Elizabeth and the Duke of Edinburgh as they set off for a tour of Kenya. It was clear to all that the King was very ill indeed and he died in his sleep on the night of February 6th, the Princess Elizabeth was now Queen.

George VI was much loved. He and his Queen had endeared themselves to the nation by choosing to stay and see the war out, they had lived by the rationing and fuel restrictions as the people had and now he was dead. The war was over though its effect was still being felt. The passing of the King ushered in a new era, the King was dead, long live the Queen.

The sight of the bereaved Elizabeth dressed in black descending the steps of the airplane to be greeted as Sovereign by Churchill and Attlee touched everyone.

In the coming days and weeks the preparation for a state funeral and then a Coronation would go ahead, amid a heated debate as to the proper title of Elizabeth. Undoubtedly she was Elizabeth the second in England, but there was a groundswell of opinion that she was Elizabeth the first in Scotland.

When the argument was lost, Ada was furious, finding it difficult to reconcile her loyalty to the Monarch and her fervent loyalty to Scotland. Other events much nearer home claimed her attention, and touched Eugene deeply. Tommy had been rushed to hospital with what was eventually diagnosed as a malignant brain tumour. There was nothing that could be done and three days later he was dead.

Gerald his son was only two years old.

Apart from a trust fund set up for his son's education, all of Tommy's wealth went to Carol.

Yet in the days and months that followed his death she became closer to the family. Tina, Famie and Lizzie gave her all the support they could, Ada too acknowledged Carol's loneliness and welcomed her frequent visits.

Betty wrote to Ada begging to come home, things were bad and she needed time out.

'She needs tae learn tae sort oot her own troubles, she cannae keep runnin' back tae her mammy every time they have a spat,' Eugene ventured.

'You're right,' Ada agreed, but still wrote to Betty saying she could come.

There was little enough room as it was but when Betty and the little one arrived we were really pushed for space. Betty took my place in the bed while I and the little one slept at the bottom.

For some time I had been feeling unwell and was finally persuaded to visit the doctor. There seemed to be a problem with my kidneys and I was admitted to hospital for tests. At least it solved the overcrowded sleeping arrangements. Betty would visit keeping me up to date with all the preparations for the Coronation, which was causing great excitement as it was going to be televised.

'Daddy is going to buy a television set,' Betty told me.

'Does mammy know?' I asked knowing Eugene's habit of springing surprises.

'Yeh, she is fine about it, but she is not too happy about him inviting all the neighbours in to watch on the day,' Betty laughed.

'I hope I get home in time to see it,' I said.

I was discharged days before the event. The newspapers were full of stories of the future Queen, songs were being written in her honour and every day Vera Lynn could be heard warbling on the radio-

In a golden couch there's a heart of gold
driving through old London town.
With the sweetest Queen the world's ever seen
wearing a diamond crown.

As she rides in state, through the palace gate
her beauty the whole world can see.
In a golden coach there's a heart of gold
That belongs to you and me.

Betty had decorated the windows with red white and blue streamers and she put red white and blue ribbons in not only her little daughter's hair but her own too.

On the great day itself the house was crowded each one stretching to see the tiny screen.

Days later in response to an impassioned letter from John, Betty decided to go home. We saw her off at the station, and as we smiled and waved we wondered what the coming days would hold for her. We knew we had not seen the last of her.

For me the days that followed were filled with a strange depression. I felt life was passing me by. I was full of vague longings that I could not put into words, not that Ada or Eugene would have listened. Now that I was older the aunts were less vigilant about my Catholic duties, though they did ask for reassurance from time to time that I was fulfilling my obligations to the church.

The truth was that I had become lax about going to mass, I had taken to reading about other religions and had ended up with more unanswered questions, so when one Sunday morning I opened the door to an elderly Jehovah's Witness I was in the mood to listen to what she had to say.

Soon I had agreed to a bible study and to begin with Ada and Aggie joined in, though Aggie found the whole thing hard going. Ada did attend the odd meeting with me, and agreed to attend the assembly that was to be held in nearby St. Andrews halls, (later destroyed by fire).

The main speaker gave a rousing speech outlining God's plan for humanity. He promised a new World Order that would sweep away all mankind's troubles and sorrows. It was just what I wanted to hear, I longed for the day to come. Soon I had agreed to be baptized as a Witness, eager to fully embrace the teachings Phyllis my mentor had taught me.

Ada was more cautious, she felt the witnesses were good people but was unsure if they held all the answers. Eugene thought the whole thing was nonsense.

'People make the world the way it is, yer mammy and me hiv made a new world fur oorsels, we came back thegither and that is a new world,' he declared and would not hear otherwise.

Ada decided she would come with me one morning as I went round the doors witnessing, not because she believed in the message but because she could not believe that I would have the courage to knock on doors and witness.

Finding the courage was harder than she knew, but it helped that I really believed what I was saying. I really did not like the 'witnessing' work; four out of five doors were slammed in my face. The work did have its lighter moments.

The theme of the message we were trying to get over to people was the state of the planet, the sorry state of mankind and God's solution. Most people on a Sunday morning were barely awake, having just tumbled out of bed often after a heavy night. One witness confronted by a huge unshaven man in a dirty vest, who stood scratching his groin, nervously asked him if he had considered the state of the earth that morning.

He stopped scratching for a moment and stared at her. She repeated the question, 'have you considered the state of the earth this morning?'

'Naw, ah hivnae been oot the back at a',' he grunted and slammed the door.

Ada took the news of my intended baptism calmly, the aunts were horrified.

'You have been Christened in the Catholic church, you can't turn your back on that,' Famie protested.

'It is what I want, I have to do this.' I could hardly believe I was telling her this.

The 'immersion' was some weeks, set to take place at an Assembly to be held in Coatbridge in the autumn of 1955. As the date drew nearer, Ada became agitated, and now and then I would interrupt a conversation between her and Eugene, she seemed troubled, he dismissive. Always the conversation would come to an abrupt halt as I entered the room, or they would lapse into Italian. I became uneasy, it was just like the old days and I began to worry that the 'fresh start' they had made was losing its appeal.

One day they rose early as did Aggie. There was a flurry of activity as they washed and dressed in their best clothes and they left the house without any explanation as to where they were going. I couldn't bring myself to ask, and resigned myself to wait till the 'bomb' dropped. When it did it was the last thing I expected.

The usual Wednesday bible study hour was over, and as Phyllis rose to collect her bag and gloves, she put a gentle hand on my shoulder and said, 'I believe your parents were married last week. I am so pleased. Did you all have a nice day?'

I stared at her not knowing what she was talking about. She smiled apologetically and said, 'you don't know about it, do you?'

'I — I know they went out somewhere, all three of them, but....'

'You did know they were not legally married?' she asked.

'Well, yes, I mean no, I thought there was something, I....'

She sat down and drew me down beside her.

'Perhaps you are wondering how I know? Well Brother Livingstone and myself are to be married, so we went along to the register office in Martha Street to put up the banns for our marriage, and that is where we saw the banns for your parents. I always knew things were not as they should be in this house, something in your mother's demeanour when she spoke to me and I could see she was a very honest and moral lady who was not at ease with herself.'

'And you guessed?' I was astonished.

Phyllis smiled a thin smile, 'I have been doing this work for many years, I have met all sorts of people, after a while you learn to 'read' people, you know instinctively that they are troubled, and often the cause of the trouble.'

She took my hand and held it in hers, 'I am so glad they have regulated the situation. It means you can go forward to 'Immersion' as their legitimate child.'

I stiffened, and withdrew my hand from hers.

'Would I not have been acceptable if I was still illegitimate?'

'All are acceptable in God's sight if they recognize their sinful state,' she said quietly.

'You say I was in a sinful state, but surely it was no fault of mine.'

'It is of no matter now, everything is as it should be,' she rose to go, 'I will see you next week. Pray about it and you will find peace,' she went out.

I sat for ages staring into the fire after she had gone. Of course I knew they were not legally married, I had known ever since Mary had hurled the accusation at Ada, that Friday night as I listened on the stairs, yet somehow I had pushed it to the back of my mind. Phyllis had brought all that all uncertainty back with her revelation.

That day, when the three of them had gone out not saying where they were going, that day Ada and Eugene had gone through a marriage ceremony, I remembered how they had been when they came home. Ada had a strange shuttered look on her face, and she had looked sharply at Aggie every time Aggie went to speak. Eugene had seemed pleased with himself. I had dismissed the whole thing as Ada being displeased with something that Eugene had done.

I thought again of what Phyllis had said about Ada. She was right, Ada was deeply moral and honest and she had instilled into all of us the virtues of honesty, fidelity, courage and integrity. I suddenly realized the pain all these years had caused her, being a 'common law' wife, recognized as a wife by 'habit and repute'. To a woman like her, not only moral but proud, it must have been an intolerable burden.

Yet she had lived under that strain. Why? For us her children? For love of Eugene? Surely love must have played its part in her decision to throw in her lot with this man who was already married, who no matter how dear to her was her intellectual inferior.

I remembered the hectoring tone of the letter from 'Ruth Martin' the agony aunt, whom I now knew to be Claire Raynor, lecturing that the relationship between a man and a woman held secrets known only to them. I realized she was right, I could see Ada and Eugene not just as my parents but as two people, two adults living out their lives. The halted conversations made sense to me now; it wasn't a harking back to the 'old' days. Ada was worried that because I had chosen to be baptized to become a witness and live by that strict moral code she wanted me to be 'right'. I felt a rush of gratitude towards her that she had taken such a big step on my behalf.

I had no idea if Lena knew about the marriage; I did know that if she knew she would say nothing of it to me, so I let sleeping dogs lie. Sometime afterwards I came across a photograph of Ada and Eugene seated on chairs with Aggie standing behind them. It had been taken on that day out, I could tell from the clothes they wore. Ada caught me looking at it and she said over my shoulder, 'Oh that was taken that day we went out. Your daddy took a daft notion and insisted we went to 'Jerome's' in Argyle Street'.

'It is nice. You should have waited till I was there and then we would all have been in it,' I said.

'Well, we can do that another time. It was only a daft idea of your daddy's, you know what he is like,' she laughed.

'Yes,' I handed her the photograph and she slipped it into a drawer. I felt sad that even now she could not bring herself to tell me it was a wedding photograph, and I knew she never would.

The time for my 'immersion' drew near. To my horror Aggie had knitted me a swimming costume, it was deep mauve and the legs covered almost to my knees. As modesty was of prime importance I knew it would meet with Phyllis's approval, but as I gazed at myself in the wardrobe mirror my heart sank. Eugene and Ada had decided against coming to the ceremony, so when I rose early on the Sunday morning they were still fast asleep in the recess bed. I filled a basin with warm water and carried it along with soap, towel and talcum powder into the little lavatory to have my customary daily all over wash. Dressed ready to go I nudged Ada gently to tell her I was leaving. She gazed at me sleepily and murmured 'good luck'.

Slightly miffed that she was too sleepy to be bothered I huffily told her that 'witnesses' did not believe in luck so her wish was in vain. Lining up with the other candidates for immersion I was shocked to find most of the young girls had chosen looks over modesty and looked very attractive indeed. I stood shivering miserably in my knitted mauve monstrosity and tried to look invisible. We had been advised to tuck our hair into swim caps, and here again all the girls looked fetching, while I bereft of my glasses, my eyes screwed up in an effort to see the steps down to the pool looked like a refugee from the naughty nineties. There were plenty of spectators, both lining the pool and in the gallery above and I felt all eyes were on me, whether in pity or amusement I dreaded to think.

As each person moved forward they were helped into the pool by two 'brothers' who after the name had been called dipped the person right under the water, from which he or she emerged to a 'new life' of service. Soon it was my turn. I found myself gripped firmly by my arms and guided into deeper water, quickly I was tilted back ducked under and came up spluttering wildly. As I emerged the woollen swimsuit saturated with water stretched down to my ankles, exposing my miniscule bust, (it was the only occasion I was grateful it was miniscule. A kindly 'sister' stepped forward, and throwing a large towel around me she quickly bore me away from public gaze.

My humiliation was complete; instead of the 'feeling of light' I had been promised as I rose from the water to the 'new life', there was the furious burning on my cheeks and the dripping sagging costume under the towel. To my chagrin Ada found the whole thing very amusing when I recounted the sorry tale to her later.

Eugene's one man business was ticking over quite steadily. Now and then he would recruit me to help, mostly on a Sunday after I had done my spell of witnessing. He was laying a patio for an elderly lady in Eaglesham, a pretty unspoilt village not far from the new town of East Kilbride. As we worked the lady of the house watched me fetch and carry bricks and mortar, hold the spirit level and generally act as labourer to Eugene's craftsman.

She insisted we break for a light lunch and came out with a tray of sandwiches and a pot of tea. Eugene as usual sat for all of five minutes and went back to work. I rose to follow but the lady caught my arm and said she wished to talk to me.

She asked about my job, I told her I worked in the offices of a department store. She asked if I was happy there, to which I replied 'happy enough'. It seemed she had a brother who was a partner in a stockbroking firm in Glasgow, and she felt I was just the sort of girl he was looking for to fill a vacancy.

Later, the job finished, she expressed her satisfaction, paid the asking price and as we said our goodbyes, she promised to speak to her brother about me. 'Don't build your hopes up,' Ada said when I told her.

Two weeks went by, I had heard nothing and decided to forget about it, but then a letter arrived inviting me for interview.

The firm had its premises on the ground floor of the Merchant's House in George Square. I became a reconciliation clerk, a grand name which meant I recorded the buying and selling of stocks and shares in a huge leather bound ledger. I quickly grew to love the place; it was an old fashioned office like something out of Dickens. It had a coal fire which was always kept well supplied with coal, and this was one of my tasks as the junior to fill the huge scuttle from the bunker at the end of the corridor. We sat on high stools at huge school like desks, and I soon discovered my ability to write with both hands proved to be useful as I could use each side of the ledger without changing my position on the stool.

Both partners had sons learning the business, Allan the nephew of my benefactor was tall, handsome and full of flirtatious charm. He was extremely clever and very serious about his work. The other son was shorter, chubby, feckless and full of grand schemes, his avowed aim in life was to be very rich, and he seemed to think that he would achieve this by doing as little work as possible.

I was still painfully shy; it was an ordeal to knock on the partner's door with the morning post, the walk from the door to the grand desks seemed like crossing a field. Allan must have inherited his charm from his mother as his father was a dour man of few words and struck terror in me. Ranald's father was a big bluff man who would growl 'good morning' if he passed you in the corridor. I developed a hopeless crush on the handsome Allan, who let me know he was aware of it and thought it very amusing.

I would die with embarrassment if I had to enter his office and often dithered about outside his door before getting the courage up to go in. On one occasion Ranald's father came down the corridor and found me pacing nervously up and down.

'What are you looking for girl?' he growled.

'N-Nothing sir.'

'You'll find it in the middle of a doughnut,' he said deadpan, and walked on.

Women were not allowed to enter the actual floor of the stock exchange (then) but we were allowed in the gallery from where you could see all that was going on. I was always running back and forth from the office to the exchange, and one day witnessed the 'hammering' of a firm who had

failed. It was a dramatic and sad occasion, as the hammer relentlessly struck the desk and the staff left the building.

Allan, Ranald, and their fathers came from a different social class. I would hear them talk of golf, deer stalking, grouse shooting. They owned summer homes, in the Hebrides, and in Greece.

I knew I could never hope to move in those circles.

The coming January would bring my 21st birthday. As a Witness I had renounced all such celebrations, but Ada said it was too important an occasion to miss and insisted she intended to hold a party.

She urged me to invite some of my new young friends in the organization but I knew they would not come. There were many young people in the local group, we would pop into a local cafe after meetings, and have coffee or soft drinks. Many of the girls paired off with boys, but there were very strict rules about relationships; if two young people had been going together for some time it was expected of them that they should marry and having a constant change of partner was frowned upon. I had a special friend, a girl who was about my age and she had had boyfriends but I never had. The nearest I had come to it was attracting the attentions of a rather plump bespeckled, earnest young man who had been a Witness since boyhood. He insisted on walking me home and turning up at my door on Saturday nights to read his excruciatingly bad poems.

I had no interest in him whatsoever, but did not know how to get rid of him. My friend suggested that she could ask her brother to pretend to be my boyfriend, she felt sure my earnest suitor would get the message. There was several things wrong with this plan. I heartily disliked her brother, he had worked his way through nearly every girl in the group except me, he was arrogant and conceited, all of which she cheerfully conceded, but still insisted on going ahead with her plan.

I pointed out to her that it was unlikely her brother would agree, and even if he did, it was even more unlikely that anyone would believe he and I were going out together.

To my surprise he said yes to the daft plan, and agreed to come to the party. The party held another surprise, Eugene had tracked down Dario Benedetti my schoolboy hero. I had not seen him since as a twelve year old he had left St. Alphonsus to go to live in Edinburgh. Now here he was, tall, with dark Italian good looks. He had brought along his accordion and his very pretty Italian wife. The aunts were delighted to see my supposed boyfriend, and they teased me all night saying the next party would be an engagement party. I had to go along with all this, how could I tell them the truth of the situation, or the fact that the 'boyfriend' in question had made it very clear that he never got serious about a girl and would never, ever, marry.

Stung by this arrogance I had replied that if I ever married it most certainly never be with anyone like him.

Despite all this undercurrent the party went with a swing, mainly due to Dario's expertise on the accordion. Tina was in great form, dancing around wiggling her hips as Carmen Miranda, and she was one of the last to leave, and went down the stair arm in arm with Famie and Lizzie still singing.

It was only a few weeks later that she was diagnosed with breast cancer. She remained in hospital for some weeks and then was sent home at her own request. It was 1956 and there was no real hope that she would beat this thing.

Lena was devastated. She held Tina so dear, and despite her growing family spent as much time as she could helping to nurse Tina. We all did what we could but it was clear Tina was sinking fast. Pat just could not cope and would disappear for hours on end, and when he did return he would shut himself in his 'glory hole' as Ada termed it.

As she neared the end, and the priest came to give the last rights, Pat left the house. He was not seen again till a week after the funeral.

Lena and Ada were furious, though Ada said she was not surprised at his behaviour. I felt a little sorry for him; it had all been too much for him to take. I asked Ada how she thought he would cope on his own, but she shrugged and said she did not care what happened to him.

Lena said she never wanted to hear his name mentioned again, and so it was to be. Two years after Tina died he turned up at our door a shabby unkempt figure with long matted hair. He stood twisting his greasy soft hat nervously between dirt ingrained fingers.

'Eadie will ye let me in? Ah need tae talk tae ye,' he mumbled.

Ada's bark was always worse than her bite; she stood aside and motioned him to come in.

'If you have come for money you are wasting your time,' she said.

He stood just inside the door, shuffling his feet, eyes downcast.

'Ah'm in a spot o' bother, ah've goat rent arrears, they are gonnae evict me and ah will hiv naewhere tae go.'

'So you do want money. I told you, I don't have any,' Ada said.

'Naw, it's no' that, it is jist that you hiv always been good at talkin' tae legal folk an' ah wondered if ye would talk tae them fur me, ask them tae gie me a chance.'

I felt really sorry for him. I thought of Tina who had loved him even though he treated her so badly. If she had been standing there she would have said as she always did to excuse him, 'ah man's a man for a' that'.

I looked at Ada wondering if she was thinking that too. She looked at me and then back to Pat and I could see she was thinking of Tina, I knew she was going to help him for her sake.

'I will do what I can. You better sit down and tell me the whole story.'

She did help him, negotiating him a move to a small flat in the Saltmarket and getting an agreement to pay off the arrears at a small sum each week.

He came back to tell her he had made the move and everything was working out, he wanted her to know how grateful he was.

'I did it for Comar Tina's memory. She was the best friend you ever had.'

'Aye ah know,' he said.

We never saw him again.

The newspapers were full of the forthcoming Christian Crusade that was due to be held in the Kelvin Hall. The famous American Evangelist Billy Graham was coming to town. He had been sweeping through the country calling people to Jesus, and thousands had heeded the call at his rallies. The office was agog with the news that Ranald intended to go to see Billy Graham and there was much teasing of him that he would convert.

'Don't be daft. I am only going out of curiosity,' he assured us all. The persuasive powers of Billy Graham were great and Ranald was no match for him. When at the end of a rousing speech Graham invited all people to 'give themselves to Jesus' by walking to the front of the podium, Ranald found himself following the crowd and pledging his life to God and Jesus.

'But you have never been in a church since you were a kid,' Allan challenged him.

'I know, but something made me get to my feet and sign that declaration'.

I decided to watch how he behaved to see if he really had changed his ways. I hoped too to get into a discussion with him about the 'Truth' which I followed. The chance came one night when we were working late. He and I got into a deep discussion about the bible, by the end of which he declared himself ready to 'jump ship' and join the Witnesses.

On recounting all this to Phyllis she warned me that Ranald sounded to her like a 'religious grasshopper', who merrily hopped from one faith to the next but had no real commitment.

She was to be proved right. One evening when we had finished work he stood elbows resting on my desk and quizzed me about the promised new world. I told him all I knew. He seemed impressed then asked, 'what about sex?'

Since even at twenty-one my sexual knowledge was one of complete ignorance, I was to say the least nonplussed by his question.

'What do you mean exactly?' I asked.

'Will there be sex in this 'new world?' he grinned.

'I-I am not sure, the bible says there will be no male and no female, so I don't think there will be sex. Anyway you won't need it you will be happy and immortal, living for ever and knowing God.'

His face fell, 'Oh I don't fancy that. What is the use of living forever if there

is no sex?'
I repeated my explanation, by this time most of the staff had gathered round and were finding it hard to keep straight faces.

Ranald stood up and shrugged, 'No, sorry, it's not for me. I think I need to keep looking. I mean a man has to have some pleasures.' He lifted his coat, swung it over his shoulder and walked to the door, then looked back and said with a grimace. 'Not that I get a lot of sex you understand. No, more's the pity, but I would like to know there was always a possibility right?' he gave a broad wink and closed the door quietly behind him.

I found it hard to 'witness' in the office after that.

Ranald was really a nice guy under all his bombast. He came to me at the end of the year with two tickets for his amateur dramatic club's production of 'The Quaker Girl'. I hadn't the heart to remind him that I did not celebrate Christmas, so I went along with one of the other girls in the office and enjoyed a wonderful show.

It reawakened my interest in the theatre, an activity that was not exactly encouraged within the 'Witness' movement.

Meanwhile I was still going out with my 'pretend' boyfriend, though the poet had long given up on me. Neither of us would admit that the 'pretend' phase had passed and we were enjoying each other's company.

That summer there had been a climate of real fear in Glasgow, there was a serial killer on the loose and the newspapers were full of the horrific details of his murders. We all lived in fear and he seemed to operate with impunity. We found ourselves watching men on the bus and looking over our shoulder as we walked down the street. Ada would be waiting at the bus stop to walk me down Garfield street to our close.

At last the police got their man - Peter Manual - who was arrested in the Woodend Bar at Garrowhill. He was tried convicted and sentenced to death.

His expressionless face stared out at us from the front pages. There was a strange atmosphere on the day of execution. Not one of us would have freed him, but we were grateful it did not fall to us to put the noose round his neck.

Though I was baptized into the Witness faith I found the life quite difficult. The injunction to 'be in the world but not part of it' was one that Jesus himself had given, subsequently it lay on all Christians whether Witness or not. Yet the Witnesses took it more seriously than most. As someone who throughout my childhood felt excluded from the 'normal' life of others, who felt there were rules to living that I had not mastered, the 'apartness' of the Witnesses should have been familiar to me and easy to follow, yet I found it just the opposite.

The role of women in the Organization was one of subservience to men. The apostle Paul's law 'I do not permit a woman to teach' was followed to the letter so only 'brothers' gave talks. The husband was the head of the family and wives were required to acknowledge them as such and obey by their decisions.

I had always bowed to authority, it had been the teaching at school, it had been the example that Ada set, yet I began to question the role of women in particular in the Organization. I could plainly see there were very intelligent women married to ineffectual men, but these far from smart men made all the decisions that affected not only themselves but their wives, children, and in many cases their female relatives.

As time went on I found this increasingly hard to take, but told myself that it was heresy to think like this and that I must be wrong.

I tentatively revealed my feelings to Phyllis and she lost no time in setting me straight.

'It is not for you to question the teachings of the bible, you need to acquire humility and understanding,' she scolded.

I resolved to try, but the doubts lingered on. After eighteen months of going out together I found myself accepting a proposal of marriage, and gazing in wonder at the engagement ring that had been slipped on my finger. I could not wait to get home to tell Ada the news. She was standing before the little mirror by the sink brushing her hair when I burst into the kitchen with my exciting news. In one swift movement she turned and hurled the hairbrush at my head hitting me above the eye.

'You will marry that lad over my dead body. Take that ridiculous ring off your finger and give it back to him.'

I dabbed at the cut above my eye and stared at her in disbelief.

She put her finger and thumb together and shook it in my face, 'You are just a silly girl who has had her head turned by that one, he is not for you, he is far too fond of himself to care for you or anyone else.'

I turned and fled into the room slamming the door behind me.

1 heard Eugene's key in the lock, and later Aggie coming home, but still I stayed in the room my eyes red from the tears that I could not stop.

Eugene came through, 'Come an' get your supper,' he said.

'I don't want anything.'

'Come on, don't be daft, ye need tae eat,' he held the door open.

Reluctantly I took my place at the table; Ada poured the tea but said nothing. Eugene reached over and examined the ring.

'Aye, very nice, an' no before time. Ah was beginnin' tae think we would have an old maid on our hands.'

I fled back to the room, my cheeks burning with shame.

The next day my prospective mother-in-law appeared at the door. Ada invited her in and they talked quietly in the kitchen before coming through to speak to me.

His mother came straight to the point, 'Your mother is not happy about the engagement, and neither am I. He is my son but I know he isn't right for you, he is too selfish, he will break your heart. You are too quiet a lassie for him, I want you to give back the ring and forget about him.'

Ada nodded in agreement, 'It is for the best, some day you will thank us,' she said.

I refused to answer them and eventually they left me alone.

'What was I to do? I did not want to break off the engagement. I did not believe he was not the right one for me.

A week later as he walked me to the bus stop he asked for the ring back. He told me his mother did not approve of me as I was Italian, 'Why can't you marry one of your own kind, she is too quiet, a nice enough wee lassie but strange'.

I felt totally humiliated and I could not wait to get on the bus, though the tears blinded me.

Ada read my face, glanced at my hand but said nothing.

I shut myself in the room once again, but to my surprise it was Eugene who came to comfort me, he held my hand and told me that I would get over this sadness, and find somebody who would be right for me.

Ada brought me a cup of tea.

'This is one of life's lesson's you must learn. You know nothing of the world, nothing of men and what they are really like. You are far to trusting of everyone. People are not always what they seem, believe me, I have said it before and I will say it again you will thank us for this someday.'

Left alone with my thoughts, I reflected on Ada's words. She was right. I knew little of the world, of men, of relationships, of sex, and it was all her fault, she had kept me in ignorance, maybe to protect me but she had left me dangerously exposed.

I thought back to when I was fifteen, kneeling on the carpet in the wee room in St Vincent Street, suddenly I noticed blood spreading over the carpet. Jumping up I ran through to Betty in a panic, sobbing that there was something terrible happening to me. She listened and laughed out loud, 'It is only your period starting you daft thing.'

'Periods?'

'Yes, periods, it means you are a woman now, every woman gets periods, they come every month, it means you can have a baby now.'

'What!'

'Well you don't have a baby if you are not married; at least not in this house,' she laughed again, 'it is just part of growing up.'

'Nobody told me,' I wailed, 'what do I do?'

She went through to her room and returned with a slim white pad, 'you use one of these, an S.T., here go and put it on,'

'How?'

'How do you think,' she giggled, 'you don't wear it on your head, that's for sure.'

'You said women get these things every month?'

'Yes till you reach fifty.'

She laughed again, 'you should see your face.'

'I had no idea.'

'That's mammy for you, at least now you know what those machines are for in the ladies toilets, when you go to the pictures.'

So here I was twenty two years old and the extent of my sexual knowledge was about periods. I felt a great resentment against Ada.

I found it difficult to attend meetings as if nothing had happened. Your personal problems were not regarded as important, it was not the thing to discuss them, your priority had to be the 'Truth' and your service.

Four months later, despite the objections to our union, we were back together. We were married in the Kingdom Hall on the 18th of March 1958.

CHAPTER 35

I had always wanted to go to Italy, and finally on 1959, a year after our wedding we did the grand tour from the Austrian border to Naples. I came back determined to get Eugene to see it all again. He had never expressed much interest in going back and was happy enough to plod along with his work, his occasional visit to the pictures and watching the little black and white television.

Eventually he gave in to my pleas and plans were made to book the trip for the summer of 1963. Ada and Aggie spent a happy time in Glasgow buying clothes for the trip, but Eugene resisted all attempts to update his wardrobe, and finally under pressure he announced he would do his own shopping. Ada said she trembled to think what he would come back with and her worse fears were realized.

Jazzy shirts in clashing colours, a loud check jacket that Ada declared was surely second hand as the pockets sagged.

'You can't wear that thing. What are people going to think?' Ada said.

'Eh, what's wrong wi' it? It has plenty pockets for ma pipe and tobacco, ma money an' ma moothie,' he said shrugging the thing on and demonstrating.

'Oh no, you are not taking that mouth organ,' Ada protested.

'Eh, why no? Folk like a bit o' a sing song.'

'Tell him!' Ada appealed to me.

'Maybe it would be better to leave it dad,' I said.

'Well if you say so, but ah don't see whit a' the fuss is aboot.'

He slipped the mouth organ into the drawer, and took off the jacket with a sigh. Helping Aggie to pack I stayed her hand as she put her whalebone corset in the case.

'Oh you won't need that, it will be far to warm to wear anything like that.'

She looked at me over her glasses, 'Ah cannae go without it, it wouldnae be decent. Yer mammy bought me this so that ah could wear one and have one in the wash.'

'Yes but she won't expect you to wear it in Italy, it will kill you trussed up in that thing.'

'Ah need it,' she said, placing it firmly back in the case.

I gave in, believing that she would soon change her mind about it once she experienced just how hot it could be in Italy in August.

But I was to be proved wrong and every morning she stood patiently waiting to be laced up in the thing. To her credit she never complained once.

Within minutes of meeting, Eugene and the two drivers of the tour bus were bosom buddies, the three were like naughty schoolboys, playing tricks on each other, doubling up with laughter and slapping each other heartily on the back.

Two days into the trip, Eugene made his way to the front of the bus to where Serifino the relief driver sat and soon their heads were together and there was much smiling and nodding. Eugene rose, turned to face the passengers and began to play his mouth organ.

Ada groaned, 'where did that come from? I thought I had hidden it where he would never find it.'

Soon he had exhausted his somewhat limited repertoire, but undaunted he pocketed the 'moothie' and launched into a rendition of 'An Old Bass Bottle'; our mortification was complete.

Walking through Florence, Pisa, Rome and Naples he would get chatting to people, telling them how long it had been since he had last been in Italy and he also told everyone he met that he was related to Mario Lanza, the famous Italian/American tenor. This was no idle boast; he really was related, as Dadee had been cousin or brother to the singer's father.

On hearing of this connection a small crowd would gather and he would be asked to sing, but they soon melted away when it became clear that Lanza's talent had not been passed on. Eugene laughed the whole thing off and would produce his 'moothie', playing as he walked and gathering a following of children. We daubed him Papa Piccolino.

In Naples he went missing and Ada was frantic as the whole company was sailing for Capri. Everyone went looking for him and he was eventually found high up on a scaffold built around a great church. There he was happily discussing the finer points of restoring frescoes.

Arriving in Capri, he elected to stay down in the piazza of lower Capri while we went up to Anna Capri to visit the boutiques. Coming back down we could hear the familiar strains of the mouth organ and there he was standing on a marble bench playing away to his heart's content. He had placed his battered sun hat upside down on the bench and people were tossing money into it.

Ada turned on her heel, pretending not to know him.

Back in the hotel, she lost no time in telling him off.

'What were you thinking of begging like that?'

'I wisnae beggin'. Ma hat just happened tae be upside down,' he grinned.

Back in Rome, we visited the Villa Borgese to see the floodlit fountains. It had been raining, and though it had not been a heavy shower, the rain combined with the spray from the fountains made the paths and steps slippy. Going down some steps to see a sunken garden, Ada slipped and fell striking her head on the marble step. She was severely concussed and needed medical treatment. We were beside ourselves with worry, but after a day or two of rest she felt well enough to attempt the journey home. We insisted that she continue to rest, and as the weeks went by she seemed more like her old self, though she complained of headaches, she stubbornly refused to see a doctor.

With both Eugene and Aggie out at work all day, Ada spent her time resting and reading. To any inquiry regarding her health she would smile and say she was as fit as a fiddle.

As the year turned from Autumn to Winter she began to suffer from bouts of weakness and she would reach out to steady herself, or collapse heavily into a seat, holding her head and complaining the room was spinning round her.

Still she was deaf to our pleas to her to see a doctor. She would complain that nobody knew what she was suffering; nobody understood what she was going through.

Our frustration and feeling of helplessness grew.

On Hogmanay she was bright and full of life, accepting an invitation to go down to a party in a neighbour's house. They invited her to play the piano and she sat there playing hour after hour, playing and singing every song she knew. Her mood was too bright, too brittle; it made both Lena and myself feel uneasy, we knew we had to get her upstairs. Upstairs she collapsed sobbing on her bed. Ada was not a drinker; she would toast the 'Bells' with a glass of wine and not touch a drop till the next Hogmanay. We put her strange mood down to fatigue. She had worked for hours cleaning the house from top to bottom to welcome the New Year, then without much to eat had spent hours playing the piano in a smoky unventilated crowded room.

Eugene grumbled that she cared too much about the house; her high standards of house keeping was often the cause of disagreement between them.

'I don't understand you woman. We bought the fireside chairs because you liked the upholstery, then you put covers over them to keep them clean, and covers over the covers on the arms to keep them clean, so you never get to see the upholstery you like. You bought yon fancy china tea set because you liked the pattern, but it's stuck in the sideboard wrapped in newspaper and never sees the light o' day, except at New Year, where is the sense in that?'

'I just like to keep things nice, you never know when you can get visitors and if the place is nice then we won't be ashamed.'

'Bugger the visitors. If they only come to see the furniture they neednae bother. This is where we live and we should enjoy the things everyday, and if they break or get dirty, we can replace them.'

'Oh so money grows on trees?'

'Och money, we will always get by, ye can always get money, but ye only get one life, you're a long time dead.'

'Oh that is typical of you, easy-oasy Joe. Who is that has had to scrimp and save to get us what we have today?'

The habit of house cleaning was too ingrained in her to ever change. Friday was devoted to top to bottom cleaning, tea leaves would be saved all week to sprinkle over the carpet in her constant battle to rid it of tiny pieces of white lint that seemed to appear from nowhere, and after the leaves were judged to have done their work she would be down on her knees with a stiff bristled hand brush, reaching into every nook and cranny till she was satisfied every trace of white lint and tea leaf was swept up. The sideboard would get beeswaxed, the brass would be cleaned, the fire-irons lacquered, beds changed and windows washed. The house finished, she would turn her attention to the walls of the close and the stairs leading to the house, these she would wash and polish to a brilliant shine. This was what I found her doing one Friday afternoon, and as she stopped to talk to me I noticed she was breathless, but she put it down to the vigorous polishing. We sat drinking tea and I noticed her clutching her abdomen now and then as if in pain.

'Is there something wrong, are you in pain?'

'Och just a twinge now and then, it's nothing.'

'Have you had it long?'

'Since Italy, it's nothing, maybe I was rubbing too hard on the walls.'

'Have you taken anything for it?'

'The usual things, you know I don't believe in pills, I just carry on with my hot water first thing in the morning, it's the grandest thing, and then I have my 'Hyjah' tea every night.'

'I think you should see a doctor.'

'I have seen him, as a matter of fact he has asked me to see him again this afternoon.'

This surprised and alarmed me. Ada did not like doctors and if she had gone without telling anyone she must be worried.

'Would you like me to come with you?'

'No I will be fine, maybe you could finish off the walls for me, while I am away?'

'Right, I'll do that,' I said, though I much preferred to go with her.

She came back quite cheerful; the doctor had diagnosed trouble with her gall bladder.

'What happens now?' I asked.

'Oh I just have to wait for a hospital appointment to see a consultant.'

In the weeks she waited on the appointment she kept herself busy, she seemed not to want to stay in the house. She visited Lena, wrote to Betty and went to the pictures. She and I went into the town and walked round Lewis's, then to Arnott Simpson's for afternoon tea.

Arnott's tea rooms were elegant and genteel in Ada's opinion and she loved the black silk clad waitresses with their white frilly aprons and pert little hats. The tables were set with fine bone china, heavy silver cutlery, silver teapot and hot water jug. She would smile with pleasure as the waitress placed the three tier silver cakestand before us with its tiny triangular sandwiches on the bottom tier, fluffy scones on the second, and cream horns, Eiffel towers and empire biscuits with thick white icing on the top tier.

'Oh this is lovely, there is nothing to beat a well set table, with the finest things.'

'Maybe daddy is right; you should use your best china and get the pleasure from it.'

'Maybe he is.'

'So will you use it?' I smiled

'We'll see.'

I knew she wouldn't.

As the time went on she was obviously feeling less well, the pain was getting worse. She was often sick, and complaining of weakness. She wanted to go to Edinburgh, ostensibly to see Jimmy and Mary, long since reconciled to her. She asked me to go along and once there she toured us round all her old haunts. She especially wanted me to see where her little flat in Elm Row by the meadows had stood.

She gazed at the rather run down building, and sighed.

'It is strange to think I spent so much time here and so much happened to me here, but time passes and nobody around here would remember me or the cafe where I worked. What is life all about eh, who knows?'
This melancholy mood was her norm in recent weeks. We turned from Elm Row and walked across the Meadows when suddenly she doubled up with pain and was violently sick several times.
Her strength deserted her and she could barely stand.
Mary and Jimmy agreed with me that we should seek medical help, but she would not hear of it. I worried about the train journey home, wondering how she would be.
'Just let me rest. I need a little rest and then I will be fine,' she whispered.
We managed to get her to a bench, where she sat eyes closed breathing heavily.
We managed the journey home without mishap. After the trip to Edinburgh, she lost all interest in going out. We tried to chase up the hospital appointment, and were very relieved when it came. She was to have an operation, but once again it was a case of waiting. Ada took to her bed, too weak, to sit up for any length of time. Her appetite was never big but now she barely ate at all. Lena and I, washing her one day, helped her slip off her night gown and our eyes met in horror over her head as we realized how much weight she had lost.
Constant pleas to the doctor for a date for the operation were to no avail. It was out of his hands, the hospital would decide. We went on pestering him till he agreed to write and try to hurry things up.
Ada did not want to go to hospital, but it was a relief even to her when eventually an ambulance was sent to take her to the Royal Infirmary which was only a few minutes from the house.
Lena by now had five children, the youngest almost three years old. She was also due to sit her final exams after studying at night school to become a tutor in dressmaking and tailoring. Ada's condition put all thought of this out of her mind. As we went to visit the next day after admission we found Ada sitting up bright and cheerful.
'I have had the operation and I feel fine, much better than I expected to feel,' she told us.
We looked at each other slightly puzzled, it didn't seem possible.
Lena went in search of a doctor.
She came back looking pale and drawn, but chatted away to Ada, who fully expected to be home in a day or two.
As soon as we had left the ward I asked Lena what the doctor had said.
'The operation she had was just a biopsy, they think she has cancer,' Lena said.
'Not at all,' Eugene said dismissively, 'yer mammy has always been a strong woman, how can she have cancer, it's nonsense.'
'It's true, daddy, the doctor says they think she has had it for a long time, but the fall on holiday really triggered it off,' Lena said, her voice shaking.
'Och, he's talking nonsense. How could that happen? Ah don't believe it, ah

cannae believe it,' Eugene said.

'None of us can, daddy, but you know how ill she has been and how much weight she has lost,' I told him.

'What are we goin' tae say tae her,' Eugene asked, accepting the truth at last.

'Ah don't know daddy, I honestly don't know,' Lena said.

Aggie was sobbing, she stood hands at her sides, letting the tears fall unchecked, just as she had done all those years ago, when Ada and I had found her dishevelled and bent, unwanted by Jimmy and Mary. Looking at her my heart went out to her. How would she cope without Ada? How would any of us cope?

Despite Eugene's reluctance to admit the hopelessness of the situation we all knew that Ada would not survive this cancer. There had been some progress in the treatment of the disease from 1956 when Tina was ill, but even now in 1964 there was a long way to go before they could claim victory over this horrible scourge.

I thought of Ada only a few months before sitting before the television shocked and tearful as we all were as we watched over and over the vile assassination of John F. Kennedy.

'What a tragedy, what a miss he will be,' she had said.

The prospect of losing her was a greater tragedy for us.

Life without her was unthinkable, and it was with heavy heart we went to see her the next day. She had been told she would need to stay in for several more tests, and seemed happy enough about it. She asked us to bring in the photographs of the Italian holiday to show to the 'lovely' nurses. She even gave them lessons in Italian as they worked round her bed. As the days went by she became more frail, she was in a lot of pain which the nurses did all they could to alleviate.

We took it in turns to be at her bedside. As she slept Lena and I would talk of her strange mood at New Year, the frantic playing of the piano, the brittle laughter and the heartrending sobs.

'She knew it was her last New Year,' I said.

'She always knew what was ahead,' Lena nodded.

Ada was heavily drugged and complained they had opened up her feet and fed lines through them. We could make no sense of it and the nurses denied all knowledge, so we had to conclude she was hallucinating. As things got worse she asked to be taken home, but the doctors would not agree. We kept up the pretence that she would be home soon and she would smile and say 'thank God'.

Eugene came every night. I took comfort in the fact that after all their troubles they had found calmer waters and a new beginning, but even now in this time of extreme sorrow the past in a most unexpected way came back to haunt us.

By a strange quirk of fate I now lived in a tenement that looked out on the back wall of the slaughter house, where Eugene had spent his truant hours and that had caused me such anguish as a child. A new general store had opened in Duke street just across the road from my flat. I called in to get some things, the shop was busy and as I queued I became aware of the young woman who was serving behind the counter. She looks like me I thought, she is older but she could pass for my sister. I watched her closely and with a shock realized that she seemed as interested in me as I was in her.

When it was my turn she obligingly went to fetch the things I wanted, and as she was wrapping them she suddenly blurted out, 'is your name Cocozza?'

'Ye-yes, my maiden name is Cocozza.'

'Is your father's name Eugene?'

'Ye-yes.'

'He's my father too, though I have never met him. I'm your half sister'.

I couldn't find anything to say. I knew she was telling the truth, but it didn't seem possible that here right where I lived was Eugene's daughter.

I fled the shop dashing across the road almost into the path of an oncoming bus. I heard the screech of brakes, and the driver yelling an oath at me. I gained the pavement and stood bent over shaking and trying to get my breath back.

A hand gripped my arm and a voice said, 'I knew it was you, what were you doing trying to get yourself killed?'

I looked up to stare at a young man who looked vaguely familiar.

He smiled, 'you don't recognize me, do you?'

I shook my head; I was still shaking not really seeing him.

Tommy, Tommy who used to help you carry the pails of Blancmange to your dad?'

I tried to focus, took in the red hair, the freckled face, older but still Tommy.

'Tommy, yes I recognize you now. I'm sorry I was distracted.'

'Aye distracted enough to nearly get yourself killed. I saw you from the top deck of the bus.'

'Oh, so that's where you came from!'

'I dashed down the stairs as soon as I realized it was you, you looked as if you had seen a ghost.'

'I think I did - a kind of ghost.'

He looked at me quizzically, 'how do you mean?'

'Oh, it's nothing, I'm all right now.'

'Ok, you don't need to tell me, it's none of my business,' he grinned.

I smiled, pulling myself together, 'so how are you?'

'Fine, fine. Do you live round here?'

'Yes, right here in this street. Do you have time for a cup of tea?' I felt I needed to make amends.

Over the teacups we exchanged our news. I told him of Ada's illness.'

'That explains why you were not looking where you were going, I suppose.'

'Yes,' I lied.

'So you are married,' he said looking at the ring on my finger.

'Yes, six years.'

He looked up and smiled, 'I had such a crush on you.'

'What!'

'See, you never knew, did you?'

'No, nobody ever had a crush on me,' I said.

'Well I did, but you never really saw me, did you? Too busy thinking about 'Flash' Gordon.'

I felt myself blush, 'yes I suppose that's true.'

'No suppose about it. All the girls were after him or my big brother,' he grinned again.

'Oh yes, your brother, he was good looking too, and he was the best climber, but neither of them took any notice of me. Anyway, 'Flash' broke all our hearts he went to America.'

'I can remember how happy that made me. Maybe some of us ordinary guys will get a look in,' I thought to myself.

He reached out to help himself to a biscuit, and shook his head in mock sorrow, 'by then you had disappeared almost overnight to Edinburgh, what was that all about?'

'You don't want to know,' I said.

'Secrets? You always had secrets.'

'Yes, didn't I.'

'Did you ever write to old 'Flash'?'

'Yes, though I'd rather not be reminded of that,' I shuddered.

'He never answered you? That doesn't surprise me.'

'Oh he answered me all right,' I said grimly.

'What did he say?' It must have been something to upset you.'

'You really want to know?'

'You bet.'

'Well, he told me he had never liked me, I was weird, I never allowed myself to get angry with anyone, too serious, too plain - need I go on?'

'Crikey! I would like to punch his jaw!'

'Needless to say I never wrote to him again, but the awful thing is, I agreed with everything he said, that had always been my opinion of myself too and he had just confirmed it.'

'Yer daft. That is a load of rubbish. He is a jumped up conceited twerp. What did you do with the letter? If you still have his address, give it to me and I will give him a dose of his own medicine.'

'I burned it. I couldn't take the chance of anyone else reading it, it would have been too embarrassing, anyway it was years ago, heaven knows where he is now.'

'I would still like to land one on his jaw, always wanted to, but I was too wee,' he laughed.

I asked about his life, he told me he was a Rep. for a whisky firm, still single, with nobody special.

'Shame you're spoken for.'

I laughed, 'yes, isn't it.'

He rose to go, and fishing out a scrap of paper from his pocket he scribbled his address. We said our goodbyes, his best wishes for Ada echoing in my ears as I closed the door. I never saw him again.

The moment the door closed behind him, the thought of the woman in the shop seized me. A million questions whizzed through my mind. How did she know about me? How was she able to recognize me? Had she sought me out, sought all of us out, watching Eugene from a distance, watching us all? If she had, how long had she been doing it? Where had she seen us? It went round and round in my head.

Was her mother still alive? Was she the only one, or were there others who could claim Eugene as their father?

I never doubted she was who she said she was for a moment; the resemblance was too strong, though she was older, nearer Betty's age. She was Eugene's daughter, I knew that. I thought of the way I had dashed out of the shop. Why had I done that? Why hadn't I stayed to talk to her, asked my questions, answered hers? For surely she must have questions too.

What was I to do with this knowledge? I couldn't tell Eugene, or Ada, I couldn't tell Lena either as we had never acknowledged Eugene and Ada's past. I knew Lena's dislike of delving into family secrets, besides this was not the time for such revelations, not the time to add to the burden she carried. I knew John would be furious if I upset her in any way.

I made up my mind that I would tell no one, and I knew that meant never going back to the shop again.

The thing lay heavy upon me, and was still fresh in my mind as I walked with Eugene to the hospital a few days later. As we walked past the ancient walls of Duke Street Prison on our way to the High Street, a man stopped us and greeted Eugene with surprise.

'My God!' It's years since I saw you, how are things?' he asked.

Eugene gripped his hand and shook it warmly, 'this is a surprise right enough, we go back a long time.'

'Aye, so how are things wi' you?' the man said again.

Eugene shook his head, 'ach no sae good, ma wife is in the Royal, we are just on our way tae see her.'

'Bella? Is she bad?' the man asked.

'Naw, naw no Bella, it's ma second wife Eadie. Aye she is bad, she has cancer.'

'Yer second wife? Oh ah didnae know. You an' Bella....'

'Oh aye fur years noo,' Eugene said.

'Cancer eh? Ah'm right sorry tae hear that,' the man shook his head. 'Aye, there is nothing can be done. Ah cannae be doin' with it. She has no' been a wife tae me, if ye get ma meanin' fur a long time, wi' this illness,' Eugene told him.

The man nodded and snatched a look at me as he heard my sharp intake of breath. I had been standing arm in arm with Eugene, during this encounter, but now I withdrew it sharply, hardly daring to believe Eugene had said such a callous thing. The man was not the only one who 'got his meaning'. I was horrified and I wanted to run off and leave him.

Instead I stood as he took his leave of the stranger, and he proceeded to walk alongside me as if nothing untoward had happened.

If he even realized that it was the first time he had ever admitted to having had another wife, he said nothing to explain it away, neither did he seem to realize my shock at his tack of sensitivity.

I sat watching him from the other side of the bed, thinking of all the pain he had caused Ada throughout their time together, all the pain he had caused to us all, the horror of the bankruptcy, of Niddrie Mains, when she had been so ill and almost lost her mind. I found it hard to think kindly towards him, but now was not the time to show it, coming on top of the meeting with my half sister and Ada's approaching death it was too much to bear.

I thought too of the young woman who was my half sister. She had lived all her life without his fatherly presence. It hurt me to think of her hurt, of her feelings of rejection.

We had sat for two hours or more. Ada was in a drugged sleep. Eugene stood up and yawned. 'Ah think ah'll go for a fish supper, want some chips?' he asked.

As the days went by the drugs became less effective, so bad was the pain. Lena and I practically lived in the hospital and we sat on in the darkened hushed ward, behind the screens round Ada's bed. She would cry out in pain, and we would beg the nurse to 'do something', but always we got the same reply - they could not increase the dosage, they had run out of options to help her.

The soft light that shone above her turned her hair to spun silver. It eased the lines etched on her face by the pain, though her white knuckles plucking at the bedclothes told their own story.

It is often the case (though we did not know this at the time) that people who are near death rally for a little while and seem to lay a new claim upon life. Such was the case with Ada.

She asked to be lifted up on her pillows, she seemed at ease, smiling at Lena's and my anxious faces.

Reaching for each of our hands she said, 'why the long faces? I am happy, Granny and Bennie have been here and they have promised to come for me later.'

We could not answer. She increased the pressure on our hands, 'I want you to sing with me.'

We stared at her.

'Sing?'

She smiled, 'yes, I want you to sing with me.' She began in a faltering voice —

Tell me the old, old story
Of unseen things above,
Of Jesus and his glory,
Of Jesus and his love.

We tried to sing as we choked back the tears. Ada went on to sing the whole hymn, then asked us to pray. She let her head fall on the pillow for a moment or two, then gripping our hands in an even fiercer grip she raised her head and whispered, 'sing the 23rd psalm, sing it with me.' Once more in her tremulous voice she began –

The lord is my shepherd
I'll not want
He makes me down to lie,
In pastures green,
He leadeth me,
The quiet waters by.

We faltered, the tears overcoming us, but she said, in a voice that suddenly regained its old strength, 'sing up, be brave, everything is all right, they told me. They are coming back for me.'
Somehow we struggled through the rest of the psalm –

Although I walk in death's dark vale
Yet will I fear none ill,
For Thou art with me,
And thy rod and staff me comfort still.

'Sing! Sing it again with me. Sing!' she dug into the flesh of our hands. We sang.
The whole episode had exhausted her, but she was content, sank back on the pillows and closed her eyes. They were, like ours, wet with tears.
Aggie and Eugene arrived shortly after, but Ada had slipped into a coma. Lena told them what had happened, Aggie sobbed into her handkerchief. Eugene, quietly reached out to take Ada's hand.
We sat, each lost in thought, the silence broken only by Aggie's sobs. A nurse came and led her away, saying she would make her a cup of tea.
The hours passed and still we sat, afraid to leave the bedside lest she die in that moment. The nurse whispered to us that she was making tea and toast and asked if we would like some. We smiled our thanks and when she came back to say it was ready, Eugene chased Lena and I through saying we had been there so long. We hurried through the welcome tea and went back to send Eugene and Aggie through, Lena saying to Eugene that the nurse was making fresh toast, and to our amazement Ada stirred and muttered, 'put some butter on it.'
We bent to speak to her but she could not hear us. It was 6am. She was gone.
We walked stiff and weary into the bright July morning, stunned by our loss, unable to accept the fact that she was gone.
It was still the custom then to bring the coffin home and it took up all the space in the little room in Garfield Street, but Ada was home where she should be, and where family and neighbours could come to pay their respects.
Mary and Jimmy arrived and as Mary came back through to the crowded kitchen she shook her head and said 'ah jist wanted tae say, Oh Eadie come away ben and hae a cup o' tea wi' us.'
As day succeeded day the serious tones were interspersed with laughter, Eugene could be heard telling jokes. I knew this always happened at times

like these, but I still resented it, I still resented Eugene.

Betty arrived; she was distraught, especially since she had not been able to see Ada before she died. The night before the funeral I sat alone by Ada's coffin. I could hear the buzz of conversation and the occasional bust of nervous laughter coming from the kitchen. Betty had taken over the proceedings, in her usual efficient manner. I gazed on Ada's face my eyes tracing every dear familiar line. The hospital had asked permission to conduct an autopsy, the final decision being Eugene's but we urged him to say no. Ada would not have wanted it and we pointed out that they knew the cause of death already. 'Well the doctor says it would help them in future cases, Eadie is gone, she will feel nothing and ah think she would want tae help them.' He went in search of the doctor to give his permission.

Now as I gazed on her still face I asked her forgiveness for the intrusion. I found a writing pad and tearing out a sheet I wrote -

'I am the resurrection and the life,
He that believeth in me, though he were dead
Yet shall he live,
And whosoever liveth and believeth in me,
Shall never die.
John 11.V 25.26'

Folding the page in two, I placed it by her hands.

I sat on and after a while I heard people leaving, heard Betty fill the kettle, heard Lena arriving, and the low murmur of their voices.

Lena came through, bringing me a cup of tea and we sat in silence for a while, then patting my shoulder, she left me.

The stillness of the room made my eyes heavy, my head drooped and then I would snap awake with a start, but I was determined not to leave her.

Around 3am Eugene pushed open the door and came to stand quietly by the coffin. He reached into his pocket.

'Ah want tae put her wedding ring on her finger.' he said.

'You mean now?'

'Aye, tomorrow will be too late. Ah talked tae yer sisters, they know aboot it.'

'Do they think you should? I mean actually put it on her finger, maybe you could put it on a ribbon, and just lay it on her chest.'

'Naw, it must be her finger.'

'I don't know if it is right to disturb her, daddy.'

'This is between yer mammy an' me. Ah want the ring on her finger, ye better go till ah'm finished.'

I stood up reluctantly.

'Away ye go, let me be.' He made a shooing motion with his hand.

Through in the kitchen, Aggie and Betty were slumped on the fireside chairs fast asleep, Lena having long since gone home to see to her children.

It was over an hour before Eugene came through, his eyes were moist. He looked at me and nodded.

'It's done, everything is fine,' he said.

Our chequered religious history meant there was no parish priest, no Protestant minister on whom we could call to take the service. It fell to me to ask a 'brother' from the Kingdom Hall if he would officiate.

Ada was not a 'witness', though she had attended some meetings, so it was not a simple matter, but after some persuasion it was agreed he would conduct the funeral.

There was little that was personal to Ada in his sermon, and this upset most of those present. At the cemetery, as we were gathered round the grave for the final reading from the scriptures, Betty distraught and overcome with grief, collapsed and pitched forward almost into the grave, Eugene and Eddie Gillan catching her as she fell.

Back at the house, Famie and Lizzie took over from us to dispense tea and drinks. The house was full to overflowing, Mary and Jimmy sitting cheek by jowl with Carol, their shoddy attire contrasting sharply with Carol's smart black suit. Carol herself seemed content to say little and surveyed the company through a haze of smoke from the cigarette held in a long mother of pearl holder.

The sponge bag Ada had used in hospital lay on the sideboard, and in the crush of bodies someone knocked it over breaking a bottle of Ada's favourite Gardenia perfume. It seeped through the bag onto the highly polished wood causing a white stain. Lena and I stared in dismay, sure we could hear Ada's voice bewailing her beloved sideboard.

Years later we both agreed that was the moment we fully accepted that Ada was dead.

CHAPTER 36

Each of us dealt with our grief in our own way. Aggie tearful and shaking, clinging to whoever was around, Eugene out all day looking for work and hidden behind a newspaper at night. He was not a drinker, and seemed to find most solace in his pipe and beloved 'Erinmore' tobacco. Lena went back to her studies, and succeeded in passing her exams. As for me within two weeks of Ada's funeral I was in Italy. I had not wanted to go, but the trip had been arranged for some time, and we had promised to take my young sister-in-law. I had been urged to go by the family, who told me 'it was for the best'.

I found it hard to revisit the places were only a year before I had walked with Ada. I felt very alone, despite the company of my husband and his sister.

For almost two years before Ada's illness we had been going through a process of adoption, we were hopeful that soon we would be approved and eventually be given a baby boy. Shortly after returning from Italy we heard we had been turned down, the reason being we were 'Witnesses' and they were reluctant to place a baby in a 'sect'.

It was a severe disappointment, especially as I was having serious doubts about being a 'Witness', though I had kept these doubts to myself. During Ada's long illness I had turned to fellow 'Witnesses' for comfort, but I found little, instead I was directed to read certain passages of the scriptures, reminded everyone died at some point, and put my hope in the 'New World'. Now Ada was gone it was expected that I would pick up the pieces and carry on, but my mind was too confused, I felt adrift a ship without a rudder. As the weeks went by I began to feel weak and suffer from bouts of nausea. Like Ada I disliked doctors and resisted the advice of the family for some time before giving in. I found to my amazement that I was pregnant. I left the surgery with very mixed feelings, I had wanted a child so badly, and now I was to have one, but I could not feel the surge of joy that I had always dreamt I would feel at such news. I longed to tell Ada, to hear her voice reassure me that everything would be all right. I wandered absently down the road not wanting to go back home, yet desperate to talk to someone. Passing a cafe I stopped to gaze in the window, the familiar display of cardboard cones, and chocolate nuggets, the advertisements for Vimto and Irn-Bru brought back memories of the cafe, the Favourite Cafe, now derelict and boarded up. Wearily I pushed open the cafe door, and minutes later sat staring into the froth of the coffee the old woman had brought me.

I looked up to find her watching me from behind the counter and as I lowered my eyes she came and put her plump warm hand on my shoulder.

'You gonna have a baby, eh?'

'Yes,' I looked up at her, 'how did you know?'

She tapped the side of her nose, 'I know,' she nodded.

'You no wanna this baby?'

'Yes, yes I do.'

'Then why you looka so sad?'

I poured out the whole story, and as I spoke she had wriggled her plump frame onto the bench opposite me, her dark brown eyes never leaving my face. When I had finished she reached for my hand and held it for a moment. 'I just wanted to be able to tell her. It doesn't matter about anyone else, I wanted to tell her.'

She squeezed my hand before letting it go, got up, puffing with the exertion of quitting the bench and once again she put her hand on my shoulder.

'Your mamma she know, she know,' she said with a smile.

My news was greeted with pleasure. Eugene puffed at his pipe saying through the smoke, 'as yer mammy always said, a life goes oot o' the world and a life comes in.'

But this particular little life was not to be, by October I lay near to death in hospital, my precious baby lost.

It was only once I was home I realized how close I had been to following Ada yet my only memory was floating on a soft, soft cloud, with every care gone. I reckoned if that was death then there was nothing to fear. Lena insisted I go to stay with her for a time so she could look after me. In truth she had enough to do looking after all her children and holding down a job, but I went for a week or two to please her.

During those long days as I sat trying to pass the time reading, my thoughts recalled snatches of conversations I had had with Ada. After my marriage, of which she still disapproved, I remembered her imploring me not to have children, she was adamant that that would not be a good thing for me. No amount a pleading on my part could get her to explain why she felt that way. In my confused, depressed state now after the loss of the baby, I began to feel that she had reached from beyond the grave to take my child. The thought drove me to distraction.

Some seven months after Ada's death Eugene came to my house saying he needed to talk to me urgently. His timing could not have been worse, that morning I had had several teeth extracted and was feeling miserable, all I wanted to do was crawl into bed and feel sorry for myself. Indeed I had been in bed when Eugene came to the door, and I promptly went back, leaving him to follow me through to the bedroom, where he perched at the foot of the bed.

I waited for him to speak.

'It's like this, ah canny be withoot a woman, ah need tae marry again,' he said watching me closely.

I was dumbstruck, staring at him as if he was mad.

'Did ye hear me? Ah canny go on like this, ah need tae marry again.'

'Mammy has only been dead for a few months,' I mumbled, my mouth still numb from the cocaine.

'Ah know, but it is the way ah am,' he said.

'Wh-who is there to marry,' I was getting really angry, not least with the inability to get my lips to move, to say what I wanted to say.

He shifted his position, pulling himself further onto the bed as if I might shrug him off.

'You're not a young man,' I managed.

'There is a lassie, a woman, she is younger than me, ah've known the family fur years. Ah've spoken tae her father, he is quite happy aboot it.'

'You mean you have spoken to him without telling us first?'

'Aye it is the way o' things. Ah've spoken tae Carla, that's the lassie, ah've spoken tae her as well.'

'What did she say?'

'She is quite happy aboot it, it will be fine.'

'How old is she?'

'Aboot forty, ah think, a young woman compared wi' me.'

'What about Aggie? Have you thought of her?'

'Ah thought she could live wi' you or Lena.'

'Have you told Lena?'

'No, no I wanted to tell you first, I thought you would understand. Ah want you tae tell Lena fur me.'

'She won't be happy about this daddy, it is too soon. We never ever dreamed anything like this would happen. As for Aggie living with Lena, that is not a good idea, Lena has her hands full as it is, with the children.'

'Then you take her, you don't have a family, anyway Aggie works, it's no as if she is totally helpless and she does bring in a wage.'

'Daddy, I still hope to have children. I lost the baby after mammy died, but I still want another one.'

'Ach well maybe it isnae meant tae be, ye have been married seven years noo and it should have happened long ago. Ye jist have tae accept these things.'

'Well if that is the case can't you just accept that your wife has died and do without?'

I felt cruel saying this to him, but he just shook his head.

'It's a different thing a'thegither.'

'Daddy, too many things have happened, mammy dying, me losing the baby, and nearly dying myself. It is not the time to go upsetting things further.'

'Ah thought you would understand, ye need tae understand,' he said.

'I just feel that you can't put Aggie out of the house. It is the only home she has known for years. We all thought you would be happy with each others company, it is what mammy would have wanted.'

'Well ah'm no happy. Ah want tae marry Carla, Aggie will just have tae go intae a home or find lodgings.'

I was really shocked, 'how can you say that? Think what it will do to her.'

'Ye cannae expect me tae ask a young bride tae share a hoose wi' somebody like Aggie, it would never work. Ah've already asked the lassie tae marry me, an' she has accepted so you will a' jist have tae put up wi' it.'

He got up, shaking his head, and reaching the door, he paused and looked at me.

'Ah honestly thought that you would understand.'

Next day Aggie sat before me sobbing into her handkerchief.

'Whit would Eadie say if she was here?'

'It wouldn't be a problem if she was here,' I said, pouring her a second cup of tea.

She put down the handkerchief and reached for the cup, clutching it with both hands.

'Have you met this woman he is on about?'

Her eyes danced, 'no but he is going to invite her for her tea, he says.'

'When?'

'Next week ah think, he told me to give the place a good clean.'

'He has a cheek, tell him to clean the house himself.' I was furious at his thoughtlessness.

Aggie put the cup down with shaky fingers, 'does Lena know?' she asked.

'No not yet,' I told her.

'What dae ye think she will say?' Aggie sniffed.

'I shudder to think,' I said.

I was right to fear telling Lena, she was absolutely furious.

'How could he think of doing such a thing, how can he betray mammy's memory?' she fumed.

'I hate the idea too. It isn't something we ever expected, especially so soon after losing mammy, but....'

'What do you mean but? But what?'

'I don't know. Maybe we should let him talk it through, listen to him, try to understand,' I surprised myself coming out with this.

'What is there to understand? Will you be happy with another woman using mammy's things, sitting where she used to sit?'

I had a quick mental picture of Carla sitting on Eugene's knee at the table, the sight made me shudder.

'No I would find it hard,' I agreed.

'I thought I knew my dad, I thought losing mammy was as hard for him as it was for us,' Lena said.

'I think it was, but he says he needs a woman, he can't live the rest of his life without one,' I said, echoing Eugene's words to me.

'Don't talk like that, I don't want to hear it, he is crazy,' Lena said.

She went through to the kitchen, leaving me alone with my thoughts. I wondered if any of us knew Eugene. I thought of the postal orders for 'Mrs E Cocozza', the secret wedding in the register office, the meeting with the old acquaintance on the way to the hospital and Eugene's callous remark that Ada had 'not been a wife to him because of the illness'.

I thought of the newly discovered half sister who knew who I was and claimed Eugene as her father. I could hear Lena noisily banging cups on to a tray, the rattle of the cutlery as she threw it down. She was the most even tempered person I knew, and rarely showed her feelings, but she was very upset about all this, and it showed despite herself.

I wondered how much she knew of Ada and Eugene's past. It was possible that she knew everything and maybe things I did not know and if she did I knew she would never tell me. I loved her dearly, but there were times, and now was one of them that I wanted to tear away her reserve and talk openly about all the things that had haunted me in my childhood and in many ways still haunted me.

She came through with the tea things, placing the tray gently down on the coffee table. I knew she was struggling to regain her composure.

'What do you think we should do?' I asked.

She handed me a cup before answering, 'talk some sense into him. If he doesn't listen and give up this mad idea, then we have nothing more to do with him,' she said firmly.

'We can't do that, he is our dad.'

'Not if he insists on marrying this - this woman.'

A week later I was summoned to meet Carla. I hesitated, knowing any such meeting would be seen as a betrayal by Lena, but I was really curious to see the woman, and I felt too that Aggie needed a bit of support.

She was plump with several chins; every finger was adorned by at least two rings, three gold chains hung round her neck and a heavy gold charm bracelet dangled from her plump wrist.

She was really quite pretty when you looked behind her roundness. She looked older than her forty something years, and had I suspected, been teetering on the brink of being an old maid, making her father anxious to have her taken off his hands.

Her eyes were beady, darting this way and that watching Aggie, then me, though her manner towards us was pleasant enough. I remembered Eugene's remark to me when I got engaged at the age of twenty two, that he had feared he had an old maid on his hands, so how much keener would Carla's father be to see her married off, it was the Italian way.

The meeting with Carla was strained to say the least. Poor Aggie had done her best with the table, using Ada's best china (how incensed Lena would have been to see it, I thought).

There was salmon sandwiches, three kinds of biscuits and a plate of luscious cream cakes. Aggie sat perched on the edge of her chair, her dancing eyes never leaving Carla's face. I poured the tea and tried to make small talk. Carla seemed intent on working her way through the spread before her, when in one unfortunate moment both she and Aggie reached for the same cream cake and Aggie fled the table in tears. Carla took no notice, placed the cake on her plate and delicately licked the cream from her plump fingers.

Eugene smiled indulgently. I excused myself and went in pursuit of Aggie whose sobs could be heard coming from the bedroom.

It was clear the situation would take a lot of sorting out, and time was not on our side.

Aggie refused to return to the kitchen and I decided to stay with her. The courtship continued. Aggie refused to leave the house. Lena and I supported her in this and tried to get Eugene to change his mind. He refused. It was stalemate.

Then out of the blue Carla asked to be released from the engagement. She had had a better offer and she was quite upfront about it, telling Eugene she did not like the house, it was too small, and he did not have enough money to keep her in the style to which she had become accustomed. The other suitor, though even older than Eugene had a thriving business and a fine house and no clinging relative to get rid of.

Eugene shrugged off the disappointment, 'Eh, it is the Italian way. You always take the better offer.'

We breathed a sigh of relief and thought the matter closed. We were wrong.

Before long another plump but less glamorous figure sat sipping tea and lobbying for our approval. She was one of two spinster sisters who lived next door. Unable to believe the dizzying turn of her fortunes, she became skittish and giggled incessantly, almost causing me to have a treacherous wish for the return of the avaricious Carla.

Aggie's despair went on and Eugene was still bent on getting rid of her. Both Lena and I had kept Betty informed about the Carla situation, but she heard about the second contender from a rather surprising source, Aggie herself. To our knowledge it was the first time Aggie had ever written a letter. Clearly losing faith in Lena's and my ability to solve her problem she had turned to Betty who she thought would be bolder in her approach.

Betty of course was no stranger to fractured relationships. Now divorced, she had a new partner and was expecting a baby. As always Betty had a way of 'managing' things and she saw an opportunity in Aggie's dilemma. She wrote to Eugene feigning ignorance of all that was going on, and told him of her plight; she was pregnant had lost her job in a local bar and with it her lodgings. She begged Eugene to take her in till the baby was born.

It was not the response Aggie had expected, not the response any of us had expected and we felt sure that Eugene would refuse her, bent as he was on marrying the giddy spinster. If it suited Betty to turn the situation to her advantage, it suited Eugene too, as unknown to us he had become weary of the simpering girlish giggler, and used Betty's request as an excuse to cool the relationship.

Within days of her arrival Betty sat opposite me, regarding me with a mischievous grin.

'I think I have found the perfect solution to our problem,' she said.

'You mean about Aggie?'

'Yes, it is so simple I'm surprised neither you nor Lena thought about it.'

'Lena wants nothing to do with Daddy's plans; she just wants Aggie to stay where she is.'

'I know, and with my idea she can. Dad wants a wife, Aggie needs a home, and the obvious answer is that he marries Aggie.'

'You're not serious!'

'I am, it is the perfect answer, don't you think?'

'No, no I don't. Aggie is not the marrying kind, she is well into her fifties and she is too old to change.'

'Has anybody asked her?'

'No, don't be daft, the very idea would send her shutting herself in the room in floods of tears. As for Daddy, don't you think if he wanted to marry Aggie he would have asked her?'

'No, not right away. He was hoping for a younger woman, or at least a woman with a bit of spunk about her.'

'Exactly! Aggie is hardly the life and soul. She can hardly look after herself never mind look after daddy.'

'Well, she certainly has surprised me in the past couple of days. She has made a decent pot of pasta soup, tackled the washing, cleaned the house and she is talking of doing the meat for the spaghetti at the weekend.'

'Really?'

'I kid you not. What do you think about me sounding out dad?'

'He will never go for it. I know he seems to have gone off the spinster next door and she has had to go away for a holiday to get over it, by all accounts.'

'For heaven's sake don't say a word to Aggie about your daft plan till you see what Daddy's reaction is.'

'Should we tell Lena?'

'No, definitely not, there is no point in upsetting her for nothing. He will turn the idea down flat and even if by some loss of his senses he doesn't, Aggie will.'

'We'll see,' Betty grinned.

She came back a few days later to say that Eugene had rejected the idea out of hand. Marrying Aggie had never entered his mind, he wanted a 'full' marriage, or nothing at all.

'Well it is just what I expected,' I told her.

'Maybe.'

'Surely you must admit defeat, I mean my knowledge of sex was woefully neglected, but I should think Aggie's would be even more so. She has led a very sheltered life, you can't expect anything else.'

'We will just have to ask her,' Betty grinned.

'Don't look at me, I could never broach the subject, it is up to you.'

'She just might consider it. The alternative is losing her home and that can concentrate the mind wonderfully, I should know,' Betty said grimly.

'It is really unfair that she is put in this situation at all. You know what she is like. We have always had to look after her.'

'Maybe that is just the point, we didn't do her any favours doing everything for her and mammy was far too soft on her.'

'You are probably right, but it is too late now for her to change.'

'Right!' Betty rubbed her hands, 'I'11 talk to her but I will need to pick my moment, so you will need to give me a few days and I'll let you know what happens.'

I expected Aggie to arrive on my doorstep in floods of tears, and tried to think what I could say to her to calm her down. Instead my visitor was a triumphant Betty and she came in grinning from ear to ear.

I stared at her, 'you don't mean to say she.....'

'Either she is just desperate to stay in the house or she has hidden depths,' Betty laughed.

'Oh please don't give me the gory details; I honestly can't believe she even considered it. What happens now?'

'I'll talk to dad,' Betty said.

I pulled a face.

'What are you squeamish about? It solves the problem if dad agrees, it is what mammy would have wanted, Aggie staying on in the house.'

'But not like that, not as daddy's wife?'

'Well maybe not, but it is the best of a bad job, you should be relieved.'

'Don't you want dad to marry again?'

'If I am honest, no, I don't think so, but it is not me you have to convince, it's Lena. She is totally against his marrying again, and when she hears about this, if it happens, well I can see her washing her hands of us all.'

'We will just have to argue the case but first I need to tackle dad and see if I can get him round to my way of thinking,' Betty said decisively.

'You might convince daddy, but we haven't a cat in hell's chance of convincing Lena.'

'Leave it all to me, trust me to fix it.'

'I think you are enjoying this and that worries me, this is people's lives we are arranging here,' I warned.

'I don't mean them any harm, it is for the best, you'll see.'

'How many times have I heard that said,' I sighed.

'So will we go to visit Lena?' Betty asked.

'If as you say you fix it and it looks like it is going to happen then we will have to go see her.'

'Right, I'll start the ball rolling,' Betty said.

'See I knew you were enjoying this,' I said with disapproval.

'Maybe I just want to forget about my own worries,' she said.

'No, no, no, that isn't right, how can you agree with that?' Lena was really furious.

'It's the answer to the problem. Everyone gets what they want,' Betty said.

'It's not what I want, the very idea is horrible,' Lena told her.

'It's going to happen, dad is all for it now,' Betty said.

'I want nothing to do with it and if it is to happen then I don't want to be told a thing. I certainly won't be there, I just couldn't be witness to it', Lena said.

'I'm not too happy about it either, but it seems the best solution,' I said.

'I thought you would feel like me. It is a betrayal of mammy's memory. When you think how she used to care for Aggie, do everything for her, and if she wasn't round we did it. How can somebody as helpless as that be of any use? She can't cook, can't do anything.'

'Well, that's not strictly true,' said Betty, going on to tell her about Aggie's transformation.

'As far as I'm concerned mammy doing all that stuff for Aggie was the worst thing she could have,' Betty finished.

I saw Lena's eyes blaze, but she just shook her head and repeated that she didn't want any involvement in what was about to happen. I watched the two of them. Theirs had always been a slightly uneasy relationship. Though Lena had gone through a rebellious stage when she was younger, she had never matched Betty's recklessness, and now Lena was a mature, confident wife and mother while Betty was still kicking over the traces, still biting at life and rejecting what she bit.

I suspected Lena did not approve of Betty's life style, but if she did, she would never say. I was the bridge between them and whatever their feelings towards each other, they were united in their regard for me, the little sister, someone to protect, to keep bad news from, someone who was not ready for the world and all its vicissitudes. It occurred to me that just as they did not really know me, so perhaps we all did not know Aggie. Betty was still trying to argue the case with Lena but it was hopeless. Lena for all her softness had an iron will and once she had set her face against something nothing would change her.

I thought on the fact that Eugene was not Betty's father, so perhaps it was easier for her to think of him marrying again, but whither this thought had crossed Lena's mind I had no idea. In any case Betty and Eugene had always had a good relationship and he had never in any way treated her differently.

We left Lena promising to respect her wishes and leave her out of the whole arrangement.

'There is still Famie and Lizzie to tell. What are they going to say?' I lamented to Betty.

'Whatever they say will have no affect on dad, you know what he is like so don't worry,' Betty said.

The wedding was to take place in December. To my horror Eugene came up with some really elaborate plans which sent Betty into a fit of the giggles and me into despair.

'We need to do something,' I urged Betty.

'Why? It is their wedding and they can have what they like,' she giggled.

'It's, it's, well just not appropriate,' I said.

'Look! Are we going to support them in this or not?' Betty scolded.

'Well, of course, but it need to be a much more modest affair, something in keeping with the finances, something......'

'In keeping with their age,' Betty finished for me.

'Well yes, they are no spring chickens. We want something quiet and dignified,' I told her.

'Dad dignified? Fat chance!' Betty laughed.

'Well, you know what I mean.'

'You don't really want this to happen at all, do you?' Betty accused.

'NO I don't. I hate the whole idea, especially when it has put me at odds with Lena; we have never fallen out before.'

'Well you're a big girl now, so lets get on with planning a reception that won't make the headlines in the 'Evening Times' for all the wrong reasons.'

'Betty 'managed' the whole thing again, convincing Eugene that it would be a good idea to save expense and hold the reception in my 'big room'. She hired tables, benches, cutlery and glasses, and in response to Eugene's request for band, hired a pianist who assured us he was up in all the latest and bygone music too.

She even arranged for my piano to be tuned for the occasion.

It fell to me to take Aggie into town to buy the wedding outfit. I was happy to do it, fearing if Betty had gone she might have for devilment allowed Aggie to give reign to her expressed wish for 'something really bright'.

I steered her toward a smart navy blue costume, with matching hat and shoes. Seeing she was a little disappointed by the 'safe' blue, I relented and found her a really pretty blouse, then bought a spray of artificial flowers for her hat.

Eugene, never known far his sartorial elegance, was pressed heavily by Betty, Aggie and me to buy a new suit, and have his monk's rim of hair professionally trimmed, rather than hacking away with the scissors as was his usual ploy.

The marriage took place at the Register Office in Martha Street, where nine years before Eugene and Ada had been married. Betty excelled herself with the catering arrangements, and friends and neighbours came along, entered into the spirit of toe occasion and the party went with a swing.

Lizzie appeared bearing a small gift and she stayed only long enough to toast the health of the newlyweds and deliver Famie's disapproval, the message being that 'Eugene should have more sense'.

None of this seemed to upset Eugene who as Lizzie departed responded to the request for a song, by offering the pianist a beer while he, Eugene launched into 'An Old Bass Bottle'.

The evening over, the last guest departed, we sat among the debris of crumpled napkins and half finished drinks, and sipped a welcome cup of tea. Eugene and Aggie went home to the little flat in Garfield Street which they would share for the coming months with the ever expanding pregnant Betty.

All that was left for me to do after all traces of the reception had been cleared away, was to figure out how I was going to rebuild the bridges I had burnt between Lena and myself.

There was some bridge building to be done with Famie too, it seemed.

The building was to take some time.

CHAPTER 37

Betty continued to share the house with Eugene and Aggie, but each time I visited I could tell that all was not well. Aggie was quiet and withdrawn, Betty snappy and ill tempered.

Getting Aggie alone was difficult, but when I did, she broke down and said Betty was being bossy and critical of everything she did. She had always been very fond of Betty, but now she wished she would go back to England and leave her in peace. Eugene as always was oblivious to any atmosphere, he went to work, smoked his pipe, snoozed over his paper, and beamed happily and contentedly at us all.

Lena and I had almost got back to our old easy companionship, as long as I didn't talk of Aggie and Eugene. I thought long and hard as to whether I should tell her about Aggie's state of mind, or whether I should speak to Betty and try to find out what the problem was. I decided on the latter course, calling unexpectedly one morning when I knew both Aggie and Eugene would be out. Betty opened the door, and said testily 'Oh it's you', turning on her heels to go back into the kitchen.

I followed her in and sat down, trying to think of the right thing to say.

'I suppose you want tea?' Betty sighed.

'Yes, fine, you sit down, I'll put the kettle on,' I said.

She looked up and grinned sheepishly, 'sorry.'

'It's OK, maybe you got out of the wrong side of the bed this morning, and you're certainly not your usual happy self.'

'Oh it's this house. The two of them drive me mad. Nothing happens, dad falls asleep over his paper, Aggie washes those damn cloths and I think I'll die of boredom.'

I gave her a long look.

'What?' she said, giving me a twisted grin.

'Well, they are as they have always been, it is just the way they are, it's a bit unfair to expect anything else.'

'Has Aggie said anything?'

'Yes, she had mentioned you are not exactly sweetness and light.'

'She didn't say that?'

'Well not those exact words, what she did say was you were being bossy and snappy.'

She sighed, 'I suppose she has a point.'

'So what's the problem?'

She was bending down to get the tea cups out of the sideboard and as she straightened up I saw her eyes fill with tears.

'I don't know what's going to happen to me. Gerry hasn't written in weeks. I think he has left me.'

'Have you written to him?'

'Of course, but I've no claim on him, we're not married, he has never mentioned getting married, so when I think of the future all I can see is being a divorcee, with a fatherless baby, and nowhere to live. I can see myself stuck

here with the two of them for ever.'
'I don't know what to say, I've never met Gerry, so I don't know how he feels about all this. If you are left with nowhere to go, you know daddy would never turn you away. You could do worse than living here.'
'I know I should be grateful, but honestly, I couldn't stand it.'
'Maybe you should go back down, just for an overnight and speak to him,' I said.
She looked at me, her face brightening, then shook her head.
'What would I use for money? The little I had is gone, and to tell the truth I'm living off dad.'
'I don't mind helping you out if you want to go.'
'Maybe I should, I'll think about it.'
She poured the tea and sat down.
'So how are things with you?'
'Fine,' I said. 'I'm having a baby,' I said casually.
'What? You're kidding?'
I smiled, 'no, honestly, I only found out last week but I don't want to tell daddy or Aggie till I feel things are going to be all right this time.'
'That's great, just be sure you take care of yourself.'
'Yes, and you should too. All this worrying can't be good for the baby. Just think if you have to stay here, the two of them can play together, they will be cousins after all.'
'Yeh, true, but I hope I won't be here.'
'Well, you can let me know if you want to go down to see what is going on.'
Gerry didn't write, he turned up at the door about two days later. Betty couldn't wait to bring him to see me. He was a giant, a gentle giant, whose ample girth shook every time he laughed which was often.
Gerry had plans for the future. He wanted to get married. The problem was finding somewhere to live and getting a job, since he had just left the army which had been his life.
Betty was happy enough to wait, now she knew things were settled. She had her baby, a boy and Aggie lavished little gifts on the tot and was an ever eager babyminder if Betty wanted a break. Before long, Gerry was back. He had found a job and place to live, but it would be some time before they could move in, and meanwhile they set the date for the wedding - June 13th. It was 1967, and I, now seven months pregnant, was maid of honour and my husband best man.
Some weeks later they moved to Stoke-on-Trent. Aggie was sole mistress in the house and it was as if a great burden had been lifted from her shoulders.
My daughter was born at the end of August and as I read through the cards showering me with best wishes, the card signed daddy and Aggie brought tears to my eyes. How I wished that Ada could have been there.
As time passed Lena was able to put her hurt and disappointment over Eugene and Aggie behind her, and was a frequent visitor to Garfield street as before.
One thing that had not changed was Eugene's driving, if anything it was

worse than ever, especially as the volume of traffic continued to grow. Lena and John decided he had to have driving lessons, Eugene thought otherwise. 'Eh, ah wis drivin' before half o' these young guys were born.'
'The difference is they have been taught how to drive properly,' Lena countered.
He was constantly having near misses and sometimes close encounters that left tell tale dents in his beloved Morris. When as we feared he was involved in a more serious accident in which both he and the other driver were injured, though not too seriously, he was banned for six months. This ban proved to be the first of many, the final one being for twenty years, but by that time there were much more threatening things happening to him. He had been complaining of a severe pain in his shoulder and thinking it was a legacy from the crash he went willingly enough to the doctor to get some pain killers. He came back to say the diagnosis was a frozen shoulder, and in his usual flippant way warned us not to come near him or we would get the 'cold shoulder'.
The pills did not work, the pain travelled up his neck and down his spine and he was referred to the 'Royal' for tests.
He proved to be a bad patient, never having been ill and did not take to being subjected to 'poking and prodding'.
Each time we visited he told of more tests and begged us to get him home. I became really upset to see the bag draining his urine, it was a deep red colour just like Ada's had been. Lena drew me outside as she saw my face.
'Don't get worried, it is nothing sinister, he is going to be all right.'
I refused to believe her and she gripped my arm and repeated her assurance, adding, 'I don't want you going in there and letting him see you are upset. I have told you there is nothing to worry about, you have to believe me.'
I nodded and composed myself to return to Eugene's bed.
I knew in my heart that everything was not all right, and decided if Lena could not or would not confide in me I would go to Eugene's G.P. and ask him.
Dr. Buckley had been G.P. to all the Cocozzas and his surgery at Bridgeton Cross was on the top floor of a four storey tenement. Eugene had never needed a doctor and so had felt no need to change to one nearer to where he lived. I had to wait for quite a while before being shown in to the small consulting room with its heavy oak desk, white enamel sink and worn leather swivel chair.
I introduced myself and explained my errand.
Dr. Buckley regarded me over his spectacles in a slightly hostile manner. 'It is not possible for me to discuss my patient with you.'
'I understand that, but I am really concerned and the hospital will tell us nothing.'
'That is a matter for them and they have the relevant information. I'm sorry I don't think I can help you.'
'Please doctor, he is my father, I need to know.'
He sighed, got up and left the room, coming back a few minutes later with a

file which he threw on the desk and thumbed through impatiently.

Finding what he was looking for, he looked up and said without ceremony, 'Your father has terminal cancer.'

'But we thought the pain was from a frozen shoulder. That is what the first diagnosis said.'

The pain is from the cancer, it is in his bones and there is nothing that can be done. You asked me what was wrong and I have told you, against my better judgement I may add.'

I stood up, feeling slightly sick.

'Thank you, doctor. Goodbye.'

'Good day to you,' he said.

As I reached the door he closed the file and laid his hands flat on it.

'It is better to face these things head on, better for all concerned,' he said in a slightly kinder tone.

'Yes, thank you, thank you,' I nodded and closed the door behind me. I walked to the tram stop in a daze. Terminal cancer - it was history repeating itself.

I told Lena when we met at the hospital that evening and I knew by her face that it was not news to her, she had known from the first.

I was angry, resenting her for treating me like a little sister who could not take bad news. When was she going to acknowledge that I was an adult, a married woman with a two year old child?

Later at home when my anger had died, I admitted to myself it was just her way of trying to save me heartache, she had always been that way and would never change.

Now that I knew, we could discuss how to manage things. Eugene was in complete denial and was getting more and more frustrated that they were keeping him in hospital. He became really tetchy, his good humour totally deserting him.

We knew we would have to take him home. The outlook was very bleak but it would not be fair to leave him to grow more and more frustrated and confused.

Aggie was in panic, 'ah dinnae ken whit tae dae wi' him, ah'm no a nurse, he is better in the hospital.'

'We'll look after him,' Lena and I said together.

We knew it would not be easy. It was indeed history repeating itself. Lena was facing final exams, just as she had been when Ada was dying. Lena had really got the taste for academic success and she had struggled to get her diplomas despite having given birth to another daughter in the five years since Ada died. Once again she was prepared to put her studies on hold to help look after Eugene. Both she and I lived outside Glasgow so it would mean constant travel to and fro.

We set up a rota, it was well that we did as Aggie just could not cope and she sat in a corner wringing her hands and weeping.

As the months went on he continued to lose weight, being unable to keep food down, but his spirits were good, he was at home where he wanted to be and was convinced he was going to get well.

'Eh, who would have thought that a frozen shoulder could take this long tae get better.'

There were at least four drugs that had to be taken three or four times a day and this was our biggest worry as he refused to take them.

'Ah hiv never taken pills in ma life till thae pain killers and thae were nae use, so ah'm no startin' noo. Just get me a bottle o' stout, yer mammy always swore that was the thing.'

He grew tired of being in bed as spring turned to summer and the sound of the street came through the open window and he struggled to get out of bed.

'Ah need tae get oot o' this hoose. Ah'll never get better lyin' here.'

He managed to dangle his legs over the side of the bed and tried to stand and we caught him as he fell.

'Och, a' that lyin' aboot has made ma legs weak. Ah'll be fine.'

We settled him in his old chair and he beamed his delight.

Next day he felt a little stronger.

A soft balmy breeze fluttered the curtains and lifted the corners of the newspaper which lay unread on his knee.

'Ah want tae go oot, never get better stuck in here.'

Lena and I held a quick confab in the lobby. We agreed he would never be able to walk outside, yet it would be nice to get him out when the weather was fine.

'We could go to the Red Cross and hire a wheelchair,' I said.

'Do you think he will agree to use it?' Lena frowned.

'We can't get him out otherwise, so we could pretend it is really for our benefit, you know say it would be too tiring to keep holding him steady all the time.'

Lena gave me a look and I grinned knowing we had little hope of convincing him.

We got the wheelchair before telling him about it. In fact the whole thing was a set up. The neighbour in the close whose piano Ada had played so long and hard that last New Year agreed she would come out of her door just as we were bringing him down the stairs, and seeing how tired he looked as he surely would, she was to offer the wheelchair which had been left behind in her house by a relative.

It worked like a charm, mainly because the effort of getting down the stairs had taken all the strength he had.

As we wheeled him up the street so many people stopped to talk to him it was like a royal progression.

To each in turn, he said he was 'on the mend'.

We took him out each day during the warm spell of weather, 'borrowing' the wheelchair on each occasion and 'thanking' the neighbour for its use.

'Fancy her havin' a thing like that in the hoose. It has certainly come in handy for me,' he would say.

One particularly fine day we pushed all the way to Alexander Park. It was full of people and colour and light was everywhere, in the flower beds, the green of the trees and the colours of the clothes people wore.

It was 1969, the new fangled transistor radios were all the rage and as we sat on a bench by the duck pond, watching small boys trying to catch 'baggie' minnows in their little nets, a young man stood back against a tree listening to his radio and the song drifted out over the pond.

> *Goodbye my friend it's hard to die*
> *When all the birds are singing in the sky*
> *Little children everywhere*
> *Think of me and I'll be there*
> *We had joy we had fun*
> *We had seasons in the sun*
> *But the dreams that we knew*
> *never really could come true.*

The words of the song cut through me like a knife and as I looked down at Eugene I saw he was crying.

I had never seen him cry openly before and I realized that just as we were playing a game of denial with him, he was playing one with us.

Across the pond the young man moved on, the music growing fainter as he went.

With the break in the weather came a worsening of his condition. His continual refusal to take the drugs meant the pain became unbearable. Aggie was almost out of her mind, and would quit the house without saying, staying away for hours at a time.

A despairing Dr. Buckley came on home visits, it was a chore for him having to come so far and he tried hard to hide his impatience with Eugene's rejection of the drugs. After several visits, he took Lena and I aside and said Eugene needed to be admitted for professional care.

'You have managed things very well but we are nearing the end now and he must be admitted.'

'He was so unhappy in the 'Royal',' we said.

'I could send him to a nursing home. I know there is a vacancy in such a place in Claremont Crescent, how do you feel about that?'

'Could we see it?' Lena asked.

'Yes, I'll arrange it as soon as possible.'

The nursing home was set in a large Victorian house, and we met the matron, who left us in no doubt it was a place men came to die.

'We try to make their last days as peaceful as possible.'

We nodded and took our leave, hardly able to believe we were arranging for Eugene to be sent there.

We sat Aggie down and told her what was going to happen She burst into tears but admitted it was a relief.

Two days later the ambulance arrived to take him in. Lena went with him and I stayed with Aggie.

The door had barely closed on Eugene when Aggie went into a frenzy, gathering up the bottled of unused pills, the tissues and the bottled water in her arms and throwing them into the bin.

'Strip the bed. Strip the bed. Throw a' thae things away. Ah dinnae want them here,' she said, her voice trembling.

I did as she asked, bundling all the bedclothes together and put them out in the lobby.

'I'll take them away later. I think you need a strong cup of tea, we both need a strong cup of tea,' I said.

'He's no comin' back, is he?' she asked.

'No, it is only a matter of time now.'

'Ah'll be by masel'. Eadie away and noo yer daddy.'

I know, but you still have us,' I said.

She let the tears roll unheeded as she always did. I sipped at my tea, but found it hard to swallow.

Visiting times were limited to one hour in the afternoon and one in the evening. We went in the evening on that first day to find him sleeping peacefully. He woke after a while, saying that the pain seemed to have eased. We knew they had given him an injection. The next day we found him quietly fuming.

'That matron refuses to let me oot o' bed. How can ah get better if she stops me from gettin' up and aboot?'

'You do need a lot of rest daddy, maybe we could ask if you could sit up on a chair.'

The matron was not amused, 'Mr. Cocozza is not being co-operative. We know what is best for our patients and he is not fit to sit by his bed at this point.'

'What did she say?' he queried as we went back to him.

'She said maybe in a day or two,' Lena said.

'Ah don't understand these people. You would think in this day and age they could cure a frozen shoulder.'

He slept a lot, his arm moving up and down in a sweeping motion. When he woke he said dreamily, 'Ah made a rare job o' plastering that wall. Of a' the jobs ah do, ah love plastering the best, there is nothing to beat a wall plastered by a man that knows how to do it and do it well.'

He still demanded to be let out of bed and matron relented and a nurse brought a high backed green leather chair. She helped him into it and covered his knees with a tartan rug.

'Look at me, lord muck wi' a' ma orders,' he grinned.

His eyes were failing and we would find him rubbing at them furiously, 'a don't know whit's the matter wi' ma eyes, but things are gettin' dimmer and dimmer. Ah spoke tae that wee nurse aboot it an' she told the matron. At least she has promised tae get an eye specialist to see me.' The eye specialist never came.

'The damn eye infirmary is just up the road, why has he no' come yet?'

We promised to find out.

Famie came and she sat erect on the edge of her chair, twisting her hands in her lap. Lena and I left her and Eugene alone for a little while. She came out very upset.

'I tried to get him to agree to see Father Macteer, but he won't do it. He just keeps saying he has no faith. He needs absolution, he must have confession,' she was terribly upset.

'We'll talk to him,' Lena and I promised.

'He cannae die without confession, tell him, tell him,' she said.

He made his feelings clear as soon as we got to his bed.

'That daft sister o' mine wants me tae see a priest. Ah told her ah have always been a widden Catholic and ah'm no' changin' noo. What do ah want wi' a priest, ah ask ye?'

We consoled Famie saying that as time went on he might change his mind and we would definitely call a priest right away.

Lizzie's visit was more laid back. She sat and talked with him recalling things of their childhood, and she made no mention of confession or a priest. As we walked along the corridor after visiting, she laughed and said.

'Famie is convinced Eugene will go tae hell if he refuses confession, but ah told her that a' the pain he has suffered these past months is bound tae count for something. God will no bar him, anyway, he has plenty that have gone before him and they will put in a good word.'

The nursing home had a small garden and as the weather grew even warmer some of the patients were wheeled out into the sunshine.

Eugene was furious that he had not been taken out.

'Ah need ye to do something for me,' he said as Lena and I sat down. 'Ah want ye to bring ma pipe and tobacco, and ah want to go out for a bit, you can push me in the wheelchair.'

'You can't smoke, not in here, anyway it wouldn't be good for you,' Lena said.

'Ah know ah cannae smoke in here, so that is why ah need you to take me oot.'

'I'll see if the matron will agree to us taking you for a walk tomorrow.'

'An' you will bring ma pipe and baccy?'

We looked at each other and nodded. He smiled. We went in search of matron.

'Very well, if the weather is fine you may take him out for a short while. I will be on leave tomorrow but I will leave word with my deputy.'

We thanked her and went to report to Eugene.

'Fine, now don't forget the things ah want.'

'Right, OK, we will see you tomorrow,' we waved to him from the door.

'What do you think we should do about the pipe?' I asked Lena.

She shook her head, 'My instinct tells me no, it will make him worse.'

'I know, but it may be that just holding the pipe and smelling the tobacco will be enough,' I said.

'Oh he will want to smoke, you can depend on it.'

'So what do we do?'

'We will take them. If we don't he will only get very upset.'

We wheeled him to the end of the very long Crescent, then round the block. Well out of sight of the nursing home we handed him the paper bag.

'Is everything here?' he asked.

'Pipe, cleaners, pouch full of tobacco and matches,' I said.

His face lit up as he settled the pipe into its familiar hollow in the palm of his hand, then drawing a cleaner from the pack scraped away at the inside of the bowl, knocking the pipe against the side of the wheelchair to dislodge the debris.

With a practiced hand he opened the pouch and crumbled the tobacco between thumb and forefinger, the pungent smell of his beloved 'Erinmore' tobacco filled our nostrils. We watched in silence as he gripped the pipe between his teeth, packed it with tobacco, and striking a match he lit the pipe, his eyes narrowed against the smoke.

He puffed at the pipe, drawing strongly to get it started; suddenly he was choking, fighting for breath. I whipped the pipe from his mouth while Lena gently patted his back. He was struggling, eyes rolling, face crimson.

Gradually he regained his breath lying back in the chair panting. As he came back to normal he looked around and seeing the pipe still in my hand seized it and dashed it to the ground.

We turned for the clinic, not one of us said a word. The whole thing had exhausted him, and we felt terrible about it, not least, because it had brought home to him and to us that he would never again be the man he was.

He seemed to lose heart after that and he slept a lot, but when he was awake, he would grip our hands and say he was afraid to die.

This was so painful for us. All his life he had scoffed at death, saying it was a natural thing, it would happen to everyone, and it was nothing to be afraid of. Ada had always feared death, not the death but the dying. She always felt she would be so afraid of the process, but she was just the opposite when it did happen.

'Yer mammy should be here,' Eugene would say impatiently.

Though his eyes were very weak he could still see us and the wide blue ceiling above him, which was the blue of a summer sky and he would lie gazing at it, clutching our hands. We were allowed to stay with him. He was slipping away, but all the time his lips were moving though it was difficult to make out what he was saying.

On the last day, he tossed and turned his eyes wild, and then they focused on the ceiling once more and it seemed to soothe him. His lips moved and we bent as close as we could. He was smiling and mumbled.

'You brought me back, under a blue Italian Sky.'

We sat while he slept his breathing laboured, long pauses between each breath. We bent to kiss his forehead, first Lena then me, it was cool like marble. He was gone.

I sat with Lena in the back of the car as John drove us into Glasgow to make all the arrangements that have to be made at such a time. It had been some time since I had been into the heart of the city. I was astonished at the flyovers, the tiered highways along which a constant stream of cars hurtled. I found it difficult to know where I was.

'This is Charing Cross,' Lena said.

'What have they done to it?' I gasped.

On the far side I could see the Mitchell Library, in front of which an ugly concrete motorway seemed to bar access. Other landmarks loomed, some standing forlorn and alone, awaiting the bulldozer that had already sealed the fate of their companions.

Glasgow, what have they done to you? WHAT KIND OF TRASHY LADY HAVE YOU BECOME with your flashy neon signs, bistros and wine bars? The bold lights winked at me and seemed to be saying, time to move on, the past has gone. It was as if the city had already forgotten her sons and daughters of Ada and Eugene's generation. The future was here and it had an ugly face.

I felt desolate and alone, Ada was gone and now Eugene and I was three months pregnant with my third child. It was time to look to the future. For me the past was not a foreign country, but a dark sombre valley, sometimes shot through with bursts of radiant sunlight.

It came as something of a surprise to us that Eugene had actually left Aggie quite comfortably off. She had the house and there were two or three substantial insurance policies, but it was not money Aggie needed it was people. Betty had come up for the funeral; she was also pregnant with Gerry's second child. She stayed long enough to help dispose of Eugene's machinery, selling it off and neglecting to share the money with Aggie, which infuriated Lena. For her part Aggie was happy to have someone to lean on, and became upset when Betty had to go back. Lena as she had done before, resumed her studies, and secured a job as a tutor at Cardonald College. It was a magnificent achievement and she was quick to point out how supportive John had been. I thought how proud Ada would have been of her, and of that day so long ago when Eugene had said, 'folk like us don't go to college', and the desolate look on Lena's face at his words. As the months wore on, it was clear Aggie was not coping living alone. Lena suggested that she sell the house and move to a new flat in East Kilbride, near to Lena and the children. When the house was sold, we had Aggie make a will and she chose to make Jimmy and Mary the beneficiaries.

Sadly the move to the new flat seemed to increase her loneliness. She developed Parkinson's disease and would be found wandering in her nightclothes. It was a difficult time for us all. Two years after Eugene's death Aggie died in the local hospital. The doctors caring for her said she just lost the will to live and turned her face to the wall.

Jimmy was to die a year later, and Mary move into a nursing home, the legacy from Aggie's will cushioning her care. I could not help reflecting how strange it was that Ada and Eugene who had struggled financially all their lives were the source of Mary's comfortable old age. This tiny feisty little woman, who ate like a bird and weighed less the seven stone, lived on well into her nineties, perfectly lucid and argumentative as ever.

CHAPTER 38

Ada often cautioned us when we were young to be careful what we wished for because we might get it. When pressed for an explanation she would say that sometimes a wish fulfilled trails unexpected consequences. One wish of mine was to have a son. I suppose Eugene would have said it was the Italian way. Through the years when I was trying for a child, I always knew that they would come. When I worked in the city I would leave the office at lunchtime to sit in George Square eating my sandwiches, or if the weather was cold in the little cafe on the corner nearby.

As I walked and sat I could feel little ghostly hands in mine, a little girl and a little boy. That lost child had been a boy, and now I had my little girl, the thought haunted me that the story was told. But in 1971 I gave birth to a boy, on a beautiful shining Sunday in May, we called him Stephen.

His father unwrapped the shawl, counted all his fingers and toes and pronounced him perfect. Only he wasn't. The story of Stephen is too important to be a footnote in this story and it is enough to say that at nine months he was diagnosed with epilepsy and mental retardation.

Ada's words – 'be careful what you wish for' - resounded in my mind.

My sisters were bewildered and sorrowful. Here was the little sister they had sought to protect and shield from the world faced with an enormous challenge. They felt helpless.

For me the future beckoned me into a world that I knew nothing of, a world whose demands had to be met and met unflinchingly.

The next decade was to bring the death of Carol and widowhood to both Famie and Lizzie, Joe dying from cancer and Eddie from liver failure brought on by heavy drinking.

Eddie's death left Lizzie alone in their high rise flat, right at the top on the twenty first floor. We were concerned at her isolation but she revelled in the solitude. She loved looking out of her window at the broad panorama of Glasgow spread out before her, and to marvel at the birds as they wheeled and dived high above her.

The lifts were often out of order forcing her to climb the interminable flights of stairs. Famie begged her to move in with her, but Lizzie dug her heels in. The enforced use of the stairs had brought the tenants together; they would chat and stop at each others flats for a restoring cup of tea and a rest before climbing some more.

But gradually the isolation seemed to be taking its toll on Lizzie, she became bad tempered, given to outbursts of swearing, something she had never done in her life. The flat next door became empty and she wanted to move into it. She was in for a mere two weeks then demanded to know why we had forced to give up her own flat. She wanted to move back, and we managed to arrange it for her, but we were seriously concerned.

When she was finally persuaded to give up the flat and move in with Famie, she lasted only a year before suffering a stroke and dying. During all these months we were preoccupied with Lizzie, Betty was battling lung cancer.

Lena and I had been down to Stoke several times to see her. She had had her lung removed and was recovering from the surgery when Lizzie died. Betty insisted on travelling up to Scotland to attend Lizzie's funeral. She had surprised us by taking instruction to return to Catholicism. We were happy for her hoping it would bring her the comfort she sought. Though it had only been a short time since I had seen her I was truly shocked at the change in her. She could barely walk, relying heavily on a walking stick. At the requiem mass she was determined to go up for communion. We watched with heavy hearts the slow painful progress of her skeletal figure to the alter rail, having to be helped to kneel to receive the host and to stand again.

On the day she was due to return to England she came to see me, sinking thankfully into a chair, weak from the exhaustion of the short walk from the taxi to my door.

I knew immediately she had something on her mind. Our conversation was at first of trivial matters, and I supposed she must be waiting for Lena who was due to arrive later. As she tried to sip her tea, she kept glancing at the clock, and said with sudden urgency, 'I have something to say. I need to say it before Lena arrives, she would never understand.'

'Understand what?' I asked.

'All this pent up resentment I have against mammy. I need to get it off my chest before it is too late. It is robbing me of any peace,' she gave me a penetrating look as if trying to judge my reaction.

I must have looked surprised, and I was, but I said nothing and waited for her to speak.

'Most of my childhood I was miserable, I never felt part of the family, I didn't seem to fit, to be accepted. I blame Ada – mammy,' she corrected herself. 'I blame her, and have always resented her for what she did, but I feel guilty, I wanted to tell someone, I felt you would understand.'

I felt a great pity welling up in me. I thought of all the times I had sensed the undercurrent of something I did not understand, all the times when the aunts by body language and something in their eyes kept Betty on the periphery.

I knew there was something different about Betty, which had been only partially answered by the doctor's revelation that she was my half-sister.

'What is it that has hurt you so much? Is it because you are my half sister? Why wouldn't you let me tell mammy what the doctor had said that day?'

'I daren't. It was a secret, damn secrets that stalked us all our lives. She would guard them so well, she would never open up to anyone,' she gripped the walking stick with trembling hands, her knuckles white. 'Whatever it was it must have been hard for her too, you know how proud she was,' I said.

'Proud! She was proud all right, but I suffered because of those damn secrets, we all suffered, all those whispered conversations in Italian, all that not letting us learn the language in case we found out. I suffered more than you will ever know, more than you ever dreamed of.' she said bitterly.

Then tell me about it if it will make you feel better. Do you want to, can you?'

'Yes, especially about my father. MY father. I wanted to talk about him.'

Just then the door opened and Lena came in greeting each in turn with a kiss. My eyes met Betty's; she gave the merest shake of her head. I knew she would say no more in front of Lena.

The next time I saw Betty she was in a coma, and as Lena and I sat by her bed I thought of all the things Betty had wanted to say that night, and now she would never have the opportunity. How I wished she had come straight to the point, instead of waiting.

It was June, the window of her bedroom was open, and the room was full of the heavy scent of roses, vases of roses also stood around the room. The heavy drone of bees made a soothing backdrop as they buzzed around the bright petals, their legs heavy with yellow pollen. All this bright beauty contrasted poignantly with the poor shrivelled form of our sister, her frame barely discernable under the covers.

The nurses arrived to check on her and they chased us downstairs to have a cup of tea while they worked. Betty's daughter, now a mother of several children herself, clung to Lena for solace, knowing there was nothing to be done. We returned to find her looking peaceful her head swathed in a bright silk scarf of vibrant reds and greens.

She died as the morning sun sent out the first tentative rays heralding a beautiful day.

She had four sons who shouldered her coffin to its final resting place. Those boys had different fathers, and as I looked at them I thought how history does repeat itself. I was tormented by the thought that she had not been able to unburden herself to me and so find the peace she so desired. I prayed that her spirit had been reunited with Ada's and only love existed between them now.

Betty's life had been one of turmoil; she was always reaching out for something and I doubt if even she knew what, or would have wanted it, if it came.

Famie was the last surviving member of Eugene's family, Tony their brother having died aged eighty six in a nursing home soon after Lizzie. Famie had been a widow for forty six years and was now in a little sheltered housing flat. She was about to celebrate her ninetieth birthday. Over the years, though she had suffered no illness, she had become frail and immobile, spending long hours just sitting. She had almost lost the ability to make herself understood, her voice having diminished to a croak. John and Lena had given her hours of care as well as seeing to all her bills and doctors appointments. John would feign annoyance at Famie's fussiness. If visitors sat on her sofa, they had to be sure to plump up the cushions and place them exactly as they had found them, Lena would be instructed by signs and motions to change the lace cloth on the television table for a clean one if it did not hang exactly to Famie's liking and she would point with a long knurled finger instructing Lena to move it this way and that till she was satisfied. John would scoff and say in a loud voice, 'yer a crabbit auld bugger'. He knew she could hear him, and they would laugh together. As we gathered round her to wish her happy birthday, behind the smiles there was real anxiety. John had suffered a stroke, and was suffering from other complications, Lena had breast cancer.

We had made the hard decision that Famie would need to go into a nursing home very soon.

As if to reinforce our decision Famie fell and had to be hospitalized, social services taking on the difficult task of telling her she would not be returning home. It would fall to Lena and I to clear her house and give up the keys.

The little house seemed to be waiting on us. Famie had not been its first occupant and she would not be the last, but each one would be old with only memories as their companions in the long hours of each day. We emptied drawers and cupboards, full of postcards and letters from long dead friends, we bundled up the hats and coats which had hung unused for years in the wardrobe, we took down the large sepia photograph of Joe in his smart army uniform, the wedding pictures of her wedding, and that of Tina's, the calendars of past years that still hung on the wall because each had a picture of the pope, or a favourite saint. They all left their ghost marks on the wallpaper. We wrapped in newspaper the crystal pear which held shrivelled cotton wool balls, and the crystal powder bowl that was full of safety pins. Guiltily we tied up the fat cushions and set them aside to be uplifted with the rest of the furniture which was going to Saint Vincent De Paul.

Lastly we swept the floor with the brush whose bristles were almost worn away, and stood in silence looking round for one last time, before we closed the door, turned the key in the lock and headed for the factor's office. It was the end of an era.

As we drove home, we were not to know that the coming months would hold so much pain.

I am so conscious as I write that there have been many deaths recorded in this story, but they at least were many years apart.

Now sadly we were to suffer the loss of four of our loved ones in the space of eleven months.

Lena was to lose John four days before they were due to celebrate their Golden Wedding and four months on I was to lose my son, aged twenty eight. The Millennium would only be three days old when Famie slipped away, and by the third week of February, the cancer had claimed Lena.

She had known her time was running out and had met the prospect with fatalistic stoicism. For a few precious weeks she and I had been able to go into Glasgow, do the shops and have lunch. John Lewis had come to Glasgow and Lena had anticipated the store's arrival with eagerness. We walked its isles together and I happily followed her to finger bales of exotic material, inspect the latest in sewing machines and discuss the merits of various threads. I watched her with a lump in my throat. She was so happy looking at these things I think she forgot for a little while at least what the future would hold.

On these outings she was no longer Lena the wife or mother, she was gloriously released, the old Lena as I had known her and I gloried in having for a brief time the sister I had known before fate dealt our cards.

When the pain became too much, she was admitted to hospital. There was another tumour in the lung.

Her family gathered round her coming from their various locations in the world. In the time I spent with her she never spoke of things in the past. I longed to ask her so much, but now was not the time to bother her with questions. On one of our outings we had gone back to the Gallowgate, gazing across at where number 206 had been. She pointed and said, 'I was born there.'

I was amazed; it was something I had not known. She turned and smiled a little smile and said.

'You know something? I always suspected I was adopted.'

'What?'

She shrugged, 'fancy me thinking that?'

She walked on and I followed, knowing she would say no more on the subject.

Her death was the last link with my generation.

It was no surprise to her family to find everything in order, everything labelled saying who it should go to.

The girls took on the heartrending task of clearing the house that had been their childhood home. I was not present, and I was grateful for that. It left my memories intact of John by the fire watching snooker, and Lena carrying in a tea tray from the kitchen and urging us all to eat.

If I was to be asked to give an example of a successful life I would cite Lena's. Fifty years of happy marriage, giving the world six children, all happy and successful by their own ability. The triumph over the lean years when money was very tight. The sheer determination she showed in spending years at night school to gain the qualifications that took her where she wanted to be. Her generous acknowledgement of John's support through it all. Her courage in the face of a dreadful illness, that challenged every ounce of strength and fortitude she had. All of that speaks of success, but it is in the enduring love for her that beats in all our hearts that is the greatest success of all.

Things passed into my keeping, family albums, familiar faces smiling out at me, each one no longer here. I felt an overwhelming desolation as I looked at each one.

Here is Da-dee, gazing unsmiling at the camera, his moustache carefully combed, here a handsome Pat McCann standing alongside a happy beautiful Tina, she full of dreams and hopes that were cruelly dashed. Here an oval portrait of Granny and Benny, this from the gravestone, and strangely never replaced.

In the albums there is a list in Lena's neat handwriting of who each person is so that future generations may know. I turn some loose sepia toned snaps over to write the names, and finish what Lena had started. The cardboard mountings are yellowed and torn round the edges; they smell of dust and decay. Yet I know these faces, I remember them, and though they may not think it now the generations to come will be influenced in thoughts, behaviour, even profession, by the natures and actions of these long dead faces.

CHAPTER 39

As I sat in the back seat of the little hired car, watching the scenery sweep by, I had to pinch myself to make sure it was all real, I really was on my way to Filignano. The trip had been meant for Lena, now I had been invited to go in her stead. It was a bittersweet moment, not only for me but both my nieces, who had invited me. We had picked the car up at Rome airport, heading straight out of the city on the toll road that would take us into the mountains. Filignano, I rolled the named around my tongue. All my life it had been a presence, yet I had never really believed it was real. It was like 'Brig-0-Doon', a mythical place that reached out to influence me and colour my thoughts.

The motorway had been uninspiring, mile after mile of garish graffiti, but now we were climbing into the mountains. Stunted olive tress hung heavy in the heat of the day.

At last the signpost pointed straight ahead - Filignano.

It was early June, very early in the season for tourists, and we it seemed were to be the only guests in the surprisingly modern hotel.

All the guide books I read before departure emphasized the remoteness not only of the village but of the region, they warned of the odd wolf and bear still roaming in the mountains, the ominous presence of snakes who were none too friendly to unsuspecting trespassers on their territory.

No train will take you there or bring you back, a bus about once a week, 'car essential' cautioned the writers.

All of this tempered my excitement not one bit.

My room at the back of the hotel looked out on the swimming pool (empty this early in the season).The large window took in the mountains beyond, they looked dark and forbidding and I could well imagine wolves and bears hidden in the thick cover of trees.

Our evening stroll that night brought curious glances from the villagers but we were met by smiles everywhere we went. Most of the shops were closed, and the drinking places too, save for one which was clearly the 'local' having old men leaning on sticks watching the passing scene.

We ventured in, leaving the ordering of our drinks to my younger niece who spoke fluent Italian among several other languages. Our every move was watched closely by the old men who, clearly bored, welcomed this unexpected diversion.

Later as we wondered down the main street we stopped to look at a plaque on the wall of a very modest house. This was the birthplace of Alfredo Cocozza whose son, also Alfredo, had become the world famous Mario Lanza. An elderly woman standing at her door came to explain the great esteem which the villagers had for Mario, not least because they held a competition every year to find the best sound alike, drawing entrants from all over the world and boosting the economy of the village and the surrounding area.

She clasped her hands in regret that we had come too early; the festival did not take place until July.

We smiled and said we had come to seek information of a less illustrious son of the village, another Cocozza, not Alfredo but Eugenio.

She threw up her hands in delight, 'Bene, bene,' she said. We smiled and said our goodbyes. In the morning we made our way to the square where we were told the records of births, deaths and marriages were kept. The square was small and the two storey block which housed the records' office and the Mayor's chambers was decked by the flag of the European Union and Italy's Tri-colare. Opposite the Municipal Building was a mound of stone, the remains of what had been a substantial building, now fenced off with a red warning sign to keep out, smaller print told it had been razed to the ground by an earthquake. I thought of Granny and her terror of being almost caught up in a quake so soon after returning to Italy all those years ago. Taking pride of place was the church of St Anthony, its façade scarred and pitted, part of it ruined and fenced off, but it was still very much in use, people were coming and going all the time.

We ventured inside, wandering around marvelling at the painted ceiling, nothing that could rival Rome, but surprising given the distressed state of the building outside.

An elderly lady came towards us, a large bunch of keys dangling from her belt. She smiled, 'Americano?'

'No, we chorused, 'Scozzese!'

Her eyes lit up, 'Ah, Scozzese, ecco -,' she spread her hands, 'Ecco', she said again.

We looked around trying to find what it was she particularly wanted us to see. She beckoned us forward to a brass plaque by the door.

'Oh!' said my niece, 'The church was badly hit during the war and was rebuilt by money raised by Scottish Children, most of whom had Italian connections.'

The old woman smiled and launched into a long explanation, most of which I understood, having frantically tried to brush up on what little knowledge of the language I had before the trip.

My niece was translating as she went along, but the old woman put her hands on my shoulder and said. 'La Signora capisco, molto bene.'

She told us that St Anthony's feast day would take place during our visit, and invited us to come to the mass on that day. Though none of us were practising Catholics we agreed to come.

We were given a warm welcome at the record office, the clerk calling others to come and shake our hands. I had come armed with as many details of Eugene's birth as I knew, and I had also brought lots of family photographs. As my niece conveyed all this information the clerk's face took on an apologetic expression.

He rattled off a stream of Italian of which I could understand nothing at all and I looked helplessly at my niece.

'He says it is unlikely that the records will still be here. Many were lost in either the war or the earthquakes.'

I felt a keen disappointment which must have shown on my face, because he stretched out his hand and took my papers from me, and with a lovely smile went off into another room.

He was gone for quite a while during which my niece, in answer to many questions, told them all about us and the fact, which was received with great interest, that she now lived in California.

The clerk returned struggling with a gigantic book at least three feet across, and as he dumped it down on the desk a cloud of dust rose up and set us all coughing.

Carefully he began to open the book, his assistant clearing the desk to make room. The pages were yellow and looked extremely fragile. He handled them reverently, his eyes scanning the columns of spidery writing.

At last he smiled and nodded, stabbing an entry with a nicotine-stained finger. Collectively we breathed a sigh of relief, smiling at him and each other. He tried to swivel the book round so that we could see and we peered over each others shoulders. The writing was faint but I could clearly make out Benniomeno Cocozza, and Benedetta, and Eugenio. I felt tears prick my eyes and before I knew it I was sobbing quite openly. The others including the clerk, smiled in understanding.

It was the strangest feeling, seeing that entry, the very beginning of Eugene's life. I just could not explain why it moved me so, but it did. I had the craziest feeling he was standing there grinning at me, that he knew I was there and he was pleased.

Efforts to find the entries recording the birth of Granny and Da-dee were unsuccessful, the clerk was sure that they had been lost in the war. He went on to remind us that there had been fierce fighting in the hills around Filignano, and the Italian Partisans had had the advantage over the Germans with their knowledge of the hills and mountains.

My niece asked if I could have a copy of Eugene's birth record. The clerk shook his head with an apologetic smile.

'He says, the records are too frail to photocopy,' she told us.

I shrugged and nodded my understanding.

We chatted on for a few minutes, and then the clerk gently closed the book and took it away.

He came back a few moments later with a beaming smile.

From behind his back he produced a sheet of paper, handing it to me with a flourish; it was a copy of the entry.

I stammered my thanks hardly daring to believe that I actually had the paper in my hand.

I felt confused and I wanted to thank him but did not want to insult him by offering money.

My niece had already seen the problem and she asked if there was a charge.

He tapped his nose and mumbled something in her ear.

'He says what he has done is against all the rules, but he wanted to make the Signora happy. He says we must tell no one in the village what he has done.'

We thanked him again and I offered my hand which he clasped it tightly in both of his.

As we left, he called us back waving our photographs which we had forgotten. He smiled, gesturing expansively with his hands, telling my niece something.

She looked at me and said, 'he wants to make an appointment for us to see the mayor. Apparently the mayor will be very interested in the photographs but he reminds us to say nothing of the copy he gave us.'

We promised to call in the next day to get the time of the appointment, if it was to take place.

Next day we were ushered into the mayor's office, his officials bringing extra chairs, offering water.

My niece did all the talking. I produced the photographs on cue and I also handed over the copy of Da-dee and Granny's wedding certificate, that unknown to me Lena had treasured all her life. The mayor read it carefully. He became quite excited, leaning over the desk and pointing to a name at the foot of the paper.

'He says the official who signed the wedding certificate is his own grandfather. It was an amazing coincidence, even more so when we looked again and realized it was also the name of the people who had originally owned the Favourite Cafe.

I could almost hear Ada's voice saying 'everything and everyone is connected', and Eugene's full of surprise saying, 'fancy that eh?'

The photographs were a big hit too. The mayor asked permission to have them copied, and of course I agreed bearing in mind the service which had already been done to me. He handed them to his assistant who hurried off to copy them. He wanted them for the folk museum he planned for the village, he wanted to display photographs of people who had left the village and tell their story. I was delighted that Da-dee, Granny and all the family would play their part. It was so right and proper that they did.

Before we left he plied us with promotional material for Filignano, and urged us to return for the Lanza Festival, to see the village at its best.

He said he regretted that all the records we had wanted to see were not available, and suggested we go to the main town, where there may be copies still in existence. He also suggested we visit the local cemetery where there were family vaults. We thanked him and with the return of the photographs we took our leave.

Next day we went to the cemetery and searched with some success for family names. I had hoped to find the last resting place of the legendary rich aunt Madalena, but it was not to be found. We mused that if she had indeed been rich she may have lived somewhere more in keeping with her status and now rested in some imposing vault, rather than in one of the whitewashed tombs in the little cemetery of Filignano.

On the morning of St. Antonio's feast day we made our way to the chapel and found it crowded. We were forced to stand at the back which allowed us to view the congregation. At one point the priest mounted the pulpit and letting his glance roam around the assembled throng launched into an impassioned diatribe.

'He is calling for eight young men to carry the statue in procession tonight, reminding them it is their duty and lambasting them for being lazy and forcing him to call for volunteers every year,' my niece whispered, highly amused.

The priest had not finished with his erring flock and he went on to threaten punishments for backsliding, even to the fires of hell. The congregation sat unmoved, possibly inured to his outburst over the years.

Wickedly the older of my nieces whispered, 'Maybe the packed house is just to hear him rant.'

We agreed that we would come down that evening to see if the threat of hell fire was enough to shame the layabouts.

We spent that day, going beyond the village to picnic in the hills, and on a mad impulse we set out to follow in Granny's footsteps and walk to Cerosuolo. We had not gone far before the heat exhausted us, and saluting Granny's strength, we turned back to get the car.

Cerosuolo proved to be one long street and as we parked the car at the far end we realized most of the inhabitants were seated at their doors, the black clad old women knitting or peeling vegetables, the old men leaning on their walking sticks, the knurled hands one on top of the other. We advanced down the street three abreast, feeling like gunfighters in a spaghetti western. Every eye was on us. We smiled self-consciously. The faces were impassive.

When we reached the end of the street there was nowhere to go but back the way we came. It was as before, watching eyes, no sound. Halfway down a voice called out, 'Americano?'

We as before, 'No, Scozzese.'

The effect though not exactly electric, was a definite thawing and several faces broke into smiles of welcome.

An old woman beckoned us over. She was sitting with a much younger woman and a little girl, who was tormenting the life out of a poor little ginger kitten.

We went across, our appointed interpreter fielding the questions and giving the answers.

We chatted on using smiles and gestures. They invited us to sit with them and I produced the photographs of Da-dee and Granny, having explained that Granny had come from this village. The old woman nodded and said the Pacitti's were a Cerosuolo family. Looking at her and at Granny it was easy to see they were of the same stock.

We asked if we could take their photograph, at which point the younger of the women jumped up giggling and throwing her apron over her face, disappeared into the house.

We did get some snaps in the end. Having been accepted by one of the inhabitants, we were showered with smiles and waves the rest of the way back to the car.

Back at the hotel we freshened up before walking down into the village to watch the procession. We were curious to see if the priest had found his volunteers. A sizable crowd had gathered outside the chapel from which the dying notes of a hymn floated out on the balmy breeze. After a few minutes the statue emerged, propped on a platform shouldered by eight men, four of whom were the same old men we had seen earlier in the local bar. Standing around watching the unsteady progress of the great statue were several young men in sharp suits and slicked back hair. The priest emerged swaying an incense burner, the crowd crossing themselves and falling into line behind. We tailed on at the end. The procession went right round the village twice, the priest intoning the rosary, the followers murmuring their response. Finally the bearers reached the flight of steps leading up to the door of the chapel. Slowly they began to climb, the legs of the old men visibly shaking. The crowd followed them in and filed into the pews. We stood at the back as before.

The priest mounted the pulpit, his angry gaze sweeping round his flock. He raised his hand, edge of palm to the watching faithful, 'In Nomini Padre, il figlio, il spirito santo.'

There followed a short sermon in which he pointedly castigated the failure of the young men to do their duty. This was followed by a hymn, a collection, a final prayer and the whole thing was over for another year.

When the crowd had all gone home, we sat on a bench beneath the mayor's window, and drank in the peace of the evening. The air was heavy with the scent of jasmine; the stars were the brightest I had ever seen. I wanted to pinch myself to make sure I was not dreaming. Suddenly a dog barked, it was echoed by another, and another till the whole valley was filled with the sound of barking dogs. It reminded me of the scene in 'One Hundred And One Dalmatians', when the doggie 'bush telegraph' sent out a message that the pups had been taken. What, I wondered were the dogs of Filignano saying that night? Had there been a wolf or a bear spotted? Suddenly I wanted the safety of the hotel.

Saturday evening at dinner we were pleasantly surprised to find several tables occupied in the large restaurant where all week we had dined in solitary splendour. It was a beautiful room, with glittering chandeliers whose light was reflected in the mirrors round the walls and the sparkling wine glasses on the tables. The tall French windows were open to the soft Italian night; moths danced a delicate ballet, bats swift flight silhouetted against the darkening sky. We were introduced to the diners who had come to have dinner and play bridge. They were retired Scots-Italians who had come home to the peace of Filignano. They lived in villas in the hills above the village, some had built themselves new houses, others had restored the old family home putting in modern facilities, but whether new or old, all had four foot thick walls to withstand earthquakes.

We were told there were several enclaves, among them French and German. A slim weather-beaten man sat down at our table and introduced himself as one of the Cocozza family. We chatted for a while and he seemed to know Eugene's branch of the family. He told me he had just completed the sale of a plot of land on the outskirts of the village to the Italian Government, who were buying up the land to build a Heritage Centre.

'I am sure there will be land belonging to you there, it would be worth your while finding out,' he said.

Out of curiosity we visited the land office. After much pulling out of giant maps, cross references, shrugs of shoulders, then nods and smiles, a triangular slice of land was traced in red ink, the map man stabbing at it and giving us a beaming smile.

It seemed I was looking at my inheritance, a piece of Italy that had belonged to Da-dee, and his forefathers before him.

Hardly daring to believe this, I just stared at the red triangle not knowing what to say. The map man nodded as if in understanding, he whipped the giant map away, rolling it up expertly as he went, and in a few moments he was back with a photocopy of 'my land', complete with instructions as to how to find it. I gazed at the map, 'Travarecce' it said. I said it over under my breath, but the little map man heard me and smiled.

'Si, si, Travarecce, ecco!' he stabbed at the map again.

We set off to find it, and as we turned to leave the office the little man had caught my niece by the sleeve and whispered something to her. She nodded and just shrugged off her sister's and my inquiry as to what he had said.

We drove out of the village - it was not far – and soon we had drawn up alongside a large expanse of overgrown vegetation, which was fenced off and bristling with red signs proclaiming 'PERICOLO TERREMOTO'.

'That,' said my niece, 'is what he was whispering in my ear. We must stay in the car.'

My wonderful inheritance was in an earthquake zone. It was not until we were on the plane back home that I was told Travarecce was also full of snakes.

What to do? I decided it would be too costly to pursue the claim through the Italian courts. What has happened to my little piece of Italy, I have no idea. It would appear the Italian Government work on the principal that if you don't come to us, we will not go looking for you. I have the map, and look at it now and then; it is all I can do. It would have been nice if we had known about the land long ago, when Eugene had been in such dire financial straits, but if he was here today, he would just shrug and say, 'Och what ye never had ye never miss.'

I suppose I echo that sentiment.

CHAPTER 40

The visit to Filignano stirred up so many emotions in me. I had walked with ghosts. People who had played out their lives in the heat and isolation of those tree clothed hills. I had traced their names with my fingers on the bronze plates of their vaulted tombs. Generation after generation and now I stood as the last of my generation. It was a lonely feeling. I returned home eager to write of these feelings and eager too to tell the whole story for the next generation who knew little or nothing of the tale.

I had now in my possession photographs, letters, missals, birth and marriage certificates that Lena had kept all those years. I needed more. I needed to find the answers to so many questions. To find if all those guesses I had made were right.

My first call was at Dalbeth Cemetery where so many of the family lie. The visit was disappointing. Dalbeth seemed to have been swallowed up by rank weeds and sycamore. It was impossible to find anything. A helpful workman shook his head when I asked him for directions.

'You have no chance'. It will be trying to find a needle in a haystack.'

Seeing my disappointment he came back to me and said,' Dalbeth is still here, it has just become part of St. Peter's now. We will be restoring it but if you phone the office they might be able to help.'

The office were very helpful, and though it took some weeks I got the references I needed to locate the grave and soon I was standing before it, shivers running through me as I gazed at the familiar names.

I also spent a day accompanied by Lena's eldest daughter combing through the records of births, deaths and marriages.

Here recorded was the marriage of Eugene aged just 19yrs, his bride aged 20yrs on March 28th 1918. In November of that year the birth of a daughter is recorded, and the end of that marriage by divorce thirty seven years later in 1955. It was in that year on March 31st he married Ada.

There before us now was the record of the birth of Benedetta Elvira Cocozza on January 27th 1928 and the stark black words recording her death on March 19th 1931 aged three years and two months.

I was intrigued by the middle name of Elvira. It had occurred many times on the bronze plates on the family vaults and somehow seeing the actual records made her real to me. All my life she had been there - a shadowy presence like a hovering angel. I had barely acknowledged her as my sister. It brought home to me the real pain Ada had felt and I identified with that pain knowing the loss of a child myself.

As we traced record after record I felt my heart would break. The words were simple enough yet behind those records was heartache and lies.

It was a strange feeling seeing the pieces of the jigsaw falling into place but there were still pieces missing that I have to this day been unable to find. That night as I lay thinking over the events of the day I thought how those events recorded had the power to shatter lives, to force people to live a lie.

How being born out of wedlock somehow seemed to make the child complicit in the sins of the parents and stigmatized them for the rest of their lives.

Now times have changed and no one seems to care. Divorce, co-habitation and births outside marriage are the norm and Chastity, virginity and fidelity the exception, so it is difficult for this generation to understand the awful shame of being a 'bastard bairn' as Mary called me so long ago.

I recalled Lena's strange admission that day we walked in the Gallowgate that she had always believed she was adopted. I found myself wondering if she knew or guessed about Ada and Eugene and chose to believe that rather than accept the shame of illegitimacy.

It was true that Betty had never been truly accepted by the aunts though they were never unkind to her. She had suffered too and I felt tears prick my eyes as I remembered her torment to unburden herself that last night she had come to visit me.

All that pain and misery because the truth could not be told. Those secrets had been shut away; now I was opening those long closed shutters letting in the rays of truth to banish the dark fears.

Even now I questioned if it was the right thing to do.

Would Ada cast it all on the fire as she had done in Niddrie Mains? Yes, no doubt she would.

So why do I write? For many reasons, none of which is malice or hatred, rather out of love.

Ada was my mother, Eugene was my father, I loved them in life and I still love them today. As an adult I can now see what it must have cost Ada to live a lie. She who was so proud, so honest in all her dealings and had to live with this knowledge. She had to endure the barely concealed contempt and disapproval from some of her relations. She found herself constantly at their mercy to keep the secret she could not bear to tell her children.

As their child I knew pain, fear, hurt and bewilderment, but love too, though seldom overtly expressed.

Can I answer the question why I had to write? I think I can. To make sense, if I could, of all the things that had happened and for our children who wanted to know.

I am anxious that they do not judge Ada and Eugene too harshly, that they understand they were just two people who played the cards life dealt them as we all must do.

We live in a very different world. We have come far in personal freedoms. Perhaps too far; history will judge.

For any reader of this story I would hope that they own it is a love story, sometimes fractured, often unhappy but a love story nonetheless.

My one regret is that all the people in this story are not here to allow me to take each of their hands in mine and tell them that none of it mattered; all that matters is that none of it changed by the tiniest fraction my love for them.

As I write I am surrounded by their faces smiling out at me frozen in time. As in all families there are triumphs and disasters but in the end we all walk alone and have to pay the price fate demands.

I miss them all. They lived, and I for one am very grateful.

THE END

Lightning Source UK Ltd.
Milton Keynes UK
UKOW05f1018210317
297151UK00001B/39/P